FEMINISTING IN POLITICAL SCIENCE

FEMINISTING
IN POLITICAL SCIENCE

Edited by
Alana Cattapan,
Ethel Tungohan,
Nisha Nath,
Fiona MacDonald,
and Stephanie Paterson

UNIVERSITY *of* **ALBERTA** PRESS

Published by

University of Alberta Press
1-16 Rutherford Library South
11204 89 Avenue NW
Edmonton, Alberta, Canada T6G 2J4
amiskwaciwâskahikan | Treaty 6 |
Métis Territory
ualbertapress.ca | uapress@ualberta.ca

Copyright © 2024 University of Alberta Press

LIBRARY AND ARCHIVES CANADA
CATALOGUING IN PUBLICATION

Title: Feministing in political science / edited
 by Alana Cattapan, Ethel Tungohan, Nisha
 Nath, Fiona MacDonald, and Stephanie
 Paterson.
Names: Cattapan, Alana, editor. | Tungohan,
 Ethel, editor. | Nath, Nisha, editor. |
 MacDonald, Fiona, 1976– editor. | Paterson,
 Stephanie, 1972– editor.
Description: Includes bibliographical
 references.
Identifiers: Canadiana (print) 20230541615 |
 Canadiana (ebook) 20230541690 |
 ISBN 9781772127324 (softcover) |
 ISBN 9781772127478 (PDF) |
 ISBN 9781772127461 (EPUB)
Subjects: LCSH: Political science—Canada. |
 LCSH: Feminism—Political aspects—
 Canada.
Classification: LCC JA84.C3 F46 2024 |
 DDC 320.50971—dc23

First edition, first printing, 2024.
First printed and bound in Canada by
Houghton Boston Printers, Saskatoon,
Saskatchewan.
Copyediting and proofreading by
Joanne Muzak.

All rights reserved. No part of this publication may be reproduced, stored in a retrieval system, or transmitted in any form or by any means (electronic, mechanical, photocopying, recording, generative artificial intelligence [AI] training, or otherwise) without prior written consent. Contact University of Alberta Press for further details.

University of Alberta Press supports copyright. Copyright fuels creativity, encourages diverse voices, promotes free speech, and creates a vibrant culture. Thank you for buying an authorized edition of this book and for complying with the copyright laws by not reproducing, scanning, or distributing any part of it in any form without permission. You are supporting writers and allowing University of Alberta Press to continue to publish books for every reader.

This book has been published with the help of a grant from the Federation for the Humanities and Social Sciences, through the Awards to Scholarly Publications Program, using funds provided by the Social Sciences and Humanities Research Council of Canada.

University of Alberta Press gratefully acknowledges the support received for its publishing program from the Government of Canada, the Canada Council for the Arts, and the Government of Alberta through the Alberta Media Fund.

To all those we care for and who care for us.

Contents

Acknowledgements XI

Introduction XV
Disrupting Political Science through Feministing?
ETHEL TUNGOHAN, NISHA NATH, STEPHANIE PATERSON,
ALANA CATTAPAN, and FIONA MACDONALD

TEMPORALITY AND THE CASE FOR TRANSFORMATION

1 | "Diversity Is Important, but Only When It Is the 'Right' Type of Diversity" 3
Canadian Political Science and the Limitations of an Additive Approach to Equity
ETHEL TUNGOHAN

2 | Being "Reasonable" (whilst Feminist and Black) within the Neoliberal University 21
NICOLE S. BERNHARDT

3 | The Fish and the Spider 31
ALANA CATTAPAN

4 | Anti-Racist and Indigenous Feminism and the Generative Power of Disruption 49
ELAINE COBURN, RITA KAUR DHAMOON, JOYCE GREEN,
GENEVIEVE FUJI JOHNSON, HEIDI KIIWETINEPINESIIK STARK,
and GINA STARBLANKET

RELATIONALITY, COMMUNITY, AND CARE

5 | Your Absence Is Not an Accident 71
Storying Feminist Friendship from Dissonance to Dissidence
KELLY AGUIRRE, MARIAM GEORGIS, and SARAH MUNAWAR

6 | Disrupting Feminism / Confronting Ableism 89
MICHAEL ORSINI

7 | **Indigenous Feminisms and Political Science** 105
   Indigenization and Epistemological Barriers to Inclusion
   EMILY GRAFTON

8 | **Feministing Online** 123
   Using the Internet to Learn New Things and Create Community
   AMANDA BITTNER

9 | **Conversations in Feminist Solidarity** 139
   Reflecting on the Political Science PHD Experience
   LINDSAY LARIOS and MANON LAURENT

10 | **Don't Be an Asshole** 157
   STEPHANIE PATERSON

FEMINISTING AND THE "REAL" WORLD OF POLITICS

11 | **Letters of Engagement** 175
   Learning from Our Efforts at Feministing Public Policy Deliberations
   JULIANNE M. ACKER-VERNEY, ALANA CATTAPAN, ALEXANDRA DOBROWOLSKY, TAMMY FINDLAY, and APRIL MANDRONA

12 | **Feministing** 191
   Lessons from Bill C-237, the Candidate Gender Equity Act
   JEANETTE ASHE

13 | **Feministing on the Campaign Trail** 213
   Dialogue with KIMBERLEY ENS MANNING, NADIA VERRELLI, and MELANEE THOMAS
   Edited by ALANA CATTAPAN and FIONA MACDONALD

GATEKEEPING, PEDAGOGY, AND MENTORING

14 | **Radical Pedagogies for the Present** 227
   Vignettes on Decolonial Feminist Potentials in the Classroom
   DAVID SEMAAN

15 | **Reworlding the Canadian University** 245
   Centring Student Leadership in Institutional Transformation
   JAMILAH A.Y. DEI-SHARPE and KIMBERLEY ENS MANNING

16 | **Photovoice as Feminist Pedagogy** 265
   FIONA MACDONALD

17 | **Learning to Relinquish Silence** 287
Feministing in Political Science as an Ethicopolitical Project
NICK DORZWEILER

(RE)BUILDING POLITICAL SCIENCE

18 | **Towards an Agenda for Feministing Political Science** 305
Intersectional Feminist Pathways
CHAMINDRA WEERAWARDHANA

19 | **"Refusal Has Been Really Important in My Life"** 315
Political Science Aunties Discuss Feministing in Political Science
Dialogue with YASMEEN ABU-LABAN, KIERA L. LADNER,
REETA CHOWDHARI TREMBLAY, and LEAH F. VOSKO
Edited by ETHEL TUNGOHAN and ALANA CATTAPAN

20 | **En Route to a Black Feminist Praxis** 331
Reflections of a Black Woman Graduate Student
TKA C. PINNOCK

Conclusions 347
Towards a Lexicon of Feministing
THE EDITORIAL COLLECTIVE

Contributors 371

Acknowledgements

THIS BOOK HAS BEEN A LABOUR in many senses of the term. Symbolically, it is a labour of love and hope—a coming together of many voices in the view that reflections on the field that we work in and live in can be better. Practically, it has been a labour insofar as it has taken time and effort that were in short supply during the turmoil of a global pandemic, with worklives and homelives in disarray. We worked hard in the solitude of our homes and institutions, via teleconference, email, texts, Facebook messages, and otherwise, to bring these contributions together, reflecting on the struggles of enacting feminism in an often exclusionary discipline while imagining—alone and together—another way, another world.

None of this would have been possible without the labour of the contributors to this volume who, in their glorious multitude, offer different perspectives and interventions that collectively challenge the bounds of political science in Canada. The contributors took a chance on us by sharing their personal and professional experiences and their subversive approaches to advocacy, research, and teaching. Doing so takes courage and trust and we are immensely grateful and honoured that they agreed to share their work with us.

We also want to acknowledge those who have not stayed in political science or the university, those who may have left because the generative capacity of the university is often outweighed by a climate that is hostile. The privileges of the ivory tower are built on the backs of those it long did not let in the door. This book is made possible by the experiences of those who have come before us, and those too who tried but were kept out and down.

There are a number of people whose insights and ideas—whose intellectual and practical labour—have contributed to the realization of this volume. Thank you also to Rita Kaur Dhamoon, whose writing has been formative in the connections we've drawn between feministing and labour; in particular, rewitnessing feministing as a kind of epistemic labour has shaped how we approached our work together. Thank you to Nicole Lugosi-Schimpf, for your heartfelt and incisive reflections on the academy that deepened our understanding of feministing. We are also grateful to Gina Starblanket for insights and thoughtful suggestions that helped us understand the scope and direction of the volume and reminded us of the communities to which we were and are accountable. Thank you to Elaine Coburn for always being a fantastic confidante, and to Paulo Ravecca for his inspiring work and solidarity. Thank you to Joyce Green, who encouraged us to consider and build upon the generative and constructive dimensions of our collective anger and frustration.

This collection also owes a debt of gratitude to those who participated on panels over several years at the Canadian Political Science Association Annual Conference and the International Political Science Association where the need for a volume of this kind emerged. We are specifically indebted to the participants on the 2017 CPSA roundtable on Feminist Praxis in Academic Careers, the 2018 IPSA panel on Critical Theory in Political Science: An Uninhabitable Home, and the 2019 micro-paper roundtable on Feministing in Political Science: Stories and Strategies from the Front Lines. Thank you to the many inspiring contributors at these events, including Sarah Sharma, Bailey Gerrits, Jennifer Mustapha, Nicole Wenger, Juanita Lee Garcia, Charlotte Yates, Cynthia Enloe, Nick Dorzweiler, Paulo Ravecca, Laura Shepherd, Robert Adcock, Lindsay Larios, Kimberley Ens Manning, Jessica Merolli, Michael Orsini, Gina Starblanket, Malinda Smith, Dempsey Wilford, and Raveena Walia.

Thank you also to those who saw us through to publication. Hannah Scott (University of Waterloo) supported us with a meticulous attention to detail as we brought the manuscript together. Negin Hamesh (York University), Tracy Morrison (University of the Fraser Valley), Eisha Ali, Lee Whelan, and Sarah Seabrook (University of Waterloo) provided us with critical research assistance as we finalized the volume.

We have also been fortunate to have a cover image provided by Lucia Lorenzi that reflects the tensions and challenges of the volume, and we want to express our gratitude for our ability to use this work. The image, titled *Still Here*, is, in her words,

> a rallying cry of rage and defiance as much as a kind of quietly resigned hope at the beginning of a global pandemic, a crisis that brought so many of our feminist methods of doing and being under pressure and into question.

Nearly four years on, some aren't still here; others yet remain, but within the tangles of precarity that loosen or tighten in different ways each day. I like to imagine those tangles as small ladders, somehow, little threads that allow us to connect, to give evidence of our presence when we are in such danger of slipping away.

A huge thank you as well to Mat Buntin, Duncan Turner, Joanne Muzak, and the team at University of Alberta Press, who saw the potential for this kind of work to make a difference, helped us shape and reshape the work as we moved towards publication, and who supported us through a long and winding process.

Finally, if this book was a labour and an artifact of our experiences and imagination, it is also reflective of the labour of our families and friends in supporting us, listening to us, and caring for us as we did this work. Thank you to those we love for imagining new worlds with us and nourishing our hearts as we did this work together.

Introduction

Disrupting Political Science through Feministing?

ETHEL TUNGOHAN, NISHA NATH, STEPHANIE PATERSON,
ALANA CATTAPAN, and FIONA MACDONALD

> The focus on feministing also involves building upon, and moving beyond, the emphasis on feminist political science as a disciplinary subfield. Most importantly, the full significance and potential of feministing is to be found in a core focus on challenging established ways of doing things, of rattling the system, and calling for meaningful, long-term, and holistic transformation.
> —CHAMINDRA WEERAWARDHANA, *Chapter 18, this volume*

> To reworld the university is to engage in intentional practices that enable the flourishing of racialized peoples—students, faculty, and staff—while simultaneously dismantling the colonial logic at the bedrock of the academy. We see reworlding generally, and coalition building specifically, as means of disrupting the current Eurocentric worldview/order that dominates higher education.
> —JAMILAH A.Y. DEI-SHARPE and KIMBERLEY ENS MANNING, *Chapter 15, this volume*

WHY DO WE FEEL a visceral need to change political science? What has led us to actively seek the transformation of the discipline? Can these transformations occur within existing structures? What *else* can we build as an alternative to political science specifically, and the neoliberal academy more generally? Are there feminist alternatives that we can use to build these other worlds?

The term *feministing* was popularized by Jessica and Vanessa Valenti through their co-founded blog *Feministing: Young Feminists Blogging, Organizing, Kicking Ass*, which operated independently from 2004 to 2019 (feministing.com). It was widely celebrated for its cutting-edge work during the heyday of independent feminist media, with a following of 1.2 million monthly visitors at its peak (Goldberg 2019). As a result, *feministing* became representative of the impact of digital activism and solidarity movements not only in popular culture but also within academic discourse (Greyser, Mukhopadhyay, and Beetham 2012; Mowles 2008). As Mowles notes, feministing.com was one of the most popular feminist blogs and stood "at the epicentre of debates around the politics of third-wave feminism and online activism" (2008, 29), while other academics adopted the parlance in praxis (see, e.g., Greyser, Mukhopadhyay, and Beetham 2012; Hearn 2015, 38).

Feministing in Political Science is a project borne out of a sense from the editorial collective and the authors of this collection that political science as a discipline, and the academy as a whole, needs to change. These changes should reflect not only the diversity of research approaches that exist within political science but also the diversity of positionalities that people who are part of the discipline hold. As opposed to locating change within a politics of identity, the changes we are animated towards emerge from the embodied knowledges of those experiencing structured precarity within the academy and the lineages of struggle from which they come. For us, the project of transformation is twofold: first, we are asserting an epistemic (re)orientation to political science that is grounded in a relational politics; as researchers, scholars, and community members, we are bound through implication, complicity, and at best through solidarities and coalition. When grounding our analyses and politics in a relational ethos and an intersectional understanding of traffics of power, the implications are manifold for the kind of political science that could support our collective thriving. This political science would: trouble the privileging of dispassionate inquiry, and support research that centres affect, care, and emotion; see the pursuit of social good through community-engaged research as not just valid but necessary; hold that markers of social and structural location such as race, Indigeneity, gender, and disability are not only variables to be examined or controlled for, but are part of interlocking structures of domination; consider experiential knowledge as legitimate; and, finally, centre more expansive and relationally accountable understandings of research ethics to ground all projects.

Second, we reflect on the manifold ways that political science specifically, and academia more generally, endorses, authorizes, legitimizes, and fosters norms, policies, and practices that are hostile to women, Indigenous people, racialized people, and other minoritized communities. Alongside such reflections, we ruminate on what new norms, policies, and practices we can collectively create to make political science and the academy a more caring space. To be clear, this orientation to care is political, particularly as we note the tight co-implication of white femininity, benevolence, and colonial and imperial violence. Hence, this ethos of care is necessarily anti-racist, anti-colonial, and pushes against the heteropatriarchal and ableist norms that have tethered care and harmful forms of white benevolence together. Our editorial collective lives and works in the Canadian context, as do most of the authors who contributed to this volume, but it is our hope that *Feministing* can inspire and compel readers to reflect on where they and their research are situated in the discipline, to think of their own experiences in the field, to connect these experiences to larger structural issues that are deeply embedded in the everyday workings of the academy, and to subsequently dream of other worlds. The latter is perhaps our most ambitious goal for our collection. Dreaming, imagining, hoping, and remaking the university might appear antithetical to how the academy functions.

After all, in a world where intellect is prioritized over affect, where being pragmatic feels like the most reasonable response to ever-increasing administrative responsibilities, and where we face the politically motivated defunding of higher education, imagining how the university could look otherwise might seem useless at best, and naïve at worst. In this volume, contributors reveal how political science enables and constrains certain forms of knowledge and certain ways of being, as well as how their work in the discipline is embedded in the broader practices of contemporary universities as corporatizing institutions.

The purpose served by dreaming and imagining in this context, as Chamindra Weerawardhana, Jamilah A.Y. Dei-Sharpe, and Kimberley Ens Manning state so powerfully at the beginning of the chapter, is to disrupt and shake up existing structures. Imagining an "otherwise" to the status quo can be a radical act insofar as it allows us to push ourselves to remember that there *are* other ways that the university can and should be. Given that higher education, in its most ideal form, is designed to open minds, to encourage students to "transgress" and to pave the way for critical and oftentimes unexpected lines of inquiry (hooks 1994; Freire

2009; Berila 2015), refusing to acquiesce to corporate visions of academia is a crucial site of resistance. Remembering that "another university is possible" (Another University Is Possible Editorial Collective 2010) and imagining what this other university could look like ensures that we are not left complacent or defeated.

If we were to present one central argument underpinning all of the chapters in this collection, it would be that feminist expertise borne out of feminist research, teaching, and theorizing—including embodied experiences, narratives, and affective realities—should be placed at the centre of knowledge production *and* praxis. All of the editors and authors of this book are feminists: we have a collective expertise in feminist politics and believe that political science as a field, and the academy as a whole, should centre feminist politics. Yet, despite the editorial collective's identifications as feminist scholars, there are distinctions in the ways we understand feministing along with our individual journeys that brought us into this collection. There are also different interventions that we each feel compelled to make. We recognize, too, that readers have different entry points in this conversation as a result of different positionalities, different levels of engagement with feminist research and praxis, and different agendas. Critically, we do not read these differences as individual, idiosyncratic, or as a neutral description of multiplicity (Bannerji 2000, 36). Rather, how we come into this text as an editorial collective, as contributors, and as readers is within a context of deep structural inequity, meaning that our coming together requires a kind of coalitional politics that attends to, rather than papers over, how power moves between us.

In what follows, we briefly discuss research that outlines the challenges that women, Black, Indigenous, and People of Colour (BIPOC) and other members of equity-deserving groups have faced in political science, followed by a discussion of the journeys that brought us together to edit this volume. Then, we identify central themes that emerge through the contributions of the various authors, while making suggestions about how the readers might engage with the collection.

The Challenges of Political Science

Numerous reports have outlined the challenges that women, BIPOC, and equity-deserving groups face in the field of political science. These challenges include but are not limited to disciplinary powerbrokers disparaging "insider" research on gender, race, and Indigeneity; the discounting of the legitimacy of experiential knowledge; microaggressions that make clear that political science spaces such as conference rooms, classrooms, and receptions are unsafe; and harrowing experiences of racial, gendered, and anti-Indigenous harassment in academic spaces. Yet within political science, the belief in objectivity and "merit" remains sacrosanct, making it harder for those critiquing the way the field operates to be heard. Sara Ahmed's (2010) trenchant observations of the way "feminist killjoys" are scapegoated for going against a "social order, which is protected as a *moral* order" (emphasis added), holds true in this regard.

In some ways, it can often appear as though a few key events can spark change (or attempts at change) to take place. For example, two significant events have been attributed to the decision by the Canadian Political Science Association (CPSA), and the Federation for the Humanities and Social Sciences (the Federation, for short) to look at and revise their respective practices and create a set of robust equity, diversity, inclusion, and decolonization (EDID) policies.[1] The first event occurred when a Black graduate student was racially profiled and falsely accused of theft at the annual Congress of the Humanities and Social Sciences (Congress, for short), of which CPSA's annual meetings are part. The following year, the Federation's prestigious Prix du Canada was given to a book about Métis people written by a group of non-Métis authors, leading to the resignation of the Federation's Indigenous advisory circle (Peters 2022).

In 2020 the Federation conducted a six-month investigation of its practices through its Congress Advisory Committee on Equity, Diversity, Inclusion, and Decolonization (2021), culminating in a report that issued specific recommendations for change. The Federation subsequently launched its Charter on Equity, Diversity, Inclusion, and Decolonization, highlighting measures to ensure gender and racial equity. In 2021 CPSA agreed to uphold the Federation's Charter, and formed an EDID committee dedicated to ensuring that organization practices fall in line (CPSA News 2021). In 2021 the Federation was able to reach an agreement with the Black Canadian Studies Association (2021), which had withdrawn from the Federation in the wake of the racial profiling incident. The agreement included promises to proactively address anti-Black racism in the Federation and its member associations, and ultimately convinced the Black Canadian Studies Association to rejoin the Federation.

While it can be comforting to present a narrative in which a few key moments are demonstrably linked to responsive change, in reality, any change within the discipline of political science and within the academy more broadly can be traced to a long lineage of struggle inside *and* outside of the academy, amidst an equally long lineage of persistent backlash, complicity, obstruction and institutional consolidation. The racial profiling at Congress is situated within long and well-documented histories of anti-Blackness within our discipline and the academy, as well as entrenched carceral violence and surveillance targeting Black people more broadly. The response of CPSA and the Federation cannot be untethered from years of non-responsiveness, or from a larger context in which the murder of George Floyd made it increasingly untenable to hold a moral position of apathy, and a context in which the mobilization for Black lives insisted on holding (and returning) the gaze. This persistent pushing up against the academy, and in particular against the discipline of political science, is further evident in a long and well-documented history of struggle against anti-Indigenous racism, particularly within the subfield of Canadian politics; this struggle far precedes the important calls to action emerging from the Truth and Reconciliation Commission.

In these ways, it is not discrete (often catastrophic) events that are the engine for substantive change; if this were the case, there is a litany of harm that should have already sparked mountains of change. Rather, it is mobilization that draws from past struggles, present circumstances, and visions for liberatory futures that constitutes the engine for change. *These are the temporalities of feministing.* Consider the numerous incidents of sexual harassment that take place in political science (see, e.g., Kelsky 2018), coupled with many reports of the chilly environment that characterizes the discipline, which pushed United States–based feminist political scientists to organize under the banner of #MeTooPoliticalScience. The combination of online activism, which saw many disclose their experiences of sexual harassment, including race-based sexual harassment in the discipline (Brown 2019), and in-person mobilization such as conference forums and workshops, led to increased awareness of the problems of harassment in political science and a desire for meaningful change. The shortcomings of institutional solutions to harassment, the backlash that victims face, and the reality that academic networks protect the powerful make change difficult. While "whisper networks" among women,

BIPOC, and marginalized communities have long existed as a form of protection (Young and Wiley 2021, 288), these networks do not directly challenge the systemic inequities that allow abuse and harassment to take place unchecked. Yet the difficulty of understanding *what* structures to put into place to combat these inequities makes it impossible to conceive of easy solutions. "Burn it all down" is an adage that many of us frequently say jokingly, but also semi-seriously, to indicate the absence of alternatives.

In the face of these challenges, many find strength and solidarity in conversation with one another. In Canadian political science, scholars come together periodically to discuss the fraught experiences women, people of colour, Indigenous, Black, and queer scholars face. These gatherings have included two pre-conference events held prior to the CPSA annual conference: a workshop in 2019 on women in political science, and a seminar in 2021 on "living and learning EDID" (discussed in more detail below). In these sessions, understanding the interconnections between lived experiences and knowledge production was a central part of the agenda. Equity issues cannot only be understood theoretically but should rather be seen as part of the *expected* results of institutional operations and disciplinary norms. When, for example, political science conventionally dismisses gender, race, sexuality, class, and other social locations as "identity politics," these become divorced from the rigorous study of politics (Bernhardt and Pin 2018). Put differently, rather than seeing ongoing racial and gender-based harassment as systemic and embedded within structures of power, they are seen as individual problems. The result places the burden of proof on equity-deserving communities to *prove* the validity of their experiences, with repercussions in the type of interventions made to the field in the name of diversity, the fields themselves (i.e., adding and mixing more diverse faculty is the solution rather than more structural transformations), and the types of research that gets rewarded (i.e., "objective" research undertaken by researchers without grounded and proximate knowledge is deemed more rigorous).

Coming Together to "Feminist"

The members of the editorial collective have all experienced and observed the challenges of being part of a discipline that at times renders the research we do marginal and unimportant, and at other times dangerous in the challenges it presents to the field. We have also had different encounters with being seen as "others" in the discipline not only because of the research that we do but also because of our distinct social locations and the struggles we centre in our work. When we came together to reflect on our experiences in the discipline, we were struck with how a sense of non-belonging resonated, as well as the overarching realization that institutions—whether our respective departments or other bodies within the university or even our professional associations—do not have appropriate policies to redress widely felt experiences of toxicity, harassment, and discrimination. Various encounters with gatekeepers and powerbrokers have made it harder for us to navigate the discipline and the academy because of the roadblocks that gatekeepers and powerbrokers have presented. And finally, the pervasive feeling of gaslighting was commonplace, where we are made to believe that there is something deficient with *us* as individuals. Gaslighting prevents us seeing the institutional and systemic issues at hand.

Despite—or perhaps because—of these challenges, we sought each other out. The workshops that we organized within CPSA allowed us to see that our experiences are reflected in others', but also, more importantly, to understand that there are differences in our experiences. These workshops prompted us to reflect on issues of power and privilege, on our resistance to *and* variable complicity with white supremacist patriarchal norms, and on the manifold ways we resist *and* leave unchallenged the power abuses of the academy. Sometimes fraught, sometimes tense, but always generative, the conversations we have in and outside these spaces (be it through Twitter/X or Instagram or Facebook, through WhatsApp or Signal group chats, between conference panels, in hallways at work, etc.) establish common ground but also reveal the messiness of a feminist politics that assumes commonality at the expense of recognizing how power structures difference. Rather than seeing these differences as departure points, we recognized the need to learn from each other, to organize alongside and in support of each other, and to fight back.

Various panels over several years, and a call for papers sent out by Fiona and Stephanie, initiated discussions on what, if anything, we can do as a collective. Our activities included engaging at various moments with colleagues, including Gina Starblanket, Tammy Findlay, and Alexandra Dobrowolsky in the beginning stages, and, for Nisha and Ethel, seeking the counsel of Rita Kaur Dhamoon. Through these conversations we came to the decision to collectively edit this collection. Aside from accepting papers through an initial call, we also approached friends, colleagues, and co-conspirators to develop chapters based on conversations and experiences that they have shared. We also recognized that writing conventional academic chapters could feel restrictive for some people and so encouraged our contributors to be creative, which is why we have chapters written as letters, chapters written with a creative structure, and chapters that were collectively produced dialogues. Our decision not to adhere to a singular format was deliberate.

Our decision to not provide set prescriptions on how to feminist is also deliberate. While all of the contributors discuss how they interpret feminism, and how they promote feminist praxis, there are differences in approach, in priority, and in the risks that people feel that they could take. In the beginning, the subtitle of the book was "A Manifesta for Change," and we imagined a framework for action, steps that we might take together for a better discipline, university, and world. But as we explore in the final pages of the collection, the contributors' different experiences and visions of what a better political science might look like are not the same, nor should they be, and we shifted away from calls to specific action, to a reflection on our different journeys and a shared vocabulary—a lexicon—to highlight points of convergence and difference, the groundwork laid for ongoing conversations, collaborations, coalition building, and imaginings.

Feministing Themes and the Invocation of Disruptive Reading

Understanding how power moves in and through feminism and in feministing consequently means that we know that readers will likely gravitate towards some chapters over others. This is not simply a matter of preference, but rather indicative that how we read is political. In this sense, we invite you to engage in a reading of this collection that is disruptive, meaning that you read for *both* coherence and disjuncture, or for those rough edges that reveal incommensurabilities. In inviting a disruptive reading from you, consider what feministing means to the practice of reading:

- That how we enter a text might shape *where* we enter the text—where we linger, and experience an affective response of connection *and* disconnection (and why);

- That how we enter shapes our accountabilities in reading the text—where we *must* linger, where we *must* probe a lack of affective response or connection, and where we might identify (and demand) new junctures for accountability;
- That as we read, we are reading for inclusions but also silences—that there are accounts that are too risky to include, particularly when the experiences of Indigenous, Black, and racialized women in the academy are often treated voyeuristically as something to be consumed. Silences also reflect people who did not see our call as inviting their response, raising important questions as to why;
- That we read these pieces as being in conversation and contestation, even in the absence of explicit conversation amongst the authors—where are the ruptures, why are they discomforting, and what are the implications for feministing;
- That we read for complicities and accountabilities—if as Vimalassery et al. (2016) write, the "act of ignoring—is aggressively made and reproduced, affectively invested and effectively distributed in ways that conform the social relations and economics of the here and now," what are the implications for feministing?

A disruptive reading of this text also invites a rejection or refusal (Tuck and Yang 2014) of the siloed thinking that organizes not just our discipline but work within the academy. It can be too easy to position the contributions to this collection as incidental side projects related to "service." In (re)witnessing the contributions (Nath, Bhandar, and Girvan 2022) in this collection through a disruptive reading, feministing also involves articulating that what is being presenced here is *epistemic labour* that is carried unevenly within our discipline and the academy; this labour contributes substantively to the health of our discipline and the academy. While contributors are reflecting on institutional service work, teaching, pedagogy, and methodology, the pieces in this collection are also engaged in profound forms of concept-work that contest and redefine core concepts within our discipline: the political, power, institutions, relationality, intersectionality, legitimacy, legibility, authority, neoliberalism, ethical accountability, intersectionality, progress, change, and justice. In this sense, one of the interventions (Nath and Allen 2022) that we can make in engaging in a critical, disruptive, and pedagogical *feministing as reading* is that we (re)witness the work of each other, but also support a (re)witnessing of our *own* institutional labour as epistemic (Nath 2020). To render visible can be reactive, but visibilizing this labour to ourselves (Dhamoon 2020) can be a radical act that enunciates that these relationally other worlds already exist.

To help guide readers on how to engage with the book, we have identified five different themes that cut across the collection (although most chapters engage with more than one). We discuss each of these themes below.

Temporality and the Case for Transformation
A critical theme that emerges in this collection is the multiple ways that different notions of time shape our experiences in both academia and political science. Time emerges in consideration of what is presumed to constitute a linear academic career—from graduate student to professor—and the shifts from short-term precarity to long-term security assumed to follow. Chapters on this theme describe longer-standing experiences of precarity that defy linear understandings of time and career progression, with racism, sexism, colonialism, and other forms of oppression looping back on themselves, making it impossible for many to ever lose the sense of the ground always shifting beneath them.

Time also emerges as a critical theme in this volume in terms of the pace of academic life, from the intense daily pressure of teaching, research, and service, to the decades-long experiences of advocating for institutional change. The intensity of the work of feministing in political science stands in contrast to the long history of both the discipline of political science and the university-as-institution, in which hard-fought efforts to make change seem to disappear like drops in a proverbial ocean. Yet the stories told in this volume show how reorienting our conceptions of time can challenge our expectations of what we can otherwise achieve, and how the moments together can turn the tide.

The contributors, individually and collectively, contribute their voices and their experiences to unravelling linear notions of time, challenging how we understand what it means to "advance" in our careers, through our disciplines and within our institutions. In her chapter on approaches to equity in Canadian political science, Ethel Tungohan explores the ways that the linear narrative of slow but steady "progress" towards equity in the discipline of Canadian political science obscures the limits of a liberal, additive approach to equity, instead calling for more significant transformations that might actually make a more equitable discipline a reality. In her chapter, tracing her experience modulating expectations of "reasonableness," Nicole S. Bernhardt suggests that the longstanding approach to an inclusionary and equitable discipline that requires BIPOC and others to simply fit in contributes to these linear narratives of progress, and not only works to replicate the already existing discipline but also takes an undue toll on those being called upon for diversity work in ways that will always feel precarious.

In other chapters, time emerges as a way to reconcile the university as a site of transformational, radical possibility—a site of mobilization—and the heavy history of a long-revered institution. In her chapter, Alana Cattapan uses two metaphors—the fish and the spider—to explore the history of the university as both a site of extractive capitalism and of the transformative possibilities of the present. It seems that both stories are true. In Elaine Coburn, Rita Kaur Dhamoon, Joyce Green, Genevieve Fuji Johnson, Heidi Kiiwetinepinesiik Stark, and Gina Starblanket's chapter on "Anti-Racist and Indigenous Feminism and the Generative Power of Disruption," the authors use their experience mobilizing at the annual meeting of the CPSA to explore a particular moment in time. Here, the authors examine how their collective contributions in a particular time and (virtual) space worked to challenge "the pre-existing structure and expectations of the discipline" and its embedded "racialized, colonial, and patriarchal inequities," drawing attention to the relationships developed and redeveloped in the process. The incident they describe, and the labour of their mobilization, presents a critical example of how collaborative interventions can shift, if only slowly, the work of doing political science towards anti-racist, decolonial, feminist practice.

Together, these contributions stress the urgency of this moment within the neoliberal academy within a longer context of structural marginalization.

Relationality, Community, and Care
Following from a long feminist lineage, the chapters in this collection converge in their iteration that feministing is grounded in intersectional embodied knowledges. Critically, this attention to intersectionality also

draws attention to *relational* understandings of power, and to what can be described as feminist (and/or otherwise) *relationalities*. In the case of the former, the chapters bring forward a focus on interacting and intersecting structures of dominance, but also leave room to consider how these structures of dominance are *reliant* on each other; they are mutually reinforcing. A relational understanding of power examines "the interactive processes of re/making, re/organizing, and managing subjugating formations of difference which operate not only in contexts of dominance but in relation to one another as well" (Dhamoon 2021, 874). Here, the chapter by Kelly Aguirre, Mariam Georgis, and Sarah Munawar beautifully lays out their diverging and converging locations within intricate and relational webs of power. Through their storying of the discipline, they reveal the distinct challenges and epistemic violences faced by racialized and Indigenous scholars within the field of politics, but simultaneously name the practices of kin-making care work and friendship that "unsettle foundations built on our backs." In their naming of the "spectre of whiteness" and of "whitestream feminism," their dialogue evokes a distinct ethic of refusal that signals an important space of tension within feministing. In his chapter, Michael Orsini examines the tensions bound up in the "unconscious ableism of feminist activism and feminist interventions," asking how disability and ableism can enable better understandings of bodily difference and diversity. For Orsini, the extraordinary contributions of disability justice scholarship should be central to the project of feministing from the beginning.

    The implications of this relational framing of power are profound in that they ultimately require challenging conversations about complicities, coalition, solidarity, and otherwise relationalities. Indigenous scholars have long written about relationality within the context of Indigenous research paradigms, describing it as an ethical imperative and relationality that is socially interconnected and premised on culturally embodied knowledges connected to land (Donald 2012; Moreton-Robinson 2017, 71). This relationality informs an Indigenous "epistemological and ethical premise that social research should begin with an awareness of our proper relationships with the world we inhabit, and is conducted with respect, responsibility, generosity, obligation, and reciprocity" (Moreton-Robinson, 2017, 71). In her chapter on Indigenous-centred feministing in political science, Emily Grafton asks whether political science can truly "make space" for the diversity and nuance of Indigenous feminisms or whether it will (continue to) be an exercise in co-optation.

Yet, as many chapters in this collection demonstrate, the neoliberal academy structurally cultivates neoliberal relationalities of distance, extractivism, competition, and abstraction. In her cogent chapter, Amanda Bittner disrupts the voice of political science, writing from her positionality as a white woman and pushing back against dominant ways of being, feeling, and relating in the academy. Speaking to the coexistence of academic success with states of depletion, unhappiness, and of feeling alone, she provides an extended reflection on her experiences of building community through online spaces, before and during the pandemic. In describing the impact of these intentional spaces of community, Bittner offers a hopeful commentary on the possibilities of disrupting institutional relationalities in the creation of spaces of care and generosity that support "belonging, purpose, and fulfillment." In their chapter, Lindsay Larios and Manon Laurent also speak to community through feminist relationships, as they engage in a conversation reflecting on their experience doing PHDs in political science. They describe the misogynist contexts in which their feminist praxis emerged, including the strictures of being situated within the discipline, particularly when one is engaged in work that is positioned at the margins. Here, they trace how gatekeeping manifests in real time in PHD classrooms, and also how entry into the discipline can be profoundly disorienting. Writing of the loneliness of doing a PHD, they note that a feminist PHD program "should actively fight against graduate students' loneliness." In laying out this assertion alongside a structural analysis of the experiences of PHD students, Larios and Laurent's chapter invites critical reflection on at least two questions: What is a feminist institution, and what are the university's responsibilities?

Finally, these chapters articulate complex iterations of a praxis of care, including intimacy and empathy, as well as the implications of presencing trauma and vulnerability within the context of disciplines and institutions that render these ways of entering or inhabiting illegible. In her chapter, Stephanie Paterson pulls all of these threads together by carefully exploring the "politics of intimacy" through an intersectional lens and considering how it both troubles and constitutes the academy. Through a series of powerful vignettes, Paterson demonstrates how the university interpellates, articulates, and acknowledges emotive experiences, including daily systemic and institutional traumas as individualized encounters. Challenging institutional relational logics that individualize emotion and empathy, Paterson reorients towards considering how social empathy, as an approach to policy and decision-making, holds transformative possibilities.

Feministing and the "Real" World of Politics
Feminist interventions in political science, particularly in Canada, have their roots in the study of "women in politics," and academic and activist interventions to address inclusion in politics and public policy. Early work focused on descriptive and substantive representation in both elected bodies and bureaucracies, exposing barriers to participation and inclusion, but also opportunities for change (for an overview, see Bashevkin 2010). Recent work in this area offers more nuanced approaches to gender and sex and intersectional politics, troubling the construction of "gender" in research and policy design (e.g., Bird 2016; Bittner and Goodyear-Grant 2017, 2018).

The contributors to this volume begin from the premise that feminist interventions in law, policy, and electoral politics are part of the labour of feministing in political science, identifying critical connections between struggles in the legislature, the boardroom, campaign trail, and the political science classroom. The chapter from Julianne M. Acker-Verney, Alana Cattapan, Alexandra Dobrowolsky, Tammy Findlay, and April Mandrona adopts an epistolary approach to report and reflect on results from a research project aimed at assessing the impacts of public policy for women since the 1970 report of the Royal Commission on the Status of Women. The series of letters, to research assistants, to feminist scholars and researchers, to students, and to their future selves, troubles the ways knowledge is produced and shared across the diverse groups with whom we engage in our work as political scientists. Jeanette Ashe's autoethnographic chapter uses both experiential and academic knowledge to understand how feministing shaped her work in drafting and advocating for Bill C-237. The bill, a private member's bill put forward by a New Democratic Party (NDP) member of Parliament, sought to amend the Canada Elections Act by addressing the political underrepresentation of women and other equity-deserving groups in Canada's House of Commons.

Through her experience, Ashe illuminates not only the challenges facing feminists and feminist interventions, such as violence, compromises, and misinformation, but also the indefatigable work and commitment of feminists and allies both within and outside of Parliament. The final chapter in this thematic section also showcases experiential knowledge, featuring a dialogue between Kimberley Ens Manning, Nadia Verrelli, and Melanee Thomas, facilitated by Alana Cattapan and Fiona MacDonald. Through the dialogue, these three political scientists reflect on their experiences running for political office. Together, these pieces demonstrate the power of political science research that centres our own experiences, offering reflexive and progressive understandings of representation.

Gatekeeping, Pedagogy, and Mentoring
The classroom is, generally speaking, the first place any future political scientist meets the discipline. It is also an important site of feministing for students, teaching assistants, and instructors ranging from those precariously employed as sessional contractors or adjuncts and those with the security of permanent positions and/or tenure. What, who, and how we teach our discipline is a reflection of the politics we study, interrogate, and work to shift.

The ongoing legacies of structural and epistemic violence built into academic institutions and disciplines, including political science, are perpetuated by generations of scholars training other generations of scholars about the norms and mores of the discipline. The pieces in this collection articulate how feministing disrupts these hegemonies of knowledge by challenging what topics and ideas are seen as sites of "legitimate" interrogation, and what methodologies are characterized as "rigorous." Put differently, in this ongoing praxis of resistance to gatekeeping, feministing both exposes and challenges the terms of legibility in mainstream political science. Contributors to the collection consider how teaching, learning, and mentoring can contest what comes to count as political science, building from other contributions in the collection that name the challenges of contesting the discipline but also why so much is at stake.

David Semaan's chapter reveals the double bind that arises from being both a graduate student of colour and a teaching assistant. His "vignettes from the classroom" reveal that the "liminal space of tutorials" offers potential for critical pedagogy, solidarity building, and feminist interrogation while also acting as a site fraught with political tension as the backlash politics of "free speech" circulate within post-secondary institutions. As his work makes clear, we are not simply "teaching politics" but are, in many ways, at the front lines of doing politics in our classrooms. Jamilah A.Y. Dei-Sharpe and Kimberley Ens Manning take up questions of solidarity and collaboration to examine how their experiences of anti-racist coalition building as a Black student leader (Dei-Sharpe) and white tenured professor and department head (Manning) have worked to challenge the precariousness and disempowerment often experienced by BIPOC students in the academy. Describing their experience of anti-racist coalition building, Dei-Sharpe and Manning interrogate both the radical, transformational possibilities of anti-racist coalition building and the need for "constant vigilance" to ensure that their work is not co-opted. Fiona MacDonald's chapter—in conversation with her students—engages with how to look inward to our own embodied experiences as a site of learning and contestation. Here, MacDonald presents her students' engagement with photovoice to centre their own lives and identities in the classroom, and to privilege and highlight embodied forms of knowledge within the political science classroom. Finally, in his chapter, Nick Dorzweiler shares some of the most difficult moments he experienced while pursuing his PHD and how engaging with feminist theory during this time impacted him not just cognitively but affectively. In so doing he reveals the complex value feminist scholarship holds for us at various moments in our careers as well as the importance of teaching feminist scholarship in our discipline.

(Re)building Political Science
Another theme that emerged throughout the chapters is the importance of pushing back against the norms and practices that have been deeply entrenched in the discipline of political science and in the academy at large. The authors have documented the many exclusions that they faced that made academia hostile terrain. Such exclusions include disciplinary backlash to their presence and to their chosen research areas; microaggressions, abuse, and harassment; the creation of a chilly climate within departments and professional association meetings; and the deliberate non-recognition of women, BIPOC, trans, and other minority scholars' expertise.

Because of the pervasiveness of these experiences, the authors understood that accepting the status quo was simply not an option—that, in fact, to stay in academia and in political science necessitates thinking of *what else* they could create. The collective epiphany that life is too short, as the COVID-19 pandemic has revealed so blatantly, and, for BIPOC academics, that many BIPOC professors are getting sick and dying young due to the multiple pressures they face (Thomas 2020), led to an urgent desire to build new ways of doing and being within the academy.

From deliberately centring Indigenous, Black, and trans feminists when teaching, as Chamindra Weerawardhana and Emily Grafton call for, to pushing the discipline to accept new methodologies and new research approaches, as our mentors' dialogue with Yasmeen Abu-Laban, Leah F. Vosko, Reeta Chowdhari Tremblay, and Kiera L. Ladner highlight, to strategically developing coalitions and using equity "brokers" to achieve important goals, the chapters in *Feministing* show the manifold actions taken by feminist political scientists to ensure that the academy works for them and their communities. Rather than accept that academia is a bastion of objectivity, neutrality, and merit, the authors puncture the myth of the impartial academy. Through their use of pedagogical, methodological, and theoretical approaches outside the convention of political science, the authors fight against practices that have long sidelined equity-deserving communities. Alongside their use of these varied approaches, the authors also write about how their *presence* in the discipline is also subversive. As Tka C. Pinnock notes in her chapter, "*our being (t)here* is not just additive but transformative, rescripting institutional practices." Hence, feministing involves seizing power to create a new way of being a political scientist and an academic. Creating "other worlds" (Spivak 2012) is thus a core part of feministing.

Yet the authors paradoxically also recognize the generative possibilities presented by the politics of refusal. As Kiera Ladner mentioned, her two mantras are both to "just do it"—that is, keep pushing to do the work that she finds important despite facing opposition—and "refuse"—that is, reject academic norms and expectations that run counter to her values. Deliberately adopting both approaches enables a more nuanced feministing ethos: we simultaneously do what we can within existing structures to pursue our goals while also trying to push for structural changes. Feministing, then, involves acts of resistance that deliberately eschew old approaches in favour of a different path, all the while keeping in our sightlines the belief that, to paraphrase the Another University Is Possible Collective (2010), a feminist, decolonial, anti-racist political science and academy is within our reach.

Conclusion

The chapters in this book highlight the myriad challenges we face, but also, we hope, highlight the joy the editorial collective and the contributors take in being subversive. There is something cathartic about putting to words our experiences. There is also something cathartic about witnessing how different contributors have fought against power imbalances and have found ways to exist in an otherwise exclusionary discipline. Taken together, all of the chapters are future oriented in that they hint at the possibilities of how much stronger and richer political science and academia could be if women, BIPOC, and other equity-deserving communities are given the opportunity to thrive under changed structural conditions. *Feministing in Political Science,* ultimately, is about thinking and working towards a better, more just political science. We hope that readers join us in this journey.

Note

1. The Federation is an organization of academic associations, universities, and colleges that promotes academic teaching and research. Its key activities include advocacy and lobbying, funding scholarly publications, and organizing events, including the annual Congress of the Humanities and Social Sciences. The CPSA is a member association of the Federation (Federation, n.d.).

References

Ahmed, Sara. 2010. "Feminist Killjoys (And Other Willful Subjects)." *S&F Online* 8 (3). https://sfonline.barnard.edu/polyphonic/print_ahmed.htm.

Another University Is Possible Collective. 2010. *Another University Is Possible.* San Diego, CA: University Readers.

Bannerji, Himani. 2000. *Dark Side of the Nation: Essays on Multiculturalism, Nationalism, and Gender.* Toronto: Women's Press.

Bashevkin, Sylvia, ed. 2010. *Opening Doors Wider: Women's Political Engagement in Canada.* Vancouver: UBC Press.

Berila, Beth. 2015. *Integrating Mindfulness into Anti-Oppression Pedagogy: Social Justice in Higher Education.* New York: Routledge.

Bernhardt, Nicole S., and Laura G. Pin. 2018. "Engaging with Identity Politics in Canadian Political Science." *Canadian Journal of Political Science* 51 (4): 771–94. https://doi.org/10.1017/S0008423918000318.

Bird, Karen. 2016. "Intersections of Exclusion: The Institutional Dynamics of Combined Gender and Ethnic Quota Systems." *Politics, Groups, and Identities* 4 (2): 284–306. https://doi.org/10.1080/21565503.2015.1053399.

Bittner, Amanda, and Elizabeth Goodyear-Grant. 2017. "Sex Isn't Gender: Reforming Concepts and Measurements in the Study of Public Opinion." *Political Behavior* 39 (4): 1019–41. https://doi.org/10.1007/s11109-017-9391-y.

Bittner, Amanda, and Elizabeth Goodyear-Grant. 2018. "Why 'Sex' May Not Be the Best Way to Understand the Gender Gap in Political Behavior." *USApp-American Politics and Policy Blog*, March 2, 2018. http://eprints.lse.ac.uk/89345/1/usappblog-2018-03-02-why-sex-may-not-be-the-best-way-to-understand.pdf.

Black Canadian Studies Association. 2021. "Statement Regarding 2022 Congress of the Humanities and Social Sciences." *BCSA News*, November 5, 2021. https://www.blackcanadianstudiesassociation.ca/uploads/1/3/7/6/137686872/bcsa_statement_to_public_-_congress_2022.pdf.

Brown, Nadia E. 2019. "Me Too Political Science: An Introduction." *Journal of Women, Politics & Policy* 40 (1): 1–6. https://doi.org/10.1080/1554477X.2019.1563413.

Congress Advisory Committee on Equity, Diversity, Inclusion, and Decolonization. 2021. *Igniting Change: Final Report and Recommendations*. March 8, 2021. https://www.federationhss.ca/sites/default/files/2021-10/Igniting-Change-Final-Report-and-Recommendations-en.pdf.

CPSA News. 2021. "FHSS' Charter EDID—CPSA EDID Committee." *CPSA News*, August 25, 2021. https://cpsa-acsp.ca/cpsa-news/fhss-charter-edid-cpsa-edid-committee/.

Dhamoon, Rita Kaur. 2020. "Racism as a Workload and Bargaining Issue." *Socialist Studies* 14 (1). https://doi.org/10.18740/ss27273.

Dhamoon, Rita Kaur. 2021. "Relational Othering: Critiquing Dominance, Critiquing the Margins." *Politics, Groups, and Identities* 9 (5): 873–92. https://doi.org/10.1080/21565503.2019.1691023.

Donald, Dwayne. 2012. "Forts, Curriculum, and Ethical Relationality." In *Reconsidering Canadian Curriculum Studies*, edited by Nicholas Ng-A-Fook and Jennifer Rottman, 39–46. New York: Palgrave Macmillan.

Federation for the Humanities and Social Sciences. n.d. "About the Federation." Accessed September 20, 2023. https://www.federationhss.ca/en/about-us/about-federation.

Freire, Paolo. 2009. "Chapter 2 from *Pedagogy of the Oppressed*." *Race/Ethnicity: Multidisciplinary Global Contexts* 2 (2): 163–74. https://www.jstor.org/stable/25595010.

Goldberg, Emma. 2019. "A Farewell to Feministing and the Heyday of Feminist Blogging." *New York Times*, December 8, 2019. https://www.nytimes.com/2019/12/08/business/media/feminist-blogs-feministing.html.

Greyser, Naomi, Samhita Mukhopadhyay, and Gwendolyn Beetham. 2012. "Gender Nerds at Heart: An Interview on Bridging the Blogging/Academic Divide with Feministing.com." *American Quarterly* 64 (4): 837–39. https://www.jstor.org/stable/41809534.

Hearn, Jeff. 2015. "The Uses and Abuses of the Political Category of 'Men': Activism, Policy and Theorising." In *Engaging Men in Building Gender Equality*, edited by Michael Flood and Richard Howson, 34–54. Newcastle: Cambridge Scholars Publishing.

hooks, bell. 1994. *Teaching to Transgress: Education as the Practice of Freedom*. New York: Routledge.

Kelsky, Karen, ed. 2018. "Sexual Harassment in the Academy: A Crowdsource Survey." https://docs.google.com/spreadsheets/d/1S9KShDLvU7C-KkgEevYTHXr3F6InTenrBsS9yk-8C5M/edit#gid=1530077352.

Moreton-Robinson, Aileen. 2017. "Relationality: A Key Presupposition of an Indigenous Social Research Paradigm." In *Sources and Methods in Indigenous Studies*, edited by Jean M. O'Brien and Chris Andersen, 69–77. London: Routledge. https://eprints.qut.edu.au/93245/.

Mowles, Jessica. M. 2008. "Framing Issues, Fomenting Change, 'Feministing': A Contemporary Feminist Blog in the Landscape of Online Political Activism." *International Reports on Socio-Informatics* 5 (1): 29–40.

Nath, Nisha. 2020. "'The Letters': EDI and Tracing Work in the Academe." Support Network for Academics of Colour Plus, Alberta Human Rights Commission Education, and Multiculturalism Fund in Collaboration with the Women Scholars' Speakers Series, University of Lethbridge. November 5, 2020, Lethbridge, AB.

Nath, Nisha, Davina Bhandar, and Anita Girvan. 2022. "Insurgent Resurgent Knowledges Lab." Unpublished paper.

Nath, Nisha, and Willow Samara Allen. 2022. "Settler Colonial Socialization in Public Sector Work: Moving from Privilege to Complicity." *Studies in Social Justice* 16 (1): 200–26. https://doi.org/10.26522/ssj.v16i1.2648.

Peters, Diane. 2022. "Has the Federation Done Enough to Address EDID Issues at Congress?" *University Affairs*, July 8, 2022. https://www.universityaffairs.ca/news/news-article/has-the-federation-done-enough-to-address-edid-issues-at-congress/.

Spivak, Gayatri. 2012. *In Other Worlds: Essays in Cultural Politics*. New York: Routledge.

Thomas, Lahoma. 2020. "A Black Feminist Autoethnographic Reflection of Mentoring in the Discipline of Political Science." *PS: Political Science and Politics* 53 (4): 788–92. https://doi.org/10.1017/S104909652000044X.

Tuck, Eve, and K. Wayne Yang. 2014. "Unbecoming Claims: Pedagogies of Refusal in Qualitative Research." *Qualitative Inquiry* 20 (6): 811–18. https://doi.org/10.1177/1077800414530265.

Vimalassery, Manu, Juliana Hu Pegues, and Alyosha Goldstein. 2016. "Introduction: On Colonial Unknowing." *Theory & Event* 19 (4). https://muse.jhu.edu/article/633283.

Young, Sarah, and Kimberly K. Wiley. 2021. "Erased: Why Faculty Sexual Misconduct Is Prevalent and How We Could Prevent It." *Journal of Public Affairs Education* 27 (3): 276–300. https://doi.org/10.1080/15236803.2021.1977983.

TEMPORALITY AND THE CASE FOR TRANSFORMATION

1 "Diversity Is Important, but Only When It Is the 'Right' Type of Diversity"

Canadian Political Science and the Limitations of an Additive Approach to Equity

ETHEL TUNGOHAN

AS A WOMAN belonging to the Black, Indigenous, and People of Colour (BIPOC) community, I have long been aware that BIPOC remain the minority in political science. Yet it has been interesting to witness shifts in the way the field has addressed issues of "diversity." Between 2006 when I first started as a PHD student in political science at the University of Toronto to the time of writing in 2023, as an associate professor of politics and a Canada Research Chair at York University, I have witnessed many seismic shifts within the profession.

These include the development of subfields, such as the race, ethnicity, and Indigenous politics section at the Canadian Political Science Association (CPSA); widespread efforts to decolonize the curriculum as seen in the syllabus created by the Reconciliation Committee at CPSA (CPSA Reconciliation Committee 2018); efforts to diversify the profession specifically and the field more generally through targeted Indigenous and Black hires (see, e.g., York University 2020; University of Guelph 2020); and the commonplace understanding (or so it seems) that the status quo simply is insufficient. Social movement organizing undoubtedly played a role in bringing this awareness, with many BIPOC communities disclosing their lived realities in public fora and demanding accountability. To be a professor of *politics*, which examines various manifestations of *power* in the state and across society, must mean also being part of efforts to hold such power into account, to speak truth to power...

...Or does it? Alongside these developments appear various instances of individuals within institutions being resistant to accountability and to change. In myriad ways, the field of political science specifically and academia more generally seems reluctant to move *beyond* established practices and norms to truly pursue structural and systemic change. Hence, many of the developments I cited—the creation of separate subsections, targeted diversity hires—still remain rooted in liberal notions of instituting change. The logic goes that adding and mixing is perfectly fine. If we add more of "you"—you being BIPOC professors, women, and other members of underrepresented communities—surely change will follow. The time span for institutional shifts, after all, are longer. Transformation cannot take place over night.

But can arguments saying that it "takes time" still hold when many of the demands for greater equity in political science have remained the same for decades now? Our dialogue with political science mentors in Chapter 19 of this volume highlights how gender and racial exclusions have persisted, even as initiatives to rectify these exclusions are promoted. In this chapter, I reflect on the question of feministing in Canadian political science, which I define as the active labour involved in overturning *structures* and *practices* of inequality in order to create a more equitable discipline. I ultimately argue against liberal modes of inclusion, making the claim that the "discipline" needs to go *beyond* adding and mixing; instead, the discipline has to consider its complicity in perpetuating settler colonial and white supremacist structures of power and be prepared to make reparations that enable transformative change.

My analysis proceeds in three parts. First, I consider how Canadian political science, as a discipline, has actually shifted by encompassing more diverse forms of research and by accommodating more diverse individuals. In this section, I acknowledge the tension between linear narratives of progress and the reality that "diversifying" Canadian political science is difficult in light of its settler colonial history. Second, I discuss attempts to institute change through the implementation of liberal policies that are intended to facilitate greater inclusion. Third, using my own encounters in these fora, I reflect on the challenges presented by these moments. In the spirit of a feministing approach, I also provide some suggestions of ways for Canadian political science to institute transformations. And finally, I conclude by thinking about the *politics* of political science, and how these efforts may be insufficient to engender lasting structural transformation.

Political Science: Then and Now

It would, of course, be unfair to characterize Canadian political science as being stagnant. Writing this chapter in 2023, it would be churlish not to acknowledge changes within the discipline. Janice Newton's (2017) historical review of the CPSA in the twentieth-century pre-war era shows shifts in the way the discipline saw the role of political scientists in Canada. As Newton shows, while CPSA was established in 1913 by a group of "mostly elite men" who considered themselves "more learned than the democratic masses and without partisan or private biases" and who could thus provide recommendations to government (40), it has since evolved into a professional organization representing political scientists from diverse backgrounds. Erin Tolley's (2017) analysis of the abstracts of papers presented at CPSA's annual conference from 1965 to 2017 shows the growing mass of gender research in Canadian political science and also the rising numbers of women assuming positions of leadership. She supports the argument Jill Vickers (2015) made in her CPSA presidential address that "feminist political science" has taken hold in Canadian political science. And more recently, Joanna Everitt's (2021) CPSA presidential address maps the evolution of the profession from being a predominantly white, male field to one where at least 50 per cent are women and where there is more representation of racialized, Indigenous, and LGBTQ+ researchers. Everitt (2021) also notes that research focus has shifted, too, to encompass areas of research beyond the discipline's conventional focus on political behaviour. Graham White's (2017) reflections on the *Canadian Journal of Political Science* (*CJPS*)'s first fifty years points to the gradual diversification of the types of research showcased in the discipline's flagship journal, corroborating Everitt's observations.

Yet even these observations are tempered by the recognition that much more needs to be done to ensure that the discipline grows. Most of the researchers cited above are well aware of the "diversity work" that still needs to be done. Everitt discusses how more effort should be put diversifying the discipline, including making the discipline more reflective of the demographic makeup of Canada and "push[ing] beyond the canon" to reflect "underrepresented voices and perspectives" (2021, 765).

Similarly, much as Tolley (2017) recognizes the growth in gender research presented in the CPSA annual conference, she warns that such gender research is predominantly featured in the "women, gender, and politics" subfields, and not in the "main" conference panels, thus showing a siloing of gender research. White's (2017) own observations of shifts within the discipline highlights that both "continuity and change" co-exist. I find it noteworthy, in fact, that White echoes Tolley's observations of the siloing of gender research in Canadian political science when he notes that the "Finding Feminism" special issue in *CJPS* serves as an "important correction to the still limited number of articles on gender" (White 2017, 32). When gender research has a better chance of being included in *CJPS* through a special issue dedicated to gender and politics, perhaps Tolley's observations of the siloing of gender research from "mainstream" research holds true. The question that emerges when reading these accounts is whether Canadian political science, both in its history and its conventional approach to "doing" political science, is resistant to change.

There are some researchers who appear to believe that the very foundations of Canadian political science make it difficult to shift the discipline. Vickers criticizes the field for resisting the use of gender as an analytical category, concluding that such resistance shows what she calls the fundamental "incompatibilities between so-called conventional political science and 'feminist political science'" (2015, 750). Debra Thompson and Nisha Nath make similar observations regarding the discipline's approach to the study of race. Thompson highlights how "methodological fuzziness, dominant elite-focused and colour-blind approaches to the study of politics, and the prevalence of ideas and foci about the nature of Canadian politics" make the field unable to see race as worthy of study (2008, 526). Nath affirms Thompson's claims, arguing that "race" has been deployed narrowly in Canadian political science to encompass a specific subset of one's identity, as opposed to being seen "as a product of social or political action, a product of multiple and competing discourses and a governmentality" (2011, 162). Kiera Ladner (2017) observes a similar dynamic when considering the field's engagement with the study of Indigenous politics. Canadian political science's fixation on examining the Westphalian state means that there are "methodological and epistemological" incompatibilities between the study of Canadian politics and the study of Indigenous politics. Elaine Coburn, Aileen Moreton-Robinson, George Sefa Dei, and Makere Stewart-Harawira (2013) make a similar point when discussing how historically, social sciences perpetuate colonial practices, making Indigenous Peoples objects of study.

Nicole Bernhardt and Laura Pin (2018) trenchantly put together all of these observations by arguing that Canadian political science's tendency to label research on gender, race, Indigeneity and on diversity as "identity politics" relegates such work to the margins of Canadian political science. Canadian political science assumes that gender, race, and Indigeneity are only identity issues. It does not recognize that inequities born out of gender, race, and Indigeneity are woven into the very institutions, structures, and histories of Canada. Indeed, Yasmeen Abu-Laban's CPSA presidential address sees the emergence of the Canadian nation-state as being tied closely to the history of Canadian political science, which was "really at heart a national venture" (2017, 895). It thus follows that Canadian political science *affirms* settler colonial ideologies because research in support of the field was undertaken to support the Canadian national project.

Hence, there is a fundamental tension between scholars on the question of diversity in Canadian political science. While I do not wish to overstate this tension, I do think that there are some researchers who embrace linear notions of progress within the field: that as ideas evolve, and as more awareness is engendered regarding the necessity of embracing diverse members of the profession and diverse types of research, the tent can be widened within Canadian political science to be more inclusive. And yet there are other scholars who disavow this linear notion of progress. If the foundations of Canadian political science are rooted in settler colonialism with all of its attendant sexist, anti-Black, anti-Indigenous, and racist praxis, then seeing "adding and mixing" more diverse bodies as a route to progress does not resolve underlying structural inequities.

Criticizing Liberal Modes of Inclusion

There are many arguments that highlight the limitations of liberal modes of inclusion. One of the most commonly cited arguments against these is the reality that additive approaches to change simply do not redress structural inequities. For instance, leaving diversity issues at the back end of syllabi renders neutral the readings that came before;

race, Indigeneity, gender, become topics of interest rather than fundamental parts of structures of power. Erin Tolley's (2020) examination of Canadian politics textbooks points to the challenges that emerge from this dynamic. She argues that while Canadian textbooks discuss diversity, these are relegated to "diversity-specific chapters" and are commonly discussed through the framework of *past* injustice; what this means, then, is that students of Canadian political science see diversity through the lens of history rather than considering ongoing manifestations of settler colonialism.

Another example of the limitations of liberal modes of inclusion is the reality that diversity in Canadian political science tends to be interpreted in limited ways. When Canadian political science still leaves intact the belief that the strengths of research on race, Indigeneity, gender should be assessed using mainstream metrics of generalizability and parsimony, then such research has to meet a much higher standard before being accepted into publication into flagship journals such as *CJPS* and the *Canadian Political Science Review* (*CPSR*). An article that I co-wrote with Nisha Nath and Megan Gaucher (2018) discovered that while research on different "diversities" has, over the years, become more prominently featured within *CJPS* and *CPSR*, diversity research that is featured in these journals is *still* predominantly focused on questions of political behaviour. This means that what we deemed "intersectional, anti-oppression" research that questions the unequal structures of the Canadian nation-state are sidelined (622). This sidelining of intersectional, anti-oppression research has led to the replication of a dynamic witnessed in other fields of political science: research that is read as critical and non-mainstream in that it discusses race, Indigeneity, gender, and so on tend to be published in specialist journals and not in general topics journals that are more widely read.[1]

Another way that Canadian political science has attempted to diversify is through including more diverse individuals within the profession. That many of these individuals tend to also do work on race, Indigeneity, gender, and so on makes these initiatives a win-win solution. The growing recognition that the field needs to diversify has led to new programs such as targeted hiring initiatives to include Black and Indigenous professors into majority-white departments and to the availability of new opportunities for funding for members of underrepresented groups.

Although I am fully supportive of these initiatives, I think that these initiatives do not go far enough. I discuss ways to ensure that these initiatives actually lead to structural transformations in the next section. The point I want to make concerns the limitations of these liberal strategies and the harms that they enact on BIPOC faculty, both as members of these committees and as job applicants. What remains painfully clear in the aftermath of these initiatives is that the few BIPOC colleagues who are placed in these committees are also forced to navigate the tricky terrain of speaking truth to power when they themselves are not protected by, for instance, the security that comes with tenure or even the security that comes with speaking as part of a group (see, e.g., McInnis 2020). These committees tend to be populated by "allies" (said with *huge* quotation marks) who see themselves as progressive by virtue of their willingness to serve on these committees. Rather than analyzing individual and institutional complicity in perpetuating unequal practices or giving space for members of underrepresented groups in these committees to speak, some "allies" perpetually centre their perspectives (McKinnon 2017). More problematically, some allies in these committees gatekeep, seeing it as their prerogative to ultimately decide what can count as acceptable and appropriate political science research. Research falling outside the mainstream orthodoxy veers too far away from "political science," and thus cannot be accommodated. The insistence on maintaining these boundaries, even within targeted hiring initiatives designed to diversify the discipline, means that only certain types of bodies are permitted access into the academy.

BIPOC scholars applying for these jobs are then forced to meet the demands placed on them to make their research legible to powerbrokers, posing their research in such a way that it is seen as sufficiently political science enough. In addition, when applying for these jobs, they are expected to show that they *can* usher in needed changes (mostly related to equity, diversity, and inclusion or EDI) to the department but do so in such a way that they do not jeopardize their "fit" within the institution (Muñoz et al. 2017).

Of course, while the presence of more diverse individuals within majority-white and -male institutions can and has led to change, what happens when such liberal modes of inclusion are promoted over and above other measures is the occurrence of a "leaky pipeline" (see, e.g.,

Gasser and Shaffer 2014; Monforti and Michelson 2008). Members of underrepresented groups leave the academy after a certain point, finding the burden of being "one of the fews" to be too big of a challenge. These groups hit a glass ceiling preventing their ascension in the academy. The glass ceiling can be measured through the dwindling numbers of racialized faculty getting promoted assistant to associate professors and from associate professors to full professors (Statistics Canada 2020) and through the virtual invisibility of people of colour in higher administrative roles (Fuji Johnson and Howsam 2020). Genevieve Fuji Johnson and Rob Howsam's (2020) research delineates, in fact, that the biggest beneficiaries of diversity policies are white women, showing that putting together different diversities lead to forms of representation that overlook race and Indigeneity. What these examples show is that change can come, but only to a point. The effect, then, of liberal models of inclusion is that underrepresented faculty would still have to conform to mainstream standards: to diversify means adding more members of underrepresented communities but leaving structures *and* practices of inequality intact.

As a faculty member of colour who has been part of many of these initiatives, I am well aware of these challenges. One challenge of liberal modes of inclusion that I would like to address, and that remains relatively underexamined, are the *tolls* that such attempts at widening the tent bring to people of colour whose presence and research are meant to bring much-needed diversity to Canadian political science. There is, in fact, a nascent body of work that highlights the harms that fall on people of colour who do diversity work within the academy, many of which highlight the challenges of facing pushback and backlash to their work, and the emotional toll of trying to transform a system that is resistant to change (see, e.g., Gutierrez y Muhs et al. 2012; Dhamoon 2020). As Rita Dhamoon (2020) puts it so concisely, "racism is a workload and bargaining issue."

Venerating liberal modes of inclusion invariably means that heightened pressure is placed on those of us who are part of underrepresented communities to do the diversity work on top of our other research, teaching, and service responsibilities. For me, I find that I become *the* voice for diversity in many spaces, including in spaces that are clearly not ready to accommodate and account for diverse bodies and voices. To be blunt, being tasked with being the voice of diversity within institutions that are, at their core, never made for me or people like me, led and populated by people who do not wish their power to be challenged, has been intensely painful. I estimate that I have spent thirty hours per week in the last academic term attending meetings for these initiatives, performing emotional labour in the aftermath of these meetings, and spending an inordinate amount of time writing, researching, and attending talks for these committees. This work comes at the expense of time I could have spent on writing or research. In 2020 and 2021 these responsibilities took place during the COVID-19 pandemic, during which my workload magnified as a result of ongoing childcare responsibilities due to lockdown provisions. That many of these committees ended up imploding or with diluted recommendations makes me lament now about time I could have spent doing something else.

Another challenge to liberal modes of inclusion that I have faced concerns attempts to push the boundaries of the discipline. Like other non-mainstream political scientists, I have also faced backlash to the research questions that I ask, the methods and methodologies that I commonly deploy, and the literatures that I cite. Much of my work tends not to be seen as part of the mainstream and thus remains largely illegible to powerbrokers such as journal reviewers. The aforementioned piece that I co-authored at *CJPS* with Nath and Gaucher (2018), for instance, faced a lengthy review process, with one reviewer being resistant to our arguments. This reviewer even became defensive, citing examples of "progress" within Canadian political science that they see as nullifying our empirical findings. As Nath sums up, the burden of proof we had to meet to satisfy this reviewer was high (personal communication, July 20, 2021). The reviewer requested that we provide "neat and tidy" (read: parsimonious) definitions of a long list of concepts (e.g., gender, social justice, privilege, etc.), perhaps because they saw these concepts as "variables" that can be placed in a causal relationship; in making this request, they conveniently ignored how these concepts are drawn from a long, established lineage of critical scholarship. After setting an impossible standard for us to meet, the reviewer then concluded that the changes that were required for our piece to be publishable were too high. In short, the reviewer set unreasonable terms that would then de facto lead to the exclusion of our work. Had it not been for the interventions of the journal editor, who was supportive of our work, this piece would have been rejected outright.

To use another example of pushback from powerbrokers, the first application I made to be a Canada Research Chair was given a "revise and resubmit." Although most of the reviewers provided glowing appraisals of my research proposal, one reviewer was skeptical of my chosen methodologies (interpretive research and participatory action research [PAR]), was doubtful of the research merits of studying migrant communities (including the Filipinx migrant community, of which I am a part), and was unclear about how examining social movements counted as political science. Why not study the United Nations instead the reviewer queried. When revising my proposal, I code-switched and used terminology that was legible. Rather than studying social movements, I claimed that I was instead studying "interest groups." Rather than using PAR, I focused on my use of interpretive methodology, which was somehow a bit more acceptable than PAR. I was successful the second time I applied. I find it highly ironic to be, on the one hand, celebrated by my funders and my institution for being a female, visible minority Canada Research Chair—my very existence, after all, signals that they have made tremendous strides in diversifying—yet also, on the other hand, be expected to fit within prescribed boundaries in order to get this position. Put differently, research diversity is celebrated, provided that the research diversity we bring fits within prescribed frameworks.

On this note, what is extremely challenging for me to navigate is the expectation that my *presence* signifies progress. I regularly get invited to speak in keynote and plenary panels, conferences, and workshops. While there are many spaces where it is clear that the organizers were genuinely appreciative of my work, there are other spaces where it became obvious that my inclusion was meant to check boxes. An example of the latter happened when a major organization recently invited me to speak for Asian Heritage Month, along with other researchers of Asian descent. The pitch was to showcase the breadth and depth of research on Asian communities, as led by Asian researchers. The organizers told me that the idea was for my fellow panelists and I to discuss our research on anti-Asian racism. Seeing that I was involved in projects that traced the effects of public policies on Asian international students and Asian care workers during COVID-19, I said yes. Against my better judgment, I felt that it would be a good forum for knowledge sharing.

Taking in good faith that the organizers genuinely wanted to showcase the breadth of research projects looking at the Asian diaspora in Canada, as led by Asian researchers, my fellow panelists and I structured our talks accordingly. What happened, however, was that while none of us formally gave an EDI talk, it essentially became one when we transitioned to the question-and-answer part of the event. Rather than asking us about our research, audience members asked my fellow panelists and I questions on EDI. It seemed as though some saw this as a prime opportunity to ask three Asian women questions they had about being Asian. We also faced harmful questions that I am still healing from. One of the questions I was asked—even if it had nothing to do with my talk—was whether "my culture led me to have imposter syndrome." (My answer: it is institutions that were never designed for me that lead me to have imposter syndrome.) I was also frustrated during and after the event because of the lack of care taken by the organizers. There was no moderation, no signals given to the audience on the types of questions that they should ask, and no offer on the part of the organizers for us to debrief.

Thus, we cannot underestimate the emotional toll that going to these events bear on us. These tokenistic modes of inclusion create aftershocks. Even now, when I think about that question and that event, I get frustrated not only because these talks exposed us, unarmed, to racism, but also because these talks show that in some spaces, BIPOC scholars only merit inclusion at certain times of the year and in certain events. That specific talk was pitched as *the* research talk for Asian Heritage Month in May. Can we conceive of inviting Asian scholars to talk in these fora when it isn't Asian Heritage Month? Of inviting Black scholars when it isn't Black History Month? Although I have since heard from audience members who thanked me for being part of this space, and who said that they felt validated after hearing from us, I remain uncomfortable with how inviting me and my panelists to speak was the organization showing to its members that it was doing "diversity work." What other initiatives *beyond* a speaker series is this organization committed to doing? And, for the majority-white audience members, I wonder whether the sum total of the diversity work that they were willing to do is listening to us speak or whether they would use the insights that we shared as the catalyst to fight for structural change. I oftentimes think that for many organizations, diversity work ends here.

In sum, including more articles on race, Indigeneity, gender, issuing public statements condemning anti-Black racism / anti-Asian racism / ongoing anti-Indigeneity / insert-statement-prompted-by-a-recent-event, endeavouring to hire more diverse workers, inviting diverse speakers to various speakers' series, and other liberal modes of inclusion simply is not the same as instituting lasting changes that will overturn unequal power structures. To put it plainly, *saying* that diversity matters and then making one or two gestures to prove that it does is not really the same as actually *doing* the hard and arduous work of dismantling inequity.

Feministing in Political Science: From Adding and Mixing to Dismantling and Transforming

The question that I face now is, well, what is to be done? Countless audits have already been undertaken on the state of diversity in academia (Smith 2017) and in Canadian political science, all leading to similar findings (CPSA Diversity Task Force 2010, 2012): there is growing demographic diversity but there appears to be a ceiling to how much members of diverse communities can ascend; there are more research projects being undertaken outside the mainstream but such research tends to be siloed into the margins of the field; while a few initiatives have led to important interventions within Canadian political science—namely, the creation of subdisciplines within CPSA to showcase diverse research—and targeted hiring initiatives, these are few and far between and, as I've already discussed, may merely serve to provide surface-level fixes that do not even begin to address deeper structural issues.

For me, the act of feministing necessitates asking hard questions that do not yield easy answers. One of the hard questions that the discipline of Canadian political science must ask is whether the field is ready to undergo the painful task of revisiting existing practices and fundamentally transforming the field. It is not enough to add and mix, hoping that the tent can be widened to encompass diverse members and diverse research. It is important to let go of ideas, practices, and research that are inequitable and consider new ways of knowing and of being.

While it is beyond the purview of this chapter to discuss in detail how to foster new ways of knowing and of being in Canadian political science, I offer the following feministing recommendations as a way to jumpstart conversations on how we can transform the discipline.

First, feministing asks that holders of power step back and hand the metaphorical gavel over to underrepresented members of the discipline. I suggest making the leadership teams of important Canadian political science bodies—be they the CPSA Executive Board, journal editorial teams, conference chairs, funding bodies, hiring committees—consist *entirely* of women, BIPOC researchers, and other members of underrepresented communities for a year. In contrast to liberal remedies of adding and mixing as a way to rectify representational imbalances, a feministing approach sees the value in ensuring that BIPOC, female, and other members of underrepresented communities who sit in decision-making bodies actually *do* have the opportunity to lead. If there is a true commitment to redressing power imbalances, then there should be an accompanying commitment to substantially do so! While I do not think that members of underrepresented groups think as a monolith, research has conclusively shown that *who* you invite to the table affects the final outcome. There is precedent for making leadership teams consist solely of underrepresented groups. The *American Political Science Review* has, from 2020 to 2024, an all-woman editorial team, which was intended to "bring a wider range of voices and scholarship to the discipline" (APSA 2019). An overview of the types of articles that have been published under the new editorial team shows that the journal has started publishing more articles that fall outside the mainstream.

Second, feministing encourages rethinking foundational concepts within Canadian political science. For example, Canadian political scientists see multiculturalism as a demographic reality, as a policy, and as a normative ideal within Canada. Yet using a multicultural lens obscures analysis of other differences that are arguably more relevant to people's lived realities. Scholars, for instance, have held that multiculturalism has obscured analysis of race and class inequities (Bannerji 2000). What would it mean, then, if we interrogate the "truthiness" of foundational concepts? How might doing so shift the questions that we ask and the research that we pursue?

Third, and relatedly, feministing involves rethinking how we teach Canadian political science. When teaching Introduction to Canadian Politics, for example, putting what is normally placed at the back end of the syllabus and placing it at the front would help students see that inequalities born out of race, gender, and Indigeneity are *part* of the foundations of the Canadian state. Starting with an understanding of how settler colonialism, white supremacy, and patriarchy are part of institutions may help contextualize later lessons on the machineries of government, or federalism. When teaching Introduction to Research Methods, to use another example, a feministing approach may involve a few weeks teaching research ethics *first*, so students become attuned to the importance of ensuring sound research ethics and become aware of the instances of social science researchers doing harm to communities.

Fourth, feministing entails enacting substantive measures to repair longstanding inequalities. Although targeted hiring initiatives are important, there needs to be more attention paid to what comes next. Hiring a more diverse professoriate is not enough; there should also be care taken to ensure faculty retention. Resources should be allocated to ensure that faculty members from underrepresented communities are truly supported. For example, there should be automatic course releases for all racialized and Indigenous faculty as a pre-emptive recognition that they will inevitably be expected to do more than their white colleagues. There should also be more start-up funding and more internal funding opportunities made available to underrepresented faculty, considering the structural impediments that make it harder for them to get external funding. And there should be ongoing check-ins, mentorship, and community networks that can facilitate the creation of "communities of care" (Francisco-Menchavez 2018) that can help support underrepresented faculty.

I recognize that these proposals will elicit backlash. Being asked to fundamentally transform the status quo through policies that actually transfer power leads to much unease. Feministing in political science, however, requires the pursuit of bold actions despite the discomfort it causes. When the same problems of a lack of diversity keep emerging within Canadian political science, perhaps it is time to move towards attempts geared not at widening the tent but at transforming structures of power.

Conclusion

In this chapter, I discussed the notion of progressive change within Canadian political science, critiqued liberal attempts at inclusion, and put forward proposals to transform the discipline through acts of feministing. I strongly believe that adding and mixing should give way to transforming and resisting. Structures can only truly transform when power actually shifts away from those who have historically held it to those who have not held it.

Yet I should also note that I recognize, of course, the tremendous power in exercising the politics of refusal. I keep reflecting on Paulo Ravecca's claims that we have to be attentive to "the *politics* of political science" (2019, 1, emphasis added). While not writing specifically about Canadian political science, Ravecca sees political science as being tied closely to national projects; far from being neutral, the field itself is geared towards promoting hegemonic beliefs regarding the nation-state.[2] When Canadian political science by its very nature is a settler colonial project that is intended to bolster the Canadian national project and, by extension, to keep intact existing structures of domination, then no amount of policy initiatives can ever transform the field. Even the structural solutions that I propose above are limited. As such, refusing to participate in these efforts at transformation may very well be the ultimate act of feministing.

Hence, feministing at its core means being strategic when acting. It means understanding the possibilities and the limitations of what can, and what cannot be done, within a given juncture, and doing what is right for oneself and one's community.

Notes

1. The *American Political Science Review*, one of the discipline's highest ranked generalist journals, in fact, recognized that such siloing is a problem and accordingly diversified their editorial board (full disclosure: I am part of the board) to ensure that the journal is more representative of diverse research in the discipline.
2. This argument closely reflects Abu-Laban's (2017) arguments regarding Canadian political science's development as being closely tied to the development of the Canadian nation-state.

References

Abu-Laban, Yasmeen. 2017. "Narrating Canadian Political Science: History Revisited." *Canadian Journal of Political Science* 50 (4): 895–919. https://doi.org/10.1017/S000842391700138X.

APSA. 2019. "APSA Announces New Editorial Team for the *American Political Science Review*." *Political Science Now*, July 26, 2019. https://politicalsciencenow.com/apsa-announces-the-new-editorial-team-for-the-american-political-science-review/.

Bannerji, Himani. 2000. *Dark Side of the Nation: Essays on Multiculturalism, Nationalism, and Gender.* Toronto: Women's Press.

Bernhardt, Nicole S., and Laura G. Pin. 2018. "Engaging with Identity Politics in Canadian Political Science." *Canadian Journal of Political Science* 51 (4): 771–94. https://doi.org/10.1017/S0008423918000318.

Coburn, Elaine, Aileen Moreton-Robinson, George Sefa Dei, and Mekere Stewart-Harawira. 2013. "Unspeakable Things: Indigenous Research and Social Science." *Socio*, no. 2, 331–48. https://doi.org/10.4000/socio.524.

CPSA Diversity Task Force. 2010. "Report and Analysis of the Questionnaire for Chairs of Department of Political Science," May 2010. https://CPSA-acsp.ca/documents/pdfs/diversity/2010_Diversity_Task_Force%E2%80%93Chairs_of_Departments_of_Political_Science-Report.pdf.

CPSA Diversity Task Force. 2012. "Report and Analysis of the Canadian Political Science Association Member Survey," May 2021. https://CPSA-acsp.ca/documents/pdfs/diversity/2012_Diversity_Task_Force_Report.pdf.

CPSA Reconciliation Committee. 2018. "Indigenous Content Syllabus Materials: A Resource for Political Science Instructors in Canada," September 24, 2018. https://www.CPSA-acsp.ca/documents/committees/Indigenous%20Content%20Syllabus%20Materials%20Sept%2024%202018[27].pdf.

Dhamoon, Rita Kaur. 2020. "Racism as a Workload and Bargaining Issue." *Socialist Studies* 14 (1). https://doi.org/10.18740/ss27273.

Everitt, Joanna. 2021. "Academic Absences, Disciplinary Siloes and Methodological Prejudices Within the Political Science Discipline in Canada." *Canadian Journal of Political Science* 54 (4): 749–68. https://doi.org/10.1017/S0008423921000883.

Francisco-Menchaez, Valerie. 2018. *The Labor of Care: Filipina Migrants and Transnational Families in the Digital Age.* Champaign: University of Illinois Press.

Fuji Johnson, Genevieve, and Rob Howsam. 2020. "Whiteness, Power, and the Politics of Demographics in the Governance of the Canadian Academy." *Canadian Journal of Political Science* 53 (3): 676–94. https://doi.org/10.1017/S0008423920000207.

Gasser, Courtney, and Katharine Shaffer. 2014. "Career Development of Women in Academia: Traversing the Leaky Pipeline." *The Professional Counselor* 4 (4): 332–52. https://doi.org/10.15241/ceg.4.4.332.

Gutierrez y Muhs, Gabriella, Yolanda Flores Niemann, Carmen G. Gonzales, and Angela P. Harris, eds. 2012. *Presumed Incompetent: The Intersections of Race and Class for Women in Academia.* Boulder: University of Colorado Press.

Ladner, Kiera L. 2017. "Taking the Field: 50 Years of Indigenous Politics in the CJPS." *Canadian Journal of Political Science* 50 (1): 163–79. https://doi.org/10.1017/S0008423917000257.

McInnis, Tatiana. 2020. "A Farewell Letter to EDI Work." *Insight Higher Ed.*, August 20, 2020. https://www.insidehighered.com/views/2020/08/20/diversity-equity-and-inclusion-offices-cant-be-effective-if-they-arent-empowered.

McKinnon, Rachel. 2017. "Allies Behaving Badly: Gaslighting as Epistemic Injustice." In *The Routledge Handbook of Epistemic Injustice*, edited by Ian James Kidd, Jose Media, and Gaile Pohlhaus, 167–74. New York: Routledge.

Monforti, Jessica Lavariega, and Melissa R. Michelson. 2008. "Diagnosing the Leaky Pipeline: Continuing Barriers to the Retention of Latinas and Latinos in Political Science." *PS: Political Science and Politics* 41 (1): 161–66. https://doi.org/10.1017/S1049096508080232.

Muñoz, Susana M., Vincent Basile, Jessica Gonzales, Daniel Birmingham, Antonette Aragon, Louise Jennings, and Gene Gloeckner. 2017. "(Counter) Narratives and Complexities: Critical Perspectives from a University Cluster Hire Focused on Diversity, Equity, and Inclusion." *Journal of Critical Thought and Praxis* 6 (2): 1–21. https://doi.org/10.31274/jctp-180810-71.

Nath, Nisha. 2011. "Defining Narratives of Identity in Canadian Political Science: Accounting for the Absence of Race." *Canadian Journal of Political Science* 44 (1): 161–93. https://doi.org/10.1017/S0008423910001071.

Nath, Nisha, Ethel Tungohan, and Megan Gaucher. 2018. "The Future of Canadian Political Science: Boundary Transgressions, Gender and Anti-Oppression Frameworks." *Canadian Journal of Political Science* 51 (3): 619–42. https://doi.org/10.1017/S0008423918000197.

Newton, Janice. 2017. "The Formative Decades of the CPSA." *Canadian Journal of Political Science* 50 (1): 37–55. https://doi.org/10.1017/S0008423917000129.

Ravecca, Paulo. 2019. *The Politics of Political Science: Re-writing Latin American Experiences*. New York: Routledge.

Smith, Malinda. 2017. "Disciplinary Silences: Race, Indigeneity and Gender in the Social Sciences." In *The Equity Myth: Racialization and Indigeneity at Canadian Universities*, edited by Frances Henry, Enakshi Dua, Carl James, Audrey Kobayashi, Peter Li, Howard Ramos, and Malinda Smith, 239–63. Vancouver: UBC Press.

Statistics Canada. 2020. "Survey of Postsecondary Faculty and Researchers, 2019." *The Daily*, September 22, 2020. https://www150.statcan.gc.ca/n1/en/daily-quotidien/200922/dq200922a-eng.pdf?st=-qcr9-NJ.

Thompson, Debra. 2008. "Is Race Political?" *Canadian Journal of Political Science* 41 (3): 525–47. https://doi.org/10.1017/S0008423908080827.

Tolley, Erin. 2017. "Into the Mainstream or Still at the Margins? 50 Years of Gender Research in the Canadian Political Science Association." *Canadian Journal of Political Science* 50 (1): 143–61. https://doi.org/10.1017/S0008423916001177.

Tolley, Erin. 2020. "Hidden in Plain Sight: The Representation of Immigrants and Minorities in Political Science Textbooks." *International Journal of Canadian Studies*, no. 57, 47–70. https://doi.org/10.3138/ijcs.57.x.47.

University of Guelph. 2020. "U of G Launches Action Plan to Combat Racism, Promote Inclusion." *University of Guelph News*, September 28, 2020. https://news.uoguelph.ca/2020/09/u-of-g-launches-action-plan-to-combat-racism-promote-inclusion/.

Vickers, Jill. 2015. "Can We Change How Political Science Thinks? 'Gender Mainstreaming' in a Resistant Discipline: Presidential Address Delivered to the Canadian Political Science Association, Ottawa, June 2, 2015." *Canadian Journal of Political Science* 48 (4): 747–70. https://jstor.org/stable/24810960.

White, Graham. 2017. "Continuity and Change: Fifty Years of the *Journal/Revue*." *Canadian Journal of Political Science* 50 (1): 17–35. https://doi.org/10.1017/S0008423917000117.

York University. 2020. "The Next Steps in York University's Plan to Address Anti-Black Racism." *YFile*, June 12, 2020. https://yfile.news.yorku.ca/2020/06/12/the-next-steps-in-york-universitys-plan-to-address-anti-black-racism/.

2

Being "Reasonable" (whilst Feminist and Black) within the Neoliberal University

NICOLE S. BERNHARDT

"WE ARE SO GRATEFUL for your voice in all of this. Your approach is so *reasonable*." My department was in crisis mode, responding to a highly publicized accusation of sexual assault by one of the department's graduate students.[1] I was a third-year PHD student who had recently helped form a graduate student Equity Committee to respond to gendered and race-based exclusions in the department and the broader discipline. As the department administration was getting a crash course in gender-based violence, safety measures, and strategic communications, I was learning how to navigate an institution that would only hear me at a particular register. It was in the midst of these fraught discussions that I was told by a white male faculty member that my voice was especially helpful and necessary because my approach was "reasonable." This purported compliment rang like the academic equivalent of the line, "you aren't like other girls." It simultaneously distanced me from my fellow graduate students who were being implicitly constructed as "unreasonable" and sought to reinforce a moderate approach to the graduate students' demands. And yet, as a Black woman graduate student, being seen as reasonable—and *reasoned*—by my department felt crucial to my academic survival. I felt simultaneously wounded and reassured. I was left wondering about the utility of being reasonable: What could I accomplish and what was being foreclosed by this imposition of reasonableness?

In examining how reasonableness is invoked in the context of the neoliberal university, particularly within the discipline of political science, I am concerned both with reasonableness in relation to equity-based claims-making and reasonableness as an ontological construction in opposition to feminism and Blackness. First, to state the obvious, claims that are determined by the institution to be "reasonable" are those claims that pose minimal disruption to the institutional status quo, are expressed dispassionately, and refrain from defaming particular members of the institution. To be unreasonable is to be upset and angry, and to demand transformation and accountability. Second, reasonableness as a particular way of *being* within the university requires conformity to institutional practices and modes of engagement. To again state the obvious, these ways of being are raced and gendered. Thus, to enter the university as a Black woman is to, as described by Sara Ahmed (2009), "embody diversity." Here, I explore what it means to simultaneously embody diversity and be read as reasonable. I share an account of my unsuccessful efforts to collectively identify and challenge department inequities using a tempered, "evidence-based," process-compliant—and above all—reasonable approach. While these efforts did not result in the changes, we (the graduate student Equity Committee) were seeking, there have been reverberations of our efforts in feminist and racialized networks that emerged following this work and the enduring significance of our documented concerns.

Forming a Committee and Gathering "Evidence"
The Graduate Political Science Student Association (GPSSA) Equity Committee formed in October 2014 largely in response to the pervasiveness of unwelcome sexual attention within our department at social events (one social in particular) and in response to graduate students voicing concerns about the broader exclusionary culture of the department. Initially, we were a small group of approximately ten feminists, composed (almost entirely) of those who had felt othered in our department by virtue of gender, race, and queerness. While we had ample accounts of how department and classroom spaces left us feeling silenced, disparaged, and isolated, we were also cognizant that these experiences could readily be dismissed as anecdotal without additional corroborating "evidence." As has been identified by feminist researchers such as Suzanne Hodgkin, in seeking to influence non-feminist decision-makers it is important to consider "the types of data that are most highly regarded by the audience [we] are seeking to persuade" (2008, 314). Accordingly, we constructed a survey asking graduate students to self-identify on the basis of equity-seeking categories and to share their experiences of inequity within the department. We compiled the responses, our analysis, our methodology, and our recommendations into a report: the *GPSSA Equity*

Survey Report 2014–2015.[2] The survey had 69 responses out of approximately 225 graduate students, a response rate we considered to be relatively strong given that many upper-year students had limited interaction with the department. The responses reflected that racialized (61%) and "female" (77%) respondents were more likely to report equity concerns than respondents overall (47%).[3]

Survey respondents were also invited to elaborate on their equity experiences within the classroom and the department. We collected accounts of how women and racialized graduate students felt that their contributions were being dismissed in the classroom and how these experiences intersected with the dismissal of particular topics, such as so-called identity politics. As Laura Pin and I would later write (inspired in large part by these experiences), "identity politics tends to be deployed as a method of controlling the boundaries of political discourse and limiting who and what gains entry into the political" (2018, 788). By dismissing analyses that incorporate gender, race, ability, and Indigeneity, these classroom and department dynamics served to narrow what qualified as political science and limit research into gendered and racialized oppression. The survey also reflected that for those of us who embody diversity this dismissal of intersectional anti-oppression studies is intimately tied to power relations within the classroom. Survey respondents described being subject to racist and sexist remarks and being talked over, interrupted, and ignored in classroom debates. The survey offered a mechanism for capturing experiences of marginalization within the department that were broadly felt, but rarely voiced. As Frances Henry and colleagues identify in *The Equity Myth*, throughout Canadian universities there is a structurally reinforced "diversity trap" that limits the ability of "racialized and Indigenous scholars to express their concerns in the normal academic setting" (2017, 20; see also Coburn et al., this volume; Dei-Sharpe and Manning, this volume). An institutional silence on race and racism renders racialized differences as inconsequential and treats accounts of racism as hyperbolic. In accounting for the racial and gender demographics of the political science graduate student body, we were attempting to disrupt this silence and evidence the salience of race and gender within our department.

Our attempts to reason with, and persuade, our department administration began with a presentation to department council in January

2015. We requested space on the agenda through official channels, prepared a slide deck, and were provided ten minutes to inform the council of the graduate students' equity concerns and our preliminary recommendations for change. As the GPSSA Equity Committee Chair at the time, I led the presentation. On behalf of the committee, I shared the disparities in graduate students' experience of the department and offered some preliminary recommendations such as incorporating mandatory equity training into both the MA and the PHD programs, providing faculty with equity training, and creating a visual display emphasizing the department's commitment to equity. The presentation was well received by the feminist faculty, who noted that many of them had not sufficiently appreciated the dynamics related to race. Yet what stands out to me as I recall delivering these concerns to a room filled of mostly senior, mostly men, and mostly white professors was the disengagement. Whereas some questioned our methods (like the size of our n) or raised concerns of faculty autonomy (are you telling us what to teach?), most just turned away or looked down at their phones or their marking until our ten minutes were up.

Crafting Reasonable Requests

Following the presentation, in the midst of a departmental year defined by a labour strike and sexual assault charges against a graduate student, we continued to press for institutional responsiveness through reasonable requests and reasoned dialogue. In May 2015 we hosted a department townhall to discuss the results of the survey; only three faculty members attended. I corresponded regularly with the department chair about department gender-based violence safety measures, provided feedback on the department's draft statement on sexual assault, declined media requests (so as not to publicly defame the department), and engaged with multiple faculty members on an individual basis who wanted to discuss and rebut the graduate students' concerns. For instance, I was cautioned by one faculty member not to "define the problem as a political issue, a local reflection of a global issue having to do with the oppression of weak and/or marginalized social groups by more dominant groups." Instead, he encouraged me to focus on the "bad behaviours you want to change." I am particularly loathe to share that in response to this guidance I *thanked* him for engaging with our report. As a graduate student dependent on faculty support in order to progress through the program and one of the only Black women in the department, I pushed myself to appear open to armchair dialogue on whether or not structural oppressions were really a "thing."

The work of the Equity Committee became increasingly time-consuming. We held follow-up meetings between Equity Committee members and department administration to discuss our recommendations in full. We passed draft emails back and forth, editing ourselves so as not to appear ardent or unreasonable. Asking one another, *Does this sound ok?* Adding the equivocations and qualifiers that women are coached to both perform and avoid: *might be helpful, could be possible, just a suggestion*. Unsurprisingly, we were able to secure the most movement in the areas that principally concerned the behaviour of graduate students. The department added equity training to the MA colloquium, the PHD dissertation workshop, and TA Day for graduate teaching assistants. We took on the labour of crafting equity-based evaluation questions, delivering orientation training, coordinating speakers, and liaising with the university's Centre for Human Rights. Opaque boundaries were drawn around the recommendations that pertained to course content, faculty members, and department administration. Without being told no explicitly, we were discouraged from arranging equity training for the faculty or using existing forums (such as the faculty retreat or the department field meetings) for equity-related discussions. By indicating a semblance of willingness, the department administration ensured that we continued to channel our concerns through meeting requests and written recommendations, rather than pursuing complaints, publicly voicing concerns, or issuing demands.

Reasonableness as Workload

The pitfalls of reasonableness started to become clear to me after I stepped down as Equity Committee co-chair in the fall of 2016. Every year graduate students in subsequent cohorts continued to voice similar concerns and few recommendations had been adopted beyond those that had been led by me personally (such as delivering equity content as part of TA Day) or by another member of the Equity Committee. Even more infuriating, the efforts we had made to make visible graduate students' concerns of inequity were now being co-opted into department equity, diversity, and inclusion (EDI) narratives as evidence that the department was already engaged in EDI. In speaking about the politics of documentation in diversity work, Ahmed describes being taught a hard lesson that a document she helped craft to capture "the racism of the university became usable as a measure of good performance" (2007, 597). So too, our Equity Committee formed to decry the *exclusionary* practices in our department was being offered by department administration as evidence of *inclusive* equity practices. This co-optation felt particularly egregious given the absence of faculty labour to attend to the concerns we raised in our report. While we were grateful to the feminist faculty who had conveyed their support for our efforts, we had not succeeded in transferring any of this work onto those members of the department who are actually paid for departmental service. As Rita Dhamoon (2020) has articulated, racism is a workload issue that is rarely recognized and compensated by universities. In trying to address the racism and sexism of our department using the more conciliatory framing of "equity" and engaging in this work as a voluntary committee, we assumed responsibility for feminist anti-racist change and allowed our work to stand in for department accountability.

In 2016 the GPSSA Equity Committee again surveyed the graduate students on equity concerns—*GPSSA Equity Survey Report* (2016–2017).[4] Once again, we received 69 responses and compiled a report where we presented both our statistical findings and paraphrased quotations from survey respondents. In this second report, we more explicitly called out racist and sexist practices in the classroom and connected these practices with course content that privileges dominant groups and ideologies. In their written comments, survey respondents described being made to feel "stupid and worthless" and "angry and marginalized" for offering feminist interventions, which were being treated as "secondary to material." The report also provided us with the opportunity to revisit the neglected recommendations from the first report. We provided a progress report on all of the past recommendations, reiterating our call for anti-oppression training for all faculty and dedicated discussions within each of the department's field committees (i.e., international relations, political theory, Canadian studies, women and politics, and comparative politics) on how consideration of interlocking power structures is being integrated into course material. The waning energy of the Equity Committee around the completion of the second—and thus far final—report is reflected in the decision to release the report without a presentation to department council as well as the decision by both co-chairs to step down the following year. I took a leave from my degree and stepped away from the Equity Committee—and the department—to start a policy advisor position. The Equity Committee continued on as part of the GPSSA but ceased taking responsibility for the labour of making the department more equitable.

Departmental Feministing

While the GPSSA Equity Committee was largely unsuccessful at effecting the sorts of changes we were seeking, our true success lay in carving out a space of resistance and alternative engagement from the norms set by the department. Returning to the claim that prescriptions of reasonableness set a particular way of *being* within the university that prioritize conformity with institutional practices and modes of engagement, the Equity Committee sought to offer a safe*r* space within the department that prioritized *affect* over reason.[5] We collectively crafted our approaches, shared insecurities, and voiced our experiences of discomfort within the department. Prior to forming the Equity Committee my social interactions within the department had been dominated by men and beer, filled with adversarial debate and highly gendered interactions. Through this committee, we carved out alternative modes of connecting that were collaborative and community-oriented. We made a space where the queer, racialized, and feminist members of the department wanted to be. We met in one another's houses, hosted feminist killjoy movie nights, and formed research collaborations that had a far greater impact beyond the department than within it. We also left a mark on the GPSSA, which began hosting more accessible and family-friendly socials, and establishing a graduate student buddy program that offered incoming graduate students the option to be paired (if possible) with a senior graduate student from the same equity-seeking group.

The reports of the Equity Committee continue to resurface with every renewed call to attend to the gendered and racialized exclusions within the department. And those of us who embody diversity within the discipline and the department continue to face requests for extra labour to mend the systems that have worked against us. Most recently, when almost every department in North America was forced to contend with the reality of anti-Black racism, this department formed a working group on Black and Indigenous studies with a mandate to support the "thriving" of Black and Indigenous faculty, students, and staff. I along with the only *six* other Black and Indigenous graduate students we were able to identify between 2011 and 2020 issued a collective statement describing, that as Black and Indigenous scholars in the department, "we have had to develop our own strategies for success, survival, protection, and self-care quite independent of what exists in this program." Further, we expressed a collective fear that "in giving our time and energy" to internal processes, "our intentions and voices may get twisted into something good the department has done rather than something it should reflect upon." Those of us who had participated in the Equity Committee and the GPSSA shared experiences with the newer graduate students of the labour we had already expended trying to shift the department and raised questions about the value of participating in additional internal committee work. As a collective we carved out space to be unreasonable and non-compliant, and yet in the subsequent individual requests for committee engagement a number of us found ourselves being drawn back into conversations where we felt deeply implicated. As I reflect on these conversations and on my own inability to effect feminist anti-racist change within the context of the neoliberal university, I recognize the power of refusing to take part within the boundaries of reasonableness.

Conclusion

While I have lost time, energy, and *productivity* to engaging in equity-driven department transformation efforts that have repeatedly failed to bring about the changes we (those of us who embody diversity) so desperately need, I am grateful that these spaces have opened up opportunities to form connections with fellow feminists and institutional "others" who are precluded from department and disciplinary networks that construe us as diverse, unreasoned, and unreasonable. I am also critically aware of how I have been compelled to subsume these efforts within my own self-marketing narrative in various EDI statements. As I continue my own academic career trajectory, I have invoked this equity-driven committee work to account for "my ongoing commitment to advancing equity, diversity, and inclusion." In embodying diversity, I recognize the need to translate my diversity into institutionally recognized committee work in order to be seen as valuable to the neoliberal university. But what am I doing when I contort my institutional battles for equity into a line on my cv? How does my continual need to be seen and valued by the neoliberal university leave me stuck performing my diversity? Ahmed instructs Black feminists to become "bad at embodying diversity" (2009, 51). Being bad at embodying diversity involves a willingness to be seen as angry and unreasonable. I struggle to eschew reasonableness. To fight against my impulse to edit my voice and meet on their terms. I find strength and inspiration in the scholarship and networks of killjoy feminists, queer voices, and anti-racism scholars that remind me of the power of being unreasonable.

Notes

1. The following is an account of my equity-driven change efforts within a political science department in a large post-secondary institution in Ontario, Canada.
2. As the report was never released publicly, I have refrained from listing the seven report contributors. I want to express gratitude for the labour of these contributors and their thoughtful analyses.
3. We used the aggregate category "racialized" to preserve anonymity. The gender identity category allowed respondents to select all that apply from "male," "female," "cis," and "trans" and included a write-in option. In retrospect these categories are both incomplete and problematic.
4. As this second report was never released publicly, I have again refrained from listing the seven report contributors—some of whom had also contributed to the previous report and some of whom were newer members of the department.
5. We used the term *safer space* to mean a space that is supportive, encouraging, and actively resistant to multiple/intersecting forms of oppression. We selected *safer* instead of *safe* in recognition that our commitment to safe space is aspirational and that we are embedded within and constituted by the same power relations we seek to resist.

References

Ahmed, Sara. 2007. "'You End Up Doing the Document Rather Than Doing the Doing': Diversity, Race Equality and the Politics of Documentation." *Ethnic and Racial Studies* 30 (4): 590–609. https://doi.org/10.1080/01419870701356015.

Ahmed, Sara. 2009. "Embodying Diversity: Problems and Paradoxes for Black Feminists." *Race Ethnicity and Education* 12 (1): 41–52. https://doi.org/10.1080/13613320802650931.

Bernhardt, Nicole S., and Laura G. Pin. 2018. "Engaging with Identity Politics in Canadian Political Science." *Canadian Journal of Political Science* 51 (4): 771–94. https://doi.org/10.1017/S0008423918000318.

Dhamoon, Rita Kaur. 2020. "Racism as a Workload and bargaining Issue." *Socialist Studies* 14 (1). https://doi.org/10.18740/ss27273.

Henry, Frances, Enakshi Dua, Carl E. James, Audrey Kobayashi, Peter Li, Howard Ramos, and Malinda Smith. 2017. *The Equity Myth: Racialization and Indigeneity at Canadian Universities*. Vancouver: UBC Press.

Hodgkin, Suzanne. 2008. "Telling It All: A Story of Women's Social Capital Using a Mixed Methods Approach." *Journal of Mixed Methods Research* 2 (4): 296–316. https://doi.org/10.1177/1558689808321641.

3 The Fish and the Spider

ALANA CATTAPAN

CHARLOTTE'S WEB was my favourite book as a child. I learned to read as my grandmother took me through the pages of her copy, the cover not yet worn, although it soon would be. There is a moment midway through the novel when Charlotte (the titular spider) tells a bedtime story to Wilbur, the pig she is caring for.

> Once upon a time…I had a beautiful cousin who managed to build her web across a small stream. One day a tiny fish leaped into the air and got tangled in the web. My cousin was very much surprised of course. The fish was thrashing wildly. My cousin hardly dared tackle it. But she did. She swooped down and threw great masses of wrapping material around the fish and fought bravely to capture it…
>
> There was my cousin, slipping in, dodging out, beaten mercilessly over the head by the wildly thrashing fish, dancing in, dancing out, throwing her threads and fighting hard. First, she threw a left around the tail. The fish lashed back. Then a left to the tail and a right to the mid-section. The fish lashed back. Then she dodged to one side and threw a right, and another right to the fin. Then a hard left to the head, while the web swayed and stretched. (White 1952, 102–03)

The cousin-spider is surprised as a tiny fish becomes tangled in her web, "caught only by one fin, and its tail wildly thrashing and shining in the sun." As the fish frantically "lashed back" the web sagged "dangerously" under its weight (102–03). The cousin-spider moved quickly, dodging the thrashing fish while throwing all the wrapping material she could muster.

The story of the fish and the cousin-spider came flooding back to me a few years ago when I was negotiating for a new position, planning to make a move from my newfound home in Saskatchewan back to Ontario for another academic job. The new position was more prestigious, but also laden with the burden of increased responsibility. I knew that the choice was right for me—it would bring me much closer to my family and my hometown and would provide new opportunities for my partner—but I wondered too what I was giving up.

As I mulled over whether to take the new position, and in the years since, I have often thought about this story, wondering whether I am the metaphorical spider, or if I am the fish. Some days I think I'm the fish; once carefree, now frantic, unwittingly bound up in a treacherous web that I didn't realize was there; task after task, refusal after refusal, slowing down my will to fight. Some days I'm the spider, underestimated, working diligently, carefully—while hanging by a thread—to reach what feel like unachievable goals. I am slowly making inroads, struggling under the weight of things, making progress bit by bit, one thread at a time.

In this chapter, I use the figures of the spider and the fish to interrogate some of the inherent contradictions of feministing in the contemporary university. For me, feministing, by which I mean the labour of *doing* feminism within and beyond political science, is inherently hopeful as it requires us to recognize the urgent need for change and to believe in the promise of a better world. To engage in feminist praxis is to work towards change, and to see this work as both necessary and possible. Still, the university-as-institution requires us to work and study in often hostile and toxic environments, ones that, as I describe below, too often serve the interests of industry while requiring more of those with less privilege and fewer resources. Feministing is always a project of persistence, and labour that seems futile, like tiny threads stretched across a stream. To engage in feministing is, as I explore in this chapter, to hold these truths at once: that academia is at once a site of violent capitalist imperialism and a space of community, possibility, and radical transformation. I begin with the fish, focusing on my hometown—Sudbury, Ontario, and the drastic cuts that took place in April 2021 at Laurentian, the local university, to interrogate how the university's longstanding connections to extractive capitalism are eroding the environmental and intellectual commons. I then turn to the spider to examine the gendered nature of academic expectations as well as possibilities for community building and collaborative care in hostile environments. I close by returning to the story of the fish and the spider and reflecting on the tentative (hopeful) future it might invite us to consider.

FIGURE 3.1 Aerial view of Laurentian University during the construction of the Vale Living with Lakes Centre, 2010. (Used with permission from Dr. David Pearson.)

The Fish

Almost exactly two years after the negotiations that led me to recall the story of the spider and the fish, Laurentian University announced that it was closing nearly seventy undergraduate and graduate programs, laying off more than a hundred faculty members. The political science department was eliminated completely. Laurentian is located in Sudbury, Ontario, and the political science department that was eliminated is the one where many of my friends and colleagues have worked, and from which my father graduated decades ago. For much of my life, Laurentian was the only university I really knew about and the only campus I had ever seen. The layoffs were part of a brutal restructuring program that occurred once the university underwent creditor protection—what was once largely publicly funded education reshaped by the corporate sector.[1]

The land on which Sudbury, and consequently Laurentian, was built, is best known for mining—spaces for the establishment and expansion of resource extraction. Atikameksheng Anishinabek people have long resided in the region, with settlers following once large deposits of nickel ore were found. Resource extraction has been the driving force of the city's economic development since the late nineteenth century, and central to its identity as a blue-collar union town. Due to the removal and processing of nickel ore, the region is also known as a site of ecological devastation, and I grew up swimming in lakes that were once some of the most polluted bodies of water on earth (Miller Llana 2020). As philosopher Alexis Shotwell (2016) describes in her book *Against Purity*, despite significant regreening and rehabilitation efforts, people in Sudbury continue to take care with what they eat and grow in the city because of the long and continued histories of toxicity. Although there are fish in the more than 330 lakes within the city limits and the waterways that run between them, she writes that "people there generally avoid bottom feeders" as their tissues can carry chemicals from the ore smelting process (Shotwell 2016, 80). Still, the regreening efforts that have occurred in Sudbury are notable. The city is internationally recognized for the cooperation between industry, community, and scientists that has facilitated the city's significant ecological rehabilitation. Lakes that were once acidified and surrounded by barren rock have become beautiful and lush, teeming with life.[2]

To no one's surprise, the mining companies have engaged in these same regreening efforts while continuing to knowingly, egregiously, do harm. In 2015 Environment Canada and the Royal Canadian Mounted Police conducted an investigation into the main mining company in Sudbury—Vale, formerly Inco—for violations of the Fisheries Act. The investigation found that, since 1963, the company allowed "seepage from smelter waste piles into waters frequented by fish" (Zembrzycki 2015), and that the company knew about the leakage "at least since 1997" (Bickis 2015). The substance seeping from the slag hills far exceeded the Fisheries Act threshold for a "deleterious" substance,[3] killing all of the fish tested within twenty-four hours of exposure (see Bickis 2015; Zembrzycki 2015). Inco/Vale invested significant funds and effort into cleaning up the very waters that it was knowingly, simultaneously, leeching effluent. Extractive capitalism is like this: as one hand gives, the other hand takes, and then takes some more. No charges were ever laid.

When first I heard about the layoffs at Laurentian, I thought immediately of my father's time as a student in the 1970s, travelling from the Italian enclave where he lived to the Laurentian campus during the school year, working in the mines each summer to pay his tuition. On days off, he and his friends would swim in "the pit," a tailings pond on Inco property just downhill from the slag piles.[4] His movements at that time were shaped by the relationships between the university and the mining industry, his leisure occurring in its waste. Here, the university, industry, and decimation of the environment are always part of the same story; they cannot be disentangled, and they are an integral part of how I have always understood the university and my place within it. Poet Rebecca Salazar describes a similar experience with the city, writing in "Acid Rain" that

> it's like we cannot get this place
> out of our systems, like we cannot
> neutralize our caustic origins. (2021, 93)[5]

Investment in post-secondary education in Sudbury has always been about "tangible research and personnel benefits" and as a space for mining-related research and innovation to occur (Bray 2010a, 22). Ralph Parker, once the senior vice-president of Canadian operations for Inco, was instrumental in the creation of Laurentian University in the first place, and served as the first chair of its Board of Governors,[6] with the company making what was reported to be "the single-largest corporate gift to an educational institution in Canada at the time," donating $2.5 million in 1962, a year before effluent likely started leeching into the city's waterways (Bray 2010a, 39). A decade before the layoffs, when Laurentian was engaged in a major capital campaign to offset a growing deficit,[7] donations from the industry were central, although much of the funds were earmarked for new initiatives (named after key donors, who are also mining magnates) including the Goodman School of Mines, and the McEwen School of Architecture. The deficit continued to grow.

When the layoffs eventually came, they came swiftly, with people "pushed into early retirement or fired during group Zoom calls without termination or severance payments" (Brabazon 2022). The layoffs didn't affect programs associated with mining, but they did affect other programs integral to life in Northern Ontario. The elimination of the entire departments of philosophy, political science, labour studies, music, and anthropology suggest that these areas of inquiry matter less to the university, making it challenging to attract people with these interests or working in these fields in the city and surrounding region. The layoffs also inexplicably eliminated the university's midwifery program, which actually brought money into the school, and was one of only three midwifery programs in Ontario, and the only one offered in French. Its elimination will have longstanding impacts on access to reproductive health care in the province, and particularly in Northern Ontario (Beaulne-Stuebing 2021; CBC News 2021a; Laucius 2021). The physics and math programs were cut entirely as well, dramatically affecting the operations and personnel of Sudbury's Nobel prize–winning SNOLAB (CBC News 2021b). The termination of the agreement between Laurentian and its federated universities also threatens the sustainability of one of Canada's oldest Indigenous studies programs, although there are new initiatives underway to preserve aspects of the program.[8]

And the layoffs certainly affect the fish. The entirety of ecology, environmental geoscience, environmental science, environmental studies, major restoration ecology, and restoration biology were cut. This includes scholars who were the heart of the regreening efforts, including aquatic ecologists and restoration ecologists now viewed as expendable (Kruzel 2021). As Dieter K. Buse (2021)—a professor emeritus of history at Laurentian—detailed for the *Sudbury Star*, the layoffs at Laurentian have been a significant step in the long, slow process of making the university a technical school, designed to serve the interests of industry. At the time of writing, the home page of the new Goodman School of Mines proclaims that they are the "entryway into Canada's Mining University."

This is not a shift away from some storied past of universities that aimed to provide public education for its own sake. The corporatization of the university, and the relationship between business interests and education, is not new. But what is new is the intensity and primacy of the relationships. It is glaring in the case of Laurentian, but the same stories are true elsewhere. Since I started thinking about this essay, the University of Alberta announced a new round of cuts while the provincial government uses funding from other ministries to create one-off public-private research partnerships that undermine the university's autonomy while enabling the corporate sector to determine research priorities (Adkin 2020; Canadian Association of University Teachers 2021). Memorial University of Newfoundland has also had its funding slashed, with a longstanding tuition offset grant rescinded, and new (further) cuts to the university's operating grant. At Memorial, operating costs have been downloaded to students with tuition doubling over the several years (Smellie 2021). A report from the Newfoundland and Labrador Premier's Economic Recovery Team provides the reason for this shift: "the province can deliver the same or better outcomes if funding came from other sources," those sources being either "students themselves" or "corporate-business partnerships" (Greene and the Premier's Economic Recovery Team 2021, 157, 160; see also Whitten 2022). More than ever before, the university is replicating logics of extractive capitalism while many within the institution, including our students (and those who cannot afford to get in) hold on to the liberatory promises of education. Perhaps I should only speak for myself, but I feel that even with an understanding of the deeply embedded industry-university relations, many of us are fish struggling in tangled webs we didn't realize were there.

Métis anthropologist and "fish philosopher" Zoe Todd has often asked a question she once heard Leroy Little Bear raise in this vein—namely, if anyone "has asked the fish what they think of the current state of the world's affairs; someone should ask the fish" (Todd 2017). Freshwater fish in particular can tell us a lot about the state of the world; they are sentinel organisms—harbingers of toxicity—telling us about trouble in the water long before it might otherwise be suspected. I imagine the fish struggling in the cousin-spider's web. If we asked that fish about the state of the world, it might have told us about the many times it had previously encountered a spider's web and gotten away safely, it might deny that it was about to be devoured. I think that if someone asked the fish in Sudbury what was happening at Laurentian University, they could have told us what we already knew—that the contemporary university is not a site of knowledge building or education per se but rather it exists in service of industry, expanding and contracting at its pleasure. Those committed to environmental and social sustainability, to knowledge for its own sake, to the study of politics, to reproductive health care, and so many others, are sacrificed in service of corporatization. One hand gives, the other takes away.

FIGURE 3.2 Louise Bourgeois's giant spider sculpture *Maman*, in front of the National Gallery in Ottawa. (Credit: Jeangagnon CC BY-SA 4.0.)

The Spider

A year before the announcement at Laurentian, we slid into the pandemic. I bought too much emergency rice. I baked too often. I filled my freezer with too many future meals. I thought of the spider again, remembering Charlotte in the novel as a small but powerful caregiver, who would have gone unnoticed but for her cleverness, but for her wiles. The gendered nature of her care was not lost on me then, or now, the older woman-spider caring for and teaching others. I shifted quickly from being concerned about getting my research sorted to finding ways to care for my students, to care for my family, to care for myself. There was an urgency to my emails, checking to see that students didn't feel undue stress, that I simply didn't feel about the rest of my work.

There are many cultural and historic precedents for envisioning women as spiders, many of which understand spiders in gendered terms, as women who are at once shrewd and diligent, wily and wise. Greek mythology explains how spiders weave their webs through the story of Arachne, a too-proud weaver who—the story suggests—did not know her place.[9] Women who kill men also sometimes referred to as "black widows," exploiting their victims in various ways—man-eaters or femme fatales—before doing away with them (see, e.g., Locker 2016). But the cunning and clever nature of spiders appears in hopeful ways too, and West African traditions often include stories of Anansi (sometimes translated to Aunt Nancy), a gender-fluid trickster spider who is able to outsmart more powerful opponents using wit and language (Benjamin 2005). Indigenous Peoples in the Southwestern region of what has come to be called the United States often include spider women or spider grandmothers in their storytelling, powerful wisdom keepers and teachers, and, in some cases, creators (see various stories in Allen 1990).

My own tradition is as a white, Italian Canadian settler, and Charlotte is the spider woman who has most shaped my own experience, and of which I am most fond. Yet my experience of academia is best articulated, perhaps, through Louise Bourgeois's *Maman* sculptures, which depict a spider carrying an egg sack full of marble eggs. Cast in stainless steel and bronze, *Maman* is exceptionally large, and one stands in Ottawa, her legs a gateway for visitors to the National Gallery of Canada. She is monumental. In the documentary *Louise Bourgeois: The Spider, the Mistress, and the Tangerine* (Cajori and Wallach 2008), Bourgeois describes her spider sculptures as a reflection of her mother—intellectual, industrious, and without emotion—though elsewhere Bourgeois says also that the spiders are, like her mother, "helpful and protective" (McNay 2010). She is at once menacing and maternal, a caretaker and a potential threat lying in wait.

The many, seemingly contradictory archetypes of the spider-as-woman reflect back, in no uncertain terms, the irreconcilable expectations I've experienced as a woman professor. On the one hand, I am meant to be *professorial*—ambitious, confident, industrious, and with a one-track mind oriented towards "excellence"[10]—a black widow of sorts, and a cunning creature diligently, hungrily working towards a goal. Academia in many ways breeds a competitive spirit that feels cutthroat because there are wins and losses and literal competitions for scholarships and fellowships and jobs. The stakes are high. I wonder when I behaved as a black widow, or when I was less generous than I might have been.

On the other hand, I know, I feel, that I am meant to be *feminine*. I am expected to be kind, generous, and to take up little space. This is reflected not only in my experience but also in students' expectations of what women professors can and should do outside of the classroom—women professors are more likely to be asked for favours such as deadline extensions, redoing assignments, and grade increases that occupy time we have allocated for research, more than their male counterparts (El-Alayli, Hansen-Brown, and Ceynar 2018). This is not to say that students should not have the chance to ask for such things, or that I mind providing them, but that the labour of those requests is unfairly distributed, and the brunt of the unseen, unvalued, unpaid labour of the academy falls to some more than others. Colleagues ask for favours too, and I distinctly remember the unfairness of the labour as one woman colleague cast me an apologetic glance leaving a too-late meeting that went well beyond schedule to pick up her children. We had both indicated to the department chair that we needed to leave, but in that moment, I was left with the decision of either neglecting my own caretaking responsibilities (a dog, not a baby) or staying because my departure would put us below quorum, and the meeting would have to end. If I left, the already long meeting, which had been deemed too important to delay, would be for naught. I am very embarrassed to say that I stayed, only to return home to a puddle of urine and a dog upset that I had put her in that position. My colleague, of course, made the right choice, but neither of us should have had to choose, and we should have been given the opportunity to participate in a meeting, an important one, that could and should have been scheduled within regular business hours. The favour was that we would stay, we could stay, because we were asked. And I did.

I am not a mother, I am in a tenure-track academic job, and I'm white and a settler, and in so many ways in an extraordinarily privileged position. But I have also come to understand that the position itself is made less privileged, less prestigious, because I and others who were not historically welcome in the university have risen through its ranks. Research in other fields demonstrates that when women "enter fields in greater numbers, pay declines—for the very same jobs that more men were doing before," and that the work is less valued, and the workers less seen as worthy of protection, or prestige, than before (Miller 2016). It is not a coincidence that the large-scale entry of women and other historically marginalized groups into the professoriate over the last few decades has been coupled with the devaluing of academic work, as well as a growing reliance on precarious and exploited labour.

There is no winning here. Those who do not comply with expectations of caregiving are seen to be gender traitors, and labelled "bitchy" or "crazy" for failing to privilege kindness above all while those that give over their time and efforts to care work within and outside of academia are not taken seriously as researchers (Berdahl 2017). In either case, the pay gap persists. And these always conflicting expectations were heightened during the pandemic, as we were forced to pivot online and to reorganize our lives, and take on not only the labour of trying to survive a pandemic but also, for those with care responsibilities, a great deal of work that was—in the before times—provided by childcare workers, teachers, family members, and others, all of whom were no longer allowed into our homes. In her book *The Juggling Mother*, sociologist Amanda Watson (2020) reflects on her experiences of gendered care work in academia including visions of "dropping the ball" and the radical potential of failure. During the pandemic, I imagined parenting professors in a mixed metaphor of juggling mother-spiders, eight limbs stretched upwards each trying to catch a different part of their lives and reaching too far, inevitably dropping some, or tumbling out of their webs (Watson 2020). I imagined a refusal of spider archetypes and expectations. Perhaps we should let the balls drop. Perhaps we could tumble towards a different future, a different university.

My recent fascination with spiders has led me to documentaries, old *National Geographic* articles, and listless depth-of-the-pandemic daylong dives into Wikipedia. There are, it turns out, two major kinds of socialization among spiders. Not all are the archetypes I have previously learned about and imagined. Many are the kinds with which we are most familiar—competitive or wily or wise. But there are, as it turns out, also a few species of what are called social spiders. They are rare—numbering around twenty-five of the approximately forty-five thousand or so known species of spiders—and work together to weave magnificent sprawling colonies of webs, to fight against predators, and to trap prey that would otherwise be too large to hunt. Social spiders collaborate to survive, but also to thrive, engaging not only in collaborative hunting and web-building but also childrearing. They challenge my longstanding assumptions about what spiders are and what they can do, and my view of spiders as solo artists, weaving their web in solitary pursuit of their goals. It is noteworthy that some live in colonies that are comprised of a large majority of female spiders. In one species, *anelosimus eximius*, approximately 78 per cent to 95 per cent of any colony are female (Goldman 2016).

During the pandemic, I joined the extraordinary online writing group described in Amanda Bittner's chapter in this volume, full of like-minded people, mostly women, mostly Canadian, mostly political scientists. As time went on, the group got broader and our relationships with one another moved beyond writing to support and survival. There was some discussion of our support in terms of "a raft of otters" (Bittner 2018), but I started, over time, to think of us as a web of social spiders weaving our work together, towards common goals. I would think of this weaving as I looked at their faces onscreen on days during the pandemic that were lonely, and when it felt too hard to keep working. I could be present for my survival and for theirs, and together we wove webs, of collaborative, supportive, academic engagement. We fought, and continue to fight, against the obstacles that we individually and collectively face, and to achieve goals that we might not be able to accomplish on our own. I would think too about the attacks on the legitimacy of the scholarship and expertise that many women, many of my colleagues have faced, recalling a line from a *BBC Earth* article that describes that social spiders congregate in part because "it is easier to defend yourself against predators in a group" (Goldman 2016).[11]

As I continue to think about the work of feministing in political science, and in the university, I think about social spiders, and the act of reimagining. Knowledge of the existence of social spiders has reshaped my understanding of what spiders can be. Perhaps the generosity and support of this writing group and the other collectives in which I engage—these rafts of otters, these webs of social spiders—can enable us to think differently about what academia can be as well. This may be, in the context of the corporate university, little more than swimming upstream, a fish struggling in a spider's web, but all we have, it seems, is each other.

FIGURE 3.3 Junction Creek, Sudbury, Ontario, 2020.
(Used with permission from Quinn DuPont.)

Conclusions

In the telling of the story of the spider and the fish in *Charlotte's Web*, there are a range of possible outcomes. Perhaps the fish might have thrashed itself free, using its energy and weight to change its circumstances, to alter its fate against the web it didn't realize was there. It might have even displaced the spider and returned to being free. As readers we are meant to sympathize with the spider, as it is Charlotte who tells the story, and the spider in it is her kin. We are rooting for the tiny spider, no matter how badly we might also feel for the fish. Feministing—that is, feminist labour in academia—is, for me, recognizing that I am both spider and fish at once, struggling against the throes of increasing corporatization and its challenges to the university as a site of public knowledge, while working steadily, with bravery and persistence to overcome the insurmountable. In the end, Charlotte's cousin-spider wins the fight, the fish "wrapped up so tightly it couldn't budge," expertly prepared for a future feast (White 1952, 103).

Notes

1. For more on the restructuring process at Laurentian, see Leadbeater 2021; Peters 2021.
2. See, for example, the final episode of CBC *Ideas* with Paul Kennedy (2019) titled "The Sudbury Effect: Lessons from a Regreened City" (https://www.cbc.ca/radio/ideas/the-sudbury-effect-lessons-from-a-regreened-city-1.5102540).
3. Slag is a by-product of the ore smelting process. After ore is processed at high temperatures, the molten impurities are poured off. In Sudbury, the nighttime pouring of the slag onto "slag piles" near the Italian enclave of Gatchell was a sight to be seen, the "17-ton slag pots tipped over like tea cups, spilling their fiery contents downhill" (Mulligan 2016). When cooled, slag becomes small black rocks, and until the regreening efforts, much of the area was marked by large hills comprised of cooled slag.
4. References to substantiate swimming in "the pit" and its composition are few and far between, and while readers are welcome to take my father's word for it, in an episode of *Ontario Today*, host Rita Celli and her guest Brian Richer speak about the same Italian neighbourhood, near where Inco/Vale dumps the slag, where "we used to go swimming in an open pit by the school...or just behind it. It is pastoral, it's beautiful, but it is actually tailings from the mine." See "Sudbury: How Hometown Is Drilled into Your Core," October 4, 2018, CBC, *Ontario Today*, https://www.podchaser.com/podcasts/ontario-today-phone-ins-from-c-13251/episodes/sudbury-how-hometown-is-drille-32281681 (at 5:00).
5. Much of Salazar's *sulphurtongue* addresses her experiences in once toxic (maybe still toxic) yet beautiful Sudbury.
6. Parker was succeeded by Horace Fraser of Falconbridge, the second-largest mining company in the region. The mining companies are so embedded in the fabric of Sudbury that only looking back do I realize the links between my own experience and the mining companies. For example, as a child, I performed in dance recitals at the Fraser Auditorium, and attended Camp Falcona, a summer camp for the children of Falconbridge employees (as a non-employee child).
7. In a chapter of *Laurentian University: A History* (2010), Matt Bray attributes this deficit to the combined effects of a small decline in enrolment and increased salary and operating costs compounded by the effects of the 2008 global economic crisis (2010b, 95).
8. The federated universities include Thornloe University, Huntington University, and the University of Sudbury. The Indigenous Studies program has historically been housed at the University of Sudbury. See discussion in Sudbury.com Staff 2021.
9. In the story, Arachne is an extraordinary weaver who boasts that she may be as good as the gods. The goddess Athena (Minerva in Roman tellings) disguises herself as an old woman and ventures out to see Arachne's handiwork, and a weaving contest ensues. Arachne's work is so beautiful and truly without fault that the goddess is infuriated, driving Arachne to hang herself. Instead of letting her die, however, she transforms Arachne into a spider, condemning her and all spiders to weave for eternity (Editors of Encyclopaedia Britannica 1999).
10. See Michael Orsini's critique of "excellence" in his chapter "Disrupting Feminism / Confronting Ableism," this volume.

11. I think of this mutual weaving with grant reports where I am asked to identify my "contribution" to co-authored articles created in community. I am compelled to list a contribution of 10 or 20 or 50 per cent or more, but I emerge feeling like I have separated a tapestry or a spiderweb into its individual threads, negating the purpose of the work. That is not how I count. That is not how I weave.

References

Adkin, Laurie. 2020. "Government Takeover of Post-Secondary Education: Upheaval at UAlberta." *Parkland Blog*, December 11, 2020. https://www.parklandinstitute.ca/government_takeover_post_secondary.

Allen, Paula Gunn. 1990. *Spider Woman's Granddaughters: Traditional Tales and Contemporary Writing by Native American Women.* New York: Fawcette Columbine.

Beaulne-Stuebing, Laura. 2021. "'Again, the North Loses Out': The Rifts and Ripple Effects from Shuttering Laurentian's Midwifery Program." *University Affairs*, May 17, 2021. https://www.universityaffairs.ca/news/news-article/again-the-north-loses-out-the-rifts-and-ripple-effects-from-shuttering-laurentians-midwifery-program/.

Benjamin, Shanna Greene. 2005. "Weaving the Web Reintegration: Locating Aunt Nancy in Praisesong for the Widow." *MELUS* 30 (1): 49–67. https://doi.org/10.1093/melus/30.1.49.

Berdahl, Jennifer. 2017. "The Crazy 'Bitch' Narrative about Senior Academic Women." *Georgia Straight*, July 15, 2017. https://www.straight.com/news/937181/jennifer-berdahl-crazybitch-narrative-about-senior-academic-women.

Bickis, Ian. 2015. "Vale under Investigation for Possibly Decades of Toxic Sudbury Smelter Run-Off." *Toronto Star*, October 23, 2015. https://www.thestar.com/business/2015/10/23/vale-under-investigation-for-possibly-decades-of-toxic-sudbury-smelter-run-off.html.

Bittner, Amanda (@amandabittner). 2018. "This is a great thread about otters and feminism. Truly an unexpected delight. Also, let me just say how grateful I am for my raft of bitches who help me stay afloat and keep me from going adrift." Twitter, November 28, 2018. https://twitter.com/amandabittner/status/1066287742269747201?lang=en.

Brabazon, Honor. 2022. "Are There Ever Really 'Financial Reasons' to Fire Faculty? Laurentian University, Academic Freedom, and the Disciplining of the Professoriate." *Academic Matters*, April 2022. https://academicmatters.ca/are-there-ever-really-financial-reasons-to-fire-faculty-laurentian-university-academic-freedom-and-the-disciplining-of-the-professoriate/.

Bray, Matt. 2010a. "The Founding of Laurentian University, 1958–1960." In *Laurentian University: A History*, by Linda Ambrose, Matt Bray, Sara Burke, Donald Dennie, and Guy Gaudreau, edited by Matt Bray, 17–30. Montreal and Kingston: McGill-Queen's University Press.

Bray, Matt. 2010b. "The Modern Age: 1985 to the Present." In *Laurentian University: A History*, by Linda Ambrose, Matt Bray, Sara Burke, Donald Dennie, and Guy Gaudreau, edited by Matt Bray, 77–97. Montreal and Kingston: McGill-Queen's University Press.

Buse, Dieter K. 2021. "Unmaking a University: Laurentian's Insolvency." *Sudbury Star*, June 26, 2021. https://www.thesudburystar.com/opinion/columnists/unmaking-a-university-laurentians-insolvency.

Cajori, Marion, and Amei Wallach, dirs. 2008. *Louise Bourgeois: The Spider, the Mistress and the Tangerine*. New York: Zeitgeist Films. https://zeitgeistfilms.com/film/louisebourgeois.

Canadian Association of University Teachers. 2021. "Academic Restructuring at the University of Alberta." *CAUT Bulletin*, March 2021. https://www.caut.ca/bulletin/2021/03/academic-restructuring-university-alberta.

CBC News. 2016. "Laurentian University Department Gets New Name, $10M in Funding." September 6, 2016. https://www.cbc.ca/news/canada/sudbury/laurentian-university-donatin-mining-1.3749337.

CBC News. 2021a. "'Destructive' Closure of Laurentian University's Midwifery Program Vexes Students, Educator." April 26, 2021. https://www.cbc.ca/news/canada/sudbury/laurentian-university-midwifery-school-cut-reaction-1.5989455.

CBC News. 2021b. "Nobel Prize Winner Says Laurentian's Physics Program Cut Means Losing Great Minds, Research Funds." April 23, 2021. https://www.cbc.ca/news/canada/sudbury/snolab-laurentian-physics-program-cuts-art-mcdonald-1.5998450.

Editors of Encyclopaedia Britannica. 1999. "Arachne." *Encyclopedia Britannica*. https://www.britannica.com/topic/Arachne.

El-Alayli, Amani, Ashley A. Hansen-Brown, and Michelle Ceynar. 2018. "Dancing Backwards in High Heels: Female Professors Experience More Work Demands and Special Favor Requests, Particularly from Academically Entitled Students." *Sex Roles* 79 (3): 136–50. https://doi.org/10.1007/s11199-017-0872-6.

Goldman, Jason. 2016. "Meet the Spiders That Have Formed Armies 50,000 Strong." *BBC Earth*, January 22, 2016. http://www.bbc.com/earth/story/20160122-meet-the-spiders-that-have-formed-armies-50000-strong.

Greene, Moya, and the Premier's Economic Recovery Team. 2021. *The Big Reset: The Report of the Premier's Economic Recovery Team*. St. John's, NL: Office of the Premier, Newfoundland and Labrador. https://thebigresetnl.ca/.

Kruzel, Hugh. 2021. "Laurentian Losing Three Key 'Sudbury Model' Researchers." *Sudbury Star*, May 13, 2021. https://www.thesudburystar.com/news/local-news/laurentian-losing-three-key-sudbury-model-researchers.

Laucius, Joanne. 2021. "Midwifery Cut Has Ripple Effect." *Sudbury Star*, April 23, 2021. https://www.thesudburystar.com/news/local-news/midwifery-cut-has-ripple-effect.

Leadbeater, David. 2021. "Laurentian University Insolvency Reflects a Structural Crisis in Ontario's Neoliberal University System." *The Monitor*, June 10, 2021. https://monitormag.ca/articles/laurentian-university-insolvency-reflects-a-structural-crisis-in-ontarios-neoliberal-university-system.

Locker, Melissa. 2016. "Killer Wives: 8 Most Infamous Black Widow Murderers." *Rolling Stone*, August 25, 2016. https://www.rollingstone.com/culture/culture-lists/killer-wives-8-most-infamous-black-widow-murderers-249561/.

McNay, Michael. 2010. "Louise Bourgeois Obituary." *The Guardian*, May 31, 2010. https://www.theguardian.com/artanddesign/2010/may/31/louise-bourgeois-obituary-art.

Miller, Claire Cain. 2016. "As Women Take Over a Male-Dominated Field, the Pay Drops." *New York Times*, March 18, 2016. https://www.nytimes.com/2016/03/20/upshot/as-women-take-over-a-male-dominated-field-the-pay-drops.html.

Miller Llana, Sara. 2020. "The Sudbury Model: How One of the World's Major Polluters Went Green." *Christian Science Monitor*, September 24, 2020. https://www.csmonitor.com/Environment/2020/0924/The-Sudbury-model-How-one-of-the-world-s-major-polluters-went-green.

Mulligan, Carol. 2016. "Accent: Lore of the Pour." *Sudbury Star*, October 26, 2016. https://www.thesudburystar.com/2016/10/21/accent-lore-of-the-pour.

Peters, John. 2021. "Shock Therapy: Public Funding and the Crisis at Laurentian University." *Socialist Project*, February 20, 2021. https://socialistproject.ca/2021/02/shock-therapy-public-funding-laurentian-university/.

Salazar, Rebecca. 2021. *sulphurtongue*. Toronto: McClelland & Stewart.

Shotwell, Alexis. 2016. *Against Purity: Living Ethically in Compromised Times*. Minneapolis: University of Minnesota Press.

Smellie, Sarah. 2021. "Memorial University to More than Double Tuition after Budget Cuts." *The Globe and Mail*, July 9, 2021. https://www.theglobeandmail.com/canada/article-memorial-university-to-more-than-double-tuition-after-budget-cuts/.

Sudbury.com Staff. 2021. "University of Sudbury Transfers Indigenous Studies to Kenjgewin Teg Institute." *Sudbury.com*, October 8, 2021. https://www.sudbury.com/local-news/university-of-sudbury-transfers-indigenous-studies-to-kenjgewin-teg-institute-4498305.

Todd, Zoe. 2017. "Fish and Indigenous Law." *The Walrus Talks*. YouTube video, https://www.youtube.com/watch?v=IhubUdR5OBg.

Watson, Amanda D. 2020. *The Juggling Mother: Coming Undone in the Age of Anxiety*. Vancouver: UBC Press.

White, E.B. (and Garth Williams, ill.). 1952. *Charlotte's Web*. New York: Harper and Brothers.

Whitten, Elizabeth. 2022. "Why Is Tuition Thawing Now? Following the Money at MUNL." *The Independent*, June 16, 2022. https://theindependent.ca/news/investigation/why-is-tuition-thawing-now-following-the-money-at-munl/.

Zembrzycki, Stacey. 2015. "What about the People? Place, Memory, and Industrial Pollution in Sudbury." *Active History*, November 5, 2015. http://activehistory.ca/2015/11/what-about-the-people-place-memory-and-industrial-pollution-in-sudbury/.

4 Anti-Racist and Indigenous Feminism and the Generative Power of Disruption

ELAINE COBURN, RITA KAUR DHAMOON,
JOYCE GREEN, GENEVIEVE FUJI JOHNSON,
HEIDI KIIWETINEPINESIIK STARK, and
GINA STARBLANKET

IN THIS CHAPTER, we share our understanding and practice of anti-racist and Indigenous feminisms in political science. We intentionally specify anti-racist and Indigenous feminisms to differentiate our work from mainstream white feminisms that reinforce the status quo; indeed, some white feminists and white feminisms participate in erasing and quashing questions of race and Indigeneity. Specifically, we reflect upon and draw out insights from an instance where we came together, in 2021, to enact a critique that would disrupt decisions made within our discipline, concerning our flagship journal, the *Canadian Journal of Political Science* (*CJPS*). We saw the matter as one that erased Indigenous voices and expertise, in a project that was all about both. We return to some of the specificities of this incident later to illustrate our argument that mainstream political science not only systemically excludes Indigenous and racialized voices but actively works to restrain and control critical Indigenous and anti-racist voices. In the first part of the chapter, we explore some of these modes of restraint and control, and in the second part we offer a typology of practices to *disrupt* hegemonies of political science that we refer to as anti-racist and Indigenous feministing. These practices of disruption emerged for us when we came together to articulate the importance of Indigenous leadership for a special issue on Indigenous politics in the *CJPS*.

In our view, the matter about the journal arose because of normalized processes of decision-making, which have been developed and deployed in a settler colonial and primarily white academic environment.[1] Systems, structures, and processes matter: they are expressions of dominant values, both designed for communities who fit the normative paradigm of those systems structures and processes and designed against those communities who are outside of normative paradigms. As Linda Tuhiwai Smith writes, "The form that racism takes inside a university is related to the ways in which academic knowledge is structured as well as to the organizational structures which govern a university. The insulation of disciplines, the culture of the institution which supports disciplines, and the systems of management and governance all work in ways which protect the privileges already in place" (1999, 133).[2] In other words, the matters we mobilized around and discuss here are systemic. Those of us who work within critical feminism draw directly from our positionalities, experiences, and relationships to enact feminist solidarity, despite and against racialized, colonial exclusions and inequities (Thobani 2021). The deployment of critical race, feminist, and anti- or postcolonial scholarship disrupts the comfortable mainstream of the discipline.[3] In the process, institutions, structures, and scholarship are all improved, for those committed to anti-racist and Indigenous feminist perspectives and to a discipline that takes these approaches seriously.

In what follows, we argue that disruption can be generative (Dhamoon 2009), its power located in the dual dynamic of embodied difference and feminist solidarity. Through our disruption we seek to nurture relationships and build a less homogenizing academy, including within political science. At the same time, we hope to cultivate a culture of welcome to scholars and students who are by definition marginalized by our heavily colonial, white, male-dominated discipline (Thompson 2008; Vickers 2015). We do this for our own intellectual and professional well-being, and for the integrity of political science scholarship. Will our disruption be tolerated, perhaps embraced, by the discipline? Could it become an effective model that challenges the routine exclusions that we have experienced?

Feministing against a Structure (and Not an "Incident")
We came together to write this chapter following our collective organizing during the 2021 annual conference of the Canadian Political Science Association (CPSA). We were prompted to mobilize to challenge the structural exclusions of Indigenous knowledges, specifically Indigenous political knowledge *by* Indigenous people and from *within* the field of Indigenous studies. We sought to refuse entrenched practices of marginalization within political science, including its peer-reviewed journals.

Our mobilization in solidarity with Indigenous knowledge holders cannot be read outside of the current chilly climates in universities for many Indigenous and racialized peoples. The chilly climate is evident in the structures of evaluation, tenure and promotion, work expectations, and publishing demands that reward participation in established, dominant knowledges and white networks. Nor can our intervention be read outside the political context of often violent racism against Black people, Indigenous people, and people of colour, since this context informs the academy, which is part of and not apart from a racially unequal settler colonial society.

Against this backdrop, the discipline of political science—including annual conferences, conventional textbooks, and the flagship journal in Canada—has often been alienating for us. The general tenor of the discipline has been hostile to critical race, anti-colonial, feminist, and other heterodox scholarship and scholars for a very long time, although there have been some hard-fought changes, often led by racialized and Indigenous women, over the past couple of decades (for helpful analyses of these dynamics in Canadian political science, see Ladner 2017; Nath 2011; Nath, Tungohan, and Gaucher 2018; and Thompson 2008). Despite progress, there is a strong cultural, institutional, and systemic bias against more critical approaches and in favour of scholarly paradigms that were introduced primarily by white men. Their work is framed as neutral, empirical, and scholarly, contrasting with critical scholars who explicitly position themselves within unequal, racialized, gendered, and colonial social locations and emphasize their commitments to challenging inequities. The structured encounter of the disruption we participated in, during the 2021 CPSA annual conference, presented opportunities for building relationships with others who have felt similarly marginalized and who have endured the familiar pain caused by the routine exclusions of our contributions and the reproduction of gendered, racialized, and colonial inequities within our disciplinary community.[4]

Our work sought to advance meaningful change towards a political science that is anti-racist, decolonizing, and sufficiently catholic in its scholarly culture to be welcoming of all. Specifically, we mobilized in response to a proposal for a special issue of the *CJPS* that was focused on Indigenous politics, led by two guest editors whose work is not principally rooted in the field of Indigenous studies. Our work addressing this "incident" emphasizes that this is less a one-time event than produced from and symptomatic of an underlying structure. In taking up this matter we therefore illuminate systemic concerns, including sexism, racism, and colonialism within the discipline, and a persistent culture of "old boys'" networks. In this section, we share insights from our conversations and relationships in the context of our advocacy, naming longstanding, inequitable practices in the discipline. We describe and analyze the erasure of Indigenous and racialized scholarship alongside the consolidation of white networks and ways of knowing; the racialized, gendered, and colonial inequities that structure "collegiality"; the isolation of Indigenous and racialized scholarship within political science as part of maintaining the "integrity" of disciplinary boundaries; and the pretention to neutrality that, together, act to produce a narrow, exclusive understandings of political science.

Erasing Indigenous Scholars and Consolidating Structures of Colonialism
One concern about the proposed CJPS special issue was that, if a few Indigenous scholars contributed, they represented the minority of authors and a fraction of the Indigenous authors who might have been interested had they been aware of the special issue. Without Indigenous editorial leadership, we saw unhappy potential for the replication of longstanding, conventional approaches in the discipline. These conventional approaches reproduce and foreground white-dominant and state-centric perspectives and priorities and reproduce Indigenous Peoples as "topics" to be studied by white experts.

Indigenous political scientists who work in close relation to the journal's editorial team, both previous editorial teams and the team then in place, had expressed their concerns about the proposed special issue, observing that it sought to centre Indigenous politics but without editorial oversight by experts in Indigenous scholarship. The concerns the Indigenous political scientists raised were ignored, even though they had been pointed out by an Indigenous member of the journal's own advisory board in a review of the proposal. Rejecting the Indigenous scholar's objections, the editorial team then in place chose to move the special issue forward. Despite attempts to raise our concerns about the lack of Indigenous editorial leadership at the CPSA conference and to explain how this was problematic for the special issue—including during a panel relevantly titled Indigenous Politics and the Problem of Canadian Political Science—it was only when we raised the matter at the annual general meeting that our critique received attention. In the day prior to the annual general meeting, we gathered about seventy signatures from political scientists who work in Indigenous politics or related fields. In the letter, we urged the journal's editors to reconsider the project. At the same time, we approached the two non-Indigenous white women scholars who had proposed the special issue to discuss our concerns and quickly received their support in the form of their agreement to step back from the project.

Following these efforts, the journal's editors agreed to pause the special issue, while proceeding with the peer review of existing submissions for publication in regular issues. The editors also agreed to review a *new* special issue proposal on Indigenous politics, now under the leadership of Indigenous scholars engaged with the field of Indigenous studies.

We were initially pleased with these developments. We had argued that Indigenous scholars should lead a special issue that would focus on Indigenous politics. This editorial leadership, we maintained, would be most likely to produce work centring Indigenous experts, critiques, epistemologies, theories, and analyses. Such leadership is critical in challenging the continued marginalization of Indigenous political science within the discipline of Canadian political science and decentring the unselfconscious dominance of white, often male scholars.

As Kiera Ladner (2017) observes in her history of Indigenous politics in the *CJPS*, most scholars in the journal have written *about* Indigenous concerns but not *from* and *with* Indigenous epistemologies and theoretical frameworks. Despite the increasing numbers of Indigenous scholars in political science, the discipline typically deploys non-Indigenous theoretical approaches to illuminate broader themes about the state and Indigenous interactions with the state (Bruyneel 2014; Ferguson 2016; Turner 2006). Indigenous Peoples and politics are inserted into colonial ways of knowing and associated theories of settler colonialism. In the face of these long-standing structural exclusions of Indigenous paradigms and theories, our mobilization was intended to move towards an anti-racist, Indigenous-directed political science.

What followed was not what we had hoped. Instead, what transpired was a familiar pattern of dismissing Indigenous feminist work in political science. After a number of formal and informal communications with the editors of the *CJPS*, it became clear that the Indigenous feminists who had proposed a new special issue would not be given an appropriate degree of scholarly autonomy and would likely be subject to more than the usual level of scrutiny and close management. Many of the editorial communications betrayed an anxiety about the professionalism, competence, and judgment of the applicant editors. Consequently, the Indigenous feminists decided to withdraw their proposed special issue rather than proceed, given an evidently fraught relationship with the editorial team at *CJPS*.

Donning Masks of Collegiality

Those who critique mainstream political science, political scientists, and institutional processes in universities often face charges that they are "uncollegial." In fact, collegiality is the capacity to work together; it does not require colleagues to agree with or like each other. Too often, collegiality is framed to distinguish between who fits into dominant (white) norms and (white) networks and who does not, with real professional consequences (Catano 2003). This raises questions: Who defines what is collegial? Whose collegial relationships are institutionalized? And which colleagues "count" in making these assessments? Institutionally, "collegiality" favours dominant, mostly white and mostly male, networks, processes, assumptions, and social norms. Indeed, the upper ranks of the academy are largely occupied by white men, and political science remains particularly male-dominated compared to other social sciences, such as sociology (Behl 2017; Bruyneel 2014; Nath 2011; Nath, Tungohan, and Gaucher 2018; M. Smith 2017; Thompson 2008; Vickers 1997). The status quo in the discipline, and in higher education generally, remains committed to the historical focuses, practices, and canonical verities of the same community that has legitimated state and institutional practices of racism and colonialism (Chan, Dhamoon, and Moy 2014; Collins 1990; Gutierrez y Muhs et al. 2012; L.T. Smith 1999). In this context, the notion of collegiality requires us, most of whom are racialized and Indigenous women, to make concessions that rarely benefit us. At times, academic freedom is used as a cover to deploy discourses of collegiality in punitive ways. To be collegial is to respect the right of colleagues to academic freedom, critics are told, so the "collegial" response to our concerns over the special issue is to remain silent and allow the special issue to proceed, despite our objections. At other times, disciplining for *un*collegiality is deployed against nonwhite, Indigenous, and other critical scholars who question the benevolence of institutions, institutions that foreground those same racialized people to signal their diversity. We were told we were behaving uncollegially by critiquing the editorial choices of the *CJPS*.

Indeed, it is only when critical scholars mobilize our own collegial networks in public ways and in large numbers, as we did at the annual CPSA meeting, that those on the margins are heard. Our inability to be heard, until we staged a major intervention at the key annual conference of our association, speaks to the routine operation of white collegial networks, and to the extraordinary efforts that those outside these networks must take if they are to make their cases and be taken seriously.

Isolating and Disciplining Critical Indigenous and Anti-Racist Feminists
Gatekeepers in political science limit open discussion about intersecting racisms-colonialisms-sexisms. In the context of meetings and conferences, gatekeeping occurs by predetermining agendas, minimizing time for discussion, holding unminuted special meetings, and shunning those who speak up. In the context of scholarly publications, gatekeeping occurs through routine processes such as selecting reviewers deemed to be impartial and competent (read: white male mainstream scholars) and avoiding reviewers whose impartiality is questioned (read: critical Indigenous scholars, Black scholars, scholars of colour, and anti-racist scholars), especially if they criticize mainstream political science. There are already risks for Indigenous, Black women, and women of colour, queer, and trans people in challenging existing relations of dominance within academia (Dhamoon 2020; Henry et al. 2017; Lorde 1984), especially when challenging the disciplinary norms. The marginalization of Indigenous and critical race perspectives is reinforced by the reproduction of subfields that exclude these perspectives from mainstream understandings of political science. The sedimentation of subfields determines the main business of political science, institutionally reproducing conventional frames of Canadian politics, international relations, political theory, and comparative politics, so that by definition, Indigenous, critical race, queer, or gender politics are outside of the "main business" of our discipline.

Institutional isolation among Indigenous and racialized women scholars, who are few in numbers in political science, increases the risk of the unofficial disciplining of marginalized scholars. When a lone woman of colour rearticulates concerns about the erasures of Indigeneity in political science to a primarily white institution, for instance, and she is subsequently summoned to "privately" discuss how she communicates with those in positions of authority, this is an attempt to discipline her. Some of us have learned that these meetings cannot be attended alone, if at all. It is not institutionally safe to do so, because racism and colonialism will be reproduced in the encounter in ways that are systemic but that fall heavily on a few, isolated, racialized women individuals. When we point this out and otherwise disrupt tactics that limit discussion of critical race and Indigenous concerns, constrain critical feminist voices, and penalize those who challenge institutional racism in its specific iterations, we are silenced. Indeed, even discussing our desire to disrupt the white male business as usual, in the company of a union representative or a witness, for instance, can be read as "uncollegial" and accordingly disciplined.

Asserting Claims of Neutrality
Historically, the academy is framed as a neutral space where intellectuals seek out objective truths ascertained through rigorous methodologies. Personal experiences and political commitments are deemed separate from the scholarly enterprise. From this perspective, the question of who contributes to a scholarly initiative about Indigenous politics is irrelevant, since the implicit proposition is that the research should be neutral and thus should speak for itself (Coburn et al. 2013). Yet Indigenous scholars have observed that the academy justifies the original and ongoing theft of Indigenous lands and the colonial assimilation of Indigenous Peoples or reduces colonialism to an historical event. There is no neutrality, but rather a deep, complicit relationship between the academy and colonial ideologies that either justifies settler colonialism or frames colonialism as "merely" historical, not as a contemporary problem. In contrast to the idea of the academy as a neutral space, separate from the broader political context, we consider settler colonialism to be a cascading catastrophe that affects all of our politics and experiences within universities, as well as outside of them.

For those who understand the academy as a site where concerned but neutral scholars seek the truth, our objections to the erasure of leading Indigenous scholars and to the marginalization of Indigenous politics as a field of knowledge are dismissed. At best, our objections are deemed a "politicized" distraction from the scholarly quest for truth. At worst, they are presented as an attack against the "good work" and "good intentions" of conscientious scholars simply trying to rigorously pursue the truth.

When we intervened to stop the special issue, we were not seen as rigorous scholars intervening in a colonial academy to rectify the systemic exclusion of Indigenous voices. Instead, we were seen as leading professional discussions astray, away from social scientific questions of methodological soundness and into the murky field of politics. In this way, anti-racist and critical Indigenous feminist interventions are often framed as engaging in dangerous "identity politics," demonstrating a failure to be objective and so to be the good social scientists that rigorous scholarship demands. The disciplining desire to hold the political and personal separate from the scholarly will be familiar to generations of feminists, who have been derided and dismissed for their attention to "the personal" and to its relationship to "the political." Yet political science, and scholarship generally, is not situated neutrally. Rather, neutrality is actually determined by colonizing white masculinity. Knowledge is deemed neutral when it aligns with white male perspectives, which are institutionalized in the discipline as paradigmatic approaches and subfields.

Contrary to the idea that universities are neutral, universities have played and continue to play an authoritative—if an increasingly complex and contested—role in assimilating Indigenous persons and extinguishing their knowledges (Grafton, this volume; Kuokkanen 2011; Simpson 2017, 171–72; L.T. Smith 1999). Our intervention is part of a rising tide of resistance to this fact, which we turn to next. Our intervention emerges from our experiences in the academy, in the discipline, in the politics of disruption, and in the conversations that animated that disruption.

A Generative Feminist Politics of Disruption

Our feminism draws from the rich and generative politics of disruption that feminists of colour, Black feminists, and Indigenous feminists have long deployed. Audre Lorde (1984), for example, wrote about creatively disrupting the master's house. Lorde reminds us that we can negotiate and renegotiate our relationships in ways that do not replicate racist and homophobic patriarchy. We can nurture each other to allow women to connect to our real power, and we can actively relate in supportive and interdependent ways with other women, all while seeking new and creative ways of being in the world. Similarly, Haunani-Kay Trask (1999, 2004) highlighted the need to fundamentally disrupt genocide, colonialism, nation-state sovereignty, and what she describes as "the color of violence"—that is, the violence of whiteness over Black, brown, red/Indigenous, and yellow/Asian people, and the violence of the Global North over the Global South. Trask emphasized the importance of protecting both Indigenous spirituality and Indigenous land, including through critical analysis and creativity. Like many others, she was critical of white feminisms that did not take racism seriously.

There is no single definition of feminism. Ours is a feminism that disrupts patriarchal theorizing and relationships while also challenging universalist feminisms that fail to account for racism, colonialism, and other systemic forms of marginalization in a white supremacist society. Our methodological orientations and theoretical approaches do not presume the neutral scholar. Unusually within political science, our analysis does not take the nation-state as an axiomatically legitimate sovereign entity, since we instead centre Indigenous sovereignties (Arvin, Tuck, and Morrill 2013). Our politics of disrupting mainstream disciplinary norms pursues an intentional transformation, as our critique interrupts and undoes the sedimented conditions that structure matrices of racism, colonialism, and heteropatriarchy, as well as our relative degrees of penalty and privilege within those matrices (Fellows and Razack 1998).

We recognize that our presence in the academy means that we are working within the master's house, which sits on Indigenous lands. We are not outside of the systems of academic disciplines and their journals, which benefit from Indigenous dispossession, the afterlife of genocide, the legacy of slavery, and indentured labour. At the same time, the very presence of marginalized and oppressed people—Indigenous, Black, and other racialized cisgender women, queer, trans, and Two-Spirit people—within institutions and structures of power has the potential to *disrupt* whiteness, masculinity, and heteronormativity, where these dominant structures naturalize and normalize white, heterosexual, and masculine authority within taken-for-granted male/female binaries (Arvin, Tuck, and Morrill 2013, 13). Moreover, the analysis and activism of critical Indigenous feminists, Black feminists, and feminists of colour disrupts hegemonic academia because we do not necessarily perform our scholarship in the ways expected by those in power. Our feminism is committed to disrupting the structures and materiality that consolidate colonizing patriarchies so as to support us and others to de-invest in systems of rule and control that threaten marginalized lives, subjectivities, and knowledges. In the rest of this section, we offer a typology of our anti-racist and Indigenous feministing, analyzing the tensions, contradictions, and potential for transformation.

Feministing as Racialized and Gendered Labour
Doing feminisms is a labour issue in the academy (Dhamoon 2020) and that labour is deeply embodied. Indigenous, Black, and people of colour are often targeted, even as they are treated as evidence of institutional diversity (Chan, Dhamoon, and Moy 2014, 19). Too often, our institutions invite us to identify as diversely situated but the same institutions are quick to discipline us when we step outside defined bounds or fail to adequately replicate forms of academic whiteness. As we explored above, institutionalized disciplining may be framed by evoking hegemonic norms of collegiality and through associated discourses about "civility," a code for dominant bourgeois sensibilities rooted in colonial notions of civilization. We are asked to perform our difference in the service of institutional Indigenization, decolonization, reconciliation, and equity, diversity, and inclusion work, while simultaneously being told to refrain from the analysis that emerges from our difference within the whitestream academy. Our identities are used as visible markers of institutional progress and change, rather than being understood as political locations that demand fundamentally new relationships, analyses, and action in and beyond the university. Yet we continue to take on this work, so that we might transform our workplace and the site of scholarship for our students. We refuse to be tokenized, preferring to engage in actions, simultaneously disruptive and generative, that emerge from our analyses.

Anti-racist and Indigenous feminist work involves quantitatively more work and an *intensification* of work. Anti-racist and Indigenous feminist work demands more hours of labour, such as sitting on various committees as "the" Indigenous or racialized representative and writing reports on Indigenous programming or on equity and diversity (Dhamoon 2020). Moreover, this work is especially emotionally, physically, and intellectually taxing. Annual performance reports and applications for promotion and tenure do not always recognize this work, both the hours it takes and the qualitatively intense forms of labour that anti-racist and Indigenous feminist work demands.

When anti-racist and Indigenous feminists have to mobilize quickly to respond to an issue—certainly the case in organizing to respond to the special issue—this burden disproportionately affects scholars who are unwell, who have responsibilities for family care, and who carry a heavy load of scholarly and administrative duties. This organizing has personal and professional costs. Time taken up protesting the lack of Indigenous expertise for the special issue, for instance, could instead be spent with those we care about or doing research. Instead, like legions of other feminists, racialized and marginalized scholars, and their allies, we contribute unrecognized, unremunerated, and unvalued labour, as we seek to open up the academy for our knowledges and voices. Moreover, the additional, intensified, time-compressed labour does not end when an incident is over. Rather, there is usually a need for subsequent meetings, debriefings, and follow-up discussions—even writing contributions like this one. There is thus a temporal continuity that marks racisms and colonialism in academic settings, beyond any single "incident." This temporal continuity has two dimensions. First, a given incident is necessarily situated in historical and contemporary relations of power and therefore operates through the weight of past and present racial divisions. Second, the labour required to mitigate racisms and colonialisms is not momentary but continuous, for instance, demanding "post-incident" relational work, which can be difficult to undertake because of family care demands, health needs, burnout, or work overload. But this supportive care after an incident is integral to how we approach our feminist labour, necessary to relationship building for our communities, and part of our commitments to look out for and care for each other. Anti-racist and Indigenous feminisms entail labour geared towards disruption, but this disruption is created so that there can be more care among us.

Feministing as Responsibility and Activism
The relationships that structure our work shape the labour we take up. Far from a static commitment, for us, feminism is necessarily a relational form of analysis and action. The deployment of our feminist practice is

shaped by the actors who embody its commitments, the particular individuals involved, and the context of racialized, gendered inequities.

During the *CJPS* special issue incident, our analysis and actions were directed towards our colleagues with whom we share responsibility for our discipline. But our own positionality is not uniform. Rather, we are diversely and unequally situated actors in hierarchical power relations, both in the discipline and in the academy. What we share is that we have all had to work against the pre-existing structure and expectations of the discipline and against racialized, colonial, and patriarchal inequities that shape but do not exhaust relationships. Moreover, we all have responsibility for our discipline, although we enact that responsibility differently based on our locations and our analyses. For the colleagues defending the special issue, responsibility towards the discipline is primarily a project of maintaining the integrity and quality of scholarship in the field as currently configured. For us, in contrast, responsibility manifests in the hard work of transforming the discipline, bringing it out of its colonial past, and pushing it to address longstanding inequities, including those reproduced in publishing practices.

Our mobilization was contingent on relationships already in place and at work; as anti-racist and decolonial scholars, we occupied an existing network of support that enabled us to move into action because our relationships were rooted in trust and safety. Importantly, our existing relationships enabled our practice; however, our generative disruption depended upon our willingness to enter into new relationships, to place our trust in the process of relationship-making, and our shared feminist commitments. Our ability to speak quickly to others, who in turn committed their support to our action, reflected the strength and integrity of pre-existing relationships. It is here that we see the greatest hope for transformation in disruption.

We will face criticism, including for our decision to write a letter to the *CJPS* Editorial Advisory Board with signatories from across political science subfields, explaining our concerns about the special issue and the exclusion of Indigenous expertise. Some will argue that if it was effective, we should not have been so vocal and instead should have engaged in private conversations to bring about change. This is a familiar appeal to collegiality. Yet we know very well that private conversations often result in nothing at all, or in resistance and antipathy to us, rather than producing change. We argue that we must learn how to sit in the discomfort that disruption produces, consciously choosing to take up disruptions that challenge and change us. Too often, we turn away from or quickly move through the discomfort produced by disruption, perhaps out of fear of our own fallibility or disposability. Yet the power of disruption is that through destabilization, new opportunities, and new ways of relating, in and beyond the discipline, are made possible.

Feministing as the Opportunity of Relationship
Political science has always been in relationship with Indigenous, Black, and other racialized cisgender women, queer people, trans, and Two-Spirit people. Often this has been a relationship of exclusion. Whiteness, heteronormativity, and masculinity have largely been defined and understood through their relationship with the racialized, queer, and feminized Other. Hence, the enactment of anti-racist and Indigenous feminisms is not only about making space for voices that have been excluded. Rather, anti-racist and Indigenous feminisms require that we unearth and dislodge the foundational logics and practices that have constructed and enabled these forms of exclusion. This demands new ways of relating, moving away from the objectification or tokenization of Black and Indigenous people and people of colour and of queer experiences and knowledges and toward our full, rigorous participation in the discipline of political science.

Inviting Indigenous and racialized people into predetermined and predominantly white spaces is not enough to transform racist and colonial institutions. Meaningful participation requires that we actively address the systemic inequities that limit the full participation of Indigenous and racialized people within these spaces. We must change academic spaces and their structures (Henry et al. 2017). As the number of racialized and Indigenous feminists grows in the academy and in political science, we are cultivating a community that enacts our own forms of feministing collegiality. This is a not an ideal of friendly or "collegial" cooperation in the service of avoiding discomfort. Rather, we develop relationships by inviting our colleagues to work with us toward structural change that is feminist, anti-racist, and decolonial.

The relationships that we envision are ones in which Indigenous people are active agents in the production and leadership of Indigenous knowledge. Our scholarly work and institutional contributions must be taken *as seriously* as those whose work maps onto the existing terrain of the discipline. Our organizing process modelled the relationships that we would like to see more broadly in the discipline, but this is challenging, since modelling something other than dominance is itself disruptive of "normal" political science. We are always in relationship and we all hold the responsibility for attending to these relationships, in ways that make space for Indigenous people as knowledge holders who count. There are important lessons here for the academy in general and the field of political science in particular.

The purpose of modelling alternatives is to cultivate relationships that do not merely exceed but actively refuse the liberal politics of inclusion deployed within many academic sites and institutions. Rather than an individualistic organizing framework, we emphasize a relational approach, where the aim is to foster good relations through active solidarity amongst allies. The issues arising from the *CJPS* special issue incident, and the deeper structure that they symbolize, teach us that we can struggle against dominance from a place of connectivity rather than in silos. Our work does not exist in isolation. Our knowledges, worldviews, politics, and histories are interconnected. Our ad hoc group of authors stands at a crossroads of multiple interlinked forms of subjugated and privileged relations of power. We mobilized our interconnections to make visible the respectful, supportive relationships that are possible across and not "despite" our differences—relationships of solidarity that vitally inform the shared work of transforming our discipline.

Feministing as a Spectrum of Transformation
Structural transformation is urgently needed. Nonetheless, the CPSA has worked to make some space for critical race and postcolonial scholarship and to take account of colonialism and genocide. Many of us—especially older scholars—did our graduate work without ever having an Indigenous or racialized professor to mentor us. Indeed, some of us had little or no instruction from women faculty. Others who form part of our network have enjoyed the benefit of working with Indigenous supervisors and mentors. These mentoring relationships heightened our expectations of the academy, emboldened our analysis and activism, and informed our

ability to envision different modes of working together and producing knowledge within the discipline.

The CPSA conference used to feature very little to no critical work about Indigenous, anti-colonial, and race themes. In recent decades, the CPSA has made changes that offer some hope for future transformation. The establishment of the Race, Ethnicity, Indigenous Peoples and Politics section of the CPSA annual conference created a home for critical scholarship, to the benefit of the discipline. The Race, Ethnicity, Indigenous Peoples and Politics section has provided a space for scholarship and for scholars who have not always found room to participate in the discipline and in the CPSA annual conference, on their own terms. The emergence of the Reconciliation Committee in 2016, in the aftermath of the Truth and Reconciliation Commission (2015), was perhaps a fairly anodyne response to colonialism and genocide. Since it was created, however, the Reconciliation Committee has developed into something more than a tokenistic, symbolic gesture, as CPSA members take ownership of the committee and its possibilities, and as the executive of the CPSA becomes more comfortable with critique, responsibility, and solidarity.[5]

There are broader changes in the discipline. Recognizing the need to remedy decades of exclusion, departments of political science have made it a priority to hire Indigenous and other minoritized scholars. There is work to be done to build a critical mass of these scholars, but these new hires have created more space for critical scholars and for their scholarship in the discipline. Now, there are cohorts of senior Indigenous scholars who teach and mentor students and colleagues in many Canadian universities. There are more students, both Indigenous and settler, who take up that scholarship as their own. Indigenous and racialized students are more positively disposed toward departments that make that space and show some awareness of the issues—especially colonialism and race inequities—that are significant in their lives. White students benefit from learning about the breadth and depth of Canadian politics and about the impact of racism, colonialism, and sexism on public policy, institutions, and fellow citizens.

In sum, while the discipline remains a site of struggle, there are positive changes, and the more political science changes, the more the momentum builds toward a scholarly tent capacious enough to include those who have long been stigmatized and excluded. Political science now admits critiques of the state, for instance, as a site of institutionalized racism and colonialism. There is now more space in political science to recognize the complicity of the discipline in theorizing, legitimating, and analyzing the policy of those colonial, racist state practices. We have some optimism about political science, even if there is much work still to be done.

Anti-Racist and Indigenous Feminisms in Practice
Our account in this chapter explores what anti-racist and Indigenous feminisms look like in practice. Our feminism is individually held but, above all, our feminist commitments are expressed in and through our relational and collective commitments and responsibilities. We mobilized around a failure to care properly for one another, especially the failure to respect Indigenous scholars as holders of knowledges that matter to our discipline. In our response to such failures, we can help to create the conditions for meaningful change. Importantly, we did not write off the discipline of political science when confronted with this incident. Nor did we despair of changing the underlying structures that shaped the marginalization of Indigenous expertise. Instead, we pushed back against a politic of disposability and came together to mobilize for change. Our collective action enacted our relations of solidarity with one another while also taking up our relationship and responsibilities to the discipline.
We acted on our shared commitments to unearthing and dislodging the white, heteronormative, colonial logics that threaten us all. Our anti-racist, decolonial feminist mode of engagement with the discipline sought to produce the possibilities for change. In so doing, we envisioned what a transformed political science might look like and mobilized that vision to confront racism and colonialism at work in the field.

What does a transformed academy look like? What is the process necessary for transforming the academy? Our answer is relationships. Decolonizing and Indigenizing the academy are futile if we do not attend to the ways we relate to one another, and to Indigenous presence, both inside and outside of the academy. Too often, decolonizing and Indigenizing efforts draw on the labour and efforts of Indigenous, Black, and other racialized scholars, who are solicited to enact visions for the academy that we did not establish and that we have not shaped. The result is an additive approach that keeps disciplinary boundaries and exclusionary measures intact and racial and colonial logics firmly in place. In delineating an anti-racist, decolonial, feminist practice, we are calling on our scholarly journals, our disciplines, and our academy to make room for our voices but, above all, to enable our voices to transform these spaces. The discipline and the university must attend to the critiques and challenges we bring forward. Our critiques must be taken seriously, and used to develop new, changed practices. Our discipline has sought to engage with Indigenous scholars and knowledges, which is an important step in meaningful transformation. Now we must go further, to nurture relationships where our voices are heard, so that critique may serve as the impetus to transformative change.

Notes

1. Emma LaRocque observes that, since the 1970s, Indigenous non-fiction writers like herself have deconstructed "the racist constructions of the dominant narrative" (2010, 90; see also Bruyneel 2014 for these constructions in political science). Opposing dehumanizing stereotypes of Indigenous Peoples, LaRocque observes, has demanded a critique of the racist (mis)use of historical sources, normalized as good scholarship. Similarly, we argue that making space for anti-racist and Indigenous feminism requires us to critique institutionalized decision-making within the university and normalized academic practices within our home discipline of political science.
2. Similarly, Joyce Green argues that the "exclusionary western canon...reproduces the kinds of scholarship that affirm the existing relations of dominance and subordination. Theory and practice that dispute this and produce alternative accounts of reality are subversive and are barely tolerated by the academy" (2001, 93).
3. As an example of the resistance to critiques of systemic inequities, consider Sunera Thobani's important book *Exalted Subjects: Studies in the Making of Race and Nation in Canada* (2007). Despite its superb analysis of Canada's systemically racist and colonial foundations, cultures, and institutions, Thobani's book is seldom adopted for Canadian political science classes.
4. As Joyce Green writes, it is "hard, painful and dangerous to take on consolidated power relations" (2001, 95).
5. In a useful example of the CPSA leadership becoming more comfortable with critique and attendant responsibilities and solidarity, former CPSA President Joanna Everitt opened the 2021 conference with a statement on the residential schools, and invited Tk'emlúpsemc historian Sarah Nickel to speak about the discovery of 215 probable unmarked graves at the site of the former Kamloops Indian Residential School. President Everitt implicated the discipline in colonialism, condemned colonialism and the outcome of one part of it—residential schools—in the abuse and deaths of children and the suffering of families and communities.

References

Arvin, Maile, Eve Tuck, and Angie Morrill. 2013. "Decolonizing Feminism: Challenging Connections Between Settler Colonialism and Heteropatriarchy." *Feminist Formations* 25, (1): 8–34. https://doi.org/10.1353/ff.2013.0006.

Behl, Natasha. 2017. "Diasporic Researcher: An Autoethnographic Analysis of Gender and Race in Political Science." *Politics, Groups, and Identities* 5 (4): 580-98. https://doi.org/10.1080/21565503.2016.1141104.

Bruyneel, Kevin. 2014. "Social Science and the Study of Indigenous People's Politics: Contributions, Omissions, and Tensions." In *The Oxford Handbook on Indigenous People and Politics*, edited by José Antonio Lucero, Dale Turner, and Donna Lee VanCott. Oxford: Oxford University Press.

Catano, Victor. 2003. "Confusing Collegiality with Congeniality." *CAUT Bulletin*, October 2003. https://bulletin-archives.caut.ca/bulletin/articles/2003/10/confusing-collegiality-with-congeniality.

Chan, Adrienne, Rita Dhamoon, and Lisa Moy. 2014. "Metaphoric Representations of Women of Colour in the Academy: Teaching Race, Disrupting Power." *Borderlands* 13 (2).

Coburn, Elaine, Aileen Moreton-Robinson, George Sefa Dei, and Mekere Stewart-Harawira. 2013. "Unspeakable Things: Indigenous Research and Social Science." *Socio*, no. 2, 331–48. https://doi.org/10.4000/socio.524.

Collins, Patricia Hill. 1990. *Black Feminist Thought: Knowledge, Consciousness, and the Politics of Empowerment*. Boston: Unwin Hyman.

Dhamoon, Rita. 2009. *Identity/Difference Politics: How Difference is Produced and Why it Matters*. Vancouver: UBC Press.

Dhamoon, Rita Kaur. 2020. "Racism as a Workload and Bargaining Issue." *Socialist Studies* 14 (1). https://doi.org/10.18740/ss27273.

Fellows, Mary Louise, and Sherene Razack. 1998. "The Race to Innocence: Confronting Hierarchical Relations Among Women." *Journal of Gender, Race & Justice*, no. 1, 335–52. https://scholarship.law.umn.edu/faculty_articles/274/.

Ferguson, Kennan. 2016. "Why Does Political Science Hate American Indians?" *Perspectives on Politics* 14 (4): 1029-38. https://doi.org/10.1017/S1537592716002905.

Green, Joyce. 2001. "Transforming at the Margins of the Academy." In *Pushing the Margins: Native and Northern Studies*, edited by Jill Oakes, 90-95. Winnipeg: University of Manitoba Press.

Gutierrez y Muhs, Gabriella, Yolanda Flores Niemann, Carmen G. Gonzales, and Angela P. Harris, eds. 2012. *Presumed Incompetent: The Intersections of Race and Class for Women in Academia*. Boulder: University of Colorado Press.

Henry, Frances, Enakshi Dua, Audrey Kobayashi, Carl James, Peter Li, Howard Ramos, and Malinda S. Smith. 2017. "Race, Racialization and Indigeneity in Canadian Universities." *Race Ethnicity and Education* 20 (3): 300-14. https://doi.org/10.1080/13613324.2016.1260226.

Kuokkanen, Rauna. 2011. *Reshaping the University: Responsibility, Indigenous Epistemes, and the Logic of the Gift*. Vancouver: UBC Press.

Ladner, Kiera L. 2017. "Taking the Field: 50 Years of Indigenous Politics in the CJPS." *Canadian Journal of Political Science* 50 (1): 163-79. https://doi.org/10.1017/S0008423917000257.

LaRocque, Emma. 2010. *When the Other Is Me: Native Resistance Discourse, 1850–1990.* Winnipeg: University of Manitoba Press.

Lorde, Audre. 1984. *Sister Outsider: Essays and Speeches.* Berkeley, CA: Crossing Press.

Nath, Nisha. 2011. "Defining Narratives of Identity in Canadian Political Science: Accounting for the Absence of Race." *Canadian Journal of Political Science* 44 (1): 161–93. https://jstor.org/stable/41300520.

Nath, Nisha, Ethel Tungohan, and Megan Gaucher. 2018. "The Future of Canadian Political Science: Boundary Transgressions, Gender and Anti-Oppression Frameworks." *Canadian Journal of Political Science* 51 (3): 619–42. https://doi.org/10.1017/S0008423918000197.

Simpson, Leanne Betasamosake. 2017. *As We Have Always Done: Indigenous Freedom through Radical Resistance.* Minneapolis: University of Minnesota Press.

Smith, Linda Tuhiwai. 1999. *Decolonizing Methodologies: Research and Indigenous Peoples.* London: Zed Books.

Smith, Malinda S. 2017. "Disciplinary Silences: Race, Indigeneity, and Gender in the Social Sciences." In *The Equity Myth: Racialization and Indigeneity at Canadian Universities*, edited by Enakshi Dua, Frances Henry, Carl E. James, Audrey Kobayashi, Peter Li, Howard Ramos, and Malinda S. Smith, 239–62. Vancouver: UBC Press.

Thobani, Sunera. 2007. *Exalted Subjects: Studies in the Making of Race and Nation in Canada.* Toronto: University of Toronto Press.

Thobani, Sunera, ed. 2021. *Coloniality and Racial (In)justice in the University: Counting for Nothing?* Toronto: University of Toronto Press.

Thompson, Debra. 2008. "Is Race Political?" *Canadian Journal of Political Science* 41 (3): 525–47. https://doi.org/10.1017/S0008423908080827.

Trask, Haunani-Kay. 1999. *From a Native Daughter: Colonialism and Sovereignty in Hawaii.* Hawaii: University of Hawaii Press.

Trask, Haunani-Kay. 2004. "The Color of Violence." *Social Justice* 31 (4): 8–16. https://jstor.org/stable/29768270.

Truth and Reconciliation Commission. 2015. *Honouring the Truth, Reconciling the Future: Summary of the Final Report of the Truth and Reconciliation Commission of Canada.* Winnipeg: Truth and Reconciliation Commission of Canada.

Turner, Dale Anthony. 2006. *This Is Not a Peace Pipe: Towards a Critical Indigenous Philosophy.* Toronto: University of Toronto Press.

Vickers, Jill. 1997. *Reinventing Political Science: A Feminist Approach.* Halifax: Fernwood Publishing.

Vickers, Jill. 2015. "Can We Change How Political Science Thinks? 'Gender Mainstreaming' in a Resistant Discipline: Presidential Address Delivered to the Canadian Political Science Association, Ottawa, June 2, 2015." *Canadian Journal of Political Science* 48 (4): 747–70. https://jstor.org/stable/24810960.

RELATIONALITY, COMMUNITY, AND CARE

5

Your Absence Is Not an Accident

Storying Feminist Friendship from Dissonance to Dissidence

KELLY AGUIRRE, MARIAM GEORGIS, and SARAH MUNAWAR

Our Storying Together

We connect through telling stories that have chosen us as their carriers and others' stories we witness. Our storying practice also marks absences and refusals. A fourth friend who participated in our initial conversation withdrew, prompting consideration of how this decision reflected thematic threads between our stories. Mariam's phrase "your absence is not an accident" took on a metanarrativity we couldn't ignore. We invite you to consider the meaningful spaces between the text and what we have chosen not to share or cannot communicate directly or at all. Such tracing around these spaces might be read to form a constellation. Constellations can be understood as navigational "flight paths," or coded interpretive *storying* guides, having layers of opacity with differential access according to your positioning and can mark fugitivity (L.B. Simpson 2017, 212–13). The following chapter outline forms one such guide.

Together, we think through how knowledge production in political science is complicit in epistemic violence and our displacements and dissociations from homelands, relations, bodies, research, writing projects. We unpack the straightening device of the white spectator as the intended audience and the spectre of whiteness that can distort our stories, rendering us invisible, inaudible, and illegible. We also take up how censoring or conforming aspects of ourselves in spaces both dominant and marginal in the academy becomes a survival mechanism. Central to our dialogue is the contention that political science is a discipline and institution whose boundaries are affirmed through the intentional absenting and appropriation of our stories.

Our title signals our decision to outwardly story this chapter as one of feminist friendship, and this friendship as an intentioned and active posture of solidarity and collaboration. It emerges from but is not determined by our disparate yet aligned experiences of dissonance as racialized women-identified scholars with/in academia, political science, and "whitestream" feminism. Our displacements and dissociations connected us, having first met with purpose to engage in this dialogue and finding resonance with each other. Yet where our conversation in the moment and the editorial process led us mirrored the process of coming to inhabit and advocate for a posture of friendship described as an ethical and political commitment and not a given, as generative and not merely reactive or born from disaffection. It is built through our myriad forms of labour for each other, what might be called care work: interpretation and naming, mentorship and advice, protection, and preservation; all responding to violence but also demonstrating love. It is a posture that can be described as dissident in the sense suggested by Elora Halim Chowdhury and Liz Philipose (2016) in that it is one which may be perceived as subversive because it is oriented otherwise, inward with *and for* each other and toward a wider reworlding.

Our Stories Apart

KELLY AGUIRRE: My name is Kelly Aguirre. I'm mestiza, of Nahua and ñuù savi descent on my father's side and my mum's family are third-generation settlers from present Russia and Wales, though our relations extend further than this. I was born in Mexico City Tenochtitlan and raised in Winnipeg, Manitoba, which is Treaty 1 territory, a gathering place and homelands of nations including Anishnaabe, nêhiyawak, and Métis. I've been living and working in ləkʷəŋən and W̱SÁNEĆ territories for over a decade.

As Indigenous, immigrant, and settler in a racialized and AFAB (assigned female at birth) woman's (able) body, I have an acute but complex sense of displacement or de-placement. I'm also autistic, and I'm queer. Both are identifiers that I'm just lately "out" with in the public spheres I circulate in, including my work. While I've come to be located within the discipline, by training and momentum, I don't consider myself a political scientist. I'm a political theorist or storyworker, understanding the work of theory as storying political life. In this I'm influenced by Hannah Arendt, Jo-Ann Archibald, and the departed Lee Maracle, among others.

It's taken time to arrive at this understanding and my present location in the university, amidst ongoing ambivalences of being "at home" here. I dwell on being valued according to metrics of utility and pragmatism, only recently factoring neurodiversity into conceptions of service and belonging that honour my capacities rather than fixate on my limitations. For example, an interest in the rhetorical and reifying power of language and adeptness at finding patterns, or what Arendt (1968) and Maracle (2015) describe as "correspondences" and "concatenations." That is, linkages that allow us to story movement, events, and phenomena, as part of a process of critical theorizing toward transformation. And so, I'm committed to asserting political theory as storytelling that matters, in Donna Haraway's (1994) multivalent sense of mattering, and so too, storytelling as political theory that matters (Aguirre 2024). Our role as storyworkers and witnesses requires a persistent ethical self-reflexivity on our methods and praxis, and this shapes and motivates my commitments as a decolonial scholar.

SARAH MUNAWAR: I also theorize through story. Everything I write must be rooted in place and begin with narrative as it is a way of enacting a relationship of witnessing with the reader/listener. Sharing my lived stories in my theorizing calls upon the reader and I to account and act ethically—to attend to the story, watch after its lessons, and be moved by it. In the summer of my third year of undergraduate studies, my father survived a severe stroke and cardiac arrest and my family transformed into a care web. The intersection of these two events marks the beginning of my path to study political theory.

The last two years of undergrad were fitting in schoolwork in between planning care shifts with my family to be with my father day and night at hospitals and rehab centres between Toronto and Brampton and attending courses at the University of Toronto. As I fell in love with political theory, I found the language jarring in its ableism. The big questions of who is a person, which ways of living were meaningful...I was facing not only in political theory classrooms but also in hospital waiting rooms. There were days I would leave a seminar theorizing Arendtian natality and then be told by doctors that my father's life as a disabled person was "no longer meaningful" and that we should "pull the plug." I was allowed to dream about Arendtian natality but not the notion of miracle in Islam to justify holding a place for my father's personhood. For Arendt, for the doctors, in my political theory seminars, my dad was no longer a legible subject.

I felt a strong conviction at a young age that I needed to hold these political theorists accountable for the harm and the trauma we experienced in those spaces. I also needed to find the moral vocabulary to articulate the unique situation of my family, and so many other families, in the netherworld of dependency care. Today, what political theory is for me is care-based knowledge and ways of knowing that I have learned from my kin and from my deen—both of which ask of me to ground my knowledge production in anti-oppressive and just practices of knowing and relating.

My life's work is to continue articulating an Islamic ethic of care and vision of disability justice. I pray that I am drawn to, and called into, spaces and relations within academia that are nourishing and respect my ways of theorizing as a Muslim, my ethics of knowledge production, and my situatedness as a mother and as a caregiver.

MARIAM GEORGIS: My work is embedded within the Assyrian story of displacement from their ancestral homeland in the making of modern states (Iraq, Syria, Turkey, Iran) in the so-called Middle East, my lived experiences of displacement via endless wars, being a refugee, and my relocation to stolen Indigenous land in Canada. I'm Indigenous to present-day Iraq, my father from a village in the north (presently, Kurdistan Region of Iraq) and my mother from Mosul, a descendant of a genocide survivor who took on a "Christian Arab" identity as a means of survival in an Arab nationalist Iraq. Today, my father's village and my mother's ancestral land in present-day Turkey are also sites of Kurdish demands for statehood.

Being Assyrian in Iraq means experiencing and knowing power from the margin of the margins. Our marginalization by and in relation to more powerful groups in Iraq and again, as we experience American violence alongside our oppressors, teaches us power and marginality are relational. I lived as a refugee, my presence illegal on the territory my ancestors once called home. Despite this history contextualizing my arrival on and complicity in the ongoing colonization of so-called Canada, my situatedness as Indigenous and my displacement shape my understanding of the interconnectedness of global formations of colonialism.

The central focus of my work is storying silences and absences. Assyrians are absent in political science, despite the field's contention (however colonially) with Indigeneity. Decolonial and Indigenous studies help articulate the questions that animate my work, but I am still absent because this scholarship is largely focused on white colonizers and Indigenous experiences of Western colonization, so, southwest Asia is rarely included. Middle East studies includes states situated on Assyrian land, yet Assyrians are rarely mentioned as Indigenous contemporary political actors because the field is premised on the characterization of this region as Arab or Muslim. So the field is sustained by the absence of Assyrian Indigeneity.

I bring in a story about a people that the world has forgotten because I cannot theorize from anywhere else; because the story of Assyrians tells us something important about how colonialism operates across different geographies and temporalities. But when you keep being *made* absent, you realize your absence is not an accident. Your absence is deliberate. It's systematic and it's systemic. When you're constantly made absent, you feel out of place. You strategize about how to be legible. Despite these strategies, however, your racially marked body and stories make you unintelligible in the academy.

White Spectres, Disciplining and Distortion

SM: This absence isn't merely a gap between fields of literature—as if political science has yet to consider the existence of Black, Indigenous, and racialized peoples and cosmologies. It is an intentional and violent absenting of the Other in citations, in classrooms, in conferences, in interpretive practices, in histories, and from lands. We are disciplined to be complicit in this violence through our instruction in "the canon" and in white-orientated modes of theorizing. In hearing your story, I empathize with your sadness. I also lead with vulnerability and openness; it is hard to live in anticipation of a reader, of an audience, who will take care of the stories we share as witnesses.

Many interpretive communities within the discipline refuse to practice an ethics of receptivity—how we hear a story, how we receive narrative theorizing matters. In the desperation to diversify our citations, to contribute something "original" to the literature, to counteract a critique, there is this refusal to see the human behind the story. It terrifies me to share my stories at a conference, job talk, or seminar, and see this total disregard, or disgust, of my Muslimness and our storied lives as relevant to the study of the "political."

I can give a brilliant presentation on intersectional Islamic thought and its potential for decolonial movement building. After it, I'm usually asked a question on how Islam, seen as only a violent tradition, can ever be used for liberation? A specific form of anti-Muslim racism in this discipline is this refusal to bear witness, to listen to what Islam offers as a critical epistemology, an anti-oppressive tradition and situated knowledge. Continually facing this rejection is demoralizing. It's important to have conversations like this, to water the communities of care that sustain us. Without them, so many of us either have left or are about to leave the discipline.

KA: Listening to you has encouraged me to reflect on my knee-jerk rejection of aspirations for a political science "inclusive" of our forms of diversity. I've been wary of seeking recognition or making space with/in these locations as the thin edge of the wedge to assimilation through various disciplinary techniques. Even if we don't want to be rendered sensible, we might get accused of conforming regardless. I just don't want to be diminished, repressed, or exhausted by an everyday struggle for subsistence when my ways of being-doing-knowing are normatively dissonant. The ethics of receptivity lacking in dominant disciplinary interpretive communities as you call them, Sarah, is sometimes also a struggle to model in the margins and interstices. That is, I also experience tensions arising from my non-normativity among critical Indigenous and racialized scholars and anxiety on their possible perception of the illegitimacy of my work or ways of doing theory. This non-monolithism is challenging to discuss as we're all often isolated from each other, and the atomizing force of the whitestream battering us makes us tired and disaffected, but also desiring of mutual recognition and holding a shared ground to withstand it. This conversation makes me feel more optimistic about the friendships that can emerge from familiar experiences of dissonance. These parallel stories are affirming, even if saying this risks playing into tropes of communities

of suffering and raises questions about sharing and aligning ourselves through trauma narratives. But I think this is imperative to connect, to help us trace our path through ambivalences and suffering, that we might form communities of purpose.

SM: I see stories as a dispositional attitude, a posture you come to inhabit when you write from the margins of political science. These stories of how we arrived at political science also tell us who we are in relationship with. Kelly and Mariam, your theorizing is place-based. There is a transparency in your intentions as scholars and it is clear how you are tied to this world through your interdependencies. Your attachments have pulled you to your research interests. We have witnessed the harm political scientists cause when we assume a view from nowhere.

Through our uncritical instruction of the canon, we inherit whiteness as an orientation and hurt others in our family, in our community, our ancestors. We are accountable for that. We are also allowed to hold our professors to account. It might threaten our material access (reference letters, grades) but we have a right to refuse, to exit, and to grieve the losses in this game of legibility, of coming to possess whiteness as an ability.

Being on the job market, you must continuously make yourself legible, palatable, for mostly white audiences. It is exhausting and damaging. As a neurodiverse person, I already spend so much of my energy masking who I am. It feels unethical to have to continually pretend, to sanitize my scholarship of Islam, of neurodiversity, of my relations, so I can get a job, a publication, or other forms of material security in academia. As a new mother, and a Muslim, I have arrived at a place where I will no longer make concessions to get through the door. It compromises my epistemic heritage, ethics, place in the Hereafter, and the traditions I pass down to my child. If the field refuses to change, if these stories are too Muslim, I won't compromise myself anymore for a job. As much as I am absenced and dislocated within political science, I am tied to this world and nested in loving, caring, and deeply nourishing relationships that hold me in place.

KA: This grief you speak to, Sarah, around compromise and accountability can be compounded by similar tensions inside relational spaces that are supposed to be ones of safety "for us, by us," or liberatory, or decolonial. These can (re)produce other normativities you're expected to conform to, including behaviourally or in your research. I've been hired in an Indigenous politics position, but I'm also interested in doing work "unexpected" of me, that exceeds an emphasis on Indigeneity. There's also an anxiousness around responsibilities to honour the struggles that shaped those pockets of air that were carved from the old white marble edifice of political science by earlier generations of activist scholars. I'm thinking here of the tenuous disciplinary "acceptance" of Indigenous politics as a legitimate field and Indigenous studies and programs more broadly. Their hard-fought boundaries are under ongoing eliminatory pressures, so when you find yourself gasping against them, feeling trapped due to any number of divergences, what do you do? The pocket of air can become a pigeonhole—one that you can still be conveniently stored in for token "EDI" deployments by the encompassing institution. Being situated in the university we need to confront dangers of not only being taken as representative and "as expected," but those that inhere in simultaneous invisibility and hypervisibility of our differences. Intellectually honest scholarship, including work critical of norms or orthodoxies in our "designated" fields, may ostracize us in a range of ways.

MG: Disciplining doesn't just happen in the mainstream discipline. Disciplining happens in the peripheries and the margins.

SM: Power hierarchies in our knowledge relations impact our trajectories as scholars. It is important for those in supervisory and mentorship roles to be responsive and attentive to the needs of Black, Indigenous, and racialized scholars. I'm grateful to my supervisory committee of radically caring women who fought for my right to share my family's stories, of Islam, of care, in my own words and on my own terms. They taught me how important it is to advise students, how to hear different stories, and how to ground our knowledge relations in caring practices. I have heard too many stories of Black, Indigenous, and racialized scholars getting damaging advice from white mentors in political science. Such advice often ignores class and cultural differences and can be harmful or toxic. It is hard to feel a conviction and moral purpose in your work and be told not to do it because the field is not ready yet. We should not have to wait for white political scientists, or departments, to do their (un)learning work, and catch up, for us to begin our careers.

I have also been made to feel as if my care responsibilities were obstacles to my career. We cannot absolve ourselves of our relations or our attachments. It is almost as if you are pressured to give up where you come from, who you are accountable to, to write about where you come from. We are pressured to create a distance from caring responsibilities and give our energy, labour, and attention to academic work. The nuances of our theorizing and abstraction of colonialism, racism, ableism, or heteropatriarchy are welcomed but stories of how such violence is impacting us, our families, is seen as messy. Whether it's taking a job somewhere else, to care for our families and materially sustain their survival, we are forced to leave our homelands and be separated from them. Normalizing this displacement, distancing, and anti-relationality is colonial.

MG: The discipline doesn't just happen in our written work, our citation practices, on syllabi. Disciplining also happens on our bodies, how we should talk, dress, what causes we take up, our beliefs. We are taught that political science is not personal. We cannot be emotional, but the dwindling number of Assyrians in Iraq, the real threat of their extinction is impossible to separate from my work. ISIS took over Mosul, my mother's hometown, and people she knew left everything and walked on foot to the north for safety. I am writing theoretical analyses of the rise of ISIS while people are dying. These racialized bodies become images consumed by us, put up outside office doors in departments to raise awareness or to perform solidarity. But for those of us who know what it is like to cross a border on foot as a child or can see ourselves or our families in that child, that image immobilizes you. It makes it hard to breathe.

At times, it becomes difficult to separate my emotional response to events happening in the region I study and come from, whether it be the "US withdrawal" from Afghanistan or anti-Muslim, anti-refugee discourses in the West. But none of this rage or grief is permissible. Academia disciplines the rage and grief out of the analysis when the state or state security is centred as opposed to human lives. Political science studies power and societies while it removes people from the story.

Bringing in the story of these "populations" that IR [international relations] loves to talk about bombing in the name of security, makes my work illegible. Being legible is an all-encompassing form of discipline that you start to feel in your body, making you feel alienated from your own body. Every time I cry at a conference, I feel my body betrayed me.

KA: When you appear viscerally emotive and empathetic, you're a model Brown Woman, while your talk is irrational and disqualified in the professionalizing or scholarly conventions of academia. Yet I've had inverse experiences in enclave spaces that valorize that model as a kind of corrective. My verbosity and inflection, or sometimes outward inexpressiveness when the mask of "engaged empathy" falls, alongside theory-mindedness, has been equated to detached intellectualism. When I present as scholarly or indeed more autistic, this can and has been disparaged or teased as "acting white" or, rather, like a white man. The concepts of whiteness as orientation or possessing whiteness as an ability, I've felt as a different kind of disciplining from within spaces that associate certain characteristics as whiteness and ironically a kind of disability. I experience dissociations, too; those instances of body betrayal you describe, Mariam, hit home. My deep internal affect is often not readable until the dam breaks. It's usually when I'm alone but it's also happened in the classroom. I've buckled under stones lobbed by students from their own places of shame or expectations of me. I've been humiliated. I've nearly quit many times. I've become quite adept at adjusting my masks to cope, or for recognition in different locales and roles, as we do to survive, until we can't anymore. I'm now thinking about these limit conditions we collide with and practices like code-switching through a lens of ableism that's also gendered and racialized. This has been helping to offset the anxieties that come with these limits and practices, but maybe it's also making me angrier.

MG: There is a model Brown Woman, who is, in some ways, allowed to be emotional or even expected to be emotional, but this emotion is seen as irrational. I think that allowance and expectation is academia disciplining racialized women, dictating their inclusion in tokenistic and stereotypical ways, perpetuating colonial narratives about these places and people. I feel that tension between being Assyrian in Assyrian spaces where I'm sometimes perceived as "westernized" or not Assyrian enough. And at the same time, in academia, I'm too Brown, I'm too Assyrian. So I'm left in this middle space where I've been dislocated from my heritage so I feel this loss, but I also can never fully inhabit my new location (nor do I want to) but these fragments—a by-product of colonization—are formative too, even as they constrain or shape my story, perspective, and scholarship.

KA: Ideas of communicability, authority, and traditionalism, being in/of or removed from "community," where and how you are "raised" and acculturated (in varying definitions), bear on us profoundly in the performativity we are expected to engage in. Being identified as "racialized women," we're still often made to perform, code, or otherwise give accounts of ourselves in academia as elsewhere, in essentializing, binary, and contrarian terms according to others' expectations of our subjectivity—where we're coming from, who we represent, our primary experiences of marginalization in relation to a dominant antagonist or antagonisms. The problem can get framed as ours and as one of double consciousness and divided loyalties, when it's mostly that in standing at intersections, we can get it from all sides.

Embodying a Feminist Posture

KA: It's interesting that none of us have used the language of feminism yet. I didn't identify as feminist for a long time. Like many Indigenous, Black, or women of colour and racialized queer and neurodiverse people, my entangled experiences and identifications didn't seem to align with the prioritization of gender. I never felt my assignment as a woman defined the constraints on my being, or my becoming, my trajectories. For example, racism and xenophobia were bound up with the misogynist violence I first endured as a child and experienced through violence targeting my father. I do now consider myself feminist as a posture rather than adjunct or adjacent ideological commitment, and I'm interested in how this might be operationalized in academia, the ways we might utilize any relative privileges we accrue not to speak for others but as we are. That we may be ignored or misconstrued are risks of putting ourselves forward, of telling stories and giving accounts. I also think of epistemic, methodological, and pedagogical implications in upholding otherwise forms of knowledge production and transmission that have been ignored or devalued in gendered terms. We've talked in the language of story today rather than feminism, but then this has long been gendered as feminine as well as raced. So, in storying perhaps we'll be classified as engaging in a "Brown Woman" feminist praxis. But we know we're just speaking as we are, to and for each other.

When I use the term *posture* I mean a kind of bearing that orients you to a certain work you're called to do. A posture is a bearing you must actively sustain, be present to, and responsive through. I wouldn't use *embodiment* to describe this as it possibly implies its incarnation or materiality in specific ways. I compare a feminist posture to my understanding of a "witnessing stance" in many Indigenous contexts, as communicated by knowledge keepers and scholars such as Sarah Hunt (2018), who has described the methodological implications of witnessing for her outside the bighouse. I've been writing on witnessing as a kind of ethical and perspectival stance academics (and political theorists in particular) consider when recounting stories of events and movements, transformative work they may be "called to witness for" and share or bring back to their communities but aren't necessarily theirs. This isn't "posturing" in the pejorative sense, but still raises questions of the rightful assumption or assignation of such a role and what it entails. Witnesses might provide commentary and heuristic guidance on interpreting what they've witnessed but are not to appropriate an authorial voice when giving their recollections of others' stories. Especially so that they're rendered comprehensible to desiring eyes or ears as Audra Simpson (2007) has written of on Indigenous ethnographic refusal. A difficulty is how in assuming such a posture we also come to disclose ourselves, it's a vulnerability we need to accept.

SM: I learned the notion of "posture of pedagogy" from Sadaf Ahmed, who helped me transcribe my birth story as a doula. There are many white women in political science who assume the posture of pedagogy as feminists but have harmed Black, Indigenous, and racialized women in the name of feminist care.

MG: White feminism has and continues to be complicit in systemic erasures of Black, Indigenous, and racialized Others. Trading on the perception that it theorizes from a place of marginality and resistance, this (em)bodied scholarship is hegemonic in its centring of whiteness in its framing of what counts as feminist scholarship. This fundamental tension explains why it is that I, like many racialized feminists, have this fraught relationship with the label "feminism." White feminism has also been extractive; its abstractions of racialized violence rely on theorizing methods that absence entire histories, lands, and epistemologies for the sake of research. In doing so, it transforms Othered knowledges into something else and makes them less accessible and recognizable by removing them from their context but also from within the reach of racialized communities. In this way, in their new form, these knowledges become no longer grounded in those lands, histories, and people.

SM: Citational justice requires us to live ethically and justly in relation to the beings, communities, and lands that inform how we learn. Diversifying our citations should not be a way to show proximity to racialized scholars and mastery over race as a category of analysis; it is a way of outlining who your theorizing is accountable to and for. Whiteness is a straightening device and white supremacy as an institution is something that we need to collectively dispossess. We inherit it. We must continually refine our ability to be aware of how we enter spaces and relations. This is access work. It's care-ethical, relational, and interdependent. It's an awareness of who is in the space and asking, What do we each need to be comfortable and how are we moving together?

MG: Until I read racialized, postcolonial, decolonial, anti-colonial, Black, and Indigenous feminist work, I did not find the vocabulary of feminism relevant, for reasons that Kelly mentioned. Joyce Green's (2007) *Making Space for Indigenous Feminism* was pivotal to me taking up that label. Kelly's conception of feminism as a posture, an embodiment, an active ethical, methodological, pedagogical ethos resonated with me because that is how I see myself as doing feminist work. It's in the research questions I ask, what I see as worth studying. It's in the things that I can't help seeing as a problem. It's in the things that I'm interested in exploring. It's in my worldview. For me, it's not a matter of just being a woman. What does that mean? Gender is at the forefront and the background of all my work, whether I use the label of feminist or not. It is uncovering what is made absent. It is having these kinds of conversations. An intersectional feminist analysis grounded in place means I write from being Assyrian—about, for, accountable to Assyrians—without having to begin with an explanation of who they are, how they are Indigenous, and why they matter. I want to not have to explain why I matter. I want my point of departure to not be a response to political science. Acceptance by the field isn't my goal, but I want to not be marginalized or oppressed or dehumanized. This means I write from my location without having to justify myself first.

KA: Not having to explain ourselves, the demand that's a disciplinary maneuver aiming to capture or *apprehend* us in various ways—including classification as feminists in immanent contention with the discipline—is a shared element of our vision of and for the field. But what would it look like to not necessarily be included or made accessible and understood, even as antagonists? I think this conversation is one opening to such imagining otherwise.

Care Work, Dissident Friendships
SM: In Islamic epistemology, there is a flesh and bone dimension to knowledge. Our relationships, how we source materials for inscription, the places we are embedded in, the lineages of knowledge we draw upon are tied to knowledge itself. I would not have a career if it was not for the incredible mentorship, care, and preservative love of women of colour in political science. They watch over me and look out for my best interests, my safety, and my happiness. From giving feedback on job talks, to hype talks after rejections, to affirming that my voice/vision as a scholar is important, they hold a place for me in this field.

MG: It's not surprising that during my PHD, the most caring relationships I built were with racialized women to whom I am so grateful for sustaining me throughout the process. What ended up being my supervisory committee was a group of caring, compassionate, supportive people, who continue to support me post-PHD. There is little institutional support for people who are unfamiliar with the structures of the academy. As in, job applications, interview preparations, job talks, how to talk and act in these settings, how to present yourself, what opportunities there are or which ones to take at different stages of your career. Learning how to navigate this is a process and a skill. There are communities of care in that way, and in my experience, it has been Black, Indigenous, and people of colour scholars who have been the ones who I've formed these dissident friendships with. Not all these spaces are safe, because there are Black, Indigenous, and people of colour spaces and academics who uphold these oppressive structures in the academy and there are non-racialized academics who do not. But the brunt of care work always goes to racialized folks to sustain each other and uplift each other because the institution does not.

SM: We do different kinds of care work in these friendships. I've always struggled with how insular and covetous social capital is in this discipline. Sometimes big decisions come down to who you know and who they know. There is pressure to perform and posture socially. What I love about these friendships is that they operate with a different logic of kin-making. There is this sense of expansiveness, of wanting your rad friends to meet your other rad friends. There is this unspoken code to look out for one another and to take care of one another. Another kind of work we perform in these friendships is interpretive labour, making sense of, naming and offering counter-discourse to violence in the academy. Interpretive labour is a way of explaining events, naming incidences of harm, identifying power. Perhaps such labours of friendship are protective as well, especially with information on predatory, racist, or toxic professors and departments. It's not just whisper networks. You embody this protection in the way that you cite and the epistemic lineages and practices you draw upon. If someone is an abuser, don't cite them or continue platforming their work, enabling their access to academic spaces and doing more harm.

KA: I think *friendship* is more resonant than *care* for me, which until recently has been a fraught term I don't take up much as it's often evoked through tropes regarding the obligations of racialized women-identified and femme people. It was a cohort of women students that got me through my PHD and perhaps their support could be called care, but maybe I experienced it then more as companionship, or rather camaraderie. This is the way that I'd like to consider a more expansive notion of friendship for the subversive and generative networks of mutual aid we've made for ourselves and can imagine expanding, to unsettle foundations built on our backs. What we've shared is a kind of dissonance in academia and political science, but we should affirm the ways we have and can further transform our dissonance to dissidence. We've refused, escaped, and evaded as much as endured efforts at our disappearance. But we've shown up for each other. We've listened to each other and have also held each other's silences. The phrase dissident friendship really connects for me. I'd say friendship, like care, brings the raced and gendered difference more fully into frame for how our work is "necessary but unwelcome" in the university that "needs what she bears but cannot bear what she brings" (Harney and Moten 2013, 26). But maybe here is not where we really talk about this.

...And Their Conversation Continues Off the Page

Much of the editorial process following our meeting and the opening of this dialogue involved shortening, removing, and shifting pieces. This process is always an attempt to freeze a continuous conversation and relationality. More importantly, this process is about making choices related to what parts of the conversation to reveal, what parts should be offered for consumption, and which to withhold. But our conversation and relationships continue off the page. It is dissonance that drives the ongoing absenting of those like us in the academy; it is dissidence that continues to presence us. Neither are accidents. The first targets us; the second, we choose.

References

Aguirre, Kelly. 2024. "Decolonization Is Also Metaphorical: Indigenous Feminist and Queer-Two Spirit Storywork Matters." In *Making Space for Indigenous Feminism*, 3rd ed., edited by Gina Starblanket. Halifax: Fernwood Publishing.

Arendt, Hannah. 1968. Introduction to *Illuminations*, by Walter Benjamin, edited by Hannah Arendt, translated by Harry Zohn, 1–51. New York: Schocken Books.

Chowdhury, Elora Halim, and Liz Philipose, eds. 2016. *Dissident Friendships: Feminism, Imperialism, and Transnational Solidarity*. Urbana: University of Illinois Press.

Green, Joyce, ed. 2007. *Making Space for Indigenous Feminism*. Black Point, NS: Fernwood Publishing.

Haraway, Donna. 1994. "A Game of Cat's Cradle: Science Studies, Feminist Theory, Cultural Studies" *Configurations* 2 (1): 59–71. https://doi.org/10.1353/con.1994.0009.

Harney, Stefano, and Fred Moten. 2013. *The Undercommons: Fugitive Planning & Black Study*. Wivenhoe, UK: Minor Compositions.

Hunt, Sarah. 2018. "Researching within Relations of Violence: Witnessing as Methodology." In *Indigenous Research: Theories, Practices, and Relationships*, edited by Deborah McGregor and Jean-Paul Restoule, 282–95. Toronto: Canadian Scholars.

Maracle, Lee. 2015. *Memory Serves: Oratories*. Edited by Smaro Kamboureli. Edmonton: NeWest Press.

Simpson, Audra. 2007. "On Ethnographic Refusal: Indigeneity, 'Voice' and Colonial Citizenship." *Junctures* 9 (December): 67–80. https://junctures.org/index.php/junctures/article/view/66.

Simpson, Leanne Betasamosake. 2017. *As We Have Always Done: Indigenous Freedom through Radical Resistance*. Minneapolis: University of Minnesota Press.

6

Disrupting Feminism / Confronting Ableism

MICHAEL ORSINI

I have found that battling despair does not mean closing my eyes to the enormity of the tasks of effecting change, nor ignoring the strength and the barbarity of the forces aligned against us. It means teaching, surviving and fighting with the most important resource I have, myself, and taking joy in that battle…

I want to write rage but all that comes is sadness. We have been sad long enough to make this earth either weep or grow fertile. I am an anachronism, a sport, like the bee that was never meant to fly. Science said so. I am not supposed to exist. I carry death around in my body like a condemnation. But I do live. The bee flies. There must be some way to integrate death into living, neither ignoring it nor giving in to it.

—AUDRE LORDE, *The Cancer Journals*

I OPEN THIS CHAPTER with the words of groundbreaking Black feminist author/writer Audre Lorde, just as I began my Feminist Disability Studies graduate class back in winter 2022. We read selections from Lorde's well-known *The Cancer Journals* in the first week because I thought it could engage the students, many of whom were new to disability studies, by thinking about disability politics from the perspective of an iconic thinker who might not be immediately legible as a disability studies scholar.

It was an experiment, one that might flop pedagogically, but it was the first week of class so I thought I could afford to roll the dice.

Lorde's work never left us.

Students who were familiar with her writing but had not thought about Lorde's foundational contributions to an emergent, intersectional feminist disability studies, were clearly moved by her work. It was a much-needed reminder for me as a white professor that disability studies as a field, much like feminist theory, is overwhelmingly white. Peppering discussion with the word *intersectional* here and there is not a substitute for doing the hard work of thinking *with* the variety of disability experience, experience that is mediated by these complex intersections but not reducible to a singular axis of oppression. Perhaps the perspective of a Black thinker was the necessary entry point for the engaged graduate students in my class, many of whom were already familiar with key texts in feminist and critical race theory.

And like many educational moments, the learning was bidirectional: it helped me to revisit my own situatedness as a white, non-disabled scholar trying to teach feminist disability studies, taking for granted that we would discuss the intellectual twists and turns in the field of disability studies as if it were removed from the everyday, mundane aspects of lives lived sometimes precariously. I also learned that disability experience, even in feminist spaces presumably more open to subverting norms around what constitutes the conventional classroom, still carries with it deep, painful stigma; critics who dismiss students as snowflakes who have been coddled in the classroom would have benefitted from learning how challenging it was for some of the students to disclose their disability to others.

These encounters with disability were feminist moments crackling with affective energy, a space of care and support, despite the technological distance of Zoom. You could feel something happen in these moments. These disclosures tapped into the desire of students to narrate experience in ways that resisted neat generalizations. And yet I could not help but think that a feminist classroom should *be* more, should *do* more. It should be a welcoming environment to share personal encounters with ableism because, as feminists, we should be working to address and to resist oppression. The students who were encountering disability in the Zoom classroom and in their daily lives recognized that their own situatedness mattered to how they move through the world. They grappled with—as many of us do—the recognition that community can be nurturing, that ableist environments are not experienced in similar ways, that their gender, race, class, and sexual identity all play a part.

Many universities are steeped in the language of excellence—in teaching, in research, in student achievement, in staff excellence. Excellence is everywhere. And they cling to a triumphant narrative that members of the university community, especially students, can work to "overcome" their disabilities so they too can partake of the excellence bounty. Despite the many strides witnessed in the university and beyond around equity, diversity, and inclusion (EDI), internalized ableism is right there, staring us in the face. It insinuates itself in discourse about the capacities of certain students to excel in the university; it announces itself in the ways that universities handle accommodation requests from students, faculty, and staff. In many institutional settings, the duty to accommodate is framed as something owed to individuals qua individuals; the accommodation (and the requester) is managed as a problem that needs to go away, lest there be any legal ramifications growing out of an unsatisfactory response to or poor handling of the request. It is the unwelcome guest at the party. Few of us want to examine this because there is great discomfort in peeling back all of the ways in which progressive forms of politics have hummed along, self-congratulatory style, with little to no regard for the kind of normative assumptions made about the bodies and minds at the heart of those struggles.

Feminism has encountered a range of challenges in recent decades within and outside academia, including its overwhelming whiteness, glaring disparities between North/South, and, most recently, transphobia. This short chapter trains its focus on the internal and perhaps unconscious ableism of feminist activism and feminist interventions, whether on the streets in protest, in institutions, in the classroom, or in the home. I deliberately began the chapter with the classroom because it is a site of radical potential. The COVID-19 pandemic has brought into relief issues related to accessibility in higher education in ways that are both affirming and infuriating. It is affirming because it has allowed many with chronic health conditions to experience higher education without having to leave their respective homes. It has been infuriating for others who decry the stubbornness of academic institutions to accommodate disabled people pre-COVID-19; suddenly, what was unthinkable or impossible has become normalized, standard operating procedure.

This chapter might serve as a call to action of sorts, a (man)infesta for feminist scholars to think *with*—and not just *about*—disability. What would it mean for feminist theory, feminist research, intersectional research to "bring disability in"? And not in the way some folks liken the oppression of people based on gender as synonymous with, or a stand-in for, the oppression of people based on disability. By "bringing disability in" I want to distance myself from any suggestion that disability can be hastily "added on" to something. Instead, disability and ableism are a beginning, an invitation to think otherwise, an opportunity to reframe social justice in ways that foreground disability experience. We need to ask deeper questions about how the constitution of gender itself is imbricated with, difficult to disentangle from, ways in which we think about oppression based on disability status. Writing more than two decades ago, leading disability studies scholar Rosemarie Garland-Thomson argued that a feminist disability studies should "augment the terms and confront the limits of the ways we understand human diversity, the materiality of the body, multiculturalism, and the social formations that interpret bodily differences" (2002, 3). And recently, Sami Schalk and Jina Kim (2020) added an important corrective to this piece, which they reference extensively, that a feminist disability studies must work to redress the dearth of racial analysis, moving toward "a crip of colour" critique.

Disability disrupts. It disrupts feminist conversations and struggles. The quality of those disruptions, however, matters for how feminists engage with the intersectional politics at the heart of social and political change. Seeing only able-bodied women provides an admittedly partial picture of how structures affect differently located individuals and communities. I am interested here in how well-meaning feminist interventions can reproduce problematic assumptions about normative ways of being in the world—normal bodies, normal minds, normal "bodyminds" (Price 2015; Schalk 2018), to use the language employed by some critical disability studies scholars.

There are important connections to make, for instance, between neoliberalism, processes of responsibilization, and their effects on marginalized women who identify as disabled. So these feminist disruptions are necessary for a critical, transformative politics that resonates in the classroom and on the streets. Without them, our politics will always be characterized by its lack, rather than by its potential to lean into the discomfort that encounters with ableism and disability might bring.

Drawing on my own engagements with the politics of disability as both a scholar and academic administrator, I reflect on some of my experience heading a university department of Feminist and Gender Studies (previously known as Women's Studies) that worked to think more critically and deeply about intersectionality, racism, colonialism, and ableism. I then move to some promising avenues of disruption that foreground disability as methodology, that imagine disability itself as a way of being and as a way of doing feminism differently. This is not an abandonment of feminist principles; it situates feminist struggle in the everyday, to highlight the connectedness of communities confronting forms of injustice that are embedded in structures and systems that are themselves difficult to dismantle. In the absence of meaningful structural change, members of harmed communities are left to fend for themselves, lauded for their resilience, for cultivating this seemingly magical quality to manage all that messes with their well-being. Members of BIPOC communities are particularly vulnerable to such claims, as explored recently in The Conversation podcast series *Don't Call Me Resilient* (Srivastava 2021).

Feministing in the University As If Disability Mattered
I came to feminism (publicly at least) when I accepted to head the Institute of Feminist and Gender Studies. I was the first cisgender man (at least I think so!) to head a department made up of scholars from the social sciences and humanities. Originally the Institute of Women's Studies, the institute decided to change its name to coincide with my arrival; it had nothing to do with me, but you can imagine the critics thought it suspicious! The institute had decided well before my arrival that it was time to shift from Women's Studies to Feminist and Gender Studies.

At the outset I was reluctant to take on this role as the person where the feminist buck would stop. Over the years, I had perfected the art of worrying, so those who knew me were hardly surprised that this new gig would bring out the worst in me. But my worries were real—I wondered why the institute needed a white guy to lead them. I wondered whether I would be a good head of a department that is normally clamouring to get their due respect.

And so, what do you do when you are a worry wart? You commiserate with friends and colleagues you love and respect. And I am fortunate to count among my friends some brilliant feminists. And when I asked one of them, well, what do I say when someone asks, "Why do you think you should be the head of the institute? Could they not find a competent woman?" (Yes, I did hear that.) My friend said, "If someone asks you why you should be the chair, answer! Address the question. Do not shy away from the questions. These are legitimate questions, and folks who ask them deserve your best answer." And so I did.

I did have to contend with some colleagues who looked askance, well-meaning progressive colleagues who seemed fundamentally stumped. "Oh, so you are going to work with the ladies?" said one. Of course, feminist women have been dealing with this kind of crap for years, but not me. One stopped me in the elevator upon seeing the announcement, looked at me and asked, "Wait, you're still a man, right?" Even prominent queer/gender studies superstar Judith Butler weighed in on the controversy of the feminist guy running the Women's Studies Department. Yes, the local *Ottawa Citizen* newspaper asked me who one of the biggest feminist thinkers was and I just said, well Judith Butler—and they contacted Butler, who promptly "yawned, metaphorically" when asked (Singer 2013).

Feminist work, I have learned, can be mundane work, too. But without that kind of commitment, units can crumble, lose resources. I was very happy to go head-to-head with committees in the university that kept lecturing us about the need to get more majors, failing to recognize the ballooning enrolments in undergraduate classes of students from other departments and faculties. That's feminist work, I countered. Educating naysayers (not to mention a few misogynists) that introductory gender studies courses are valuable for students—full stop. So again, not terribly sexy, but necessary to challenge the bullshit that dictates that the only way you can "count" is through the number of majors enrolled in the program.

Feministing is, for me, inseparable from a broader commitment to social justice. And this is where disability justice comes in. I watched as the institute began to think more deeply about its social justice orientation, its need to think more critically and deeply about intersectionality, about racism, about colonialism, about ableism. Well-meaning feminist interventions can reproduce problematic assumptions about normative ways of being in the world—normal bodies, normal minds. It is a curious gap in feminist thinking given the trailblazing work of feminists to sensitize all to why we need to resist efforts to control women's bodies.

Even the term *ableism* was coined by a feminist organization in the 1970s. Ableism refers to a "network of beliefs, processes and practices that produces a particular kind of self and body (the corporeal standard) that is projected as the perfect, species-typical and therefore essential and fully human" (Campbell 2009, 5). The body and self are implicated in projects of neoliberalism that seek to reshape notions of ability, capacity, performance, success—keywords for our current age and for a future oriented away from disability (see Fritsch 2016).

Confronting ableism is admittedly uncomfortable and messy. Uncomfortable because the feminist movement has a history of confronting suggestions that women can't do what men can do with claims that women have similar or even superior capacities (see Lowrey, n.d.). What happens when feminists abandon the rhetoric of strength and the language of "overcoming" in the face of adversity? As disability studies scholar Eli Clare (2009) makes clear, the notion of overcoming has been a central trope in narratives of disability, which centre stories of disabled people moving past their disability, accomplishing great things "despite" their disability.

Where are feminists when it comes to debates about accessibility in the university and beyond? Better yet, where is disability and access in the ubiquitous discourses of EDI? With all the talk about EDI champions and leads, is the subject imagined by the EDI bureaucratic complex almost always able-bodied? And if they are disabled, what type of disability figures prominently in the public imagination, and in representations of disability? It's most likely a person with a physical disability. Disabilities that are cognitive or exist in a grey zone of physical *and* mental health are not narratable. Barriers to access for disabled people in society are understood in particular ways.

As Jay Dolmage describes in *Academic Ableism*, there is a deep, complex history that helps to explain how disability is handled in totalizing institutions such as universities: "Disability has always been constructed as the inverse or opposite of higher education. Or, let me put it differently: higher education has needed to create a series of versions of 'lower education' to justify its work and to ground its exceptionalism, and the physical gates and steps trace a long history of exclusion" (2017, 3).

Numerous observers have lamented the problems when institutions try to *institute* something, when they try to mandate initiatives using those three magic letters, E, D, I. I have had some experience with encountering brick walls of resistance when asking questions about accessibility at the institution that employs me. I have written emails. One went like this:

Dear XXX,

I appreciate that this is a most busy time for you, but I was hoping to draw your attention to the need for the University of Ottawa to take seriously its commitment to supporting accessible events for people with disabilities as part of our broader commitments to robust Equity, Diversity, and Inclusion (EDI) policies.

Currently, any financial costs associated with ASL [American Sign Language] interpretation or captioning services must be assumed by the organizers of events. Without any support from Central administration, this means that given limited budgets internally within units or Faculties, accessibility needs may fall by the wayside. I have organized an upcoming event for the Institute of Feminist and Gender Studies on Equity, Diversity, and Inclusion (see attached) at which we will have ASL interpretation and captioning but could not obtain any support to defray these costs, so have stretched the Institute's limited resources to ensure such funding.

I have reached out to a number of people on campus, including members of the Human Rights Office, in this regard, who have suggested that they will bringing these issues to the attention of decision-makers in the University.

I am asking that the University give serious consideration to creating a dedicated fund to which members of the University community might turn for assistance in covering costs associated with making UOttawa events accessible to the community.

I did get an acknowledgement that my email was received; its reception was another story. Because, well, there really is no official response. Because officially institutions are not responsive. Because any kind of response would invariably need to dance around the uncomfortable truth that universities, like many institutions, are designed to look after and cultivate particular bodies and minds. How can we claim to be inclusive (even in the most anodyne liberal way) and yet conveniently ignore the exclusionary effects our decisions have on members of the university community?

What might feministing look like if the stories that populated the collective imaginary centred the bodies and minds of people made most vulnerable by the neoliberal conditions of success? What would happen if we departed from the narrative arcs of success, overcoming, and strength? How might this reshape the grammar of feminist politics? Few sites of struggle, of course, are without ableist logics that constrain, confine, and define what it means to live in a particular body or mind. And feminists should be particularly attuned to confronting ideas and ideals associated with bodily capacities. Much feminist energy has been rightly devoted to ensuring that women can maintain control over their bodies and minds.

Following critical disability studies scholars, the notion of "flourishing," which has been developed in and for disability communities, can be useful for reimagining feminist praxis and for thinking anew about an ethic of care that recognizes the labour associated with mutual forms of support and aid (see Piepzna-Samarasinha 2018, among others, for an illuminating discussion of this). This ethic of care centres the creative capacities of disabled people, who are not cast as objects of pity or charity, but active knowers and innovators (see Hamraie and Fritsch 2019). Feminists who may be unfamiliar with disability politics and the complex histories of disability can do well to think through what flourishing might mean for a feminist movement that integrates disability experience in a meaningful way, in a way that transforms not just disability but feminism itself. The barriers that disabled people experience when they encounter structures and institutions designed for non-disabled bodyminds are not a mirror of the barriers experienced by generations of women trying to break the glass ceiling. These are qualitatively different experiences that are irreducible to quick comparison.

Anita Girvan et al. (2020) provide a rich discussion of what it would mean to care otherwise. Gesturing toward a "poetics of care," the authors suggest that a future oriented to different forms of relationality, different forms of caring, can hold promise for lives interrupted by the corrosive effects of racial capitalism. Modelling such a relation in the article, they describe how they forged "epistemic friendships," which "are more political than standard notions of friendship" (Girvan et al. 2020, 727). They add, "Epistemic friendships are attentive to location and committed to resisting incorporation into dominant norms. They are centred on the knowledge of those typically ignored or silenced and are based on shared politics and communities of support. Friendships can sometimes be exploitative, abused, and fraught with unspoken power dynamics, but our active commitment to bonds of dissidence underlies our poetics of care. Our approach is supportive, collaborative, and rooted in relational accountability based on the limits of our own ways of knowing—learning that lifts up (rather than tears down) IBPOC folx" (Girvan et al. 2020, 727). In *Living a Feminist Life*, Sara Ahmed reminds us that feminist movements, at the heart of which are the dissident friendships discussed above, are always in movement, as it were:

> A feminist movement thus requires that we acquire feminist tendencies, a willingness to keep going despite or even because of what we come up against...If we tend toward the world in a feminist way, if we repeat that tending, again and again, we acquire feminist tendencies. Feminist hope is the failure to eliminate the potential for acquisition. And yet once you have become a feminist, it can feel that you were always a feminist. Is it possible to have always been that way? Is it possible to have been a feminist right from the beginning? Perhaps you feel you were always that way inclined. Maybe you tended that way, a feminist way...Or maybe feminism is a way of beginning again: so your story did in a certain way begin with feminism. (2017, 6)

Disability as Feminist Methodology

Julie Avril Minich (2016) provides an important discussion of the sudden interest in disability studies, remarking that one should be careful about how disability is integrated in academia. She prefers to think of disability studies as a methodology, as "a mode of analysis" that is not defined by its object of inquiry. She adds,

> The methodology of disability studies...involves scrutinizing not bodily or mental impairments but the social norms that define particular attributes as impairments, as well as the social conditions that concentrate stigmatized attributes in particular populations...And I must emphasize that this scrutiny of normative ideologies should occur not for its own sake but with the goal of producing knowledge in support of justice for people with stigmatized bodies and minds. In other words, I argue for naming disability studies as a methodology rather than a subject in order to recommit the field to its origins in social justice work.

As Minich continues, this rethinking would help to expand the boundaries of the field and, I suggest, bring feminist thinking into more productive engagements with disability studies scholarship. A number of areas of study, she adds, can benefit from more consistent engagement, including "fatness, STDs, mood disorders, addictions, non-normative family structures, intimate partner violence, police brutality, neurological differences, pregnancy, cancer, aging, asthma, and diabetes." For instance, embodied experiences of fatness often turn around notions of what a body is supposed to look and feel like, and how fat people transgress those boundaries, and presumably do so in deliberate ways. Although fat people experience ableist and unwelcoming environments, unlike disability, fat embodiment is the object of societal disgust and moral revulsion because it is presumed that fat people have chosen to live in ways that pose risks to their health and/or disability status. Recently, there has been interest in merging fat-positive perspectives with a broader social justice agenda, not to mention a greater need to think about the racial origins of fatphobia in society (see Herndon 2002; Strings 2015; on disability and fatness, see McPhail and Orsini 2021; Mollow 2014; Mollow and McRuer 2015).

Critical race scholarship has been central in rethinking the relationship between race and disability. As Nirmala Erevelles argues, "rather than conceiving of 'disability' and 'race' as interchangeable tropes in order to foreground the ubiquity of oppression, the categories of race/ethnicity and disability might be better invoked to demonstrate how they constitute one another through social, political, economic, and cultural practices that have kept seemingly different groups of people in strikingly similar marginalized positions" (2015, 148).

As Moya Bailey and Izetta Autumn Mobley explain in a key text, intersectionality needs to "attend to disability" because "racism, sexism, and ableism share a eugenic impulse that needs to be uncovered and felled" (2019, 21). They view this "myth of the strong Black woman" as a form of persistent ableism: "The myth suggests that Black women are uniquely strong, able to endure pain, and surmount otherwise difficult obstacles because of their innate tenacity. Black women are disallowed disability and their survival is depoliticized...There is a productive tension in recognizing the critical connections of the celebration of survival in the context of the demands made on Black bodies to transcend all suffering.

The logic of Black hypervisibility produces subjects that are barred from weakness—and disability in Western thought as figured through non-normative bodies is the ultimate sign of unsuitability" (21). Mel Y. Chen (2021), in an article titled "Feminisms in the Air," uses the term "incipient intersectionality" to capture how they understand a broader embrace of this framework in the wake of the COVID-19 pandemic, a development they welcome. As Chen explains, "one of the core contributions of a feminist analysis has been the examination of what was often an implicit racialized gendering of a purported division between public and private" (22–23). The phrase "feminisms in the air" drew specific attention to the twin catastrophes of COVID-19 pandemic and the forest fires engulfing parts of North America, including California and British Columbia, among others. The public injunction to "stay indoors" from public health officials so as to avoid inhaling deadly smoke from the fires, versus the warning to "stay outdoors" to limit the possibility of COVID-19 infection, is a good illustration of the contested public-private divide that has been central to feminist theorizing. In Chen's formulation, however, greater attention is paid to the ableist assumptions associated with the capacity to breathe air, which is not lost on individuals living with multiple chemical sensitivity such as Chen.

Conclusion

My feminist hope—no, I am not being cruelly optimistic here!—is that colleagues with whom I work and interact will appreciate that feminist work should be rooted in the principles of disability justice, and that some of the most radical, game-changing work is happening in disability justice communities that might not identify as explicitly feminist (Piepzna-Samarasinha 2020). Our work should centre, as disability justice pioneers Sins Invalid (n.d.) remind us, the most marginalized members of communities. With all of the intersectional talk—and there is so much talk—that permeates academic and civil society spaces, there is remarkably little attention to ableism and to disability politics. Rather than slap a million (or millions of) wrists, what can be done collectively to address this important absence? What would a more robust model of feminist action look like if it recognized the ways in which axes of oppression are mutually constituted? We can't think feminism without grappling with race, and we can't think disability without thinking gender. As Jake Pyne (2020) discusses, often painful histories of disability oppression—namely, the regulation of children who were deemed autistic and in need of behaviour therapy to rid them of their autistic traits—are intertwined with efforts to regulate transness in children.

We have many feelings about this work, affective attachments that are difficult to sort through. As Robin Wiegman (2016) discusses in a sobering account of feminist work in the university, attending to these attachments and to feelings of institutional betrayal or disappointment, can be emotionally and politically exhausting. I imagine a similar challenge when thinking about the disruptions that are necessary to bring disability and ableism to the forefront of feminism, and the discomfort it might engender for non-disabled folks. These disruptions will mobilize an array of feelings. As former graduate student Lucia Hulsether explained in a roundtable discussion on institutional feelings and feminist studies, "We cannot transform the university without transforming the desires that it forms in us. The university is an affective economy as much as it is a political and intellectual one; it shapes what we experience as pleasurable, disgusting, terrifying, hopeful, alluring. Our pleasures and pains with respect to academic life are neither essential entities nor transparent windows into the good; they are indicators of what we have learned to value. They can deceive" (Bashore et al. 2015, 231). Transforming the university and imagining a feminist university devoted to promoting social justice and confronting ableism will require us to unlearn some of the ideas that govern university life, ideas that naturalize differences in ways that gloss over the realities of interlocking forms of oppression. As Lorde reminds us, in the place of sadness we need to imagine rage, righteous rage, and fly, like the bee flies.

References

Ahmed, Sara. 2017. *Living a Feminist Life*. Durham, NC: Duke University Press.
Bailey, Moya, and Izetta Autumn Mobley. 2019. "Work in the Intersections: A Black Feminist Disability Framework." *Gender & Society* 33 (1): 19–40. https://10.1177/0891243218801523.
Bashore, Katie, Heather Berg, James Bliss, Kellie Cauley, Emerald Christopher-Byrd, Ayla Engelhart, Adrian Hernandez-Acosta, Lucia Hulseher, Stephen Molldrem, Sandy Placido, Mairead Sullivan, Christina Siobhan Wells, and Lindsey Whitmore. 2015. "Practicing Institutional Feelings: A Roundtable." *Feminist Formations* 27 (3): 217–36. http://www.jstor.org/stable/43860821.

Campbell, Fiona Kumari. 2009. *Contours of Ableism: The Production of Disability and Abledness*. Basingstoke, UK: Palgrave Macmillan.

Chen, Mel Y. 2021. "Feminisms in the Air." *Signs: Journal of Women in Culture and Society* 47 (1): 22–29. https://doi.org/10.1086/715733.

Clare, Eli. 2009. *Exile and Pride: Disability, Queerness and Liberation*. Cambridge, MA: South End Press.

Dolmage, Jay Timothy. 2017. *Academic Ableism: Disability and Higher Education*. Ann Arbor: University of Michigan Press. E-book. https://doi.org/10.3998/mpub.9708722.

Erevelles, Nirmala. 2015. "Race." In *Keywords for Disability Studies*, edited by Rachel Adams, Benjamin Reiss, and David Serlin, 145–48. New York: New York University Press.

Fritsch, Kelly. 2016. "Cripping Neoliberal Futurity: Marking the Elsewhere and Elsewhen of Desiring Otherwise." *Feral Feminisms*, no. 5, 11–26. https://feralfeminisms.com/cripping-neoliberal-futurity/.

Garland-Thomson, Rosemarie. 2002. "Integrating Disability, Transforming Feminist Theory." *Feminist Formations* 14 (3): 1–32. https://doi.org/10.1353/nwsa.2003.0005.

Girvan, Anita, Baljit Pardesi, Davina Bhandar, and Nisha Nath. 2020. "Poetics of Care: Remedies for Racial Capitalism Gone Viral." *Feminist Studies* 46 (3): 717–28. https://doi.org/10.1353/fem.2020.0021.

Hamraie, Aimi, and Kelly Fritsch. 2019. "Crip Technoscience Manifesto." *Catalyst: Feminism, Theory, Technoscience* 5 (1): 1–34. https://doi.org/10.28968/cftt.v5i1.29607.

Herndon, April. 2002. "Disparate But Disabled: Fat Embodiment and Disability Studies." *Feminist Formations* 14 (3): 120–37. https://www.jstor.org/stable/4316927.

Lorde, Audre. 1980. *The Cancer Journals*. San Francisco: Aunt Lute Books.

Lowrey, Kathleen. n.d. "Disability and Social Movements." *Project Citizenship*. Accessed September 23, 2023. https://projectcitizenship.com/disability-social-movements/.

McPhail, Deborah, and Michael Orsini. 2021. "Fat Acceptance as Social Justice." *Canadian Medical Association Journal* 193 (35): E1398-99. https://doi.org/10.1503/cmaj.210772.

Minich, Julie Avril. 2016. "Enabling Whom? Critical Disability Studies Now." *Lateral* 5 (1). https://doi.org/10.25158/L5.1.9.

Mollow, Anna. 2014. "Disability Studies Gets Fat." *Hypatia: Journal of Feminist Philosophy* 30 (3): 199–216. https://www.jstor.org/stable/24542067.

Mollow, Anna, and Robert McRuer. 2015. "Fattening Austerity." *Body Politics* 3 (S): 25–49. https://www.db-thueringen.de/receive/dbt_mods_00027196.

Piepzna-Samarasinha, Leah Lakshmi. 2018. *Care Work: Dreaming Disability Justice*. Vancouver: Arsenal Pulp Press.

Piepzna-Samarasinha, Leah Lakshmi. 2020. "Still Dreaming Wild Disability Justice Dreams at the End of the World." In *Disability Visibility: First-Person Stories from the Twenty-First Century*, edited by Alice Wong, 250–61. New York: Vintage Books.

Price, Margaret. 2015. "The Bodymind Problem and the Possibilities of Pain." *Hypatia* 30 (1): 268–84. https://doi.org/10.1111/hypa.12127.

Pyne, Jake. 2020. "'Building a Person': Legal and Clinical Personhood for Autistic and Trans Children in Ontario." *Canadian Journal of Law and Society / Revue canadienne droit et société* 35 (2): 341–65. https://doi.org/10.1017/cls.2020.8.

Schalk, Sami. 2018. *Bodyminds Reimagined: (Dis)ability, Race, and Gender in Black Women's Speculative Fiction*. Durham, NC: Duke University Press.

Schalk, Sami, and Jina B. Kim. 2020. "Integrating Race, Transforming Feminist Disability Studies." *Signs: Journal of Women in Culture and Society* 46 (1): 31–55. https://www.jstor.org/stable/4316922.

Singer, Zev. 2013. "U of O Prof's Post a Real Gender Bender." *Ottawa Citizen*, July 29, 2013. A1.

Sins Invalid. (n.d.). Sins Invalid website. Accessed November 8, 2023. https://www.sinsinvalid.org/.

Srivastava, Vinita, host. 2021. "Listen to 'Don't Call Me Resilient': Our Podcast about Race." *The Conversation*, January 27, 2021. https://theconversation.com/listen-to-dont-call-me-resilient-our-podcast-about-race-149692.

Strings, Sabrina. 2015. "Obese Black Women as 'Social Dead Weight': Reinventing the 'Diseased Black Woman.'" *Signs: Journal of Women in Culture and Society* 41 (1): 107–30. https://doi.org/10.1086/681773.

Wiegman, Robyn. 2016. "No Guarantee: Feminism's Academic Affect and Political Fantasy." *Atlantis* 37.2 (2): 83–95.

7 Indigenous Feminisms and Political Science

Indigenization and Epistemological Barriers to Inclusion

EMILY GRAFTON

THIS CHAPTER TAKES UP THE WORK of feministing in political science through an analytical lens of the theories of Indigenous feminisms. As universities increasingly take on projects of academic Indigenization,[1] those intersections of Indigeneity and gender have become more prevalent in Western-dominated disciplines such as political science.[2] Indigenization is a process that centres Indigenous ways of knowing in Western-centred institutions and intends to effect positive change towards the various settler colonial inequities and harms that Indigenous Peoples face. While Indigenous feminisms are integral to understanding the intersections of Indigeneity and gender in any Canadian political arena, they also provide insights into a serious deficit associated with Indigenization. The process of Indigenization in neoliberal contexts can encourage the co-optation of Indigenous knowledges, which is a deficit that might reinscribe colonial inequities instead of transforming them. I argue that Indigenous-centred feministing in political science illustrates this co-optation.

This chapter explores the debates of Indigenous feminisms within broader Indigenous liberation movements tied to the Missing and Murdered Indigenous Women and Girls (MMIWG) crisis, which is one of the clearest examples of the systemic settler colonial harms towards Indigenous women in Canadian society. This crisis is one of gendered colonial violence that is the result of concurrent and mutually reinforcing forms of oppression, including oppressive settler state relations (colonialism) and oppressive gender relations (heteropatriarchy) (Kuokkanen 2019, 12). The National Inquiry into MMIWG (NI-MMIWG) was announced in December 2015. Its Final Report, *Reclaiming Power and Place*, was submitted to the Canadian government in June 2019 with 231 Calls to Justice. These calls remain largely ignored by the Canadian state and society, much like gender-based colonial violence against Indigenous women.

This chapter argues that the inclusion of the settler colonial politics of the MMIWG crisis and Indigenous feminisms, brought into the discipline of political science through processes of Indigenization, illustrates the oft-overlooked complexities of Indigenous knowledge systems in the academy. These knowledge systems are often incompatible with Western knowledge systems—due to differing epistemological orientations—and, partially due to this difference, Indigenization practices routinely result in the co-optation of Indigenous knowledges (Grafton and Melançon 2020, 145). This chapter asks, Can the discipline adequately address the complexity and nuance of the debate on Indigenous feminisms that arises from an epistemological orientation that is not Western-centred? Will Indigenous-centred feministing advance the theoretical lens of Indigenous feminisms related to Indigenous liberation, or will this process make these theories vulnerable to the tactics of Indigenization, namely co-optation?

Indigenizing the Academy: Deep Colonising as Co-optation

At this point, Indigenization of the academy is a well-entrenched practice of centring Indigenous ways of knowing in predominantly Western-oriented university institutions. For many, Indigenization processes attempt to balance settler colonial premises that exclude Indigenous Peoples and Indigenous ways of knowing from institutional functions. These processes, therefore, typically address colonial inequities by including authentic Indigenous presence in physical space, teaching and curriculum, research, and decision-making (Grafton and Melançon 2020).

Indigenization is one remedy to settler colonial inequities; others, such as decolonization, anti-colonization, and reconciliation exist, too. Settler colonialism is a complex system of political-economic activity resulting from a foreign power(s) invading a nation and imposing its economic, political, and social practices. The invaded nation is pressured to assimilate, and languages, political systems, and cultures might be eroded, replaced, or altered to those of the colonizing power (Frideres and Gadacz 2012). In Canada, a significant result of settler colonialism is a depletion of Indigenous controls of lands and resources—which are the main objective of any colonial project—and, in the eyes of the settler state, Indigenous nationhood or sovereignty is reduced (Green 1995).

This invasion means that colonial forces—to varying degrees—circumvent colonized peoples' autonomy. Indigenous Peoples, however, do exercise agency, resistance, and the continuation of Indigenous-centred languages, cultures, and ways of knowing. We might refer to this as Indigenous difference: epistemological and ontological orientations that, while diverse in its specific land-based relationality, are exclusive to Indigenous Peoples.

Settler colonialism has far-reaching implications, and thus, Indigenization often has a broad agenda. It relies on Indigenous Peoples' resistance and the continuation of Indigenous knowledges: this is the Indigenous presence that encourages decolonization through Indigenization. These processes can result in positive outcomes that can include advancements towards reconciling or decolonizing colonial inequities. However, Indigenization practices have also earned various criticisms; this chapter is limited to those deficits resulting from neoliberalism's regular practice within university structures. While neoliberalism in the academy has many facets, specific to Indigenization are the ways neoliberal budgets (influenced in Canada by decreasing government spending and increasing institutional service provision) encourage competition amongst faculty to gain external dollars to support research (Changfoot et al. 2020; Last 2018). Indigenization in this highly competitive environment forces faculty to compete for research dollars tethered to the seemingly progressive pursuits of Indigenization. These pursuits often include the redevelopment of curriculum or research practices to centre those traditionally marginalized Indigenous knowledge systems within disciplines, such as political science, that are traditionally produced by and reproduce Western knowledge systems. One result of the pursuit of Indigenization-related funding in this competitive neoliberal environment is an increase in projects that co-opt Indigenous knowledges.

There are various structural reasons that such co-optation of Indigenous knowledges occurs. Deborah Bird Rose argues settler colonial structures are prone to what she calls "deep colonising" or a double bind: colonial systems simultaneously erase Indigenous difference while attempting to gain Indigenous knowledges (1996, 6–7). This double bind emerges in practices intended to decolonize that, instead, reinscribe colonization. However, this process of deep colonising is often misunderstood as a "negligible side effect" of colonial "progress" and, in this way, might be a concealed process as well as a proposition that minimizes or dismisses the actual harmful impacts that these effects have for Indigenous Peoples (Rose 1996, 7–8).

The co-optation outcome from neoliberal Indigenization is akin to deep colonising. Should we understand the erasure of Indigenous difference as a "side effect" of colonial "progress," as Rose (1996) observes of settler society, then the co-optation that results from Indigenization is similarly an extension of the colonial project that diminishes Indigenous difference. Here, neoliberal approaches to Indigenization both erase (or assimilate) Indigenous presence while accessing (or co-opting) Indigenous knowledges to further the colonial project.

Gina Starblanket and Elaine Coburn explain that when Indigenous knowledges are brought into neoliberal Western spaces, commodification can occur (2020, 98–99). These are deep colonising practices, where settler presence is built on nuanced Indigenous erasure. As Starblanket and Coburn write, "the long-standing nature of the settler state's drive to engage selectively with Indigenous relations—denying the existence of Indigenous laws, governance, and jurisdiction, while simultaneously appropriating Indigeneity for its own purposes" (87). The settler drive to selectively use Indigenous knowledges to serve colonial inequities is deep colonising in practice and, in this way, it commodifies Indigenous knowledges to assimilate Indigenous Peoples (see also Coburn et al., this volume).

One pressing matter at the centre of these commodification practices concerns Indigenous and Western knowledge production, which arise from two very different sources. Much conflict and harm come from these disparate knowledge sources, fostered through Indigenization practices that result in "inhospitable" environments for Indigenous knowledges and a lack of tangible and beneficial change (Gaudry and Lorenz 2018, 220). The conflict arises because Indigenous knowledge systems are accessed through knowledge sharers and language guardians, are passed intergenerationally, often orally and through ceremony or other culturally appropriate teaching modes, and are earned through relational actions of community-centred contributions and the respectful handling of protocols. Western knowledge might be found in books, stored in libraries or on bookshelves, and taught in classrooms or shared through conferences. It can be accessed through conversation, reading, tuition payment, or internet searches. Indigenous knowledges can be said to be lived or experiential, while Western knowledge is abstracted from non-personal knowledge (Bartlett et al. 2007, 2375). These are two very different epistemological orientations to knowledge production—experience versus abstraction—and access—community versus academia.

This epistemological conflict is deeply embedded in colonialism. Rauna Kuokkanen writes that land use can illustrate this conflict: neoliberal capitalism relates to lands through extractive purposes, and Indigenous worldviews relate to lands through caretaking and kinship relationships (2011, 286). Because land and resources are the cornerstones of colonial projects, this epistemological variation is significant. Colonial projects practice deep colonising to commodify Indigenous worldviews to access land and resources, and this practice extends to all exercises of Indigenous erasure under colonization.

As Indigenization practices become routinely applied in neoliberal academic environments, several deep colonising issues arise. While most post-secondary institutions consistently claim they implement Indigenization for purposes of transformative change, this rhetoric routinely does not translate into substantial change that benefits Indigenous communities. Instead, the status quo that erodes Indigenous difference remains intact (Gaudry and Lorenz 2018, 220). This status quo remains because "the academy is also a central site of ongoing colonialism" (Cote-Meek 2020, xv). Universities rely predominantly on Western knowledge sources that consistently exclude Indigenous ways of knowing (Kuokkanen 2007, 5). Indigenous knowledge systems are an inherent challenge for these Western-orientated knowledges (Battiste 2013). Here the deep colonising emerges: Indigenization, while meant to undo colonialism, is co-opted and commodified in support of settler colonialism. Indigenization regimes that foster truly decolonial approaches that radically transform dominant power relations within the academy are typically "off the radar" at universities (Gaudry and Lorenz 2018, 223).

This analysis is rooted in the scholarship cited and my lived experience as a woman, citizen of the Métis nation, and faculty member in a political studies department who has worked on post-secondary administrative files of Indigenization. In my faculty role, I have been called an "EDI hire," and at times folks are surprised that I teach "real political science" as opposed to, I suspect, those courses concerning feminist theories or Indigenous Peoples. These kinds of colonial, racist, and misogynist comments are longstanding practices in academia intended to minimize the scholarship of gendered and racialized minorities and those with "marginalized" knowledge systems (Coburn 2020, 435; Cote-Meek 2020, xv). For example, Kiera Ladner writes that political science does not account for Indigenous experiential knowledges but instead engages with Indigenous Peoples vis-à-vis the state apparatus and, also, casts Indigenous difference as apolitical, cultural expressions (2017, 166–67, 172). My experience reflects the deep colonising of Indigenization: I was hired to fill a knowledge gap (which I do), but often my scholarship is minimized unless it relates to the state and, additionally, those deep colonising pressures to support the continuation of colonial inequities can arise. Related to my experiences, I am deeply concerned about the co-optation of Indigenous feministing in political science in this era of academic Indigenization.

Indigenization and the Systemic Marginalization of Indigenous Women: Searching for Liberation Strategies

The MMIWG crisis is an example of the potential for the co-optation and commodification of Indigenous knowledges through academic Indigenization. Bridging Indigenous resistance writings into academia is not new, but political science has largely omitted substantial take-up of both Indigenous-related scholarship (Ladner 2017) and feminism (MacDonald and Dobrowolsky 2018). This section will consider the gender-based violence that Indigenous women face in settler Canada and those differing responses that take the shape of a debate concerning Indigenous feminisms as related to broader Indigenous liberation strategies. I argue that the differing epistemological orientations to Western and Indigenous ways of knowing are clearly articulated in this debate and, therefore, this debate is prone to the co-opting forces of Indigenization's deep colonising.

The MMIWG crisis results from the intersections of settler colonialism and gender that shape contemporary Canada (Bourgeois 2017). Settler colonialism is founded on patriarchy, a system of social organization that supports male dominance and female subordination (Green 2017). Patriarchy works in tandem with heteronormativity (Snyder 2018), a method of social organization and behaviours that prescribe heterosexuality as a normalized social construct. These co-occurring oppressive systems, or heteropatriarchy, are damaging to members of society: they restrict, dismiss, and invalidate individuals who do not fit into the social constructs of gender binaries (male or female) or dominant heterosexuality (Juschka 2014). Critical to the MMIWG crisis, these socially constructed gender roles and behaviours result from colonialism and, as Starblanket (2017) explains, are antithetical to traditional Indigenous gender roles.

In Canada, the MMIWG crisis is thus a result of colonialism and heteropatriarchal intersectional systems of oppression. These origins of discrimination against Indigenous women are longstanding in Canada and originate from early colonial encounters amongst Indigenous peoples and European colonizers, which led to particular stereotypes of Indigenous women that continue to inform Canadian society (Wilson 2018). For example, settler colonial encroachment on Indigenous Peoples' lands and the degradation and devaluation of these lands have been reproduced and upheld through social constructs concerning Indigenous women's bodies (Kuokkanen 2019, 17). This social reproduction fosters dehumanizing stereotypes of Indigenous women as hypersexualized and sexually disposable (Eberts 2017, 82). These stereotypes normalize the devaluation of Indigenous women, as occurred through settler-based exploitation of lands, waters, and animals (Kauanui 2008, 285), and colonial projects rely on this devaluation through stereotypes for support and justification (Baskin 2019, 2088). Additionally, settler colonialism is an economic and political imposition of power exercised in Canada primarily through the enforced mechanics of mercantilism and extractive capitalism's use of land-based resources (Starblanket and Coburn 2020, 94). Because Indigenous women's sociopolitical standing and influence in traditional Indigenous communities challenged the settler colonial access to lands and resources, "the colonial state sought to erase Indigenous women" (Starblanket and Coburn 2020, 98).

Today, Indigenous women face normalized gender-based discrimination rooted in and sustained by these historic settler colonial processes of stereotyping and erasure (Carter 1993). The most tangible example of this discrimination is the Indian Act, which, since 1876, has legally subjected First Nations women to a different standard to maintain Indian status than men (Gabriel 2011, 185). The Indian Act systematically elevated men and undervalued women through membership rules that allowed, as one example of many, men to retain Indian status when marrying those without Indian status but enforced women's loss of status in such circumstances (Barker 2008, 262–63; Emberley 1993, 87). This discrimination has led many women and their children to lose their status, which diminishes access to a whole host of specific rights and intends to eliminate Indigenous difference. While Indigenous women have to varying degrees successfully exercised agency to dispute various discriminatory laws, the Indian Act remains, as do the assimilative tactics of colonial stereotypes. Here, the "double jeopardy" of the dual colonial and gender inequalities that Indigenous women face are made systemic by the Canadian state (Eberts 2017; Kuokkanen 2019, 3–4).

These stereotypes and legislated sex discrimination foster wider societal violence against Indigenous women (Bourgeois 2017), and this broadly encompasses Inuit and Métis women, though they are not legislated under the Indian Act (Eberts 2017, 94). The normalization of these stereotypes and resulting violence also deflect criticism from the state to the victim, which restricts societal moral outrage to the MMIWG crisis (Bourgeois 2017): these stereotypes effectively devalue, silence, marginalize, and make Indigenous women invisible.

A debate has emerged in response to this colonial-enforced gender discrimination: that of Indigenous feminisms. The co-occurring forms of oppression, heteropatriarchy and colonialism, are consistently ignored in Canada (Bourgeois 2017). While Indigenous women have long been involved in Indigenous liberation movements (Kuokkanen 2019, 3), there remains longstanding hostility and opposition to feminist analysis and organization within Indigenous liberatory mobilization strategies (Green 2017, 2). Kuokkanen writes, "Instead, most studies present the project of indigenous self-determination as a phenomenon outside of gendered political structures and relations of power or processes of gendering in society in general" (2011, 226). Many argue that Indigenous liberation, however, ought to be understood as a project deeply tied to gender (Ladner 2009, 63); otherwise, heteropatriarchy will be reproduced by these liberation movements (Kuokkanen 2019; Starblanket 2017). As will be discussed, the responses to the gender-based discrimination and colonial-enforced violence of the MMIWG crisis as related to broader Indigenous liberation sits at the centre of the debate surrounding Indigenous feminisms. This chapter asks, Can political science recognize this complex and nuanced debate, or will Indigenization's "deep colonising" lead to the co-optation of those Indigenous knowledges that construct these debates?

What Are Indigenous Feminisms?
As Indigenization is encouraged by the neoliberal temperament of the contemporary university to draw Indigenous knowledges into academic processes in ways that commodify, Indigenous feminisms present a set of complexities for the discipline of political science to attend to in its feministing pursuits. While all feminisms are multifaceted, we can summarize these as sharing a few generalized characteristics: first, feminisms are concerned with transformative action (so, not static theory); feminisms attempt to undo systems and structures that support male dominance and female subordination (anti-patriarchal); and, finally, feminisms are not homogenous. There is a multitude of theories and analytical practices within feminisms, and these are regularly in flux as they respond to evolving social and political realities and histories.

These characteristics are at the core of Indigenous feminisms, which further include defining features that are both anti-colonial and Indigenous-centred. Beginning with anti-colonialism, Indigenous feminisms bring together two critiques, feminism and anti-colonialism (Green 2017, 12). As a movement tied to colonial experience, Indigenous feminisms resist and attempt to overcome those normalized stereotypes of colonial heteropatriarchy (Kuokkanen 2019, 16). Indigenous feminisms are tied to decolonization through connections to specific nations' relationality to lands (Green 2017, 4).

Turning to the Indigenous-centred nature of Indigenous feminisms, much like Indigenous cultures, these have specific connections and relationships to lands. Indigenous-centred relationships to land are complex, place-based, and specific to nationhood (Battiste and Henderson 2000). Indigenous feminisms are, therefore, also placed-based and specific to territory and, in these ways, tied to Indigenous identity and rights (Green 2017, 4–7) and reflective of the diversity of all Indigenous differences across what has become Canada.

Indigenous feminisms are further shaped by traditional or ancestral approaches to societal organization. It is commonly understood that traditional Indigenous society is matrilineal, and gender social forms are egalitarian (Barker 2008, 262), though some contest this universality (LaRocque 2017, 132). Indigenous feminisms are attentive to traditional social organization concerning gender (Kauanui 2008, 284). These aspects of Indigenous feminisms are innately tethered to Indigenous ways of knowing.

Why Are These Divisive Theories and Practices?
Indigenous feminisms are a controversial theory and practice, partly due to the differing epistemological orientations to how knowledge is produced. Many Indigenous women do not identify as feminists (LaRocque 2017, 122; St. Denis 2017, 58) and those who do often face stigmatization from broader Indigenous communities (Starblanket 2017, 27). As a citizen of the Métis nation, the intersection of decolonization and gender and the resulting debates on Indigenous feminisms are both personal and intellectual. Like others, I work, study, live in a society framed by Western knowledge, and am part of a family and communities that are Indigenous. These two worldviews—Western and Indigenous—often conflict in our society (Battiste and Henderson 2000, 11–17). The following section is informed by my attempts to grapple with these opposing epistemological orientations. In addition to the scholarship, it is informed by the many Indigenous women who advise, mentor, and share kinship with me. But there is much that I do not know because it is not yet—and maybe never will be—shared with me. Because Indigenous knowledge systems are created in community and shaped by those changing values specific to place, it is impossible to know all the positions that might take up this debate. Therefore, a diversity of opinion exists beyond the following summaries of scholarship and my personal placed-based experiences in the regions of Treaties 1 (Winnipeg, Manitoba) and 4 (Regina, Saskatchewan) in what has become Canada.

Opponents of Indigenous Feminisms
Those in opposition to Indigenous feminisms frame their arguments as acolonial and anti-Western. I frame those in opposition to Indigenous feminisms as resurgents or those who wish to re-establish traditional gender norms and social knowledges as one means to decolonize society.

A key aspect of resurgence is political mobilization grounded in the revitalization and reclamation of traditional knowledges and practices, which is foundational to movements of Indigenous liberation (Simpson 2017).

Resurgence in the debate of Indigenous feminisms centres on conceptualizations of traditional social norms of gender. Many argue that Western-based and Indigenous societies understand gender differently. For example, traditionally, women held positions of great authority in Indigenous communities (St. Denis 2017, 46–47). The project of colonialism dismantled these roles to some degree through those earlier discussed colonially imposed heteropatriarchal norms (Baskin 2019, 2085). Part of liberation, thus, then requires a return to these arrangements of societal organization.

Resurgents frame these traditional gender norms to pursue Indigenous liberation as antithetical to Indigenous feminisms (Barker 2008, 260). They might argue that the concept of feminist equality is Western-framed and, as such, is irrelevant to Indigenous resurgence and liberation struggles (Green 2017, 3). Some might argue that Indigenous feminists are assimilated into Western thinking (Smith and Kauanui 2008, 241). For example, Indigenous resurgents might argue that they strive for a traditional social organization centred on egalitarian principles and that Indigenous feminisms struggle to achieve equality with men's rights (St. Denis 2017, 48–50). In these ways, it might be argued that Indigenous feminisms are built on Western theory that will not liberate Indigenous Peoples but instead reproduce Indigenous people's oppression. Furthermore, resurgents might argue that the social conditions of heteropatriarchy, the MMIWG crises, are a system of colonial oppression. It could, thus, be argued that the work of liberation is not required to use a gendered lens of analysis: once decolonization is achieved, existing heteropatriarchal issues will be resolved (Kauanui 2008, 283) as those traditional gendered social relations at the centre of resurgence movements have survived the attempts of colonial assimilation (St. Denis, 2017, 47).

Finally, it might be argued that gender inequality is not the only or most important form of oppression tethered to Indigenous liberatory movements. Many forms exist, such as colonization, racism, economic disparity, land dispossession, and others (Emberley 1993, 90; St. Denis 2017, 48–50). In this way, it is understood that a feminist lens might discount these other forms of oppression, limiting the success of broader Indigenous liberation movements through a feminist analysis of gender.

Proponents of Indigenous Feminisms

The proponents of Indigenous feminisms have several counterarguments founded on anti-colonialism and Indigenous ways of knowing, which positions these arguments as suitable for Indigenization's deep colonising co-optation. Central to Indigenous feminisms is an understanding that those who ignore or marginalize gender as one component of colonial oppression will limit broader liberation movements because heteropatriarchy and colonialism are co-occurring forms of oppression that support one another (Snyder 2018). If gender justice is not woven into Indigenous liberation movements, patriarchy will be reproduced because of the male-centred nature of Indigenous liberation movements that ignore Indigenous women and 2SLGBTQQIA+ communities (Kuokkanen 2019, 6). In fact, some argue that it is not a given that Indigenous communities were free of gendered violence and inequities or that this violence can be explained (away) by colonialism (LaRocque 2017, 132). Additionally, to ignore a feminist analysis is to dismiss the colonial legacies of gender oppression (Starblanket 2017, 35), as well as the intersectionality of contemporary feminism that takes up a range of analyses according to class, race, (dis)ability, location, and more (MacDonald and Dobrowolsky 2018, 8–10).

Next, some argue that the resurgence of traditional understandings of gender has evolved inaccurately to place male and female genders alongside Western-based dichotomies. This dichotomy has significant limitations for understanding gender on a spectrum, as it is central to the NI-MMIWG's approach to dismantling gender-based violence against Indigenous 2SLGBTQQIA+ individuals, who are so often ignored due to heteropatriarchal norms. Starblanket explains that traditional Indigenous communities were not organized exclusively around a binary of male and female tasks but, instead, according to an individual's skills and interests as complemented by community needs (2017, 29). This dichotomy results from heteropatriarchy and therefore will not provide liberation from colonization but will instead reproduce it.

Additionally, some who take up Indigenous feminisms argue that traditional approaches to gender are generalized or essentializing (LaRocque 2017, 135; Starblanket 2017, 27). Essentialism means one or two characteristics are reductively used to define a whole. Regarding traditional women's roles, this essentialism often rests on frameworks of motherhood, which is not always narrowly understood as the biological ability to procreate; it can also include the nurturing of community to support broader struggles for nationhood or liberation (Anderson 2011). While such conceptualizations of motherhood can empower many women and their wider communities (Starblanket 2017, 31–32), these roles can also reproduce heteropatriarchy, which can reduce women to their biological anatomy, sex, motherhood, or other "traditional" ideas of gender (LaRocque 2017, 135). This reduction might not address or dismantle systems of heteropatriarchy oppression but instead—as deep colonising does—uphold them.

In addition to biological essentialism, various critiques are suspicious of the accuracy of contemporary understandings of traditional Indigenous gender roles. Some argue that contemporary notions of women's traditional roles are "mythic" (Green 2017, 13) and "reified" (LaRocque 2017, 125), and actively subordinate women through social practices (Starblanket 2017, 31–32). It is perhaps impossible to truly know what authentic gender roles looked like (Baskin 2019, 2074), but contemporary understandings of traditional roles are critiqued for how they empower men and disempower women (Baskin 2019, 2074; Starblanket 2017, 33).

By countering the insidious ways that colonial heteropatriarchy marginalizes Indigenous women and 2SLGBTQQIA+ individuals, Indigenous feminisms argue that a gendered analysis is integral to responding to the MMIWG crisis and to establishing broader Indigenous liberation in the face of settler colonial genocide. These arguments, much like those of resurgents, use Indigenous-centred knowledge systems to resist the imposition of Western colonial harms to foster strategies for liberation. The foundation in Indigenous worldview makes Indigenous feminisms potentially vulnerable to the deep colonising of Indigenization's commodification practices.

Conclusion: Indigenous Feministing in Political Science?

In light of this context of colonially informed and disproportionate gender-based violence that Indigenous women, girls, and 2SLGBTQQIA+ individuals face in Canada and the two disparate responses in favour of and opposition to Indigenous feminisms, the question arises, What challenges exist for feministing in political science when the intersection of Indigeneity is included? Political science is a discipline that studies state power relations and political systems of oppression but also has widely ignored Indigenous-related scholarship and feminisms. In an environment of neoliberal Indigenization, this chapter asks, Can the inclusion of Indigenous feminisms in political science advance these debates as they relate to Indigenous liberation, or will Indigenous knowledges be co-opted through Indigenization?

I would like to pull on a thread that is woven through the two opposing arguments of Indigenous feminisms: re-matriarchy. Re-matriarchy is a movement of resurgence to reclaim traditional roles that validate Indigenous women's political and social power as matriarchs. Remember that at the centre of the debate are the colonial connections between lands (a key target for colonial empires) and women that resulted in damaging stereotypes and ongoing attempts of erasure. This embodiment of the colonial enterprise legalized the devaluation of Indigenous women in settler society and normalized gender-based discrimination and violence, leading to the MMIWG crisis. In opposition to Indigenous feminisms, one response is to return to traditional matriarchal roles or resurgence. A second response is Indigenous feminisms, which argues that such resurgence movements essentialize gender, reproduce heteropatriarchy, and hamper broader liberation movements. This political mobilization also includes re-matriarchy as it combines two critiques, feminism and anti-colonialism. Thus, both sides of the debate position their response to colonial, gender-based violence as an Indigenous-centred and anti-colonial approach: they are not, in fact, so diametrically opposed.

This debate is fuelled by a dialectical model typical to Western-centred epistemology: it is a Cartesian-endorsed binary of truth that positions a claim either in support or opposition to Indigenous feminisms, ignoring other ranges of possible understanding. Often, such dualisms are unstable and cannot adequately support the range of overlapping and competing concepts at the centre of any matter (Bleiker and Campbell 2016, 203), which I argue is the case here, evidenced by the common thread of re-matriarchy. We might cast our gaze as previous postcolonial theorists have to hybridity theory (Bhabha 1994) to understand better and describe the Indigenous difference in settler colonial Canada beyond those conforming binaries. While such binaries help us to illustrate the substantial differences between the conflicting and differing epistemologies of

Western and Indigenous knowledges, these binaries also generate false opposition for those cultural spheres of Indigenous communities in settler colonial Canada that, in practice, express a range of comparative and conflicting analyses of decolonial, reconciliatory, resurgent, and even neocolonial approaches to discourse, governance, and life (Hubbard 2008). Therefore, the debate is mired in Western-based epistemological binaries that falsely position paths to liberation as oppositional when—in fact—they overlap in substantial ways in the focus of re-matriarchy and, in this way, similarly take up anti-colonial analysis through Indigenous knowledge systems.

Can political science make the space to include this spectrum of debate of Indigenous feminisms in its authentic forms, or will those deep colonising co-opting forces of neoliberal applications of Indigenization further marginalize and polarize debates concerning the MMIWG crisis and Indigenous feminisms? That Indigenous knowledges are place-based or situational, and thus not normative, and that they do not have a Western orientation remains a significant obstacle for a discipline such as political science. Understanding this debate requires a shift in how it operates as a binary because, as demonstrated, the overlap of resurgent re-matriarchy is clearly at the centre of both perspectives within this debate: it is a thread that binds, not contests. In essence, the binary fostered through Western orientations to knowledge has resulted in a repetition of colonial thinking—or deep colonising—that eclipses notions of Indigenous liberation informed by Indigenous ways of knowing. As the debate evolves— hopefully in the riddance of this Western orientation—political science faces an opportunity to support this evolution or, if not, it will defer to the well-trodden path of academic Indigenization's conformity.

Notes

1. I use the term *Indigenization* as shorthand in this chapter to refer specifically to academic Indigenization.
2. This chapter characterizes knowledge that is not Indigenous-centred as Western. This is an imprecise practice that excludes variations within Western-centred knowledge and those non-Western knowledge systems that are not Indigenous-centred. Additionally, it dismisses, as binaries do, the diversity of Indigenous knowledge systems throughout the world. *Western* is used to reflect a culturally dominant way of knowing that is rooted in Enlightenment thinking and prevalent in settler colonial Canada.

References

Anderson, Kim. 2011. *Life Stages and Native Women: Memory, Teachings, and Story Medicine.* Winnipeg: University of Manitoba Press.

Barker, Joanne. 2008. "Gender, Sovereignty, Rights: Native Women's Activism against Social Inequality and Violence in Canada." *American Quarterly* 60 (2): 259-66. https://www.jstor.org/stable/40068533.

Bartlett, Judith, Yoshitaka Iwasaki, Benjamin Gottlieb, Darlene Hall, and Roger Mannell. 2007. "Framework for Aboriginal-Guided Decolonizing Research Involving Métis and First Nations Persons with Diabetes." *Social Science and Medicine* 65 (11): 2371-82. https://doi.org/10.1016/j.socscimed.2007.06.011.

Baskin, Cyndy. 2019. "Contemporary Indigenous Women's Roles: Traditional Teachings or Internalized Colonialism?" *Violence against Women* 26 (15-16): 2083-101. https://doi.org/10.1177/1077801219888024.

Battiste, Marie. 2013. *Decolonizing Education: Nourishing the Learning Spirit.* Saskatoon: Purich Publishing Ltd.

Battiste, Marie, and James (Sa'ke'j) Youngblood Henderson. 2000. *Protecting Indigenous Knowledge and Heritage: A Global Challenge.* Saskatoon: Purich Publishing Ltd.

Bhabha, Homi K. 1994. *The Location of Culture.* New York: Routledge.

Bleiker, Roland, and David Campbell. 2016. "Poststructuralism." In *International Relations Theories: Discipline and Diversity,* edited by Tim Dunne, Milja Kurki, and Steve Smith, 96-218. Oxford: Oxford University Press.

Bourgeois, Robyn. 2017. "Perpetual State of Violence: An Indigenous Feminist Anti-Oppression Inquiry into Missing and Murdered Indigenous Women and Girls." In *Making Space for Indigenous Feminism,* 2nd ed., edited by Joyce Green, 253-73. Halifax: Fernwood Publishing.

Carter, Sarah. 1993. "Categories and Terrains of Exclusion: Constructing the 'Indian Woman' in the Early Settlement Era in Western Canada." *Great Plains Quarterly* 13 (3): 147-61. https://www.jstor.org/stable/23531720.

Changfoot, Nadine, Peter Andrée, Charles Z. Levkoe, Michelle Nilson, and Magdalene Goemans. 2020. "Engaged Scholarship in Tenure and Promotion: Autoethnographic Insights from the Fault Lines of a Shifting Landscape." *Michigan Journal of Community Service Learning* 26 (1): 239-63. https://doi.org/10.3998/mjcsloa.3239521.0026.114.

Coburn, Elaine. 2020. "'Theorizing Our Place': Indigenous Women's Scholarship from 1985-2020 and the Emerging Dialogue with Anti-Racist Feminisms." *Studies in Social Justice* 14 (2): 429-53. https://doi.org/10.26522/ssj.v14i2.2295.

Cote-Meek, Sheila. 2020. Introduction to *Indigenizing the Canadian Academy: Critical Reflections,* edited by Sheila Cote-Meek and Taima Moeke-Pickering, xi-xxiii. Toronto: Canadian Scholars.

Eberts, Mary. 2017. "Being an Indigenous Woman Is 'a High Risk Lifestyle.'" In *Making Space for Indigenous Feminism,* 2nd ed., edited by Joyce Green, 69-102. Halifax: Fernwood Publishing.

Emberley, Julia V. 1993. *Thresholds of Difference. Feminist Critique, Native Women's Writings, Postcolonial Theory.* Toronto: University of Toronto Press.

Frideres, James S., and René R. Gadacz. 2012. *First Nations in Aboriginal Peoples in Canada*. Don Mills, ON: Pearson Canada.

Gabriel, Ellen. 2011. "Aboriginal Women's Movement; A Quest for Self-Determination." *Aboriginal Policy Studies* 1 (1): 183-88. https://doi.org/10.5663/aps.v1i1.10137.

Gaudry, Adam, and Danielle Lorenz. 2018. "Indigenization as Inclusion, Reconciliation, and Decolonization: Navigating the Different Visions for Indigenizing the Canadian Academy." *AlterNative: An International Journal of Indigenous Peoples* 14 (3): 218-27. https://doi.org/10.1177/1177180118785382.

Grafton, Emily, and Jérôme Melançon. 2020. "The Dynamics of Decolonization and Indigenization in an Era of Academic 'Reconciliation.'" In *Indigenizing the Canadian Academy: Critical Reflections*, edited by Sheila Cote-Meek and Taima Moeke-Pickering, 135-53. Toronto: Canadian Scholars.

Green, Joyce. 1995. "Towards a Detente with History: Confronting Canada's Colonial Legacy." *International Journal of Canadian Studies* 12 (Fall): 85-105.

Green, Joyce. 2017. "Taking More Account of Indigenous Feminism: An Introduction." In *Making Space for Indigenous Feminism*, 2nd ed., edited by Joyce Green, 1-20. Halifax: Fernwood Publishing.

Hubbard, Tasha. 2008. "Voices Heard in the Silence, History Held in the Memory: Ways of Knowing Jeanette Armstrong's 'Threads of Old Memory.'" In *Aboriginal Oral Traditions: Theory, Practice, Ethics*, edited by Renee Hulan and Renate Eigenbrod, 139-53. Halifax: Fernwood Publishing.

Juschka, Darlene M. 2014. *Political Bodies / Body Politic: The Semiotics of Gender*. New York: Routledge.

Kauanui, J. Kēhaulani. 2008. "Native Hawaiian Decolonization and the Politics of Gender." *American Quarterly* 60 (2): 281-87. https://www.jstor.org/stable/40068536.

Kuokkanen, Rauna. 2007. *Reshaping the University: Responsibilities, Indigenous Epistemes and the Logic of the Gift*. Vancouver: UBC Press.

Kuokkanen, Rauna. 2011. "Self-Determination and Indigenous Women—Whose Voice Is It We Hear in the Sámi Parliament?" *International Journal on Minority and Group Rights* 18 (1): 39-62. https://doi.org/10.1163/157181111X550978.

Kuokkanen, Rauna. 2019. *Restructuring Relations: Indigenous Self-Determination, Governance, and Gender*. New York: Oxford University Press.

Ladner, Kiera L. 2009. "Gendering Decolonization, Decolonising Gender." *Australian Indigenous Law Review* 13 (1): 62-77. https://www.jstor.org/stable/26423117.

Ladner, Kiera L. 2017. "Taking the Field: 50 Years of Indigenous Politics in the *CJPS*." *Canadian Journal of Political Science* 50 (1): 163-79. https://doi.org/10.1017/S0008423917000257.

LaRocque, Emma. 2017. "Métis and Feminist: Contemplations on Feminism, Human Rights, Culture and Decolonization." In *Making Space for Indigenous Feminism*, 2nd ed., edited by Joyce Green, 122-45. Halifax: Fernwood Publishing.

Last, Angela. 2018. "Internationalization and Interdisciplinarity: Sharing across Boundaries?" In *Decolonising the University*, edited by Gurminder K. Bhambra, Dalia Gebrial, and Kerem Nisancioglu, 208-30. London: Pluto Press.

MacDonald, Fiona, and Alexandra Dobrowolsky. 2018. "Introduction: Transforming and Transformational Gender Politics in Turbulent Times." In *Turbulent Times, Transformational Possibilities?: Gender and Politics Today and Tomorrow*, edited by Fiona MacDonald and Alexandra Dobrowolsky, 1–20. Toronto: University of Toronto Press.

National Inquiry into Missing and Murdered Indigenous Women and Girls (NI-MMIWG). 2019. *Reclaiming Power and Place. Executive Summary of the Final Report of the National Inquiry into Missing and Murdered Indigenous Women and Girls*, vol. 1. National Inquiry. https://www.mmiwg-ffada.ca/wp-content/uploads/2019/06/Final_Report_Vol_1a-1.pdf.

Rose, Deborah Bird. 1996. "Land Rights and Deep Colonising: The Erasure of Women." *Aboriginal Law Bulletin* 3 (85): 6–13.

Simpson, Leanne Betasamosake. 2017. *As We Have Always Done: Indigenous Freedom through Radical Resistance*. Minneapolis: University of Minnesota Press.

Smith, Andrea, and J. Kēhaulani Kauanui. 2008. "Native Feminisms Engage American Studies." *American Quarterly* 60 (2): 241–49. https://doi.org/10.1353/aq.0.0001.

Snyder, Emily. 2018. *Gender, Power, and Representations of Cree Law*. Vancouver: UBC Press.

Starblanket, Gina. 2017. "Being Indigenous Feminists: Resurgences against Contemporary Patriarchy." In *Making Space for Indigenous Feminism*, 2nd ed., edited by Joyce Green, 21–41. Halifax: Fernwood Publishing.

Starblanket, Gina, and Elaine Coburn. 2020. "'This Country Has Another Story': Colonial Crisis, Treaty Relationships, and Indigenous Women's Futurities." In *Canadian Political Economy*, edited by Heather Whiteside, 86–102. Toronto: University of Toronto Press.

St. Denis, Verna. 2017. "Feminism Is for Everybody: Aboriginal Women, Feminism and Diversity." In *Making Space for Indigenous Feminism*, 2nd ed., edited by Joyce Green, 42–62. Halifax: Fernwood Publishing.

Wilson, Kara Jo. 2018. "Confronting Canada's Indigenous Female Disposability." *Canadian Journal of Native Studies* 38 (1): 153–63.

8

Feministing Online

Using the Internet to Learn New Things and Create Community

AMANDA BITTNER

I LIVE ON AN ISLAND in the middle of the North Atlantic. My university is the only one in the province. I do not have a large collection of colleagues from other institutions nearby. I have wonderful women colleagues in other departments at the university, and I have known some of them since our faculty orientation in 2008. These women helped me to survive my early years in academia.

When I began my tenure-track job at Memorial University of Newfoundland and Labrador in 2008, I was the most junior member, youngest member, and only woman in my department, amongst twelve or thirteen men. The men were kind—we went out for drinks, celebrated holidays, and talked about our research. But I felt my gender in a way that I had never experienced before. I had always seen the world through the philosophy of merit: I thought that if I just worked hard enough I could do anything. Others would value me, I thought. Instead, my colleagues organized golf games amongst themselves and didn't invite me. They asked me to decorate the political science corridor and choose paint colours. I felt like someone's wife and not like a colleague.

I felt like a little girl, out of place and out of my league. Imposter syndrome was taking over my entire being. Then, in a curriculum change exercise, my colleagues wanted to delete the sole gender and politics course in the calendar (nobody had taught it for years). I asked why we didn't just offer it. They told me our students were not interested in this topic. I asked how we knew this if we hadn't offered it. I could see that my questions irritated them. *Why was I so pushy?* Even though I was not an expert in gender and politics, I felt like I had to show them that this was an important part of the political science curriculum and that it should be taken seriously. I pushed some more, then I volunteered to teach a course on gender and political behaviour (I did have expertise on the latter, if not the former). I created the course, designed a brand-new syllabus in a part of the field I knew almost nothing about, and offered it. The course was full immediately.

The course was full, it went on to be a huge success, and I have offered it many times since then. And yet, over the years, everything still felt like an uphill battle. I felt like I had to work harder, faster, longer, and to develop entirely new areas of expertise in order to have my voice heard. I felt undervalued and alone.

I knew from my friends in other departments that the problem wasn't me. They also felt overworked and underappreciated. They also were teaching more than their colleagues. They also were doing more service than their colleagues. They also had students crying in their offices, disclosing personal traumas. They also were doing the lion's share of academic care work (not to mention the bulk of care work in their own homes) and they were burning out, too. The problem is endemic. I'm a white woman and have all kinds of privilege that others do not. The situation was bad for me, it is worse for others. While my women colleagues at Memorial were the key to helping me survive those early years, I don't recall any of us having any actual solutions to these problems.

The isolation that came from living and working on an actual rock in the middle of the North Atlantic led to strong connections forming between me and my women colleagues across the university, but it also led to me seeking information and community elsewhere. Not even deliberately: I didn't wake up one morning and say to myself, "Bittner, you need to learn more about the world and you need to find your people on the internet," even though that would have been strategically wise. I think I just went where the wind took me, and the wind showed me that off my rock, all kinds of incredible stuff was going on. The world was my oyster, so to speak, if we want to take these ocean metaphors dangerously further.

In this short autobiographical chapter, I walk through three main themes that jump out to me when I think about the way that the internet has shaped my ability to do feministing in my career. First, it has helped me to do some of my own learning and foster personal connections; second, it has allowed for community building and isolation busting in the context of a global pandemic (here I highlight and describe the SMASHLab online writing group a bunch of us created); and third, there are so many ways that this type of feministing is taking place online, and I describe some of the things our colleagues are doing. Ultimately, my argument in this chapter is that it is only through collaboration and community building that we are able to foster a better learning and working environment for all. And this activity, therefore, is feminist disruption, as through it we are able to change the way the system works.

Learning and Connection

The internet, and social media in particular, have shaped who I am as an academic today. An academic who lives on an isolated island, who was oblivious to a lot of issues even though I was aware of others. I am still these things. But through the internet I have been exposed to so many new ideas, new colleagues, new research, new connections. I have been able to find and build community via Twitter (now X), Facebook, Instagram, Slack, and, as a result of the pandemic, Zoom. These are tools that I use regularly now to communicate with others, and through these tools I have learned so much.

Twitter taught me the term *misogynoir*. Twitter taught me that Sara Ahmed and her incredible work exist (e.g., Ahmed 2016) and that my experience of the academic institutional environment was real and experienced around the world, too. Twitter taught me about intersectionality, about decolonization, about reparations, and introduced me to work by El Jones (2014), Robyn Maynard (2017), and Desmond Cole (2020). Twitter taught me about the gendered pay gap in universities and taught me that academics doing what they do best (research) could make important changes, like what Michelle Dion did with the gender pay gap through her research and leadership within the faculty union at McMaster (McMaster, 2016).[1]

In addition to the learning I was able to do over on Twitter, I benefitted from some serious community building that was taking place on Facebook. I was lucky enough to join an online writing group—I forget exactly how I got into this group, but I am confident it was either Melanee Thomas (e.g., 2018) or Erin Tolley (e.g., 2015) who told me about it and helped me get in. Erin Cassese and Mirya Holman (2018) describe the benefits of writing groups, and the one that I was in with them was *just* an online discussion forum in a Facebook group, and while the premise was simple, the experience was absolutely transformative.

I met a whole bunch of brilliant emerging scholars doing research in gender and political psychology and developed what I expect will be lifelong friendships with many of these incredible people. Online, in our "secret" Facebook group (secret because it was unsearchable, not secret because we were secretive), we talked about productivity tools, workflow, how to handle challenging situations at work, deliberated research questions, approaches, and methodology, we read each other's drafts, gave advice on academic work, troubleshooted all kinds of stuff, and discussed the discipline broadly. All of this was asynchronous, we didn't actually "meet" online, we just logged in from our own time zones and read each other's posts and responded to one another.

This group taught me about community and the benefits of gentle accountability. It taught me about how to create space and hold space for others. It taught me about mentorship and sponsorship and enthusiastic and non-competitive support of others. After I left my marriage in 2019, I stopped using Facebook because I couldn't handle engaging online with my past and present, and so I no longer get to interact with those writing group friends every day like I used to. I miss them, but I'm so grateful to the community they created. I benefitted from their friendship in countless ways even beyond those that I listed above. I had been tired and burned out for a long time when I joined, and this group gave me strength and life.

Isolation and Community Building in a Global Pandemic: The SMASH Lab Writing Group

When the pandemic hit, it felt as if we were all on our own islands, isolated in our homes, without the people and communities on which we depend. Many of us were trying to take care of kids and also do our jobs, from makeshift desks in corners of cramped homes. The pandemic laid bare what has already been true in academia for a very long time: the burdens of care are not distributed equally or equitably. The burnout that was already manifesting or underway for so many women and Indigenous, Black, and people of colour academics became more visible, and the need for systemic change became clearer even for those who hadn't already realized the extent of the problem.

At the same time, the need for community, for collective commiseration, troubleshooting, listening, and being there for others has also become much more apparent. Juggling an impossible set of tasks, trying to make things better for our students, our colleagues, our partners, our children, our parents, many of us have been lost, alone, frustrated, and completely overwhelmed throughout the COVID-19 pandemic. Reaching out was the only real option.

---

us02web.zoom.us
Join our Cloud HD Video Meeting

Reminder for tomorrow: Amanda Bittner is inviting you to a scheduled Zoom meeting.

Join Zoom Meeting
us02web.zoom.us/j/4019819747?p...

Meeting ID: 401 981 9747
Passcode: 257922

Amanda Bittner · Jan 12, 2021, 7:58 AM

Early in the pandemic, with Erin Tolley and Jennie Sweet-Cushman (e.g., 2018), I began to use Zoom every day. I already used online meeting software for teaching, meetings, seminars, public talks, even family gatherings. But during the pandemic, we logged in for two hours a day, 10:30 to 12:30 NST, to work "together" in silence. At the end, we chatted for a few minutes, discussing what we worked on and challenges we were facing. Over time, the group grew. We got Zoom-bombed, and then we got better at using Zoom. Folks came in, folks left, depending on what was happening in their part of the world. Work patterns ebb and flow for academics even under "normal" circumstances, depending on whether it's a teaching semester or a research semester, and the need for community changed depending on the severity of COVID-19 in our respective regions, and the particular lockdown/work from home/live at work situation we were in.

Everything is so hard. This is not optimal learning, teaching, or living.

Amanda Bittner · Feb 1, 2021, 4:54 AM

We saw our colleagues' kids pop in for kisses and to have their own connected classrooms managed, some of our colleagues got pregnant and had babies, some lost family members, some celebrated divorces, some got new jobs and fancy research grants and research chairs, some started and finished entire books within our Zoom community, and we all collectively celebrated and mourned these professional and personal events together, while holding space for the research, providing advice to each other, sharing tips and tricks and strategies for how to be there for others, including our family, friends, colleagues, and students.

The group has grown since its inception in March 2020 when there were three of us—on any given day now there are probably about twenty people who log in, and there are about forty "regulars" who come most of the time. The name of the group has shifted over time, and conversations about what to call it started to arise when colleagues wanted to thank writing group members in their acknowledgements sections of publications they worked on while in the daily writing Zoom. Before we settled on the SMASHLab (a nod to smashing the patriarchy, and a name coined by my Memorial Political Science colleague Sarah Martin), folks were putting "Amanda Bittner's online writing group" in their acknowledgements. This was a name that definitely needed fixing: it may have been my Zoom account, but this was in no way my group. I am so grateful to all the folks who joined and made it what it was and what it continues to grow into.

Anyone who wanted to work communally and silently for a couple of hours was welcome to join us, and I would regularly re-up the invitation via Twitter, and folks in the group invited others from within their own networks. All were welcome, students, faculty, non-academic people, anyone.

> Just wanna reiterate yet again how grateful I am to all of you. I really enjoy seeing your faces and knowing how kind you are every day.
>
> ♥ 2
>
> Amanda Bittner · Jun 2, 2020, 4:52 PM

What happens in the SMASHLab? As mentioned above, the main goal is to work silently for two hours each day. For many parts of the pandemic, the two hours in which we met online were the only two hours of research (or any work at all) folks were able to do, given the incredible pressure cooker that was "lockdown" combined with pivots to online teaching, home schooling, caring for loved ones with COVID-19, and everything else. The online Zoom space was there for us to meet and silently encourage one another, and to feel like we weren't all on our own. At the end of the two-hour writing session, we would check out with updates on what we were working on, we would get advice from each other, and just share general life joys and sorrows. So much of our conversation was taken up with discussing challenges in the discipline. Generally speaking, we help each other with issues related to teaching practice, research practice, inequities in academia, and so on. We teach each other our own tips and tricks, and we have all learned from one other, not just traditional professional skills, but we also learned how to be open-hearted and generous and kind from our colleagues.

We've had the opportunity to meet new people from around the world and have watched each other adapt to the behaviours that are our group norm, involving encouragement, solidarity, generosity, and kindness. These are not group norms for most of academic life, and we learned this behaviour from each other, and foster it together.

> You are amazing. They are lucky to have you zooming in with them. So many things you can't control, weird department quirks and random shit nobody can keep track of and that has nothing to do with you. So deep breaths, and do your best and don't worry about the rest.
>
>
>
> Amanda Bittner · Feb 4, 2021, 3:40 PM

These are gendered ways of behaving. They are not the norm of the academic community at large, but they are a better way of "doing business." Acknowledging the reality of life, being honest about the struggles, being supportive of one another allows us to thrive and grow. The regular academic pressures and incentives don't go away with a culture of care, but the culture of care allows us to weather the storms a little easier, and it allows us to care for ourselves, care for others, and ultimately, we are better at our jobs if we are allowed to be whole people rather than competitive automatons.

In addition, we have organized workshops for the whole group, either (a) seeking to teach each other things that some of us already had expertise in (e.g., teaching pedagogy and innovations); or (b) we brought in experts to guide us in workshops related to productivity, work-life balance, and planning. We have an ongoing Twitter DM group for all SMASHers; folks regularly post questions and respond to each other with advice, as well as make posts of encouragement, celebratory posts of each other's work and professional news, informational bulletins about things we believe others will find interesting, and the odd video of otters or other empowering memes. Folks in the group have become friends, and they have made each other gifts and sent them in the mail to each other. Knitters and cross-stitchers sent their work as gifts, and while nobody joined this group in hopes of receiving gifts, friends want to take care of each other and delight in bringing joy to their people.

I generally would prefer to downplay my role in all of this—truly, this space would not be what it is without everyone else, and the skills and personality that they bring to the SMASHLab—but I was reminded recently that facilitating the daily Zoom does take some work. In the winter of 2022, I had a particularly challenging teaching load (I taught 3.5 courses that semester), and I really couldn't log in each day or facilitate breakout sessions. Colleagues stepped in and helped to manage the process and make sure folks were able to breakout at the end to do checkouts. Logistics-wise, then, what we needed was a Zoom account, a clear timeslot in which to meet, a group of people who want to join, and then commitment to actually showing up and doing the work.

Personally/professionally, I have benefitted so much from this group. Pre-pandemic, I believed that I was an introvert. It turns out, that's not actually true at all. I need people, and I need to feel part of a community. I like to learn, and this group taught me a lot. Sarah Martin (e.g., 2020) and Alison Smith (e.g., 2022) really upped the care culture early in this group with their suggestions about how we could do daily checkouts at the end of our writing sessions, and many of their personality traits and styles of behaviour have been deeply embedded into the way in which we now interact as a group. I got to know colleagues from across disciplines who I hadn't come into contact with before the pandemic. My teaching improved from hearing the things these colleagues were doing in their classrooms. My research program improved as I learned to prioritize my gut and do work that felt meaningful and important rather than sticking with the "same old stuff" I always did.

Members of the SMASHLab talk a lot about the problems in the university system as it is right now. We spend a lot of time noticing and thinking about the various ways in which racist, colonial, misogynistic systems create narrow ways of thinking and doing, oppressing us, our colleagues, and our students, and collectively we talk about ways to make change. Some of us have come together to submit grant applications for projects seeking to foster anti-colonial and anti-racist teaching and training, some have done webinars together, some are working on research that seeks to disrupt existing pathways of power. There is so much potential for collaboration within this group, and I would not be surprised to see full-blown collaborative research programs emerge from the cross-pollination that occurs on a daily basis. I have benefitted from the ideas and initiatives of my colleagues, and I love having a group that I can talk to about all the things that make my job challenging, and all the things that make my job a total delight. These colleagues and these relationships are what make my job wonderful.

The SMASHLab is ongoing. I am writing this chapter while a bunch of people are staring at me through my computer screen, working on their own projects. In about twenty-five minutes, our Zoom for the day is done and we're going to check in to discuss how our work went, and maybe troubleshoot larger problems we may be having.

What Are Others Doing?

The SMASHLab is one example of community building online, and although I've seen others on Twitter and Facebook, there are so many other ways that people are engaging to build supportive, insightful, and care-filled community online. Isolation in academia occurs regardless of where one lives, regardless of what global health emergencies uproot our lives. The challenge of this work is continuously reaching out to one another across divides and at the times we might feel most alone to find the others who are in it with us.

The important thing about community building is that we do it together. It is work, but it is work that benefits us. There are many political scientists who are doing this important work, some outwardly and openly, and others quietly and behind the scenes. I am grateful to the scholars who make the discipline better, make our professional practice better, and help to build community amongst political scientists. This. Is. Feministing.

There are colleagues who dedicate time and energy writing newsletters to provide mentorship and encouragement to those who might need it. One important example of this work is the #MHAWS newsletter (Mirya Holman's *Aggressive Winning Scholars Newsletter*), which unapologetically critiques the structures and institutions that allow racism, sexism, and harassment to flourish within the academy while mentoring and encouraging both junior and senior scholars. Similarly, in the *Academia Made Easier* newsletter, Loleen Berdahl provides insights from her time as a department head and administrator, and tips and tricks to achieve better work-life balance and prioritize mental health and rest and recovery.

On Twitter, Raul Pacheco-Vega provides threads about how to do academia well, support people in teaching and training, and place their health and well-being ahead of the culture of workaholism. (His website and blog are also essential teaching tools that many of us benefit from, for our own research but also when training our students). Twitter is also where Max Liboiron shares their insights into teaching, training, and research, showing others how to develop feminist and anti-colonial processes and practices. Another critical example on Twitter is the work of Nadia Brown, whose feed amplifies the work and successes of Black scholars and creates space for scholars of colour. Her organization of #PSSistahScholar meet-ups is well known among our colleagues on Twitter, and her work with others on making better the discipline by shining a light on #MeTooPoliSci has been instrumental in raising awareness about the way we think about the behaviour of our colleagues and the institutions that shield sexual harassment, assault, racism, and other harmful behaviour.

There are other innovative virtual communities being built. In her podcast, *Academic Aunties*, Ethel Tungohan makes note of problematic systems and practices central to academia, interviewing and chatting with scholars who are women of colour, reflecting on the various ways in which academic norms have a disproportionately negative effect on women and people of colour. The episodes are funny, thoughtful, and do a good job of addressing how white scholars (people like me) can be better allies and can make the community better and more liveable for all. Another innovation has occurred through the work of a small group of scholars who came together to create the website womenalsoknowstuff.com (WAKS) to promote the work and voices of women. Through their Twitter account and website, WAKS has encouraged us all to think about asking women experts, assigning women's research, and amplifying the voices of women academics more broadly. They have made visible the many ways in which women's voices are not the norm and have highlighted how we can champion one another.

I could list many more scholars who are doing this work and fill this page with social media feeds you should follow. But I will inevitably leave people out and then feel bad about it. There is something to be said for falling down rabbit holes on your own, and following new people who do work that is different from your own, with perspectives different from your own, and lived experience different from your own. Follow Black scholars. Follow Indigenous scholars. Follow young scholars. Follow women. Learn from them, amplify their work, integrate their work into your own, and build on it. Invite them to workshops. Invite them to writing retreats. Collaborate. There's a saying (and the origin is not clear), "If you want to go fast, go alone; if you want to go far, go together" (Whitby 2020). The more we do with others, the more we connect with others, the better our work becomes, and the better we feel about our work, our jobs, our place in the discipline, and our connection with our respective communities.

Community building, changemaking, these are feminist activities, as they disrupt the traditional ways in which academic knowledge is built, and more importantly, they disrupt the types of things that academics have been told to value. My colleagues were going to cancel gender and politics because they thought it wasn't important. My intervention in that was minimal, but I think it set me on a path where I was willing to work and push to make things better, to fix the problems I saw, and to foster spaces that would allow us all to have a better work environment. It's funny how our real lives influence our research trajectories: me being the only woman in my department led me to think about the importance of gender, and it kickstarted a career where gender became a core component of my research agenda. The COVID-19 pandemic taught me a lot about myself and my own needs, and it catapulted a communal and community style of working that I'm not sure I will ever veer away from. Who knows what the future will bring?

Conclusions

My life has changed substantially over the last few years. Between 2015 and the present, my department has hired incredible women. There are now seven of us, out of a department of fourteen faculty members. The mere presence of these women has changed my professional life, and it has changed the nature and style of conversations and discussions we have as a department.

You guys I had a dream last night that we had an in-person writing retreat!! After a night of Covid-induced insomnia it was such a treat to dream about that! One day folks, one day.

Amanda Bittner · Nov 23, 2020, 5:51 AM

Because of my online communities, I have been able to be a better colleague to the folks at home, and with my new women colleagues in my department, we developed a weekly writing group and we worked together to create a series of writing retreats for colleagues across the university. We applied the lessons I learned online in the Facebook writing group to life in person. We applied for and secured funding for snacks and lunch, in order to help foster community outside of our writing activities. Many of these colleagues have gone on to organize similar activities in their own networks, spreading the word that collective community building was beneficial and valuable. This was pre-COVID-19, of course, and while the pandemic isn't really over (will it ever be?), I'm grateful that these in-person activities have slowly begun to start up again. Frankly I'm desperate for a multi-day in-person writing retreat.

So much of this chapter has chronicled my own experience as an academic, and, as political scientists, for the most part we are not taught to write this way. Indeed, it contradicts the norms in my corner of the discipline, where most of my work involves designing and administering surveys, conducting multivariate quantitative analyses, creating some pretty graphs and tables, and then describing them and drawing implications for our understanding of human behaviour. Doing political science "differently" feels weird and has me second-guessing everything.

Doing things differently, however, also gives us new perspectives and a new take on old issues. Building and benefitting from community online has been something that I have grown into, and it is something that I am so happy to have the opportunity to have learned to do. I am grateful to the Gender and Political Psychology Facebook Group for teaching me so much about building community connections across borders. I am grateful to the women I work with in my own department for growing into community building with me, and for showing me how to work with others to foster community generously, kindly, and with deep insights into the beauty that others hold and how we can find it. I am grateful to the random people I have met via Twitter, who I sometimes also get to meet in "real life" who have shown me so much that I wouldn't have otherwise noticed or seen. I am grateful to the community of scholars who seek to put care and collaboration front and centre, and who are able to pass this on to other scholars.

Community building is work. It is labour. But it also makes work better and it makes our jobs better. As the dialogues and collaborations in this volume suggest, connecting with others, sharing joys and disappointments, troubleshooting problems that affect us individually but are systemic and experienced by most of us, this is extremely rewarding work, and through relationships we are able to feel a sense of belonging, purpose, and fulfillment that we cannot get on our own, working in silos. We benefit. Our research benefits. Our colleagues benefit. Our students benefit. We learn, we teach, we train, we mentor. This is how knowledge is transferred.

Because of these online communities, I have learned to be a better academic, a better scholar, and a better ally to my colleagues. There has been risk to being public and, in particular, public with the vulnerability and critique of the way things are: I have been raked over on Twitter, and I have received terrible messages in my DMs. I have been Zoom-bombed. Still, I am committed to learning and to building community and I am confident that this is the only way I can do my job and feel like a whole person. And I know there are others like me, who have experiences like me, and who think that this work is important. I don't feel so alone.

During my job interview in 2007 one of my now-colleagues asked me, "Are you a feminist? What would you say if I told you I was a masculinist?" Being confronted by this hostile, argumentative style of misogyny in a job interview is a tough thing for a young, naïve, early career researcher (I was twenty-seven). I won't disclose exactly how I responded because it's not something I would counsel someone else to say in a job interview. I will simply say that in retrospect I am grateful to him for that question because it primed me to think about gender from day one of setting foot in that corridor as his colleague. I am a feminist. And it turns out, feminism has influenced my work more than I ever would have predicted as I finished up my doctorate. Community building is feministing. Collaboration is feministing. Centring a care culture is feminist disruption against patriarchal institutions in academia. My PHD didn't teach me that. My colleagues did.

Note

1. For more amazing feminist institution-busting work by Michelle Dion, check out her work with Sarah Mitchell (2020).

References

Ahmed, Sara. 2016. *Living a Feminist Life*. Durham, NC: Duke University Press.

Berdahl, Loleen. n.d. *Academia Made Easier*. Accessed September 23, 2023. https://loleen.substack.com/.

Cassese, Erin C., and Mira R. Holman. 2018. "Writing Groups as Models for Peer Mentorship among Female Faculty in Political Science." *PS: Political Science & Politics* 51 (2): 401–05. https://doi.org/10.1017/S1049096517002049.

Cole, Desmond. 2020. *The Skin We're In: A Year of Black Resistance and Power*. Toronto: Doubleday Canada.

Dion, Michelle L., and Sara McLaughlin Mitchell. 2020. "How Many Citations to Women Is 'Enough'? Estimates of Gender Representation in Political Science." *PS: Political Science & Politics* 53 (1): 107–13. https://doi.org/10.1017/S1049096519001173.

Holman, Mirya. n.d. *#MHAWS: Mirya Holman's Aggressive Winning Scholars Newsletter*. Accessed September 23, 2023. https://miryaholman.substack.com/.

Jones, El. 2014. "Black Sheroes." In *Live from the Afrikan Resistance!* Winnipeg: Roseway Publishing.

Liboiron, Max. n.d. *CLEAR*. Accessed September 23, 2023. https://civiclaboratory.nl/author/maxliboiron/.

Martin, Sarah J. 2020. "The Political Economy of Distillers' Grains and the Frictions of Consumption." *Environmental Politics* 29 (2): 297–316. https://doi.org/10.1080/09644016.2019.1565461.

Maynard, Robyn. 2017. *Policing Black Lives: State Violence in Canada from Slavery to the Present*. Halifax: Fernwood Publishing.

McMaster University. 2016. "Poli Sci Prof Wins OCUFA Award of Distinction." *Daily News*, March 8, 2016. https://dailynews.mcmaster.ca/worthmentioning/poli-sci-prof-wins-ocufa-award-of-distinction/.

Pacheco-Vega, Raul. n.d. *Raul Pacheco-Vega, PHD*. Accessed September 23, 2023. http://www.raulpacheco.org/blog/.

Smith, Alison. 2022. *Multiple Barriers: The Multilevel Governance of Homelessness in Canada*. Toronto: University of Toronto Press.

Sweet-Cushman, Jennie. 2018. "See It; Be It? The Use of Role Models in Campaign Trainings for Women." *Politics, Groups, and Identities* 7 (4): 853–63. https://doi.org/10.1080/21565503.2018.1531771.

Thomas, Melanee. 2018. "In Crisis or Decline? Selecting Women to Lead Provincial Parties in Government." *Canadian Journal of Political Science* 15 (2): 379–403. https://doi.org/10.1017/S0008423917001421.

Tolley, Erin. 2015. *Framed: Media and Coverage of Race in Canadian Politics.* Vancouver: UBC Press.

Tungohan, Ethel, host. n.d. *Academic Aunties.* Podcast. Accessed September 23, 2023. https://academicaunties.com/.

Whitby, Andrew. 2020. "Who First Said: If You Want to Go Fast, Go Alone; If You Want to Go Far, Go Together." *Andrew Whitby,* December 25, 2020. https://andrewwhitby.com/2020/12/25/if-you-want-to-go-fast.

Women Also Know Stuff. n.d. *WomenAlsoKnowStuff.* Accessed September 23, 2023. https://womenalsoknowstuff.com.

9 Conversations in Feminist Solidarity

Reflecting on the Political Science PHD Experience

LINDSAY LARIOS and MANON LAURENT

COMMON ADVICE for PHD students throughout their studies is to talk to someone who's been through it. Entering into our PHD program in the same cohort, we quickly found solidarity and support in each other. This chapter documents our ongoing conversations about what it means to be in academia and our feminist politics. In this chapter we reflect on our early encounters with feminism in the university, navigating feminism in the discipline of political science, the importance of finding our feminist allies, and lastly the structural and institutional challenges we continue to encounter as we move into new academic spaces. This chapter is a reflection of the friendship that sustained us through this process and a gesture of solidarity to others who have had these experiences, and to future feminist scholars who may otherwise feel alone.

Coming to Feminism

New conversations, new encounters. Conversations in corridors and classrooms. Puzzling through. Feeling out. Must-find-my-people conversations.

LINDSAY LARIOS: I'm a white woman who grew up in a rural, Canadian community. I'm the first in my family to go to grad school. The second to go to university—my mom did her bachelor's when I was four and she was pregnant with my sister. I remember playing on the floor and watching movies while she sat on the couch with a pile of textbooks. I was likely well into my twenties before I started connecting any of these early experiences to my idea of feminism, but this is where it started— the idea that women exist in and can succeed in all kinds of spaces. When I think about feminism now... it's so much more expansive. It's about resisting gender oppression in all its forms, as inseparable from other forms of oppression, and in particular the ways in which power and domination become entrenched in our institutions and norms. I'm indebted to scholars like bell hooks (2000), and a wide range of feminist mentors who introduced me to these texts and ideas, for helping to shape these ideas. It's also about community building. Building community outside of these institutions. How we're in relationship with each other. How we care for each other. Building strength and capacity within communities so we can resist these institutions.

MANON LAURENT: I agree that feminism is about fighting structures of gender oppression, building a society based on equal, respectful, and mindful relationships. I grew up in France, in a relatively privileged white family, but my parents made an odd couple. My mother is nine years older than my dad, has a higher level of education, and has always earned more money. My mum is a fighter. It felt as if to succeed in a patriarchal society, she had to hide her feelings, to be rational rather than emotional. I want to believe that in a feminist society we can be both, rather than one or the other. We can build relationships and communities where emotion and reason are not in opposition. These are the kinds of feminist values I carried with me in my undergrad.

LL: In my undergrad I did a student placement at an organization doing community-based research and policy work. The organization was approached by a nonprofit that provided support to newly arrived refugee families to write a report on the impact of their programs. Their funding was about to expire, and they hoped such a report would help them demonstrate why it should be renewed. I was tasked with interviewing program participants and other community stakeholders and writing the final report. It was my first time doing this kind of qualitative research and I was really impacted by it—in particular, the idea of learning about a policy or program by talking with the people most affected by it. At the end of that semester, I presented the findings back to the organization, their stakeholders, and funders. Although I'm sure a myriad of factors were involved, the funding for the program was renewed and it was energizing to feel like the work I did had a small part in that. I was making connections between my research and my activism in a way I had never considered before, and I began to imagine research as a form of feminist praxis.

ML: It's such an inspiring story! You could literally change the lives of people who most need support. It was great to be entrusted to do this kind of work early in your academic trajectory. What do you mean by feminist praxis?

LL: Feminist praxis refers to the bringing together of feminist theory and action (hooks 2000). The idea that feminist theory cannot be separated from political struggle—it emerges from those struggles and works to resist and change conditions of oppression. Understanding this work as an active ongoing struggle is what feministing means to me. It's something you do. It's work. For students learning about feminist theory, it's powerful when they can begin to apply these critiques to the different contexts they're in.

ML: This is very true. In my experience at university, feminism was a political struggle before a theory. I attended a fairly elite institution specialized in political science. In the first year of my master's degree, some students created a feminist organization. A few months after its creation, the organization became the victim of an intimidation campaign by a group of students who called themselves *Osez le masculinisme*.[1] They levied misogynist and homophobic comments over social media and planned demonstrations targeting the feminist student organization. Other student organizations formed a support group and spoke up against these actions. As the president of the local student union, I joined the support group and signed a press release denouncing the "noxious sexist ambiance" in my university. The press release spoke not only to the actions of these students, but also the pervasiveness of rape culture on campus more broadly—for example, sports teams named *Les Violleyeurs*,[2] *Les Mi-putes mi-soumises*,[3] and *Les Pom-putes*.[4]

LL: That's terrible. Did the university ever issue a response to any of that...?

ML: Well, the university knew about the sports teams' names and was not doing anything about it. There were also several rumours of indecent exposure from professors, which the university tried to shut down. After the press release came out, the university filed two complaints with the police: one against the misogynist group for wrongful use of the university name and logo on their social media, and one against the feminist collective for libel. The support group did not have any formal or institutional existence, but the student unions did. Thus, as the president, I was summoned to the police and pressured to give the names of the members of the feminist collective.

LL: That's a lot for anyone to deal with, let alone for a first-year grad student.

ML: The whole process—press release, complaints, police investigation—took several months. I was summoned to the police during my second semester exams. Those were probably the most stressful exams ever, since I had two oral exams with profs who also held administrative positions and most likely participated in the decision to file the complaints to the police. In the end, I did not give any names and the complaints were dismissed without formal consequences; however, the whole ordeal had profound consequences for me. Just because I signed a press release to denounce a sexist environment in my university, I was questioned by the police and worried about getting my degree at all. And at the time, the university did not do anything about the rape culture, the sports teams' names, and so on. It's a long story, but it was really the moment feminism intersected with my university experience. I was denied the right to stand up for my feminist beliefs or even just a safe space to study.

LL: That's pretty shocking, really. This story feels so symbolic of the ways in which institutions attend to their own interests above those of students. I mean, the fact that you were being formally pressured by the same people that were then evaluating you as a student...Did anything ever change?

ML: A few years after, another feminist organization was created. And this year (2021), female students from my former university started sharing stories of the sexual abuses they survived on the Facebook page of the new organization. The leaders of that group even met with the new administrators of the university to put in place measures that would support survivors and create a safer space to study. I was contacted by a former student union leader from my university to write an op-ed on our story; however, honestly, I'm still not feeling strong enough to fight back after what happened nearly ten years ago.

LL: So that experience made you hesitant to participate in future organizing?

ML: I have not given up on organizing, and taking on feminist fights, but I am longing to build a community where I feel that I belong and I don't have to fight to work, study, and express my opinions or feelings...

LL: What strikes me about these two stories is how we each entered into feminism (at least in the university context) as being fundamentally about enacting change. But also about how universities can be spaces that open doors to explore these ideas and develop the skills and networks to put them into practice, but at the same time, really toxic spaces that feel threatened by this work and punish those who speak out against that. I think we both entered into political science with the idea that it could be a space of critical analysis and debate about relations of power. And yet, as with many long-established disciplines, the field of political science quickly felt as much about the maintenance of certain power relations as it did about critical interrogation of these dynamics.

Finding Feminism in Political Science
Tearful conversations. Venting. Ranting. Conversations over coffee and tea. While sipping wine. Solidarity conversations. Burn-it-all-down conversations.

ML: When I met you, you were finishing your master's in social work. In France, we only have vocational training to become a social worker. So I was curious about your research and how it was so grounded in people's lives. I wondered why you chose to leap from social work to a PHD in political science.

LL: I had always been focused on policy work and advocacy. So I was looking for a program that would expand my knowledge of policy processes, actors, and institutions, and expand the tools of analysis I could bring into these conversations. Pivoting to policy studies (as a subfield of political science) allowed me to do that, but also brought its own challenges. I think we've each struggled to situate our interdisciplinarity and our feminism within political science, concurrently seeking validation while also resisting the boundaries of the discipline.

ML: When I started my PHD in Canada, I was told that I was not doing political science. It was unsettling, I did a BA and MA in political science in France. However, the boundaries of the discipline shift depending on the national academic context. In France, I'm doing "political sociology"; in Canada I was told I fit best in "comparative politics"; finally, in China—which is where I do my fieldwork—people think of my work as "government studies." These boundaries are very difficult to make sense of. As I think we've both experienced, this is especially true when you study a topic at the margins of the discipline, such as the politics of parenting, motherhood, or care work. And even truer when you use narrative and immersive research methods, when you want to give life to the stories of your informants.

LL: Feminist values shape the questions we ask and the way we approach answering them.

ML: I feel that the patriarchal foundations of political science are not discussed enough in class. I remember when studying for our comprehensive exams, I first learned the English word *tantrum* because of a footnote in a book on voting behaviours from the 1960s. The author was explaining that male voters are rational, except when their wives throw "tantrums," and they vote irrationally to appease them.

LL: Right, like why are we still holding up this misogynist, not to mention racist, garbage as somehow core to the discipline?

ML: I feel that we have to uncover/discover the foundations, the boundaries, and the underlying assumptions of the discipline by confronting them ourselves. This process is often unpleasant, and sometimes it seems that we are not supposed to find what we are finding.

LL: I don't think I had a good sense of these disciplinary divides or what the margins of the discipline even were until I started my PHD...I remember during one particularly heated class discussion on political representation and gender, a classmate dropped the line, "Women are their own worst enemies." He said it so casually, like an amusing little quip to emphasize his point. Remarks I would have never imagined hearing in a graduate class. Aren't we beyond this? I guess I was naïve. Was this a joke? Was this a challenge? I remember looking around the classroom, locking eyes with other female students, with you. Blood boiling. Like, I can't do this again. I shut down. I had no more words. Now I wish I had the words to respond. I wish I were braver. The discussion pressed forward like an interesting and amusing debate—as if abstract, not deeply personal for half the class. I remember thinking, is this what it's always going to be like? It's one thing to learn the history of the discipline, but if we're not critically interrogating that history and challenging those values, we're maintaining them. This classroom comment, implying women policymakers act against their own interests, is grounded in this idea of women as irrational. That students feel confident making these kinds of claims signals we're not doing enough to challenge these ideas as a discipline.

ML: That makes me relive our frustration during our classes. I remember this moment also, and so many more. It was helpful to be able to share with you after these kinds of moments (see Bittner, this volume).

LL: So much of navigating this is about finding your people, your allies.

ML: Right. And even then, it can be hard to find your place. My first time attending the annual Canadian Political Science Association (CPSA) conference in 2019, we were invited to a pre-conference workshop titled Women in Political Science Leadership Program. In the morning, one day before the official conference started, we entered a large room with many women scholars. Most of them knew each other and were hugging and greeting each other. I felt overwhelmed by the sense of community they shared. As I knew very few of them, I took some breakfast treats and retreated to a seat in the room. Coming from the French academic context, I'm not used to expressing feelings in professional settings, so I was intimidated by the excitement that everyone expressed. I was preparing for a formal conference, not really bracing for such an informal bonding experience. I felt that in a way I could belong here, but I was missing so much in terms of context and norms. During the introductory speech of the workshop, they mentioned so many names and events that I had never heard of. It felt like they were celebrating the creation of a new safe space within the CPSA, but I didn't know and I still don't quite know how I fit in this space. I am still struggling to know if I fit in political science, if I understand what political science is in Canada, or anywhere. That said, I feel that academia benefits from more informal and warm spaces like these. I think my development as a young scholar has been greatly facilitated by the supportive relationships that I encountered.

Building Feminist Relationships

Conversations in the metro. In the pool. In the library. Surrounded-by-books-and-papers conversations. Across-oceans conversations. Encouragement. Celebration. Commiseration. You-can-do-this conversations.

ML: What really became obvious to me is how we survived our PHD program by sticking together.

LL: PHD programs are known for being competitive, almost individualistic, journeys. And certainly, that perspective was imparted on us by different faculty members we encountered, and students as well. But I think pretty early on we rejected that. Reflecting back, the role that active feminist mentoring, peer support, and collaboration had in opening up spaces where we could thrive was huge.

ML: During the first years, we developed a closer friendship. Debriefing after courses in the metro on our way home. We could vent about comments made in class—like the one you mentioned earlier. We could share ideas and progressively puzzle through what was being asked of us as graduate students. When the comprehensive exams got closer, we shared our reading notes and discussed articles together. We met every week in cafés for months to make sense of the reading lists. I could not have gone through this intense learning process without our critical discussions. This process seemed absurd, learning so many old references with little context, and with very little connection with our own research. It helped to make sense of it by working together.

LL: There are so many moments in the PHD that can feel so isolating. Comps is definitely one of them. It opened so many questions for me on how to situate myself in the discipline and if I still even wanted to. Another friend of mine wrote an incredible piece on this (Batac 2021), and although our experiences are very different, a lot of what she reflects on resonates with me—the search for the scholarly home, and how isolating that can be.

ML: Thank you for sharing that article with me! I really like that she tells the story of her struggles and anxieties. We never read about how research can be a painful process, and how it is a strenuous process. It reminded me of an article I read on loneliness during the PHD process (Chao et al. 2016). The authors talk about how PHD students experience loneliness in three distinct ways: loneliness related to time management, relationships (in particular because relatives often cannot relate with the PHD process and rarely understand our research topic), and finally, place in society. Here I feel that mentoring and peer support is really crucial, to set long-term goals together, to structure work sessions every day, to build yourself a supportive community. I was so energized when we defended our proposals just a few weeks apart with matching colourful blazers!

LL: It was really wonderful to be able celebrate these milestones together!

ML: It was harder to keep in touch during the fieldwork, especially when I went to China for nearly a year.

LL: For sure things shifted when you relocated, whether to China or France. When the pandemic started, we were both immersed in dissertation writing. Zoom became a really useful tool for us to connect and work alongside each other. To maintain a sense of community when we couldn't physically be together.

ML: This is what it means to me to have a feminist graduate program—research from the start should be a collective process. A feminist PHD program should actively fight against graduate students' loneliness. It is about creating space to learn, reflect, and write together.

LL: And I think that can be modelled for grad students in different ways. In part, it's the culture of the program. But it also relates to mentorship in other academic contexts too.

ML: I remember being so fascinated when you told me that you joined a research project where everyone participated in a retreat to do some autoethnographic reflection to better understand the position from which each of you engaged with the topic. I think it is exciting to join a collective research project where all researchers get to know each other better to produce knowledge together. Feminist research is not just about the broad topic or the final product, but it should also be about the process to produce research and the consequences of the research in the real world.

LL: I've been fortunate to be part of a number of wonderfully collaborative research teams or working groups. I feel like I've learned more from these experiences than any class I took during my PHD. That project is interesting because I got involved with it at a time when I had a few different opportunities pop up and I needed to decide what I wanted to commit to over the next few years. Honestly, one of the deciding factors was that this was an opportunity to work on an interdisciplinary research team of feminist scholars and I felt like I needed that community. What was important about that team was that it wasn't just that we were all interested in feminist research questions, but that feminism was reflected in the organization and collaborative processes we engaged in as a team. We had weekly meetings to check in and engage in collaborative analysis. We had bi-annual retreats where we actively engaged in reflexivity and relationship building. Co-authorship and co-ownership of data was clearly stated and maintained regardless of one's role in the team. These kinds of supportive working environments and relationships are so important for junior scholars. The challenge, of course, is how to sustainably create these spaces and opportunities for reflexive and inclusive engagement within neoliberal institutions that tend to compel us to do more with less (Mountz et al. 2015).

Organizing Feminist Spaces
Unpaid, underpaid conversations. Between co-authors, collaborators, co-conspirators. Between friends. Over email. Over Zoom. How-the-work-happens conversations. What's-next conversations.

LL: Another thing we've discussed is our relation to our institution. As graduate students, we navigate the established procedures in order to "survive," while slowly being incorporated into the institution through teaching positions and student government. While these roles open up new relational spaces, they do not shift the relations of power. Like it's great that there's a student union—but when you talk about your experience as president of your student union, the power differential between the union and the university was clearly massive. The same could maybe be said about student associations more broadly.

ML: Well, when I entered university, I did not expect much, but I joined a student union in my first year because they were mobilizing against the privatization of higher education. During my time in university, I participated in struggles against the rise of tuition fees, rape culture, low wages for TAs and RAs, and unpaid extra hours. Whether the fight was lost or won, I always learned so much during these collective actions. I learned about university administration and student democracy, and also about the necessity to organize directly with affected communities, the power of collective action, and our craving for solidarity. I believe that our teaching should foster students' activism. When I was a student, I often felt that professors considered students' fights childish or irrelevant. Like there was a gap or a wall between students and professors, as if we were not working and studying in the same space, the same institution. Only recently I have met more professors who recognize students' struggles as legitimate and share their own fights with their students, whether it be working conditions or racial discrimination.

LL: Teaching as a PHD student felt like this liminal space where we were at once both student and instructor—at once struggling to meet the demands of the institution and at the same time enforcing them in our own classrooms. As I prepared for my class, I remember constantly being warned that as a young female instructor my students would likely challenge me or wouldn't take me seriously, so I have to be firm and strict. This really freaked me out. First, because I don't like confrontation and I'd spend my preparation time dreaming up sarcastic remarks that students might throw at me. Second, because it didn't feel like the kind of instructor I wanted to be. I ended up being super lucky and I was gifted with this amazing group of students who embraced the class and the content enthusiastically. And the "strict" rules I had worked to establish early on ended up being things I really didn't care that much about, or found myself wanting to be more flexible on as I began to figure out who I was as an instructor. While I would consider that an overall positive teaching experience, I find myself reflecting a lot on what I should have done differently and what I aim to do differently in the future.

ML: The graduate program is where I learned to be a teacher. Throughout the pandemic, I taught students at different academic stages (BAS, MAS). In my experience, online teaching was especially difficult for first-year students who have just arrived at university, sometimes even in the city. They do not know anyone, often do not really understand how the university works. I really felt for them. I spent my year trying to connect with them and create space for them to connect with me and each other because I knew how important that is. I really struggled this year because I felt most of my colleagues focused mainly on how to make sure students "learn content," how to evaluate students, how to make sure they do not cheat even though they take their exams online... Then, when growing student mental distress was finally acknowledged, the response was to be more flexible and reduce the students' workload. I agree that we need more flexibility during this period; however, I do not think that fewer courses, less content (which often means less contact) is a good answer to students' mental distress. We need to rethink our relationship with our students, provide more support, and create online space for mutual support among students. Instead of just reducing the workload, we need to create more relationships, but we need the support of the institution to do that. As a sessional instructor with a thesis to write, I really struggled to find a balance—preparing and giving courses, providing support and creating space for students, while also writing my thesis, participating in events, publishing…I feel PHD students are constantly torn apart by the conflicting demands of the different roles we occupy.

LL: Absolutely. We have to acknowledge how so much of this is structural. As grad students ourselves, we're best positioned to understand the challenges our students are facing, but we're not resourced in a way that enables us to respond. Jacqueline Potvin and Kimberly Dority do a great job of interrogating this tension, grounding it within the broader context of the "injustice of current hiring practices and working conditions within higher education" (2022, 4) for PHD students and sessional instructors who are constantly told that these teaching positions are opportunities to enhance one's CV and demonstrate that we can apply innovative pedagogy. And while it's wonderful to receive emails from students expressing appreciation for our support throughout the semester or how thankful they were to have a class taught through an intersectional lens, it takes a lot of additional work to provide that level of support and do those kinds of revisions to course material. This is clearly the case for racialized instructors and faculty who we know also end up taking on this kind of intensive work (Dhamoon 2020). If we want to talk about feminist, anti-racist, decolonializing pedagogies, we need to not only consider what gets taught but who takes on that work and whether or not their work conditions actually support them when they do so.

ML: I remember learning about Paulo Freire, Ivan Illitch, and the idea of "reconstructionism" in education (Ozmon and Craver 2008). This really imprinted on me, I became convinced that education should be about "promoting change," seeing people as agents of change. Education should *not* be about teaching people how the world has been, is, and will always be, but rather about teaching people how to change the world for the better, to convey the idea that the world is ever-changing and that we can directly influence this change.

Unfortunately, the institutional support isn't always there to engage in this kind of work (Rodriguez 2018), but I'm encouraged by the number of people interested in the idea of a feminist, anti-racist, decolonizing university and pedagogical practices.

LL: I'm feeling more cynical these days. Maybe I'm just burnt out. I don't know what a feminist institution looks like anymore. At the forefront of my mind is the recognition that universities, as institutions, don't care about students. There are great people within them that do...but it can take a profound amount of work to find those people, have them see you, and work to change anything, even at the individual level. And I say this as someone who had a very supportive supervisor who continuously went to bat for me and made me feel like I wasn't ever going to be alone facing these challenges. Not all students have that. So many close friends and colleagues of mine, of ours, have had to face navigating their PHD programs, navigating their universities, feeling alone. And now that I've been through it, I think back on those experiences and my heart aches because I know that when you're in it you don't necessarily see the institutional barriers. You're just desperate to get through it, to survive. Or you see them, but it feels like there's nothing you can do. And then so often the hopelessness and the anguish and the stress that being confronted with these barriers has on students, and the long-term mental health impacts, are felt as individual failures. Unless you have family members or friends who have been through it, nobody really prepares you for what a PHD program is. And of course, this affects racialized students more; of course, this affects students from working-class backgrounds more.

ML: I totally agree, even with very supportive supervisors I did not always feel prepared. When I moved back to France, I joined a collective of PHD students. It's like a support group. We organized several workshops to share some horror stories about the PHD process in France and our tips to get out of difficult situations. During our discussion, we came across a handbook for self-defence in academia (Le Collectif du manuel 2021). This handbook talks about how hard it is to build a good mentorship relationship with a supervisor, about how we need to learn to say "no" to some opportunities to care for ourselves and avoid burning out, about the urgency to create supportive spaces, and finally about the necessity to keep a way out so that the PHD does not become an ordeal.

LL: That's really valuable information. At the same time, we can't lose sight of the university's responsibility: What is it that makes "self-defence" necessary in the first place? A friend of mine withdrew from their PHD and recently they showed me their first-year course schedule—it was the most intense schedule I had ever seen and nobody told them it was too much. They are one of the brightest people I know whose hard work and enthusiasm for their research, learning, and teaching was more than I could ever muster, yet a lack of institutional guidance and inflexibility when it came to student mental health meant they didn't continue. And I can think of many people who have been on the brink of making that same decision. Knowing what I know now and reflecting on the kind of support I had, I know these situations don't have to happen.

ML: So how do you envision your relationships with your students moving forward?

LL: Now, when I think about what my role is as an instructor for my students, I can't help but think that it's about creating safe spaces for them to learn and helping them navigate and survive these institutions. Resourcing them to be engaged community members. Future collaborators. More people who are invested in this political work. Building that community of critically engaged scholars, students, activists, neighbours. We need that.

Conclusions

In this dialogue we share our personal experiences discovering that feminism is about enacting change and questioning the boundaries of the discipline. In discussing our PHD experiences, we choose not to focus on simply providing concrete and instrumental advice about how to choose the right supervisor, secure the appropriate funding, or select the most efficient reference software. For many students, they can follow all this advice perfectly, but still face a myriad of institutional boundaries shaped by gender, race, ethnicity, sexuality, ability, socioeconomics, and other marginalizations. We write as an act of solidarity, in recognition of the community and relationships we developed along the way and their pivotal role in supporting us in moving forward in our scholarship. The need for feministing the discipline of political science does not end after graduation. More caring, feminist institutions, we believe are beneficial to everyone, and for many students, they are not just beneficial but a matter of survival.

Notes

1. Literally translates to *Dare masculinism*—a play on the name of a French feminist organization called Osez le féminisme (https://osezlefeminisme.fr/).
2. Men's volleyball team. A contraction of two French words: *violeur* (rapist) and *volleyeur* (male volleyball player).
3. Women's rugby team. Literally translates to "half-whore/half-submissive"—a play on the name of a French feminist organization called Ni putes ni soumises ("neither-whore nor-submissive") (https://npns.eu/).
4. Cheerleading team. A combination of the French word for *pompom* (cheerleader) and a French slur meaning whore (*putes*).

References

Batac, Monica Anne. 2021. "'Failing' and Finding a Filipina Diasporic Scholarly 'Home': A De/Colonizing Autoethnography." In "The Im/Possibility of Finding Home in Academia: Personal Narratives of Transnationally Minoritized Scholars in Higher Education," special issue, *Qualitative Inquiry* 28 (1): 62–69. https://doi.org/10.1177/10778004211006705.

Chao, Marina, Carlotta Monini, Signe Munck, Samuel Thomas, Justine Rochot, and Cécile Van de Velde. 2016. "Les expériences de la solitude en doctorat. Fondements et inégalités." *Socio-logos*, no. 10, 1–20. https://doi.org/10.4000/socio-logos.2929.

Le Collectif du manuel. 2021. *Manuel d'autodéfense universitaire* (manuel_v2-0-1_integrale.pdf). https://zici.fr/manuel_univ.

Dhamoon, Rita Kaur. 2020. "Racism as a Workload and Bargaining Issue." *Socialist Studies* 14 (1). https://doi.org/10.18740/ss27273.

hooks, bell. 2000. *Feminist Theory: From Margin to Centre*, 2nd ed. Boston: South End Press.

Mountz, Allison, Anne Bonds, Becky Mansfield, Jenna Loyd, Jennifer Hyndman, Margaret Walton-Roberts, Ranu Basu, Risa Whitson, Roberta Hawkins, Trina Hamilton, and Winifred Curran. 2015. "For Slow Scholarship: A Feminist Politics of Resistance Through Collective Action in the Neoliberal University." *ACME: An International Journal for Critical Geographies* 14 (4): 1235–59. https://acme-journal.org/index.php/acme/article/view/1058.

Ozmon, Howard A., and Samuel M. Craver. 2008. *Philosophical Foundations of Education*, 8th ed. London: Pearson.

Potvin, Jacqueline Marie, and Kimberly Dority. 2022. "Feminist Pedagogy in the Neoliberal University: The Limits of Precarious Labour." *Atlantis: Critical Studies in Gender, Culture, and Social Justice* 43 (1): 56-68. https://journals.msvu.ca/index.php/atlantis/article/view/5567/4748.

Rodriguez, Celia O. 2018. *Decolonizing Academia: Poverty, Oppression and Pain*. Halifax: Fernwood Publishing.

10 Don't Be an Asshole

STEPHANIE PATERSON

IN MY FIRST YEAR OF UNIVERSITY, I lost my two grandmothers and an uncle. Most of my professors were understanding and accommodating. One, however, was a dick. Despite the documentation I provided, they outright accused me of lying and refused to make any accommodations. As I have progressed through my academic journey, I have often reflected on this experience, and many others, and continue to use it as an example of what not to be. This experience very likely informs my research, which most recently concerns care, empathy, and emotions in policymaking contexts. "Neutral" bureaucrats and "objective" researchers are represented as ideal, but do they have to be? To ask a core question from feminist political science, can institutions, in this case the university, be caring and/or empathic?

As I think about what feministing means to me, I can't help but centre concepts such as intimacy and empathy. As professors, we are not merely conduits of knowledge, translating ideas from others to our students and fellow researchers. Paulo Ravecca conceptualizes political science as "a place of human interaction," revealing "that what happens 'there'—or rather, here—affects its inhabitants and the knowledge that we can or cannot create" (2019, 4–5). In other words, political science is not simply about a body of literature; it is a relational practice that shapes how that body of literature is taught, critiqued, and expanded, and who gets to engage (or not). From this perspective, thinking about how we engage others and what we can say or feel (intimacy), as well as how we respond (empathy), can help us understand how power circulates, reinforcing or troubling hierarchical social relations that are embedded in the practice of political science.

In this chapter, I present three vignettes based on my personal experiences to consider the ways in which intimacy and empathy are reflected in institutional affective practices, helping or hindering institutional transformation. I suggest that intimacy can disrupt hegemonic affective practices, and enable new forms to emerge, forms that are premised on kindness and empathy.

To do this, I draw on three concepts, including the politics of intimacy (Durnová 2018), social empathy (Segal 2007a, 2007b, 2018), and design justice (Costanza-Chock 2020). The chapter begins with a brief overview of the politics of intimacy and social empathy, followed by a discussion of the vignettes. I close with a discussion of how design justice, an approach to decision-making and design that centres empathy, can foster change.

Assholes in/and the Academy
Faculty are what policy scholars refer to as "street-level bureaucrats" (Lipsky 2010). Street-level bureaucrats are those who deliver services to the public. In addition, street-level bureaucrats often have a high degree of discretionary power, occupying positions where policy texts and service mandates must be interpreted and implemented. It is this discretionary power, often obscured behind rules speak, that has brought considerable attention to the role of street-level bureaucrats in policy processes and outcomes, since it shapes the everyday experiences of political subjects, fuelling processes of inclusion and exclusion, or, perhaps more accurately, violence (e.g., Dubois 2010; Spade 2015).

Faculty represent the "front face" of the university (and, indeed, the discipline), often the primary point of contact for potential and prospective students. As university employees and as political scientists, we are required to interpret and implement university policies, ranging from academic regulations to student support, and professional norms and discipline-specific content. As such, as we embody and perform our disciplines, symbolically representing political science and its practitioners, constituting what the discipline *is*, and *who* is included, even beyond *what* we teach (e.g., Ahmed 2019; Henry et al. 2017; Ravecca 2019).

In large part, our discretionary power (and a healthy dose of ego) leads to a high number of assholes. We all have stories of assholes who claim to be "just doing my job," while serving to silence, marginalize, and/or invisibilize colleagues and students (see also Klein 2011). Professors like the one described above, for example, who refuse to make accommodations for students with or without disclosure; those who refuse to diversify their reading lists because "it's the canon"; or those who file code violations for the most minor offenses, without care or concern for context or consequence. The list goes on. We all know them, work with them, and perhaps, sadly, have even been them.

Let me be clear, I'm not talking about the professor who has high standards and expectations for their students. Rather, I'm talking about those professors who are either outrightly malicious, or those who have their heads so far up their own asses that they seem to care nothing of anyone else around them. They adhere to "the rules" like a lifeboat and remain so unreflexive and rigid that they fail to see the potential harm caused by such rules and practices. When we are assholes, we reproduce those exclusionary practices that have served to keep BIPOC folks out. Uncritical acceptance and application of bureaucratic rules and processes, as well as professional practices, including curriculum choices, run the risk of perpetuating harm on already vulnerabilized communities and closing off space for transformation.

The reverence for the "tough" professor runs deep and is encoded in professional practices. In contrast, kindness is perceived as personal weakness or violating professional norms yet is also expected—required?—among mostly female faculty, especially BIPOC and/or queer folks, who are expected to mend the seams of a broken system without acknowledgement or compensation (Ahmed 2019; Dhamoon 2020). What I'm referring to is not just about being nice. It actually requires a fundamental rethinking of the academy and, importantly, the discipline of political science.

How to Spot (and Avoid Being) an Asshole: The Politics of Intimacy and Social Empathy

Universities are not often thought of as intimate spaces (see also Ravecca 2019). Yet the literature on emotions demonstrates how public spaces are constituted in emotional landscapes (Orsini and Wiebe 2014) and are sites of emotional negotiation and contestation (Ahmed 2013; Harding and Pribram 2002). Emotional and experiential knowledge inform our understandings of policy and politics and are embedded in institutions through institutionalized affective practices that coproduce meanings and positionalities (Durnová 2018, 11).[1] This is what Anna Durnová (2013, 2018) refers to as the "politics of intimacy."

In contrast to conceiving of intimacy as a basis of relational closeness, Durnová explains, "Intimacy is understood…as the deeply personal and emotional experience with one's body and mind that is shared in a way, that is often unspoken or invisible and difficult to articulate but that seeks to be acknowledged as such in a collective" (2018, 2). It describes the political acknowledgement of personal and emotional experiences, subsequently reflected in institutional affective practices. For Durnová, emphasis is on the articulation of emotional experiences as the basis of knowledge and decision-making. Intimacy, then, requires shifting the boundaries between public and private to make visible what had been previously invisible. She suggests that there is a "mutation in public power where intimacy reveals circumstances under which emotional experience is given voice in the policy procedure and when it is understood and accepted as relevant by those in power" (2018, 5).

If the politics of intimacy offers a lens for illuminating institutionalized affective practices and shared meanings, social empathy (Segal 2018) as affective practice promises to facilitate the acknowledgement of emotional experiences. To be sure, feminist scholars have argued that empathy is necessary for social transformation (Collins 2000; Hemmings 2012). Importantly, social empathy is not an individual trait or disposition; rather, it seeks to institutionalize empathy in policy and decision-making practices and processes (Segal 2018). It requires "deep understanding" of the structural bases of power and oppression, including social and political structures, and asks for change (Larios and Paterson 2021; Paterson and Larios 2020). Social empathy necessitates listening and perspective-taking, aiming to understand how someone else *feels* and to embed these perspectives in decision-making and institutional design. It thus offers a normative ideal for institutional design, discussed in more detail below.

Before considering how we might cultivate social empathy in our discipline and the academy more broadly, I turn now to three vignettes to exemplify how the politics of intimacy constitutes (and troubles) the university, and how social empathy might help us transform it.

Intimate Encounters: Institutional Affective Practice as Othering

Vignette 1: The Problem with Disclosure[2]
I knew from the tone of her email that whatever she needed to tell me was important. And as we sat down in my office the next morning, and she asked me if it was okay to close the door (something I rarely do), I could see that her bottom lip was already quivering. The tears started shortly after. In the following moments, she disclosed to me what she had recently endured: the most intimate trauma. In the end, and after performing the service of pointing her to appropriate campus services, we were both crying, and I asked if she needed a hug. She nodded in response. After the hug, she reluctantly asked if it was okay to miss today's class, and if she could have until the end of the day to submit her assignment. I told her to take as much time as she needed, and that we could discuss the paper at a later date. She started crying again. She told me she hadn't expected to be greeted with kindness.

Branch, Hayes-Smith, and Richards observe that, "the combination of an elevated risk for sexual victimization as well as the vulnerability for repeat contact with perpetrators leaves college campuses uniquely dangerous for female students" (2011, 56). Sexual violence on university campuses gained widespread public attention around 2015 due to a number of highly publicized incidents, often involving high profile faculty, at various universities in Canada and the United States. Despite significant changes to university sexual assault policies across the country since this time, students remain frustrated with administrative responses to the crisis (Salvino, Gilchrist, and Cooligan-Pang 2017). In Quebec, where I work, for example, emphasis remains rooted in "law and order" approaches that privilege disclosure and campus safety rather than addressing the ways in which universities (re)produce the power relations and structural bases on which sexual violence is premised. Importantly, even where "single-window" offices exist, students often confide in trusted faculty or staff for guidance and support (Branch, Hayes-Smith, and Richards 2011; Hayes-Smith Richards, and Branch 2010; Jones, Chappell, and Alldred 2021). Since sexual violence is differentially experienced along intersectional lines, and since gender norms shape students' perceptions and expectations, disclosure to faculty frequently means reliance on BIPOC and queer faculty (Branch, Hayes-Smith, and Richards 2011).

Before exploring the politics of intimacy in this case, I want to move to vignette 2, which, as I will discuss, reveals a similar emotional logic.

Vignette 2: Yeah, I've Been an Asshole Professor Too
"Nothing on this course outline speaks to me. Is this what feminist politics is? Mostly white ladies talking about barriers to elected office??? Where does caring and community building fit into this? What about multiple oppressions? What about the experiences of Black or Indigenous or trans men and women? Where are they?"

We let these comments just hang between us for a few minutes. I had to stop myself from defensively giving her the same excuse I hear when challenging my male colleagues on why there are so few women or queer scholars on their course outlines: "But it's the canon." After a moment, I simply said, "You're right. I'm sorry. I can't change the syllabus at this point in the course, but I can address this issue in my remaining lectures. Thank you for coming to me, and I'm sorry you had to."

Universities are filled with assholes. I know; I am one. Not intentionally, of course. But assholeism is so ingrained in the institution that it's invisible, unless and until you're on the receiving end of asshole behaviour or inane rules. "Institutional reproduction" they call it. Yet, much like sexual violence, colonialism and racism have become pressing issues for universities and colleges. In the wake of the 2015 Truth and Reconciliation Commission, political science departments across the country, with the support of the Canadian Political Science Association, have been struggling (or, perhaps more accurately, resisting) to Indigenize the discipline. In addition, in light of the Black Lives Matter movement and a highly publicized anti-Black altercation occurring at the 2019 Congress of the Humanities and Social Sciences, universities more broadly have worked to establish equity, diversity, and inclusion and anti-racist initiatives (see Tungohan, as well as Dei-Sharpe and Manning, this volume) to attract and retain more diverse faculty and students.

Part of this task requires rethinking curriculum (e.g., Chan, Dhamoon, and Moy 2014; Chang 2002; Gaudry and Lorenz 2018; Henry et al. 2017; Yee 2011). Indigenous activist Jessica Yee's (now Danforth) (2011) edited collection *Feminism for Real: Deconstructing the Academic Industrial Complex of Feminism* clearly examines how academic feminism has reduced struggles of inequality to those between "men" and "women," silencing and marginalizing groups along the lines of Indigeneity, race, sexual and gender diversity, and disability, and, ironically, limiting space for activism and progressive change both within and beyond the academy. The vignette above reveals these marginalizing effects (Chan, Dhamoon, and Moy 2014; Henry et al. 2017; Ravecca 2019). Indeed, Henry et al. write, "Systemic exclusion and discrimination take place through the canons and the pedagogical and methodological paradigms of most disciplines, which tend to marginalize certain knowledges, epistemologies, and scholars. Such academic contexts also make it difficult to create sustainable scholarly communities and to find role models and mentors (Luther, Whitmore, and Moreau 2003; Mahtani 2004; Monture 2010; Smith 2010)" (2017, 6–7).

From the perspective of the politics of intimacy, we want to understand how the university enables, constrains, or channels the articulation and acknowledgement of emotional experiences. In the cases of both sexual assault and harassment and systemic racism, the university forces individualized actions and responses, perpetuating the gendered, colonial, and racist structures in which it is embedded. The politics of intimacy in these contexts disarticulates racism, colonialism, ableism, homo- and trans-phobia, and so on from the institution itself, responsibilizing individual students and faculty for accommodations, redress, or change. More generally, students—those whom the institution renders most vulnerable—are reliant on the goodwill of individual faculty to make changes and respond to their claims, affirming their "deservedness" for accommodations or "special treatment." Against that asshole professor, whose attributes form the normative basis for professional practice, these students have no space in which to articulate their experiences and have them acknowledged and validated, which potentially nurtures disengagement and further marginalizes and silences those students.

Even where professors are not assholes, faculty might not have been trained in how to deal with such situations and will likely experience intense emotional reactions through "vicarious trauma," compounded by the uncertainty of "doing the right thing" (Branch, Hayes-Smith, and Richards 2011). In these contexts, fear, sadness, or rage are constituted as "other," anomalies that must be reconciled within the broader confines of the institution. These vignettes offer examples of the "intimacy of [personal life] running up against an institution" (Durnová 2018, 206), where "private" events are mediated by bureaucratic processes (Ahmed 2019).

Vignette 3: When Your Job Just Doesn't Care About Your Personal Problems

It had been a rough week. My dad's cancer was rapidly progressing and my mom, quite understandably, was unravelling. I had been travelling frequently to Southwestern Ontario to try to help out and to just spend time with my dad in the last few months of his life. It was starting to affect my work and my ability to fulfil my commitments. Deadlines came and went, and I was regularly missing department meetings and meetings for various research projects. I was on autopilot in the classroom, simply a body in a space, barely managing to pull myself together to teach.

I thought I had been doing just fine that day. I ran the seminar, and we had a productive discussion. When I noticed two students hovering after class, I assumed they wanted to carry on the conversation. But something told me this was different. They purposely waited until everyone had left and we were alone. I looked up at them and smiled, hoping to signal that I was ready to talk. They smiled back, warm smiles filled with concern. And then they asked me a question I was in no way prepared for: "How are you doing?" In that moment I was completely overwhelmed. I took half a second to compose myself, but it was futile. I cried; I slumped over and cried, a full-on ugly cry. In unison they stepped forward and hugged me, whispering words of comfort. I thanked them and apologized profusely for my lack of professionalism. They both smiled ironically, when one noted, "um, you're human."

This vignette is similar to the first two in that it constitutes particular emotionalities "outside" the academy, but it also reveals the emotional discourses and institutional affective practices that constitute the profession, and how these get lodged in the university. In this case, my grief was limiting my ability to do my job as prescribed by professional standards. Similar to the students in the previous vignettes, I was vulnerabilized by the institution, since my only options for reprieve involved a significant loss of pay. Moreover, such measures would only relieve me of in-class teaching responsibilities; they would not relieve me of supervisory work and informal mentorship, research commitments, or grant administration. Much or our work is liminal in that it moves within and beyond the institutions in which we work.

Perhaps more concerning is that the vignette above focuses on a relatively temporally bounded period of grief or trauma. But what about the trauma that informs our everyday lives: colonialism, misogyny, racism, homophobia, transphobia, ableism, and so on, many of which are embedded in university practice (Dhamoon 2020; Henry et al. 2017; see also Ravecca 2019). By keeping these systems hidden, they remain firmly in place. The norm of objectivity and keeping our personal lives out of our work lives (I'm sorry, but is that even possible??) enables the reproduction of white heteropatriarchy that informs the university.

But this is not just about professional norms; it is also about representation, demonstrating how emotional and professional discourses constitute particular spaces and the bodies that inhabit them. As a (white settler) woman, I fear any display of any emotionality (is it possible to be "unemotional"??) will undermine my credibility and authority. To be sure, comments on my course evaluations often suggest that I am biased; one particularly imaginative person noted that I "verbally castrate men," where another questioned the utility of the "critical feminist bunk" that I "peddle." And yet, my whiteness affords me certain allowances with respect to emotional outbursts (see Thompson 2017 for a discussion). Thus, the politics of intimacy here is complex, shaped by intersectional power relations that normalize "appropriate" emotional expressions across social groups.

Within the academy, the politics of intimacy are structured such that emotional expression can only ever take place between individuals, limiting the acknowledgement of such expressions through the institution. A social empathy approach would entail not just actions at the individual level, whereby we subvert the rules of the institution to achieve particular goals, but also those of decision-makers at all levels of the organization. It would require a people-first approach that considers how university processes differentially position folks.

Social Empathy as Institutionalized Affective Practice: Design Justice and the Academy

The vignettes above reveal the ways in which the politics of intimacy in the academy limit the responses necessary to acknowledge and address emotional experiences. Despite important steps forward, emphasis remains on individual initiative, responsibilizing those rendered most vulnerable by the university. As a result, not only are responses ad hoc and uneven across the academy, but the work required to formulate responses is rarely required of (or denied by) white men. To remedy this, some have called for remuneration and performance evaluation procedures that integrate such work (e.g., Dhamoon 2020). In addition, I suggest we need to rethink how policies and professional practices are designed. I suggest we need to start from social empathy.

Social empathy is an approach to policy and decision-making that anchors empathy and kindness (e.g., Paterson and Larios 2020; Segal 2018). Social work scholar Elizabeth Segal claims we must extend empathy beyond an interpersonal disposition to "include the social and political structures of our society" (2007b, 335). Gerdes et al. explain, "because policymakers and those in positions of economic and social power are often far removed from the day-to-day experiences of people who are poor, it is sometimes necessary to help them to understand what it means to live in poverty. The more empathy policymakers have, the more likely they are to relate to the lives of the people affected by social policies and programs" (2011, 125). Thus, social empathy "describes the insights one has about other people's lives that allow one to understand the circumstances and realities of other people's living situations" (Segal 2007a, 75). Most importantly, "empathetic individuals, if they are in decision-making positions, can use their empathy to guide their course of action" (Segal 2007a, 76).

For Segal, social empathy is not simply a goal; it is also a process. Segal's social empathy framework includes three steps, including *exposure*, wherein policymakers learn about people's differences and interact with those who are different from themselves; *explanation*, which requires policymakers to gain an understanding of what makes people different and what differences mean for lived lives; it also requires them to reflect on the lived experiences of others; and *experience*, which requires that policymakers participate in the day-to-day experiences of others, which, in turn, allows folks to envision themselves in that situation; in such situations, people are less likely to judge and can acknowledge the complexity of people's lives (Segal 2007b, 335–36; see also Segal 2007a, 2018; Paterson and Larios 2020, 4).

As Lindsay Larios and I have previously argued, step three, while laudable, is problematic in terms of generating empathy since many experiences remain "unknowable" outside of firsthand experience. As a white settler woman, for example, I will never experience systemic racism or the deleterious effects of colonialism. Indeed, there is much that I might simply not see, even as I participate in the day-to-day experiences of diverse folks. Moreover, the social empathy framework seems to take as given that decision-makers are white, middle-class, cisgender straight men without disabilities. Thus, to this framework, I would add a fourth and a fifth step. The fourth step is what we have called *empathic policy analysis*, which centres emotional discourse analysis as a policy analytic, and which is beyond the scope of this chapter (see Paterson and Larios 2020; Larios and Paterson 2021 for discussion and application). The fifth step is what I would call *expansion*, which transforms institutional governance in ways that displace those who have historically held power in decision-making, instead centring diversity and diverse experiences. This is the goal of design justice.

Unlike "design thinking," which asks policy developers to consider and ideally involve the "end user" (Clarke and Craft 2018), design justice starts from the premise "nothing for us without us" (Costanza-Chock 2020). The Design Justice Network articulates ten principles that inform the approach:

- We use design to sustain, heal, and empower our communities, as well as to seek liberation from exploitative and oppressive systems.
- We center the voices of those who are directly impacted by the outcomes of the design process.
- We prioritize design's impact on the community over the intentions of the designer.
- We view change as emergent from an accountable, accessible, and collaborative process, rather than as a point at the end of a process.
- We see the role of the designer as a facilitator rather than an expert.

- We believe that everyone is an expert based on their own lived experience, and that we all have unique and brilliant contributions to bring to a design process.
- We share design knowledge and tools with our communities.
- We work towards sustainable, community-led and controlled outcomes.
- We work towards non-exploitative solutions that reconnect us to the earth and to each other.
- Before seeking new design solutions, we look for what is already working at the community level. We honor and uplift traditional, Indigenous, and local knowledge and practices. (Costanza-Chock 2020, 6–7)

Design justice, anchored in intersectional and anti-oppression perspectives, fosters social empathy by centring those who are most often excluded from decision-making processes. As an institutional affective practice, it would provide fora for expressing and acknowledging individual and collective emotions that can then be addressed institutionally. Such an approach would shift the politics of intimacy away from individuals to the collective. At the same time, however, we must be careful to not simply offload the work of transforming the academy onto marginalized faculty. Thus, while we must rethink university governance, we must also do so with Rita Kaur Dhamoon's (2020) recommendations for recognition and remuneration (see also Tungohan, this volume, for suggestions).

In closing, we don't have to be assholes. As we think about what feminist praxis within the academy means, I suggest that we use the politics of intimacy as a lens to understand the ways in which emotional discourses differentially position folks therein. To embed the care work that many of us are already doing in institutional affective practice, I suggest, requires social empathy as a policy orientation, and design justice as a framework for institutional change.

Notes

1. The term *institutionalized affective practice* builds on both Durnová and Wetherell. Durnová's work emphasizes the institutionalization (and "normalization") of practices. For Durnová, institutionalized practices describe "how meanings become consolidated in a practice through actors' entitlements or through rejections of [state] entitlements" (2018, 11). In contrast, Margaret Wetherell's (2012) work on "affective practice" focuses more clearly on "emoting and the performance and modification of affect" (Wetherell, McConville, and McCreanor 2020, 15). Wetherell defines affective practice as "a figuration where body possibilities and routines become recruited or entangled together with meaning making and with other social and material figurations" (2012, 19), which are "bound up with established power regimes and conditions of possibility set by social relations more broadly" (Wetherell, McConville, and McCreanor 2020, 15). Thus, both concepts complement each other and, combined, emphasize both institutionalization and emotion.
2. The events described in this vignette are not specific to one person or event, but rather a composite of several such meetings over the span of my career.

References

Ahmed, Sara. 2013. *The Cultural Politics of Emotion*. New York: Routledge.

Ahmed, Sara. 2019. "Why Complain?" *feministkilljoys*, July 22, 2019. https://feministkilljoys.com/2019/07/22/why-complain/.

Branch, Kathryn A., Rebecca Hayes-Smith, and Tara N. Richards. 2011. "Professors' Experiences with Student Disclosures of Sexual Assault and Intimate Partner Violence: How 'Helping' Students Can Inform Teaching Practices." *Feminist Criminology* 6 (1): 54–75. https://doi.org/10.1177/1557085110397040.

Chan, Adrienne S., Rita Kaur Dhamoon, and Lisa Moy. 2014. "Metaphoric Representations of Women of Colour in the Academy: Teaching Race, Disrupting Power." *Borderlands* 13 (2): 1–26.

Chang, Mitchell J. 2002. "Preservation or Transformation: Where's the Real Educational Discourse on Diversity?" *Review of Higher Education* 25 (2): 125–40. https://10.1353/rhe.2002.0003.

Clarke, Amanda, and Jonathan Craft. 2018. "The Twin Faces of Public Sector Design." *Governance* 32 (1): 5–21. https://doi.org/10.1111/gove.12342.

Collins, Patricia Hill. 2000. *Black Feminist Thought: Knowledge, Consciousness, and the Politics of Empowerment*, 2nd ed. New York: Routledge.

Costanza-Chock, Sasha. 2020. *Design Justice: Community-Led Practices to Build the Worlds We Need*. Cambridge, MA: MIT Press.

Dhamoon, Rita Kaur. 2020. "Racism as a Workload and Bargaining Issue." *Socialist Studies* 14 (1). https://doi.org/10.18740/ss27273.

Dubois, Vincent. 2010. *The Bureaucrat and the Poor: Encounters in French Welfare Offices*. New York: Routledge.

Durnová, Anna. 2013. "Governing through Intimacy: Explaining Care Policies through 'Sharing a Meaning.'" *Critical Social Policy* 33 (3): 494–513. https://doi.org/10.1177/0261018312468305.

Durnová, Anna. 2018. *The Politics of Intimacy: Rethinking the End-of-Life Controversy*. Ann Arbor: University of Michigan Press.

Gaudry, Adam, and Danielle Lorenz. 2018. "Indigenization as Inclusion, Reconciliation, and Decolonization: Navigating the Different Visions for Indigenizing the Canadian Academy. *AlterNative: An International Journal of Indigenous Peoples* 14 (3): 218–27. https://doi.org/10.1177/1177180118785382.

Gerdes, Karen, Elizabeth Segal, Kelly Jackson, and Jennifer Mullins. 2011. "Teaching Empathy: A Framework Rooted in Social Cognitive Neuroscience and Social Justice." *Journal of Social Work Education* 47 (1): 109–31. https://doi.org/10.5175/JSWE.2011.200900085.

Harding, Jennifer, and E. Deidre Pribram. 2002. "The Power of Feeling: Locating Emotions in Culture." *European Journal of Cultural Studies* 5 (4): 407–26. https://doi.org/10.1177/1364942002005004294.

Hayes-Smith, Rebecca, Tara N. Richards, and Kathryn A. Branch. 2010. "'But I'm Not a Counsellor': The Nature of Role Strain Experienced by Female Professors When a Student Discloses Sexual Assault and Intimate Partner Violence." *Enhancing Learning in the Social Sciences* 2 (3): 1–24. https://doi.org/10.11120/elss.2010.02030006.

Hemmings, Clare. 2012. "Affective Solidarity: Feminist Reflexivity and Political Transformation." *Feminist Theory* 13 (2): 141–61. https://doi.org/10.1177/1464700112442643.

Henry, Frances, Enakshi Dua, Carl E. James, Audrey Kobayashi, Peter Li, Howard Ramos, and Malinda Smith. 2017. *The Equity Myth: Racialization and Indigeneity at Canadian Universities*. Vancouver: UBC Press.

Jones, Charlotte, Anne Chappell, and Pam Alldred. 2021. "Feminist Education for University Staff Responding to Disclosures of Sexual Violence: A Critique of the Dominant Model of Staff Development." *Gender and Education* 33 (2): 121–37. https://doi.org/10.1080/09540253.2019.1649639.

Klein, Kate. 2011. "On Learning How *Not* to Be an Asshole Academic Feminist." In *Feminism for Real: Deconstructing the Academic Industrial Complex of Feminism*, edited by Jessica Yee, 171–76. Ottawa: Canadian Centre for Policy Alternatives.

Larios, Lindsay, and Stephanie Paterson. 2021. "Fear of the Other: Vulnerabilization, Social Empathy, and the COVID-19 Pandemic in Canada." *Critical Policy Studies* 15 (2): 137–45. https://doi.org/10.1080/19460171.2021.1927777.

Lipsky, Michael. 2010. *Street-Level Bureaucracy, 30th Anniversary Edition: Dilemmas of the Individual in the Public Service*. New York: Russell Sage Foundation.

Luther, Rashmi, Elizabeth Whitmore, and Bernice Mary Moreau, eds. 2003. *Seen But Not Heard: Aboriginal Women and Women of Colour in the Academy*. Ottawa: Canadian Research Institute for the Advancement of Women.

Mahtani, Minelle. 2004. "Mapping Race and Gender in the Academy: The Experiences of Women of Colour Faculty and Graduate Students in Britain, the US and Canada." *Journal of Geography in Higher Education* 28 (1): 91–99.

Monture, Patricia. 2010. "Race, Gender and the University: Strategies for Survival." In *States of Race: Critical Race Feminism for the 21st Century*, edited by Sherene Razack, Malinda Smith, and Sunera Thobani, 23-36. Toronto: Between the Lines Press.

Orsini, Michael, and Stephen Wiebe. 2014. "Between Hope and Fear: Comparing the Emotional Landscapes of the Autism Movement in Canada and the United States." In *Comparing Canada: Methods and Perspectives on Canadian Politics*, edited by Luc Turgeon, Martin Papillon, Jennifer Wallner, and Stephen White, 147-67. Vancouver: UBC Press.

Paterson, Stephanie, and Lindsay Larios. 2020. "Emotional Problems: Policymaking and Empathy through the Lens of Transnational Motherhood." *Critical Policy Studies* 15 (3): 273-91. https://doi.org/10.1080/19460171.2020.1752760.

Ravecca, Paulo. 2019. *The Politics of Political Science: Re-Writing Latin American Experiences*. New York: Routledge.

Salvino, Caitlin, Kelsey Gilchrist, and Jade Cooligan-Pang. 2017. *Our Turn: A National, Student-Led Action Plan to End Campus Sexual Violence*. Montreal, QC: Student Society of McGill University.

Segal, Elizabeth. 2007a. "Social Empathy: A New Paradigm to Address Poverty." *Journal of Poverty* 1 (3): 65-81. https://doi.org/10.1300/J134v11n03_06.

Segal, Elizabeth. 2007b. "Social Empathy: A Tool to Address the Contradictions of Working But Still Poor." *Families in Society: The Journal of Contemporary Social Services* 88 (3): 333-37. https://doi.org/10.1606/1044-3894.3642.

Segal, Elizabeth. 2018. *Social Empathy: The Art of Understanding Others*. New York: Columbia University Press.

Smith, Malinda. 2010. "Gender, Whiteness, and 'Other Others' in the Academy." In *States of Race: Critical Race Feminism for the 21st Century*, edited by Sherene Razack, Sunera Thobani, and Malinda Smith, 37-58. Toronto: Between the Lines Press.

Spade, Dean. 2015. *Normal Life: Administrative Violence, Critical Trans Politics, and the Limits of Law*. Durham, NC: Duke University Press.

Thompson, Debra. 2017. "An Exoneration of Black Rage." *South Atlantic Quarterly* 113 (3): 457-81. https://doi.org/10.1215/00382876-3961439.

Wetherell, Margaret. 2012. *Affect and Emotion: A New Social Science Understanding*. Thousand Oaks, CA: Sage Publications.

Wetherell, Margaret, Alex McConville, and Tim McCreanor. 2020. "Defrosting the Freezer and Other Acts of Quiet Resistance: Affective Practice Theory, Everyday Activism and Affective Dilemmas." *Qualitative Research in Psychology* 17 (1): 13-35. https://doi.org/10.1080/14780887.2019.1581310.

Yee, Jessica, ed. 2011. *Feminism for Real: Deconstructing the Academic Industrial Complex of Feminism*. Ottawa: Canadian Centre for Policy Alternatives.

FEMINISTING AND THE "REAL" WORLD OF POLITICS

11 Letters of Engagement

Learning from Our Efforts at Feministing Public Policy Deliberations

JULIANNE M. ACKER-VERNEY, ALANA CATTAPAN, ALEXANDRA DOBROWOLSKY, TAMMY FINDLAY, and APRIL MANDRONA

SOME FUNDAMENTAL CHALLENGES of feministing in political science include that it requires rethinking what constitutes labour in the discipline, legitimate sites of research, and methodologies considered "rigorous" to the exclusion of others. Over the last four years, we have been working on a research project that used the occasion of the fiftieth anniversary of the Royal Commission on the Status of Women to reflect on how far public policy for women has come, and how far it still has to go.[1] As the Halifax-based arm of the project—called Changing Public Engagement from the Ground Up—we collaborated with specific, underrepresented communities to pilot a series of four engagement "exercises." The Halifax team has been comprised of professors at various stages in their careers, as well as a number of students who have come and gone over the course of the project.[2]

Our aim was to generate insights into how groups of women and girls often left out of policymaking engage in the policy process (or would like to engage), and why some resist public policy efforts altogether.[3] The four exercises were (1) a sharing circle with Indigenous women and Indigenous people who are gender diverse; (2) an interactive simulation with girls and young women; (3) a first-voice panel organized and led by women with disabilities and Deaf women; and (4) two podcast episodes on rural women's issues.[4]

As the project comes to a close, we reflect on our experiences. We write here as four faculty members and one graduate student/research assistant/community activist who have been working on this project throughout. In many ways this project on "ground up" public engagement has also been a project about how to do feminist research from the ground up while working within and against the constraints of universities, budgets, timelines, and disciplines to think about what responsive, ethical, feminist work on public engagement looks like. This chapter contributes to feministing in several ways. Most importantly, it engages in feministing through openly sharing and candidly reflecting on our attempts at generating more meaningful and inclusive public engagement from the ground up for a range of groups. Moreover, it looks at the iterative and affective process of research, not only taking into consideration what occurred for research participants, but also for our research team, those who have supported us, as well as our broader scholarly communities. We engage in feministing through the highly collaborative, dialogic, and self-reflective process involved in drafting the series of letters that make up this chapter. The use of letters references feminist herstories of both exclusion and inclusion.

Feministing Knowledge Production and Mobilization in the Discipline of Political Science

Here we aim to contest conventional forms of knowledge dissemination in political science, which have historically relied on one or a few authors describing a project, beginning with a question asked, and then ending with a question answered. In this work we have focused less on conclusions and more on process, asking what we are able to understand about our experiences by engaging collaboratively and collectively (Karach and Roach 1992). We began the work for this chapter with two conversations that enabled us to discuss the project from our own social location and positions on the research team, listen with intention, reflect, and then engage in collaborative, generative meaning-making. By actively listening,[5] and assessing the project, and one another's experiences, together, we recognize the nature of our own understandings, at once necessarily subjective and partial.

There are some precedents for conversation as academic writing, with interviews and roundtables enabling a dialogue of a sort. However, those publications that tend to be prized (and published) are those where well-known scholars provide their wisdom to their audiences, typically through an interviewer or interlocutor who brings the sage to the masses (see, e.g., Monroe et al. 1990; Rorty, Nystrom, and Puckett 2002; Waltz and Fearon 2012). In our conversations, no one led the interview; rather, we co-created a list of questions that encompassed the research project's objectives, methods, contributors, participants, outcomes, and repercussions in ways that aimed to spark substantive reflection. After two weeks to gather our thoughts, we collectively shared our responses in two, in-depth conversations that, combined, lasted approximately four and a half hours. These semi-structured meetings took place via two recorded Zoom sessions, scheduled a week apart, which in turn allowed us to clarify and reconsider some of our initial comments.

After the conversations, we drafted letters from the transcripts,[6] writing to four audiences intrinsic to this work. The choice of using letters to convey our ideas was one thoughtfully made and speaks to the historically gendered nature of the epistolary form. Letter writing has long been considered a "ladylike hobby" through which social ties might be maintained within the confines of one's home, while enabling letter writers to capture the nature of their experiences (Luu 2019). Letters are themselves dialogical in that they are part of a real (or imagined) exchange, directed as a subject that will, or at least may, respond. Letters are also perspectival, as Nisha Nath (2020) describes, in that they mark a particular time in space but recognize others—written at one time, read another. Correspondence can be a site of advocacy as well, and one that tells us something about how labour circulates—what is counted as work and what is merely seen as informal exchange.

Letters can also be a site in which care, gratitude, and affection are articulated. For example, the love letter is a vulnerable, self-reflexive form of writing that is intimate, thoughtful, and labour(ed). Moreover, O'Malley and colleagues hope that "methodologies of radical love might allow us to cultivate prophetic visionings for the promise of our fields...Further, it might allow us to find ways to shatter the idols of standardization and testing, of 'scientific' research and 'best practices'" (2018, 580). We position these letters as a way of explicitly dismantling divisions that prevent relationship building and mutual care in research. We offer letter writing, in this context, as a form of feministing. We intend to challenge where lines get drawn between public and private, evoking the classic feminist contribution of how the "personal is political."

Our commitments to self-reflection, advocacy, and care as feminist researchers made letters an ideal way to convey our thoughts and thus, the chapter proceeds with letters to four core constituencies: project participants/community members; feminist researchers; students who worked on the project; and our future selves. These are letters full of gratitude, care, articulations of our self-perceived failings, and critical, probing questions about what might have been. They are also letters serving as sites of solidarity, inviting people into academic spaces (and challenging the lines between academic and community work), while thinking through our accountability to the communities with whom we work, and to one another, as we look to the future.

Dear Research Participants,
Thank you. Thank you for participating in the research that we have been collaborating on over the past few years. You include women with disabilities and Deaf women, women living in rural areas, young women and girls, and Indigenous women and Indigenous people who are gender diverse. Your participation has led us through a research process in which we have been able to hear your stories and communicate the findings about engagement in public policy. We hear your voices even as we wind down this project and carry this experience with you into the rest of our projects, careers, and lives.

Thank you too for allowing us into your community spaces, whether that was by teleconference, within the walls of a meeting room, living room, or on a university campus. We are grateful for the resources and knowledge you shared. We see the openness with which you approached this work, and we are thankful for your generosity.

We thank you also for allowing us to bear witness to your experiences. We have shared the results of the project in our writing, and we have used these publications to raise the profile of girls and women in academic and community-focused publications (Cattapan, Acker-Verney, et al. 2020; Cattapan, Dobrowlosky, et al. 2020; Dobrowolsky, Findlay, et. al., 2022). We have also given presentations at conferences, in classrooms, and at community-led events, specifically to share what we have learned from the time we have spent with you. We respectfully share these learnings and experiences through our conversations with students, peers, and other colleagues. We are keenly aware that we also benefit from publications and presentations, to varying degrees, as individual women scholars, but we are motivated by our desire to share information that will positively affect your communities now and in the future.

As we thank you, we must also acknowledge the shortcomings and the context of this work. We acknowledge the legacy of harm done to members of historically marginalized communities in the name of research, well-meaning or otherwise, historic and recent. We have learned from you that participating in present-day research takes place in the long shadows cast by deeply rooted systems of wrongdoing, injustice, and injury. Research spaces are not always safe spaces. We have also heard, and taken to heart, the disappointment and frustration some of you have expressed while participating in the research-related activities we have led. You have, at times, called us out on the privilege and power we hold as white, settler women. We write this to you to be accountable, to learn from our mistakes, and encourage others to learn from them as well. We recognize that this letter is only one small measure of accountability, and we need to do more.

We aimed to engage in research that was reflexive, embraced reciprocity, and engaged with you in the ways that you preferred, advocating for the changes you want for your lives and your communities. And although we were not always successful, we hope that you came to think of yourself and your experiences as important to the work, and that you had space and capacity to ask questions, and to be heard. Thank you again for working with us and for sharing how you build community, how you challenge exclusion, and how you make change.

Dear Feminist Scholars and Researchers,
This letter is difficult to write because it is a letter and not a book. Our discussions about what we owe to one another and to participants and students have implications that reach well beyond this chapter. This is a difficult letter to write as well because we have many more questions than answers. The big question is, How do we do right by participants, by their communities, by our students, by one another? How do we embrace intersectionality in our methods and writing? How do we convey our findings in the ways we promised to ethics boards and universities and granting agencies while being true to the work and creating something of value for participants? Fittingly, the working title for this chapter was "1,000 Questions."

This project began from a commitment to addressing what we knew to be an exclusion in, and the perpetuation of harm through, policymaking processes in Nova Scotia. We knew, and still know, that women with disabilities and Deaf women, Indigenous women and Indigenous people who are gender diverse, women living in rural communities, and young women and girls are often left outside of policymaking, including policy consultations, in areas that might affect them. We set out wondering how to use our capacity and resources to address these exclusions, to give women and girls the opportunity to engage in policymaking in their own ways, on their own terms. We care about the communities we live in and alongside. We came by this research with a view to reallocate resources and support the work of others. Indeed, the project allowed us to direct resources to the sharing circle, a space of reflection sought by participants in the Walking with Our Sisters Memorial, and to a self-organized panel by women with disabilities and Deaf women.

Collaboration with participants and community members in setting up the various engagement exercises confirmed some of what we already knew—namely, that conducting ambitious feminist research is exceedingly difficult. And it is exceedingly difficult because the strictures of academic institutions require timelines, budgets, and publications that do not always match the more flexible approach needed for responsive, community-oriented work.

We wanted to work with communities that have historically been seen as difficult to reach, or who have been ignored by those engaging in policy consultations and research, without putting an undue burden on those communities to participate in this work. As a group of white, settler academics, we too found some of these communities difficult to recruit, to find for collaboration, and relied on allies and colleagues with closer ties. In the case of the sharing circle with Indigenous women, we relied heavily on one Indigenous colleague to organize the event and bring people together. In some cases, students and members of the research team were able to bridge these gaps by drawing from their own communities, but we wanted to engage people on their own terms without yet knowing how to meet them in their own spaces.

We also wanted to co-develop the project and its questions in conversation with the constituencies with which we were planning to work. Navigating the research ethics process at several different academic institutions required us to make choices as to the order of things and the nature of the work that we were hoping to collaborate on over time. This is partly a problem of our own making, as we should have planned differently, but the timelines for an alternative project of this kind may not have accommodated a different approach.

As we wrote up the results of this work, we also found ourselves questioning how to best reflect the diversity of participants' experiences and not to reduce them to the social identity on which the engagement exercise was focused (i.e., women with disabilities and Deaf women, Indigenous women and Indigenous people who are gender diverse, women living in rural areas, girls and young women). We were committed to engaging in feminist intersectionality in this project, but our focus on four groups underrepresented in the policy process meant that we necessarily emphasized certain aspects of identity, while minimizing others (Levac and Denis 2019). We did not create much space in the engagement exercises that would have allowed people more nuanced articulations of their lives. Public health restrictions related to COVID-19 kept us from bringing participants together, at the end of the project, to engage in discussions about the nature and consequences of their exclusions from policymaking processes.

A critical part of feminist research is reflexivity and while this project has been challenging, now we consider greater challenges based on the many (1,000?) questions that inspire this work: How we might have engaged differently, and better, and what else there is to do? How can we continue the collaborations that we have started, and how can we do right by participants? Here, in these reflections, we continue to do the difficult work of articulating our self-perceived successes and shortcomings, and then returning to do it again.

As part of this iterative process, we must call upon one another to recognize our responsibilities to the individuals and communities with whom we work. This means recognizing our own power and the very real, felt, and lived implications of these positionings for ourselves and others, as well as our capacity to make positive change. It takes labour to reject the neutrality of structures that claim otherwise. This requires considering what it means and looks like: to hold each other accountable; to find the small openings in policy, procedure, and bureaucracy and to make the openings bigger so that others may find them; to recognize how these spaces are unsafe; and to create a sense of urgency where unresponsive systems suggest none exists.

Feministing in political science also requires the rejection of "feminism" that still has a stronghold in many areas of academia—the kind that, on one hand, has enabled feminist academics to resist and repair the harm perpetrated by the patriarchal academy (e.g., unrecognized labour, lack of representation, lack of child care, pay inequity), but on the other hand has often worked to disproportionately benefit cisgender, white, settler women. It is our responsibility to continue to push against the visible and invisible barriers so that others may be seen and heard. In the context of our professional roles this means constantly evaluating how we do research on policy engagement on the ground, and calling out institutional processes that cause harm, whether that is student financial policy or policies which dictate how communities are engaged by universities.

Dear Students,

We are writing to you at the end of this project to which you have provided so much: your time, skills, expertise, creativity, curiosity, patience, enthusiasm, and reflexivity. We write with tremendous appreciation for all you have given. In thinking about the multiple ways that you made this work possible, we are wondering if we did enough for you, and with you, and if we were able to teach and collaborate with you in ways that reflect the feministing of the discipline. In other words, we wonder if we were able to embody a feminist ethos, to move feminist research from noun to verb.

We want you to know that we are incredibly grateful for who you are and what you brought to the project. The intergenerational aspect of this project in particular taught us a lot. At the level of the pan-Canadian team, we range from young students to people in their eighties; we are women working together across decades. Locally, you were students from two different universities, from different disciplines, backgrounds, and social locations, and with different levels of research and community-based experience. Some of you identified as women, others as men, and others as nonbinary. Some identified as queer. Some identified as living with disability. Some identified as settlers, some as racialized, and some as Indigenous. We were really fortunate to have had a circle of mentorship where roles could be contested and reshaped. The experiences of mentorship felt multidirectional and collaborative.

You mentored each other, developing your own dynamics and taking on supervisory roles among your peers. Much of our work together was "mentorship in action," which happened accidentally, as you witnessed us navigating publishing and peer review, or university ethics procedures, or designing research by trial and error. You learned about academia by watching us maneuver through bureaucracies and obstacles and helping us through them.

As university professors and/or scholars, we must acknowledge that we work in institutions, and under granting rules, where we have little control over crucial elements of your working conditions, such as compensation and pay scales. We have tried to compensate you fairly, respect your time and energies, and ensure that you benefit from our work together. We also recognize that we have benefitted enormously from your underpaid labour. We've been thinking a lot about your hard work and wondering how we can do feminist work that does not replicate the kinds of unfair and inequitable labour practices that support it.

There are other challenges in our relationship too. You held dual roles as employees and students, often working for, and taking classes with us, at the same time. This must have been difficult to navigate as you tried to juggle and prioritize multiple demands from us at different times in the project, and you did remarkably well with it. And even though you were juggling all of this at once, you did an extraordinary breadth of work. Some of this work is more visible, and easier to measure than others. It is plain to see all the outreach work you did, the collaborations you engaged in, the networks you forged, the events you organized, and the writing you did. But we cannot calculate the emotional labour or grasp all the time that you were spending thinking about this project outside of your paid working hours, or account for the stresses you were encountering alongside us. In a community-based project like this, the lines between researcher and participant are often blurred, and for those of you from marginalized groups (both historically and presently), your personal experiences sometimes became integral to the engagement exercises. Again, we benefitted from who you are and the work you did, in ways that we are only beginning to find words to describe.

We also know that there are complex questions of authorship and ownership at play. You contributed to work that will inform publications long after you've finished your work on the project. We want to give you due credit for your contributions, and you have a right to consent to any publications with your name on them. At the same time, asking you to review drafts and make revisions is not fair when you are no longer an employed member of the team.

One of the things we keep coming back to is the tension between, on the one hand, our shared commitment to self-reflection and critique as fundamental to intersectional praxis, and on the other hand, the importance for you, as researchers in training, to recognize and articulate your own strengths and accomplishments. We want to critique our work without undermining your exceptional contributions to the project. As we aim the critical lens at ourselves, you should be proud of what you led, organized, designed, and produced.

Your contributions were even more impressive given that most of you were undergraduate students. Our aim was to provide all of you—graduate or undergraduate—with meaningful opportunities so you could rise to the challenge. Co-authoring papers, travelling to conduct research, and presenting at conferences are not typically the purview of undergraduate students, and given that these skills require you to "put yourself out there," we wonder if we asked too much of you.

As we reflect on your work and our gratitude for it, we have also considered how this work together has led you to understand norms of "behaving correctly" in the discipline, and about our potential complicity in the "disciplining" of students through publishing and conference presentations. We hope that our work together was not only about the research but also about pushing the boundaries of what counts as political science and policy research, while emboldening you to do that with us. Yet we fear there were times when efforts to break the parameters of our fields were overshadowed by the harsher realities of academia, where paternalism can masquerade as mentorship, and competition reigns over collegiality. How much should we have tried to protect you from this ugly side of academia? How much of the unvarnished experience should we expose you to, and how much space should we allow for you to respond on your own? Is it the job of faculty members to prepare students for the "real world"? And what is this "real world"? From a feminist perspective, isn't this exactly what we're trying to change?

We also need to start asking more about what students want out of the work. What is your goal for this work? Do you want a publication? Do you want to improve your writing? What will make you happy and fulfilled? We can employ different students with different kinds of goals and tailor that work to meet your goals and check in constantly to revisit and revise when necessary. We can emphasize that "success" has many definitions, and that there are multiple pathways you can take if you want to continue working in research, both academic and in community, without promoting one over the other.

We recognize the work you've done and continue to do to make us better scholars, better mentors, and better colleagues. Our discipline and our universities need to recognize that nurturing and caregiving of students like you—who not only engage in feminist research but engage in the feministing of research—are vital to our work.

Dear Future Selves,
Dear Julianne, Alana, Alexandra, Tammy, and April,

This project began as we thought about how to bring people together to contest conventional approaches to public engagement in policymaking and to find ways to bring in people who are often underrepresented in those processes. And as we concluded, we came together to talk about the work, reflect on how we distributed our labour among us and about the mental, emotional, and intellectual energy we each invest so we can feel good about what we've done and so we can do better next time.

The project did a lot. We carried out four engagement exercises with four different groups of women, interrogating in both process and form how public engagement occurs, who initiates relevant conversations, and in a broader sense, how those left out of policymaking are heard. We know, and have talked about, how as the people conducting this research, we had to initiate the conversations and seek out relevant groups—based on our knowledge, and our preconceptions—making us question what ground-up policymaking looks like. Do ideas in and around public engagement truly come from community if we are prompting their generation? To what extent is it useful for the relevant communities to be heard by us for this work? In what ways might we be benefitting our participants and, at the same time, doing harm?

As we carried out the project and wrote reflexively about our experiences, thinking about the lessons we learned, our unanswered questions, and our continued goal to do good work that makes a difference in the lives of people who are part of historically marginalized groups, we tried to be responsive, listen to participants, and engage openly however we could. We supported students, however imperfectly, and found ways to facilitate new opportunities for them while being conscientious of the other demands of their lives. We approached publication with a range of audiences in mind—writing for those amenable to our work and those who might be more resistant, in addition to communicating our findings in more accessible ways to communities that may use them. We wrote and published in ways that worked, we hope, to honour those who participated in our research, and in support of future engagement practices that reflect their involvement, concerns, and needs. We checked and double-checked our processes and decisions around acknowledging participant involvement and were thoughtful about authorship. We worked with kindness and open-hearted honesty. We should be proud, and we are proud, of how we collaborated and the care we showed to one another.

The project was good in other ways too. We wanted to raise the profile and amplify the voices of women with disabilities and Deaf women, young women and girls, rural women, and Indigenous women. It is safe to say that in some ways, we did. We learned—and shared—the ways that the people who participated in the project think about public policy and their ability to influence its development. They shared stories to illustrate how public policies empower or constrain their lives and communities. The sharing of those stories was a gift, and we have been honoured to receive them, and to bring them to others. Some of those stories and their telling involved feelings of distrust and anger at the wrongs perpetrated in the name of "progressive policy," and though we were caught off guard by that anger, our ignorance an indication of our white settler privilege, those stories too were a gift, and will help us see better, hear better, and speak better as we move forward with our work.

The work we did together was meaningful, challenging, and a site of learning for all. We cannot capture it all here—the ways our voices and experiences were written into and out of drafts and the conversational, supportive, and productive nature of our exchanges in their many forms. We cannot capture the way that this conversation is made visible and audible in "track changes" or in the options of computerized screen readers to hear pitch changes for revisions, deletions, and so on. We cannot replicate how the process of engaging one another through the writing helped us to learn about one another's experiences of this project. There is risk and vulnerability in this kind of self-reflexive work. By thinking about research and our collaboration in this way, we open ourselves to criticism, and we may be giving critics words to hurl back. But with all of us together in this work, it does not feel risky—it feels powerful. There is collective power in knowing how to be better, how to be stronger, how to be more thoughtful in our engagements.

Conclusion

In writing a series of letters speaking to the lessons we learned from an engaging (on many levels) research project, we have attempted to interrogate our professional and personal identities, as well as political understandings of what we do, who we are, how we perceive ourselves, and how others perceive us. These letters engage even more deeply (individually, collectively, and in concert with our professional, political, and personal selves), serving to pinpoint and evaluate the nature and extent of our contributions as well as our fundamental limitations. We are a well-intentioned group, and so, we *hoped* to be, and *worked on* being, progressive and inclusive, as well as thoughtful, kind, and generous, in our research, and with each other.

At the same time, this is also a sharply, critical group. We did not hold back in identifying when and how our research project and team showed ignorance, avoidance, or a lack of awareness and how these interactions typically epitomized the various powers we wield and privileges we hold. These letters identify how we feel we missed the mark. We also want to acknowledge that there inevitably have been things left unsaid, as well as realizations and comprehensions that have been lost, may only be revealed later, or may be left unrealized. Our fear is that our reflections here on the "work" of feministing comes across as belaboured, self-indulgent, or self-satisfied. Our hope is that it contains some valuable reflections and serious, substantive contributions.

This chapter, like other chapters in this volume, is an attempt to shed light on our disciplinary boundaries, on both the promise and pitfalls of academic research, how we continue to be shaped and affected by them, as well as how we are working not just to broaden our respective fields but break through and break down the restrictions. We began this work with many questions, and we have perhaps ended with even more. We are still asking ourselves how to enact feministing in political science (and across other disciplines).

What this project and our reflections on it have taught us is that this kind of work requires more learning and unlearning. It also requires courage and creativity on the part of researchers to, for example, develop modes of amplifying voices and mechanisms for intentional listening, or to take the time to genuinely develop the relationships that lead to meaningful collaboration. It also requires engaging in care work, and creating time and space for self-reflection, which all may involve professional, political, and personal risk. This is not easy work. Feministing in our experience means not only thinking but acting. Feministing in political science might mean an ongoing practice of continuing to identify and name what was wrong with what we did before, and specify how we can, and intentionally try, to do better the next time.

Notes

1. The broader research project, funded through a Social Science and Humanities Research Council of Canada Partnership Development Grant, is titled Engendering Public Engagement, Democratizing Public Space, and is led by Barbara Cameron at York University. See Policy4Women, https://policy4women.com/rcsw50/.
2. Research assistants on this project have included Julianne M. Acker-Verney, Sophie Boileau, Jewelle Carroll, Michael Fong, Veronica Gore, Katheryn Lewis, Jennifer O'Keefe, Megan Nichole Poole, Kenya Thompson, Meva Learmond, Emily Truesdale, and Keisha Wilmot.
3. The project explicitly focused on the experiences of self-identified women and girls, although at least one of the exercises included people who are gender diverse as well. Here, we move between relevant terms, trying to capture both the focus on the marginalization of groups of women and girls in public policymaking, while addressing the experiences of participants.
4. The podcasts, created by Jennifer O'Keefe, and supported by the project team, focus on the work of the Antigonish Women's Resource Centre (Antigonish, Nova Scotia) and the Second Story Women's Centre (Lunenburg, Nova Scotia), examining the challenges of funding, community organizing, and barriers to women's participation in public life in rural Nova Scotia.
5. We learned a lot about listening from our sharing circle, led by Mi'kmaw filmmaker and educator Catherine Martin. She began the circle by encouraging us to listen deeply without thinking about our own response in advance.
6. Transcripts were created following the two meetings by research assistant Megan Nichole Poole.

References

Cattapan, Alana, Julianne M. Acker-Verney, Alexandra Dobrowolsky, Tammy Findlay, and April Mandrona. 2020. "Community Engagement in a Time of Confinement." *Canadian Public Policy* 46 (S3): S287–99. https://doi.org/10.3138/cpp.2020-064.

Cattapan, Alana, Alexandra Dobrowolsky, Tammy Findlay, and April Mandrona. 2020. "Power, Privilege, and Policy Making: Reflections on 'Changing Public Engagement from the Ground Up.'" In *Creating Spaces of Engagement*, edited by Leah R.E. Levac and Sarah Marie Wiebe, 226–52. Toronto: University of Toronto Press.

Dobrowolsky, Alexandra, Tammy Findlay, Julianne M. Acker-Verney, Alana Cattapan, Jennifer O'Keefe, April Mandrona, and Jewelle Carroll. 2022. "Reimagining Policy Spaces: Toward Accessible and Inclusive Public Engagement." *Canadian Review of Social Policy* 82: 83–105.

Karach, Angela, and Denise Roach. 1992. "Collaborative Writing, Consciousness Raising, and Practical Feminist Ethics." *Women's Studies International Forum* 15 (2): 303–08. https://doi.org/10.1016/0277-5395(92)90108-8.

Levac, Leah, and Ann B. Denis. 2019. "Combining Feminist Intersectional and Community-Engaged Research Commitments: Adaptations for Scoping Reviews and Secondary Analyses of National Data Sets." *Gateways: International Journal of Community Research and Engagement* 12 (1). https://doi.org/10.5130/ijcre.v12i1.6193.

Luu, Chi. 2019. "The Ladylike Language of Letters." *JSTOR Daily: Lingua Obscura*, January 10, 2019. https://daily.jstor.org/the-ladylike-language-of-letters/.

Monroe, Kristen, Gabriel Almond, John Gunnell, Ian Shapiro, George Graham, Benjamin Barber, Kenneth Shepsle, and Joseph Cropsey. 1990. "The Nature of Contemporary Political Science: A Roundtable Discussion." *PS: Political Science & Politics* 23 (1): 34–43. https://doi.org/10.2307/419775.

Nath, Nisha. 2020. "'The Letters': EDI and Tracing Work in the Academe." Support Network for Academics of Colour Plus, Alberta Human Rights Commission Education, and Multiculturalism Fund in collaboration with the Women Scholars' Speakers Series, University of Lethbridge. November 5, 2020, Lethbridge, AB.

O'Keefe, Jennifer, host. n.d. *Changing Public Engagement from the Ground Up*. Podcast. Accessed September 28, 2023. https://www.changingpublicengagement.com/.

O'Malley, Michael P., Nina Asher, Brandon L. Beck, Colleen A. Capper, Catherine A. Lugg, Jason P. Murphy, and Reta Ugena Whitlock. 2018. "Asking Queer(er) Questions: Epistemological and Methodological Implications for Qualitative Inquirers." *International Journal of Qualitative Studies in Education* 31 (7): 572–94. https://doi.org/10.1080/09518398.2018.1455996.

Rorty, Richard, Derek Nystrom, and Kent Puckett. 2002. *Against Bosses, Against Oligarchies: A Conversation with Richard Rorty*. Chicago: Prickly Paradigm Press. https://core.ac.uk/download/pdf/5015698.pdf.

Waltz, Kenneth, and James Fearon. 2012. "A Conversation with Kenneth Waltz." *Annual Review of Political Science* 15 (1): 1–12. https://doi.org/10.1146/annurev-polisci-020511-174136.

12 Feministing

Lessons from Bill C-237, the Candidate Gender Equity Act

JEANETTE ASHE

PARTISAN FINGERPRINTS are all over Bill C-237's demise. Bill C-237—An Act to Amend the Canada Elections Act (Gender Equity)—was a private member's bill put forward by a New Democratic Party (NDP) Opposition member of Parliament (MP) designed to address the political underrepresentation of women and other equity-deserving groups in Canada's House of Commons.[1] Though private members' bills forwarded by opposition MPs rarely pass, a backbench revolt saw 23 of 184 Liberal government MPs vote in the affirmative for Bill C-237, forcing Prime Minister Justin Trudeau to kill the bill on the one-year anniversary of the election in which he positioned himself as a feminist.

I tell the story of Bill C-237 by drawing upon the autoethnographic approach to better understand feministing in political science and explore how feminist political scientists (FPS) dedicate themselves to making parliaments and other institutions more gender and diversity sensitive.[2] I recount how I worked with feminist scholars, MPs, parliamentary staff, women's and LGBTQ+ committees, and activists to draft and champion Bill C-237. My account relies on a series of semi-structured interviews with the bill's sponsor, my husband and former NDP MP Kennedy Stewart, as well as data from my calendar, emails, notes, Hansard, and media.

I begin by outlining the problem of women's descriptive political underrepresentation and providing background information on Bill C-237. I then move to tracing the bill from its conception to rejection, highlighting the arguments thwarting the effort and the counterarguments supporting it. I conclude by offering reflections on my experience of feministing and discussing recent developments to increase women's and other groups' representation. Telling stories of big political wins may be more popular but imagining C-237 as a feminist act toward advancing gender transformation reminds us that political losses can also reveal valuable lessons prompting future success.

Using Autoethnography to Explore Feministing

Feministing is feminist political science in action. FPS are necessarily both scholars *and* activists "because they are feminists" seeking to "influence the real world of politics" (Campbell and Childs 2014, 3–4, 6). FPS start by recognizing politics is gendered and masculinized, and then move to exploring why this might occur and how it might be remedied. For example, FPS recognize the legislative underrepresentation of women and equity-deserving groups results from biased party selection processes. Parties disproportionally select straight, white, men candidates even though more than enough women and people from equity-deserving groups come forward to secure their fair share of candidacies (Ashe 2020b).[3] FPS have long advocated for sex quotas to address this lack of demand for women and candidates from other underrepresented groups.

Drawing upon the autoethnographic approach, I explore feministing in political science by painting a picture of how I, along with other FPS, sought to increase gender equity in Canada's Parliament with Bill C-237. Autoethnography, in this case, involves examining, describing, and analyzing ("graphy") my personal experience ("auto") to better understand the masculine culture of parties and Parliament, and the challenges in transforming these institutions into more gender and diversity sensitive spaces ("ethno") (Ellis, Adam, and Bochner 2011, 273). Shulamit Reinharz reminds us that the "purpose of feminist research must be to create new relationships, better laws, and improved institutions" (1992, 175). Such feminist interventions in politics are at odds with those mostly men political scientists who instructed me "one cannot be both a political scientist and an activist."

Being a FPS married to a politician is odd. I am always "doing" politics, but much of this work is behind the scenes and invisible. More than once the cringeworthy phrase "behind every great man..." has been directed my way. As annoying as it is to be referred to as "parliamentary spouse" or "first lady of Vancouver," the rare access I have been given to the inner workings of the political machine has broadened my understanding of real-world politics—these insights add to my work and shape what I pursue as a FPS.[4] Working closely with political insiders, I am appreciative of Louise Chappell and Fiona Mackay's concept "feminist critical friends," which captures the "aspirations and dilemmas of many feminist academics" who are "'entangled' with the institutions and organizations of governance" and with the feminist legislators who "work on the inside...to unsettle the gender status quo" and "re-gender powerful... political institutions" (2021, 334).

Telling the story of Bill C-237 without fear of academic or personal reprisal reflects my considerable privilege. As a white, professional, PHD-educated, cisgendered, and settler woman, I continue to benefit from colonial institutions and relationships, and though not enough, I direct my feministing at recognizing, challenging, and dismantling these, including parties' selection processes, where sexism, racism, and Indigenous-directed racism are institutionalized. Writing this essay has been challenging; it has resurfaced several incidents of physical and verbal violence directed at me and other feminist activists by men whilst defending quotas for women and other marginalized groups—driving home the extent to which those in power are prepared to resist change.

Why FPS Care about Addressing Legislative Underrepresentation

Descriptive representation is an essential step toward creating more gender- and diversity-sensitive parliaments. Anne Phillips argues, "there is no argument from justice that can defend the current state of affairs: and in this more negative defence there is an argument from justice for parity" (1998, 232). The "politics of presence" matters not only for reasons of justice but for matters of legitimacy and policy, with descriptive representation linked to substantive representation insofar that women legislators tend to advance and support legislation to a greater degree than men.

Canada's Parliament has never descriptively reflected the population from which it is drawn. While recent elections have seen the House of Commons become more diverse, women, BIPOC, LGBTQ+ people, and other marginalized groups such as people living with disabilities, young people, and working-class people are still underrepresented relative to their proportion of the general population. Women's representation in the House of Commons, while increasing, is doing so at a slow pace. Following the 2021 federal election, women made up 30 per cent of MPs—this is only a one-percentage point increase from 2019 and a four-percentage point increase from 2015. Women's representation in the House is below the Canadian provincial and territorial average of 34 per cent. Canada currently ranks 62nd out of 193 countries included in the Inter-Parliamentary Union's 2023 ranking of women in national legislatures, dropping from 48th in 2015 (Inter-Parliamentary Union 2023).

Political parties are the main gatekeepers to most parliaments insofar as women's and other groups' descriptive underrepresentation is linked to party selection processes where party selectors choose a smaller set of candidates from a larger pool of aspirants (Ashe 2020b, 2020d). Party selection processes are not neutral. If they were, the proportions of different groups holding legislative seats would closely match the population from which they are drawn (Phillips 1998). Party rules and practices, created by and for the "in-group" (white, professional, straight men), reinforce existing gender, sexualized, race, and class power structures with the "out-group" (women, BIPOC, LGBTQ+ people) disproportionately filtered from the processes (Ashe 2020d, 297–98).

In the 2021 federal election, women accounted for a record 43 per cent of candidates, a mere one-percentage point increase from the 2019 federal election and far short of their over-fifty per cent representation in the general population. Whereas the NDP and Liberals select more diverse slates than the Conservatives and Bloc, in all parties, men, in particular white men, are overrepresented (Johnson et al. 2021). While there are many reasons why the proportion of women seeking candidacies is lower than men, women still come forward in high enough numbers to fill their fair share of candidacies, but party selectors disproportionally select men over women, and they tend to select women in less winnable seats, especially women who identify as BIPOC (Ashe 2020d; Thomas 2019). In other words, FPS must continue addressing the lack of demand for women candidates amongst party selectors as undersupply is not the main underlying cause of legislative imbalance.

Sex quotas offer a fast-track solution to women and other groups' descriptive underrepresentation by creating a temporary demand for women amongst party selectors (IDEA, n.d.).[5] In the more than 120 countries employing these tools, some entrench reserved seats or legal candidate quotas in their constitutions, some in their election laws, with some leaving this work to political parties. No formal constitutional, legislative, or party-initiated quotas are used at the national level in Canada.

Arguments against quotas in Canada have long been debunked—including that they are too difficult to apply in our single-member district electoral system, would not work with parties' decentralized selection processes, and undermine the principle of merit (Franceschet 2021, 126–32). British Colombia's NDP has successfully used a party quota, the Equity Mandate, for close to two decades and, in 2017, the New Brunswick Legislature implemented legislation financially incentivizing parties to select more women (Ashe 2020d; Ashe and Stewart 2012; Everitt and Albaugh 2022). Rather than relying on informal practices, these institutionalized commitments appear essential to ensuring legislatures are more diverse.

The Life and Death of Bill C-237

Bill C-237 is modelled after laws used elsewhere, including in France and Ireland. It is designed to increase the representation of women and other equity-deserving groups by incentivizing parties to select more diverse candidate slates (Standing Committee on the Status of Women 2018). Like many other FPS, I view quotas as the best solution to expediently address the systemic problem of women's political underrepresentation.

Opportunities for feminist interventions in Parliament rarely appear. Once elected, Kennedy's academic work on women's political underrepresentation readied him to address longstanding democratic inequities. Then, as he puts it, "I met you, we wrote some articles on it, and you did your PHD on it, so it's been something we talk about a lot." While in Parliament he sought institutional change to increase women's representation, arguing efforts "needed to be formalized; otherwise we'll see [parties] boasting about having diverse candidate slates but actually selecting women in unwinnable seats, and nothing will change."

Parliament's rules, practices, structures, and outputs are rife with "organized masculinism" that make them comparatively unwelcoming, non-inclusive spaces (Ashe 2020a, 5; Erikson and Verge 2020, 3). #MeToo's "arrival" on Parliament Hill increased public exposure to long-endured gender-based harassment of MPs and staff. Mona Lena Krook's (2020) research, for which Kennedy was interviewed, finds violence against women in politics takes place across established democracies, including Canada's, and negatively affects women's right to fully participate in their work and their willingness to seek re-election (Ashe 2020a, 7). Kennedy notes he saw daily sexism directed toward women colleagues. He recalls being in the House when Prime Minister Trudeau accidentally elbowed MP Ruth Ellen Brosseau in the breast and watched as some MPs "flipped it on her, saying it was her fault...I saw how quickly people turned it on her." He witnessed "so much misogyny" and "heard so many comments by men...and gender-based heckling that you don't pick up on the recordings." This happens when "women MPs are trying to do their job," for example, when "MP Megan Leslie asked questions, they'd yell so loud but when a man MP asked similar questions it wasn't nearly as vitriolic." During gender sensitivity training, "a lot of my men colleagues sat there with their arms crossed and huffed."

The sexist behaviour and violence directed against women MPs continued outside of the House: "On green buses that transport MPs, Senators, and staff around the Parliamentary district, a lot of younger women in our caucus were sexually harassed. On one occasion I intervened when a MP asked a younger woman MP to sit on his lap." When two women colleagues were sexually assaulted by two men MPs, he was not surprised: "I saw sexual harassment all the time. Men act like they are immune—it's been going on so long and is often fuelled by alcohol," and the code of conduct does not effectively address it. Too, were many incidences of racism: "I remember sitting in on the Indigenous Affairs Committee...we were all white guys. This is the highest decision-making body in the land and it's all old white guys."

Bringing in C-237 was a needed feminist intervention toward changing Parliament, but from the get-go, there were challenges. For example, when Kennedy said he wanted to bring in quotas, men MPs supported the idea only when women MPs were in the room, but many opposed them when they left: "Their true colours showed. And I'm in the NDP—the most progressive party on this front!" Reading Bill C-237 below, it is not straightforwardly a quota; rather, it is framed as a financial incentive for parties to diversify their candidate slates. Omitting the word *quota* was a purposeful compromise and reflects members' resistance to the term.

First Reading and Recorded Division
Bill C-237 was first read in the House of Commons on February 25, 2016, debated after the second reading on May 10, October 10, and October 18, with the second reading recorded division held on October 19, 2016. Table 12.1 shows that despite some cross-party support from the Liberals, Bloc

Québécois (BQ), and Greens, Bill C-237 was "negatived" with 68 yeas to 209 nays. Discussed in later sections, getting 23 Liberals and 5 BQ MPs to support the bill involved considerable effort, and led to extensive debate within party caucuses about the role parties should play in women's political underrepresentation.

TABLE 12.1: Bill C-237 Vote Details

Party	Yea	Nay	Paired
Liberal	23	127	0
Conservative	0	78	0
NDP	39	0	0
BQ	5	4	0
Green Party	1	0	0
Total	68	209	0

Source: Parliament of Canada, "Vote no. 32," 42nd Parliament, 1st Session, October 19, 2016, https://www.ourcommons.ca/Members/en/votes/42/1/132.

The justification for Bill C-237 is in its Preamble:

Whereas Canadians are committed to achieving gender equity in all aspects of political, economic and social life, including representation in Parliament; Whereas equal access to Canada's democratic institutions is a question of social justice; Whereas women have never held more than 26% of the seats in the House of Commons or constituted more than 29% of the candidates in a federal election since first acquiring the right to run for office in 1920; Whereas the systemic underrepresentation of women in politics is not caused by a lack of willingness to stand for elected office, but rather by barriers within the process used by political parties to select candidates; Whereas currently, under the Canada Elections Act, political parties are eligible for a reimbursement of up to 50% of their election expenses provided they meet certain conditions and can at any time decline to receive this public subsidy; And whereas all political parties lack an adequate incentive to promote parity in the candidates they nominate for a general election. (Canada 2016)[6]

In terms of substantive clauses, Bill C-237 sought to amend several sections of the Canada Elections Act, notably s. 437 (1), requiring parties to state the number of women and men candidates on their candidate lists, and s. 444, including a change to the formula by which parties are reimbursed for election expenses, which would reduce their public subsidy if they failed to meet a minimum threshold of women on their candidate lists. After every election, all parties are compensated or reimbursed for expenses based on how many people they elect, with Bill C-237 seeking to substantially reduce a party's reimbursement if less than 45 per cent of candidates are women.

The focus on reducing public funds to offending parties was taken because private members' bills cannot contain provisions for the spending of public funds as money bills are reserved for the government. Bill C-237 was allowed to proceed as it merely adjusted how already allocated funds are distributed. Still, as explored more below, some, like Liberal Parliamentary Secretary for Democratic Institutions, Mark Holland, would continually claim, Bill C-237 was unconstitutional, and from day one Kennedy says, "he just tried to come up with reasons the Liberals shouldn't support it. They were all 'BS,' and he knew it" (Canada 2016).

Strategy

Private members' bills from opposition benches rarely come to the House for a vote, and if they do, they almost never pass, and if they do pass, according to Kennedy, they are "like Tragically Hip Day or flag day," and symbolic as opposed to substantive. In 2015, however, Kennedy believed Bill C-237 had a good chance of passing not least because three factors widened the window of opportunity for its success: drawing a low number in the "MP lottery," previously winning a private member's vote, and serving in Parliament with a feminist prime minister.[7]

First, following the 2015 election, Kennedy drew "30" of 338 in the MP lottery—giving him an opportunity to trigger a vote in the House by putting forward a bill or a motion before Parliament dissolved. He wanted to introduce a bill related to democratic reform, and at the time I was working on a sex quota project, so I suggested a bill on sex quotas. Although supportive of sex quotas, Kennedy knew it would be a challenge to bring members onside: "We'll never get quotas: no one in the House supports [them], including my own caucus. The word [*quota*] alone sets them off." Given this, we began looking at other countries' legislation in this area, observing some successfully use the term *incentives* to persuade parties to select more diverse candidates.

Second, in the previous Parliament (2011–2015), where Stephen Harper's Conservatives formed a majority and the NDP formed the Official Opposition, Kennedy put forward Private Members' Motion-428 to bring electronic petitioning to the House of Commons.[8] Behind the scenes, M-428 involved garnering support from a broad range of organizations—from the Preston Manning Institute to the Broadbent Institute, securing endorsements from FPS—national and international, and gaining cross-party support—with all NDP (94) and some Liberal (33), Green (2), and BQ (4) MPs supporting it, as well as 8 Conservative MPs (Stewart 2017). E-petitions passed by two votes and was the only vote Harper lost during the 41st Parliament due to a Conservative backbench revolt. It was reasonable to imagine a win under Trudeau, especially on a bill that reflects his government's gender equity rhetoric and symbolism.

Thus, the third reason Bill C-237 stood a chance was the presence of Canada's first openly feminist prime minister who had just appointed the first federal sex-balanced cabinet—Trudeau's government would likely be "friendlier" than the last given Harper never described himself as a feminist; rather, he initiated gender equity rollbacks (Dobrowolsky 2020). Strategically, C-237 was designed to appeal to Trudeau's feminist rhetoric. Leading up to the First Reading, Kennedy was hopeful that "they'd go for it because it'd get more women in the House and [Trudeau had] been talking about it, obviously with Cabinet. I thought this would appeal to them" because "Trudeau said he was a feminist prime minister and with half the cabinet women, it'd be tough to vote down; it'd test his feminist credentials." Plus, "it was so mild." Also, electorally it would be a good move for the Liberals because it would strip tens of millions of dollars from the Conservatives. While it would also strip some money from the Liberals, the amount was small in comparison to what the Conservatives would lose, and it was thought this electoral advantage might be enough to get them to support it.

Initially only a few other people were involved with getting the bill off the ground including parliamentary staffers Andrew Cuddy, Lauren Reid, and Krystal Smith, with outside support from several FPS. Upon drafting Bill C-237, the House of Commons Clerk Office's legal team deemed the bill to be "in order." Absent from early conversations about the bill was Kennedy's party, and one reason for this was the strong degree of party centralization exerted over MPs' motions and bills: "Whenever I tried to do something even a little controversial, their first reaction was to try and shut me down" and "they would try get me do one of their leftover bills that wouldn't go anywhere." Later in the process, women MPs in the NDP's caucus championed the bill, including the critic for the Status of Women, Sheila Malcolmson, who spoke several times to the bill, as did Sherry Benson. During the drafting stage, we engaged with parties' women's committees and the NDP's LGBTQ+ caucus.

When Kennedy initially presented the idea for the bill to the NDP caucus, then party leader Thomas Mulcair was not fully on board but refrained from speaking against it for fear of backlash from women members, who made up close to half of the caucus. At this point the party was in turmoil. The 2015 election resulted in the NDP losing its Official Opposition status and at the April 8–10, 2016, convention, the party voted out Mulcair as leader and rejected the Equity Mandate that we designed to increase the diversity of its candidate slates.[9]

In early 2016, while doing a fellowship at Birkbeck, University of London, and working on a gender equity project with Rosie Campbell, Sarah Childs, and Joni Lovenduski, I mentioned the opportunity to bring forth a Canadian gender bill to Sarah, who at the time was working on her groundbreaking report *The Good Parliament* (Childs 2016). In Portcullis House we began drafting ideas for the bill. In February 2016, while at the Men and Masculinities conference in Bristol, FPS in attendance discussed the bill's potential. During this period, I was also interviewing British Labour MPs and staff about their party's all-women shortlist seats, and they gave advice on how to pitch the bill and avoid, as much as possible, likely obstacles such as internal (members) and external (media) backlash against party sex quotas (Ashe 2020b).

Drafting and Readings
My notes and email correspondence from February 2016 reflect several iterations of the bill's incentive formula before we settled on the final 45-45-10 model. For clarity, as laid out in the bill, "If the difference between the percentage of male and female candidates on the list of candidates of a registered party for the election exceeds 10%, the amount that

is provided for in subsection (1), after having been reduced under subsection (2) if applicable, is reduced by the percentage that is determined by subtracting 10 from the difference between the percentage of male and female candidates and dividing that resulting percentage by four" (Canada 2016). The formula is further explained during a second reading debate speech on May 10, 2016: "Under this new law, if party A puts forward 45% women candidates and 55% men candidates, the party loses none of its public subsidies. However, if party B puts forward 25% women candidates and 75% men candidates, then the public subsidy is reduced by 10%" (Canada, *House of Commons Debates*, May 10, 2016b). Emails during February 2016 also include discussions of the bill's wording. For example, in an exchange with Fiona Buckley, we discuss lessons learned from Ireland's quota legislation, such as "talking up the language of incentivization," and "highlighting it's not prescriptive in dictating to parties how they go about their candidate recruitment and selection strategies and tempering the word 'penalty' by also using 'financial consequence' and 'financial condition.'" In another email, I write that although we wanted to, we did not add "winnable seats" to the bill, noting "as warned, it's too much and would lead to its immediate defeat, as would a stricter financial penalty and calling it sex equity rather than gender equity—apparently Canada's House is not ready for 'sex'!" In correspondence with Kennedy's office and parliamentary council, our request went through to replace the term *gender parity* with *gender equity*. This decision reflects input from the transgender community and activists such as lawyer Adrienne Smith—insofar that parity implies 50 per cent women and 50 per cent men, and not all people identify with this binary. This email represents the final change before certified copies were made and before the bill appeared on the Notice Paper mere days before the bill was read for the first time in the House. FPS wrote me with advice for the bill's introduction, for example, to pack the public gallery with representatives from women's organizations and people sympathetic to gender quotas because "politicians love playing to the gallery! It might have an impact on diluting some of the opposition."

Shortly after the bill's February 2016 introduction, I began sending emails to FPS in Canada requesting supporting quotes—below is an excerpt taken from my email to Amanda Bittner: "The bill has had its first reading and will come up for its first hour of debate later this Spring where it will face the all-important vote to move it to committee. We need to build all the momentum we can to persuade Trudeau to move this bill through Parliament and I hope you will help."

Like all FPS' responses, Bittner was extremely positive, and her supporting quote was one of many on the bill's promotional website: "The biggest barrier to women's representation in legislatures is party recruitment and nomination practices. Research shows, time and time again, that when women run, they win. As such, legislation that encourages parties to recruit more candidates from diverse backgrounds is highly desirable and likely to lead to increased diversity in the House of Commons."[10] During this period, we engaged in other feminist activities to increase support for the bill. For example, on May 20, 2016, Marjorie Griffen-Cohen and I wrote an op-ed titled "More Women in Politics? There Is a Way," in which we state, "This is a bill that should be passed easily. A feminist has proposed it and the party with the power in the House of Commons is led by a feminist. And, it is 2016."

On May 10, 2016, when Kennedy moved Bill C-237 be read a second time and referred to committee, he highlighted the endorsers and supporters, and gave a shout out to the many FPS involved with drafting and refining Bill C-237's text:

> Supportive organizations include Samara, Leadnow, YWCA Toronto, FairVote Canada, ACTRA, Groupes Femmes Politique et Démocratie, the Canadian Council of Muslim Women...[and] Jerry Dias from Unifor. Donna Dasko, co-chair for the Campaign for an Equal Senate and past national chair of Equal Voice also supports this bill.
>
> I have also heard considerable support for the bill from Canadian academics, including Jeanette Ashe, Sylvia Bashevkin, Karen Bird, Amanda Bittner, Marjorie Griffin Cohen, Avigail Eisenberg, Lynda Erickson, Penny Gurstein, Fiona MacDonald, Sharon McGowan, Susan Prentice, and Melanee Thomas...
>
> Finally, I would like to thank my parliamentary colleagues for their support, especially my Liberal, Green, and NDP colleagues who have jointly seconded this bill, as well as Conservative Senator Nancy Ruth and Liberal Senator Mobina Jaffer for their public endorsements. It is a truly cross-partisan effort. (Canada, *House of Commons Debates*, May 10, 2016b)

He also thanked international political scientists Rosie Campbell, Sarah Childs, Liz Evans, Fiona Buckley, and Meryl Kenny "for their assistance in drafting this bill and helping me ensure it in no way interferes with internal workings of parties" (Canada, *House of Commons Debates*, May 10, 2016b).

To persuade MPs to support Bill C-237, we sent them all information packages, which included a list of endorsers and positive media stories along with a link to the campaign's website. The lobbying efforts of MP Anita Vandenbeld (chair of the Liberal women's caucus, chair of the all-party women's committee, and member of the Standing Committee on the Status of Women), and MP Pam Damoff (vice-chair of the Standing Committee on the Status of Women) helped persuade many of their Liberal colleagues to at least consider supporting C-237, including MP Nathaniel Erskine-Smith, who said without the partisan "BS" it could pass. At the same time, other Liberals worked against it, such as parliamentary secretary to the minister of Democratic Institutions, Mark Holland, who Kennedy said was "assigned" to kill the bill—to be sure, the minister of Democratic Institutions, Maryam Monsef, looked forward to its defeat "with glee." The Conservatives were less inclined to support it—for example, from the outset Conservative MP Michelle Rempel-Garner gave Kennedy a flat out "no" response when asked to consider the bill.

There were also several senators championing the bill. As noted, Senator Donna Dasko, founder of Equal Voice, was very supportive. Strangely, Equal Voice held back its endorsement until the evening before the second reading vote, which caused division among Equal Voice board members, with some leaving over the organization's lack of enthusiasm. One Equal Voice staffer suggested that the organization was hesitant to endorse the bill for worry that it would lose government funding.[11]

Just days before the debates at second reading, Kennedy's office and major media outlets received a manila envelope from an undisclosed sender containing a "leaked memo" wherein Minister Monsef instructs the government to reject Bill C-237, despite saying it would be a free vote. A CTV News (2016), headline captures the flavour of this and other media stories: "Liberal Cabinet Advised to Oppose Gender Equity Bill."

During Oral Question Period on May 10, 2016, aware of the government's leaked dictate, Kennedy was given permission by the NDP House Leader Peter Julian to ask Minister Monsef, "Will the government support getting my bill to committee and work with us, so together we can take another step for gender equality?" Minister Monsef replied, "Mr. Speaker, I appreciate the honourable member's efforts. We take note of his private member's bill and will study it on its merits when it is debated in the House. Our government supports the idea of more women and people of various genders participating in the political debate in the country. This is clearly a commitment that our government and our Prime Minister have shown. We look forward to continuing the leadership on this front" (Canada, *House of Commons Debates*, May 10, 2016a). Later that same day, when the House was debating whether to send Bill C-237 to committee for study, Kennedy restated his willingness to adjust the bill to meet the Liberal's demands to get it to committee where it could be further discussed: "I would like to say that at the very least I hope we can send the bill to committee as it is an important first step to making our Parliament more gender equal. As I have explained to colleagues, I am open to making changes to improve the bill, with the overall objective of having it made law, and increasing the percentage of women elected to Parliament in the next and subsequent elections" (Canada, *House of Commons Debates*, May 10, 2016b). Learning of the leaked memo a few days before the second reading speech gave us time to strengthen our responses to criticisms directed at the bill. Hansard debates reveals six main reasons for opposing the bill: it violates the Constitution; disadvantages smaller parties; excludes transgendered people; works against Canada's single-member plurality electoral system; weakens democracy; and undermines merit. To counter these arguments, Kennedy stated during the second reading debate,

> According to the Law Clerk's office, "Bill C-237, if found to infringe subsection 15(1), which in our opinion it does not, could be considered an affirmative action measure and thus saved by subsection 15(2), since it strives to promote consideration of a disadvantaged group—women—in politics and public life. In this sense, the legislation could be seen to have an ameliorative purpose and fall within the ambit of subsection 15(2). It is our opinion that Bill C-237 does not infringe the indicated sections of the Charter of Rights and Freedoms."...
>
> To recap, the candidate gender equity act, one, works in other countries like Ireland, France, and Portugal; two, is Charter compliant; three, does

not interfere with internal party democracy; four, works under any type of electoral system; five, provides incentives for parties to select more transgendered and non-binary candidates; and six, was designed by experts. (Canada, *House of Commons Debates*, 2016a)

Following the speech, unpersuaded, many Liberals and all Conservatives stuck to their party lines. However, breaking ranks with her caucus, Vandenbeld spoke to the merits of Bill C-237 and dispelled her party's efforts to discredit it. She spoke of the Liberal's history of being active in nomination processes, for example, by appointing women candidates and putting in place nomination spending limits (Canada, House of Commons Debates, May 10, 2016c).

Although the second vote on Bill C-237 was initially set to occur later than October 19, 2016, the government expedited it to stop it from gaining more traction. Leading up to the recorded division, we were worried that the Liberals were going to whip the vote. Looking to my emails, on October 17, 2016, just two days before the second reading, Kennedy received word from Minister Monsef that the bill would not be whipped. In a last-minute cross-party effort to secure more support for the bill, an email exchange with Vandenbeld and Damoff reveals several Liberal cabinet ministers and backbenchers were leaning toward voting for the bill, and on the opposition side, the BQ, Greens, and NDP were supportive, with even a few Conservatives leaning "yes" or abstaining. There is also a request to work on a few of their undecided colleagues and raise it at the next day's caucus to which Vandenbeld and Damoff replied "yes."

The Vote

During Oral Question Period on the day before the vote, Kennedy asked Minister Monsef if the Liberals would support the bill. By this point it was publicly known that the Liberals were going to kill Bill C-237 and Monsef replied, "I cannot support the member's bill, I believe it is important to wait until the Special Committee on Electoral Reform proposes changes to the election system, and then we can address this conversation through a different means" (Canada, *House of Commons Debates*, October 18, 2016a). On the same day, during Private Member's Business and Adjournment Proceedings, Kennedy gave his last speech before the vote: "I would ask members to take a look around the House of Commons. This is a place of moments. This is the place where we decided women should get to vote. This is the place where we decided that women should become people in the eyes of the law. This is where we decided that First Nations people should get to vote. This is a place of moments, and we are having a moment right now" (Canada, *House of Commons Debates*, October 18, 2016b). Knowing the government's position made the bill's defeat less surprising but not less disappointing. Reviewing its rejection, even a few years later, involves going over the strategy, which includes identifying champions and objectors. From the beginning, we knew it was important to build cross-party support for the bill as we needed Liberal votes to get it to committee. Outside of the NDP caucus two of the strongest champions for the bill were Liberal MPs Vandenbeld and Damoff. Green Party leader Elizabeth May and women members in the BQ caucus were also fully behind it. Looking at the result, twenty-three Liberals and five Green Party MPs supported the bill. Liberal MPs were later disciplined for supporting C-237 despite claims by the government that it was a "free vote." The BQ was divided along gender lines, and, as with the Liberals, there was considerable conflict in their party over the bill.

A few days after the bill's defeat, I sent the following email to supportive FPS:

> I thought I'd write to give you an update on Bill C 237…In case you haven't already heard, it did not pass. Due to a procedural trick by the Liberal government the vote came earlier than expected and we had less time to persuade Liberal backbenchers to support it than we thought (the Conservative official opposition was always against it, so we didn't put any resources into persuading them). The Liberal Minister for Democratic Reform ended up whipping the vote—advising the cabinet to vote against it. The parliamentary secretary and the Minister for the Status of Women voted against it. Trudeau missed the vote. But 23 Liberal backbenchers did support it—a backbench revolt by Canadian standards.

Reviewing this, I am deeply grateful for the post-vote media commentary of FPS—not only do they discredit the Liberal and Conservative critiques of the bill, but they also challenge Trudeau's and the Liberal's commitment to feminism, and they again firmly entrench the problem of women's underrepresentation and the solutions to it. One example is Shannon Proudfoot's interview with Melanee Thomas: "To advance weak Charter arguments against a measure aimed at improving the involvement of women in politics while talking so much about feminism makes the Liberal commitment to equality look like 'a veneer,' Thomas says. 'There's a big talk on diversity, and the action is really underwhelming,' she says. 'And in this case, I would say it's insulting.'" Offering further insight, Vandenbeld observes that Trudeau's sex-balanced cabinet "just glosses over structural barriers that still remain" (2017, 103). Despite some gender-sensitive policies under Trudeau, such as parental leave for MPs, the gendered nature of Parliament is still very much intact (Ashe 2020c, 87–88).

Conclusion

The spirit of Bill C-237 continues. The Standing Committee on the Status of Women's (2019) recent report *Barriers Facing Women in Politics* includes sex quotas as a possible remedy for women's underrepresentation, with witnesses encouraging the House to revisit Bill C-237. In 2017 New Brunswick's Legislature implemented a bill financially incentivizing parties to select women candidates and following the 2020 British Columbia provincial election, the BC NDP's Equity Mandate is now celebrated by the party for its role in electing the country's first women-majority caucus. In 2021 the federal NDP's executive reversed the party's position by adopting an equity mandate to ensure intersectional diversity on its candidate slates.[12]

Bill C-237 led to heated inter and intra-party debates about women's systemic political underrepresentation. During the 2021 federal election, unprecedented media attention was paid to candidate diversity. Parties' candidate slates were more diverse than the last election, raising the question of the necessity of Bill C-237. While candidate diversity is increasing, parties still tend to select women and BIPOC candidates to run in unwinnable seats. Thus, a future Bill C-237 might be stronger by requiring parties to field women and members of equity-deserving groups in winnable seats. Campaigning for Bill C-237 has given the idea of quotas in Canada more traction. Since its defeat I have been contacted by several legislators interested in resurrecting the bill. To this end, Bill C-237, like other bills that needed a few tries to succeed, such as the transgender rights bill, C-16 An Act to Amend the Canadian Human Rights Act and the Criminal Code, could be revisited in the House of Commons.

Bill C-237 reflects immeasurable efforts by parliamentary and legislative staff, women's caucuses and committees, democratic organizations and activists, and FPS. I have attempted to find the right balance between my voice and their voices, and Kennedy's role, and I am reminded that institutionalizing gender and diversity sensitivity reforms requires a commitment by all parties and by all MPs, including men MPs, who still dominate our legislative bodies. Institutional change is difficult, especially feminist-led institutional change in highly partisan spaces. We had in place many elements of a winning sex quota campaign—for example, the support of cross-party MPs, women's committees, progressive organizations, and FPS, but, despite all efforts, we could not secure the support of the government. Although Bill C-237 failed, perhaps the fact that this and future efforts to bring legislative equity has helped grow the network of feminist political scientists with whom I worked and continue to work makes this a winning story after all.

Notes

1. Equity-deserving groups include women, BIPOC, LGBTQ+ people, young people, working-class people, and people living with disabilities (PLWD).
2. Gender and diversity parliaments include greater diversity amongst its members not only in terms of gender but in terms of other identities; "equal and effective participation"; and institutional responsibility to address gender and diversity deficits (Childs 2016, 6).
3. A "fair share" of candidates occurs when a group's representation in candidate pools and legislatures proportionally reflects its presence in a country's population (Ashe 2020d, 301).
4. When Kennedy was sworn in, I was given a pin inscribed with "parliamentary spouse." In 2018 he was elected mayor of Vancouver.
5. Quotas fall into one of three types: (1) "Reserved seats (constitutional and/or legislative), (2) Legal candidate quotas (constitutional and/or legislative), and (3) Political party quotas (voluntary)" (IDEA 2022). Bill C-237 is type (2).
6. Only white women received political rights in 1920; the percentage of women reflects the 2015 election results.
7. At the beginning of every parliament there is a private members' lottery in which all MPs other than cabinet ministers participate to establish the order of precedence for private members' business (bills and motions).

8. Like Bill C-237, I worked closely on e-petitions. Kennedy Stewart's words in Parliament on the subject: "Madam Speaker, when my wife Jeanette Ashe, who is a political scientist, first brought the e-petitions motion to my attention, we started to do quite a lot of research on it" (Canada, House of Commons, 2012).
9. At the 2016 and 2018 conventions, the Burnaby South Electoral District Association introduced an "Equity Mandate" motion to institute a quota requiring the party's pool of candidates to have a proportion of women, BIPOC, LGBTQ+ people, and PLWD equal to their groups' proportion of the population, with an allowed variance of up to 10 per cent for each group.
10. See Bittner and others' endorsements at "The Candidate Gender Equity Act," archived at https://web.archive.org/web/20180327172414/https://www.equalseatsforwomen.ca/endorsements.
11. Personal correspondence with a former Equal Voice member.
12. Personal correspondence with an NDP party official.

References

Ashe, Jeanette. 2020a. "Assessing Gender and Diversity Sensitivity at the Legislative Assembly of British Columbia," December 30, 2020. http://www.cwpcanada.ca/media/48946/cwp-report-bc-gd-sensitive-audit-2020-final-e.pdf.

Ashe, Jeanette. 2020b. "Canada's Political Parties: Gatekeepers to Parliament." In *The Palgrave Handbook of Gender, Sexuality, and Canadian Politics*, edited by Manon Tremblay and Joanna Everitt, 297–316. Cham, UK: Palgrave Macmillan.

Ashe, Jeanette. 2020c. "Gender Sensitivity Under Trudeau: Facebook Feminism or Real Change?" In *Turbulent Times, Transformational Possibilities? Gender and Politics Today and Tomorrow*, edited by Fiona MacDonald and Alexandra Dobrowolsky, 68–99. Toronto: University of Toronto.

Ashe, Jeanette. 2020d. *Political Candidate Recruitment: Who Wins, Who Loses and Underrepresentation in the UK*. New York: Routledge.

Ashe, Jeanette, and Kennedy Stewart. 2012. "Legislative Recruitment: Using Diagnostic Testing to Explain Underrepresentation." *Party Politics* 18 (5): 687–707. https://doi.org/10.1177/1354068810389635.

Campbell, Rosie, and Sarah Childs. 2014. "Introduction: Deeds and Worlds." In *Deeds and Words: Gendering Politics after Joni Lovenduski*, edited by Rosie Campbell and Sarah Childs, 1–14. Colchester: ECPR Press.

Canada. 2016. Bill C-237, *An Act to Amend the Canada Elections Act (Gender Equity)*, 42nd Parliament, 1st Session, 2016. https://www.parl.ca/legisinfo/BillDetails.aspx?billId=8118999&Language=E.

Canada, House of Commons, *Hansard* 83, 41st Parliament, 1st Session, February 17, 2012. Orders of the Day (Kennedy Stewart, NDP). https://openparliament.ca/debates/2012/2/17/kennedy-stewart-4.

Canada, *House of Commons Debates, Hansard* 52, 42nd Parliament, 1st Session, May 10, 2016a. (Maryam Monsef, Lib). https://www.ourcommons.ca/DocumentViewer/en/42-1/house/sitting-52/hansard.

Canada, *House of Commons Debates*, Hansard 52, 42nd Parliament, 1st Session, May 10, 2016b. (Kennedy Stewart, NDP). https://www.ourcommons.ca/DocumentViewer/en/42-1/house/sitting-52/hansard.

Canada, *House of Commons Debates*, Hansard 52, 42nd Parliament, 1st Session, May 10, 2016c. (Anita Vandenbeld, Lib). https://www.ourcommons.ca/DocumentViewer/en/42-1/house/sitting-52/hansard.

Canada, *House of Commons Debates*, Hansard 92, 42nd Parliament, 1st Session, October 18, 2016a. (Maryam Monsef, Lib). https://www.ourcommons.ca/DocumentViewer/en/42-1/house/sitting-92/hansard.

Canada, *House of Commons Debates*, Hansard 92, 42nd Parliament, 1st Session, October 18, 2016b. (Kennedy Stewart, NDP). https://www.ourcommons.ca/DocumentViewer/en/42-1/house/sitting-92/hansard.

Chappell, Louise, and Fiona Mackay. 2022. "Feminist Critical Friends: Dilemmas of Feminist Engagement with Governance and Gender Reform Agendas." *European Journal of Politics and Gender* 4 (3): 321–40. https://doi.org/10.1332/251510820X15922354996155.

Childs, Sarah. 2016. *The Good Parliament*. Bristol: University of Bristol. http://www.bristol.ac.uk/media-library/sites/spais/images/grc/GoodParliament%20SinglePage%20Report.pdf.

CTV News. 2016. "Liberal Cabinet Advised to Oppose Gender Equity Bill." *CTV News*, May 11, 2016. https://www.ctvnews.ca/politics/liberal-cabinet-advised-to-oppose-gender-equity-bill-document-1.2898141.

Dobrowolsky, Alexandra. 2020. "A Diverse, Feminist 'Open Door' Canada? Trudeau-Styled Equality, Liberalisms, and Feminisms." In *Turbulent Times, Transformational Possibilities? Gender and Politics Today and Tomorrow*, edited by Fiona MacDonald and Alexandra Dobrowolsky, 23–48. Toronto: University of Toronto.

Ellis, Carolyn, Tony Adams, and Arthur Bochner. 2011. "Autoethnography: An Overview." *Historical Social Research* 36 (4): 273–90. http://www.jstor.org/stable/23032294.

Erikson, Josefina, and Tania Verge. 2020. "Gender, Power and Privilege in the Parliamentary Workplace." *Parliamentary Affairs* 75 (1): 1–19. https://doi.org/10.1093/pa/gsaa048.

Everitt, Joanna, and Quinn M. Albaugh. 2022. "The Origins of Gender Targeted Public Finance Measures: The Case of New Brunswick, Canada." *European Journal of Politics and Gender* 5 (1): 127–44. https://doi.org/10.1332/251510821X16354220366241.

Franceschet, Susan. 2021. "Gender Quotas and Women's Political Representation: Lessons from Canada." In *Women, Powers, and Political Representation*, edited by Roosemarjin de Geus, Erin Tolley, Elizabeth Goodyear-Grant, and Peter John Loewen, 125–32. Toronto: University of Toronto Press.

Griffin, Marjorie Cohen, and Jeanette Ashe. 2016. "More Women in Politics? There Is a Way." *Vancouver Sun*, May 26, 2016. https://vancouversun.com/opinion/opinion-more-women-in-politics-there-is-a-way.

International Institute for Democracy and Electoral Assistance (IDEA). n.d. *Gender Quota Database*. Accessed September 25, 2022. https://www.idea.int/data-tools/data/gender-quotas.

Inter-Parliamentary Union. 2023. "Monthly Ranking of Women in National Parliaments" (as of October 1, 2023). https://data.ipu.org/women-ranking?month=10&year=2023.

Johnson, Anna, Erin Tolley, Melanee Thomas, and Marc André Bodet. 2021. "A New Dataset on the Demographics of Canadian Federal Elections Candidates." *Canadian Journal of Political Science* 54 (3): 717–25. https://doi.org/10.1017/S0008423921000391.

Krook, Mona Lena. 2020. *Violence against Women in Politics*. Oxford: Oxford University Press.

Phillips, Anne. 1998. *The Politics of Presence*. New York: Clarendon Press.

Proudfoot, Shannon. 2016. "The Liberals Killed a Bill Promoting Gender Parity in Politics: They Were Wrong." *Maclean's*, October 24, 2016. https://www.macleans.ca/politics/ottawa/the-liberals-killed-a-bill-promoting-gender-parity-in-politics-they-were-wrong/.

Reinharz, Shulamit. 1992. *Feminist Methods in Social Research*. New York: Oxford University Press.

Standing Committee on the Status of Women. 2018. *Barriers Facing Women in Politics*. House of Commons of Canada, 1st Session, November 28, 2018. https://www.ourcommons.ca/Committees/en/FEWO/StudyActivity?studyActivityId=10006162.

Stewart, Kennedy. 2017. "Empowering the Backbench: The Story of Electronic Petitions." In *Turning Parliament Inside Out: Practical Ideas for Reforming Canada's Democracy*, edited by Michael Chong, Scott Simms, and Kennedy Stewart, 58–79. Madeira Park, BC: Douglas and McIntyre.

Thomas, Melanee. 2019. "Parties Not Voters to Blame for Slow Rise of Women MPs." *Policy Options*, October 30, 2019. https://policyoptions.irpp.org/magazines/october-2019/parties-not-voters-to-blame-for-slow-rise-of-women-mps/.

Vandenbeld, Anita. 2017. "Breaking the Parliamentary Glass Ceiling." In *Turning Parliament Inside Out: Practical Ideas for Reforming Canada's Democracy*, edited by Michael Chong, Scott Simms, and Kennedy Stewart, 98–101. Madeira Park, BC: Douglas and McIntyre.

13 Feministing on the Campaign Trail

Dialogue with KIMBERLEY ENS MANNING, NADIA VERRELLI, and MELANEE THOMAS
Edited by ALANA CATTAPAN and FIONA MACDONALD

THE POSSIBILITY OF FEMINIST PRAXIS in political science is attributable, at least in part, to the hard work of women who have taken to the campaign trail. Those who have put their names forward, wrangled volunteers, knocked on doors, and called potential donor after donor, have made important inroads in long-exclusionary halls of power. The engagement of women in politics has slowly enabled the study of women and politics, and it has often been in the conference rooms and classrooms where women and gender and politics is studied that feministing in political science has been possible.

As legislatures and institutions diversify, so too has the study of women and politics, with representation and its absence recognized and challenged time and again. On November 15, 2021, we gathered three feminist political scientists who have also run for political nominations and/or political office to hear their reflections of feministing on the campaign trail. Kimberley Ens Manning, a white anglophone settler in her late forties, ran twice for a nomination run by the Liberal Party of Canada in Montreal, in 2018 and 2019. At the time she ran, Kimberley was working as an associate professor at Concordia University and was living with her male partner and three children (ages 6–7, 10–11, and 13–14). Nadia Verrelli, raised by working-class, immigrant parents, was the NDP candidate for the riding of Sudbury in the 2021 federal election and finished a close second in her race. Prior to running she was an associate professor in the Department of Political Science at Laurentian University. Melanee Thomas is a professor in the Department of Political Science at the University of Calgary. She ran in two elections before starting her PHD program, as the federal NDP candidate in 2004 and 2006 in Lethbridge, Alberta.

Each of these feminist political scientists had their own experiences on the campaign trail, but it is in the exchange between them that the similarities and differences most effectively emerge. The conversation was a true dialogue—an exchange between the participants guided by relatively few questions from the convenors/editors (Alana Cattapan and Fiona MacDonald) that looped back on itself, built on key ideas, and was rich with opportunity to pause and laugh and/or shake our heads in disbelief. The dialogue as it appears below is edited and, in some places, reorganized slightly to highlight the key themes that emerged and for length.

On the Experience of Running

NADIA VERRELLI: It was my first time running and it was shorter than a normal campaign. It was a whirlwind, it was hard work, it was exciting, but overall, I think it was a good experience. It was eye opening and surprising how I had to discuss issues, which issues I was able to discuss, and which ones I wasn't. I quickly found out that while I was the candidate, I had little to no control over what the agenda was, what the platform was, what issues I should be stressing, and how I stressed them. Being an academic all my life, it was really hard for me to stay in that (candidate) bubble and relinquish control over how I'm portrayed and relinquish control on how my campaign is run and portrayed.

KIMBERLEY ENS MANNING: I will qualify my remarks by saying that I was never actually an official candidate. I ran twice, one run which resulted in a nomination election in December of 2018 and a second that resulted in a nomination election in September 2019, both on the Island of Montreal. But I didn't win either nomination contests. I never became the official candidate for the party in the ridings I contested. In a sense, however, they were the real campaign because by anybody's standards they were safe seats. Whoever won the nomination was going to take the seat, so they were both highly contested.

While I have always been interested in the possibility of one day running for office, the real thing that got me into the arena was my participation in the 2017 Senate committee hearings regarding Bill C-16, legislation to protect gender identity and gender expression in the human rights code. I had an extraordinarily positive experience. I saw firsthand behind the scenes, both senators and elected officials working across party lines to try and get this legislation passed and also working with members of vulnerable communities, particularly trans folks, in a way that was very respectful and important. Despite the fact that there was still some opposition within the Senate, what really stood out to me was the way in which a kind of progressive view of politics could actually be championed and struggled for. And so, for me, seeing that was very inspiring.

MELANEE THOMAS: My experiences that led me to seek out the candidacy was my job in government relations. I was a new grad, freshly twenty-two, and working in policy advocacy at the Alberta legislation under the Klein government. We were trying to advocate for progressive politics on behalf of a diverse set of social groups. It was just losing every single day, and I knew I needed to get out of that job. I had already applied to and been accepted to grad school, so I had my "out" for September, but I knew I couldn't keep doing the work for much longer.

I remember I was helping out Shannon Phillips at the time [who is now an NDP member of the Legislative Assembly in Alberta] and she got a job organizing for the federal NDP in rural Alberta. And driving to the middle of nowhere sounded way more pleasant than doing a job I hate. She asked me to run, and I said no a few times. And then we were in Lethbridge where I knew people and she outed me to the constituency association as a potential candidate. I was like, "I never said yes to this!" That was in 2004. The nice way of framing it is open minded, another way of framing this is naïve as to what the campaign would actually involve.

But I ran twice. I ran in 2004 following a minority parliament (which we hadn't seen in decades), so the constituency association asked to renominate me just so I could literally run a paper campaign because they knew I was going to grad school. The constituency association president was a retired professor, so they kind of understood what was going on in that context. Our goal was just to get 10 per cent of the vote, and we got 9.7 percent the first time around. The second time around, in 2006, we did get it [the 10 per cent] and all I did was leaflet drops and forums. I didn't do any door knocking.

On Constructing a Public-Facing Image

NV: My team was very careful to make sure that I didn't come off as the arrogant professor so there was this quiet push to downplay my academic training or my knowledge. I suspect that part of that is being female, because the other two people on the ticket—one Green member that was a professor at Laurentian University, and the Conservative that was a family doctor—were referred to by their earned titles. It wasn't uncommon that they, or hosts of the debates, would remind the public of their credentials. I'm not sure that it's any different in the classroom. I still feel that as a female political scientist in a very male-dominated part of political science, I am still fighting for recognition, or respect, in the classroom that my male counterparts don't have to.

In addition, we were a close riding, and I was seen as a major challenger for the Liberal seat, so I became a target, and in a very passive aggressive way. My integrity was questioned, and I wanted to respond but I was told not to and that I would lose focus. The fact that I wasn't allowed to respond to questioning about why I was running, my integrity, and my knowledge of Canadian politics really frustrated me. As for asserting more control, this is what I advised my current team, if I do run again, I am not going to be that naïve, new candidate who doesn't know what she's doing, I'm actually going to have a say. So, for example, when press releases were being put out on my behalf and there would be direct quotes, I learned that candidates' quotes aren't really their words, someone writes it for them. And it's given to you. A couple of times I was reading it over and thought that it didn't sound like me. It was grammatically incorrect. I would point that out, and they would respond, "don't worry about it because the everyday person understands it." But I would say that I don't speak this way and I certainly don't write this way. So I had to compromise on that, which sounds minor, but it was grammatically incorrect. So there was a lot of giving up, not just control, but giving up the image that they're portraying.

KEM: I say this also knowing fully well as a nomination candidate, you have a lot more freedom in what you do and how you do it than you do once you become the official candidate for a party. With that being said, the second time I ran, I hired a smart campaign manager who had extensive campaign leadership experience, and whose opinion I valued at times more than my own. If I were to do it again, I would be much more assertive on certain points. Just to give one example, my campaign manager wanted to present me in materials as a kind of mom figure, but a big part of my work in both my research and my activism is actually in deep tension with the political representation of the mother. In my campaign poster in summer 2019, my campaign manager asked me to wear a white button-down shirt. In 2018, by way of contrast, I had worn (in a campaign video) a beautiful green suit that a mentor had handed down to me years earlier and that I had worn on my first day of teaching at Concordia and to some of my first academic conferences. It was a meaningful piece—I was physically trying to embody the work I was doing. But he wanted the mom image. I felt like I was really the white mom up on the poster and that didn't feel good; it was highly problematic. So, yes, there is a whole terrain there that you're negotiating and subject to and trying to find your way through and it can be super challenging.

On Messaging

NV: One thing I found frustrating with central [the central office of the party] was that I felt they weren't listening to me. We had somewhat of a role in developing the plan for Northern Ontario, but what I was hearing at the door as to what was important to the people of Sudbury was different from the messaging they wanted me to get across and wasn't really reflected in the central platform.

MT: My experience was a bit different, a little bit more like a nomination campaign because the stakes were so low. But this idea of the central party not knowing how to speak to local issues, I did my best. I remember thinking, I will speak the language, and I just took the core of the book and not the messaging they gave me. I remember in 2006, looking at the messaging and reading one or two sentences as part of a forum and I was like, "no." It was just so wrong, and I remember thinking, they're not watching close enough, it's not competitive, they don't care if I am quoted in the local paper speaking about a core policy but not using their language for it.

NV: On that point too, Melanee, with messaging, there was also a real sense of pride that 80 to 90 per cent of the NDP candidates in Northern Ontario were women. But the issues and how we discussed them did not have a feminist angle. One of the main issues that I put up in the forefront during the nomination was violence against women because it was a topic that was important to me, and since the pandemic we have seen an increase in violence against women, especially in Sudbury. But it was a non-issue during the election. I kept on and was constantly told we would bring it up when the time is right, but it did not appear in any campaign material. When we talked about childcare, it frustrated me that it's 2021 and we are still talking about it as a women's issue as opposed to a family issue. When we say that a nationalized daycare system will help women, rather than families, we are reinforcing that idea that women are primary caregivers and that there is an obligation for women to take care of it. So, while we took pride in the NDP having the most diverse slate of candidates, it wasn't necessarily reflected in the messaging on the ground.

On Feeling (Un)safe

MT: I remember door knocking being a demoralizing experience as a young woman—the misogyny and the age bias. We don't talk about the age bias in politics very much, but there was hostility. Also, I couldn't go alone very often because it wasn't safe. And if I went with a friend of mine, people thought we were risible—as in "it's hilarious, you idiot, that you think you can do this." It was mocking in a nasty kind of way.

And your credibility gets maligned, right? It's one thing to have it happen during the campaign, but I still experience it, especially that open letter after Jason Kenney.[1] Because can you imagine trying to tell a political scientist that they can't do their job because they were a failed candidate when they were twenty-two, and that the person speaking, it is somebody who denied people dying of AIDS in hospice access to their family members, as if I somehow, I was the immoral one. But that this is still used as a stick to hit us with is interesting.

NV: I know this term is overused but it's so true, there is a lot of mansplaining telling you how you should feel. There was this one incident on the campaign where someone charged towards me. His language wasn't gendered but I'm sure he felt confident charging towards me because I am a woman. It was frightening, to say the least. I was told by senior leaders in my campaign not to worry about it, he's harmless, he has mental health issues, things like that, which didn't take away from how I felt, how vulnerable I felt in that situation. What was also interesting but so discouraging, was that it was the only time I was brought to tears during the campaign. The next day, my campaign manager did advise me to make a police incident [report] because the team was advised that he will be at future debates. I didn't know what to expect, at that point I wasn't feeling safe with him around.

In trying to report the incident to the local police officer, they kept diminishing my experiences and the officer kept saying to me, "well it's not as if he broke the law, he didn't do anything criminal. I don't know how you want me to report this." Then she put me on hold and when she came back, she told me that now that I am a political figure, they will take down the report. My thoughts were, "Oh my god, if I wasn't a political figure, I would have no recourse." So it started with me being told that he's harmless and that my feelings and sense of security being compromised didn't matter. I don't like to be patted on the head. I don't like to be told I'm overreacting. No one likes to be talked down to and there was quite a bit of that, telling me how to feel, how to approach things as if my opinion, my lived experiences, didn't matter. I don't know how we go about changing that.

KEM: I don't think there's any time when I was campaigning that I ever felt unsafe. So I just want to say that I'm really sorry you had that experience because as political scientists who study gender and politics, we know that politics is less and less safe for women, online and physically as well. What you went through is awful and I'm really sorry.

On the Implications of Feminist Campaigning for Political Science
NV: I started sensing before I ran, and when I started teaching in Northern Ontario, that people want to learn about political science, but in a localized setting, in the sense where they want to know how this struggle between the federal and provincial governments affects them directly. The difference with the campaign and the classroom is how you word it. I think it's very important to talk about the divisions of power and

who has the ability to do what, but at the end of the day, the average citizen doesn't care, they just want the job done. So, when I go back to teaching, this is something that I foresee myself stressing more. And if I do run again, it's more of that.

On the ground, it is so real and so tangible. As I mentioned before, we had somewhat of a role in developing the plan for Northern Ontario, but on the central plan, what was important to the people of Sudbury wasn't really reflected in the central messaging. When I would go back to my campaign manager and say this message is not resonating, the response would always be, "this is what central wants you to do." So this idea of the centralizing of power, that is something I am going to bring into the classroom. It is real in the House of Commons, when we see the power of the leaders, but it's so real on the campaign. For instance, one of the main messages coming out of the NDP campaign in this last election was to tax the super-rich or let the super-rich pay. And I kept telling them, this idea of the super-rich, doesn't resonate here with people in Sudbury, because more often than not, the people in Sudbury don't encounter the super-rich. So telling, you know, a miner that the NDP is looking to tax the super-rich, the miner would respond with, "I am fighting for retirement benefits, I am fighting for my child to have a future here, because there is nothing going on in Sudbury, what are you going to do then?" That message wasn't taken. The centralization of power, of control in the hands of the leader, was so tangible and real for me in this election.

KEM: I think for me it's a little hard to separate out how my experiences as a candidate have transformed my teaching of political science. But when I taught Introduction to Comparative Politics at the beginning 2020, for the first time in a couple decades, it was coming from having just emerged out of two very exciting grassroots campaigns, where I was able to break out of my academic bubble in a really profound and meaningful way and build lifelong relationships with people in communities that would never have otherwise happened.

For me, coming back into the classroom with those foundational experiences and my own sense of community and my own sense of Montreal in its incredible complexity and multiplicity, knowing that I needed to teach much differently as a consequence. Like really, what does this mean for teaching at Concordia, where you have a lot of first-generation students, where you have students coming from many of the communities where I was campaigning and knocking on doors? I was also coming out of the women's studies classroom. Being principal of the Simone de Beauvoir Institute and teaching in women's studies classes, really shifted my thinking about how I need to be teaching. Coming back in and designing an Introduction to Comparative Politics class, I really wanted to shift the narrative around, I really wanted it to be more about how it is my students can be connecting to the various concepts and struggles. The campaigns had these ripple effects out beyond the simple win or lose of the election itself in my classroom work, in my community work, and in my research.

MT: There are two things that immediately come to mind for me on how this changes how I think about political science. This is the benefit of having gone through it and then designing research projects based on the experience where in Canadian political science, we have very detailed explanations about what's going on with the individuals in elections, and we've got reasonably good explanations of what is going on nationally, and we ignore the middle. We have ontological problems. We like to think that districts don't matter, and that district campaigns don't matter. [But] districts matter, what candidates are doing matters.

And this brings me to my second point, which feminists will understand well. The embodiment of the representative matters. There is sexism that structures Canadian politics from top to bottom, just like white supremacy does and you can see it as a candidate in ways that you cannot see it with the preferred empirical methodological tools. There's a lot of geography but we don't think about the sexism, we don't think about who the candidate is and how that matters. But you know that on a campaign, like when you're the candidate, you know.

On Possibilities for Change

MT: When I think about how campaigning could be better, two things come to mind. One is that none of this is going to change until we dismantle the system of problems. It's super easy to want to tackle the system and sexism but there's some stuff that isn't going to be fixed if you don't do that. And the other thing, we need to rethink how we do politics as work because the workload expectations for candidates and for representatives are wrong. I think they are morally wrong to say that this person, because they do this job, has no right to privacy, no right to be able to have a boundary between their public and private life, has no right to expect a forty-five-hour work week, etc. Feminist theory can come up with a number of interventions that would actually make this stuff easier. And if you think about how and who representatives are supposed to be, I don't think they are supposed to be superhuman and I don't think they are supposed to be necessarily exceptional. But everybody should be able to do it if they are so inclined, I think it should be accessible in that way. The way we do, the way that we think about the work of the job, it's got some real issues with it.

KEM: I will say that for the most part, both of my two experiences were extraordinarily positive and life-giving for me. But again, I just really want to stress, I am the anomaly because there are so many people, including women, trans, nonbinary, people from first-generation Canadian families, etc., who, for all kinds of reasons, wouldn't think about running, and if they do want to, the steps that are necessary for engaging at this level are just too high. And I think if we want to talk about equity and diversity and inclusion and anti-racism work, there's just a real disconnect in terms of when we think about our political institutions, both the campaign itself and putting oneself forward as a candidate. As parties, you're trying to encourage a greater diversity of candidates. And, if you're saying okay, well, this is the campaign book and here are all the talking points and here are all the positions, and you have to stick to the script, that in itself denies that encouragement because there's no way of pivoting or speaking to, through, and out of a candidate's own experience, own knowledge, and own capacity. And so, you're in effect losing the very thing that diversity is supposed to bring into being.

Also, the amount of time, energy, money, support, informal networks, formal networks, job flexibility, childcare, etc., that is needed is extensive. From what I have seen municipally, provincially, and federally, there's still a lot of work to do to understand the party system in our country because there's still this very strong discourse of "you just have to want it badly enough." And that discourse feels like a major form of gaslighting for the many people who would love to participate and to go out there and advocate on the issues that are top of mind for them, but simply aren't able to because the structural barriers are too high. We just don't talk about this enough.

NV: I agree with both Melanee and Kimberley, it is still a money game. One thing that was told to me when I won the nomination was to begin making a rolling list of all the contacts you can reach out to and ask for money, and I told them what you told them. My network isn't that big, and even if it is, at best we are talking about small donations. But there was this constant pressure to raise money. And just how the election played out here, it was quite obvious which campaigns had money and which ones didn't. On what I could change—again this is just picking up on what both Melanee and Kimberley are saying—there is a disconnect on what central thinks is best for all of Canada versus what matters to the local community. So I would say more conversation with local candidates. And be ready to change or alter your message. It's kind of like our research: we start off with research questions and then as you dig in and you do your experiment or what not, you realize, wow, I'm going down the wrong road, I need to go down this way. There isn't, there isn't that opportunity to do this in campaigns.

Note

1. In November 2019, then Alberta Premier Jason Kenney dismissed comments by NDP Opposition leader Rachel Notley who had quoted Melanee Thomas, stating that "it is so sad over there that they're now resorting to quoting NDP candidates like Ms. Thomas as objective sources." In addition to Thomas's own tweets about this, a number of organizations released statements supporting her, including the University of Calgary and the Canadian Political Science Association. See discussion in Andrew Jeffrey and Nadine Yousif, "Why Experts Say Kenney's Critique of a Calgary Professor Is a Strike against Academic Freedom," *Toronto Star*, November 26, 2019, https://www.thestar.com/calgary/2019/11/26/jason-kenney-criticism-melanee-thomas-academic-freedom.html.

GATEKEEPING, PEDAGOGY, AND MENTORING

14 Radical Pedagogies for the Present

Vignettes on Decolonial Feminist Potentials in the Classroom

DAVID SEMAAN

THIS CHAPTER PRESENTS a series of vignettes that offer insight into my experiences of challenging dominant narratives of race and gender in the classroom. These vignettes are only some examples of creating solidarities through mentorship with students of colour and allies. I am currently a PHD candidate; however, I have been working as a teaching assistant (TA) for a few years now. I am also a settler of colour, my family originating from Lebanon. As a settler of colour, I have extensively reflected on my particular position as a settler on Indigenous land, while still operating within a matrix of white supremacy. Through these vignettes, I want to demonstrate what my students have also reflected on in the multiple identities they embody and their situatedness in the broader colonial landscape. As a racialized teaching assistant, a precarious employment position of its own, I am tasked not only with teaching content but also with the often unrecognized work of mentorship that students seek out. TAs are not typically recognized as instructors, mentors, or organized workers. At least if we are, it is not reflected in our pay. At a large university like York, TAs are the first and often only point of contact with the course. We not only grade students' assignments but deliver the content in tutorial, grade, and manage our workload. Students of colour seek this mentorship especially from graduate students of colour often because they see us as a roadmap to learn from and an example of possibility in an academic space where they see so little of themselves elsewhere.

Overall, this chapter highlights the potential for critical pedagogy found in the liminal space of tutorials as sites fraught with political tension and room for critical feminist interrogation. This work involves a degree of care and investment in our students, charged with the political dimension of creating space, particularly queer, racialized, and woman-identified students in the classroom. Students bring both their academic acuity and personal experiences with them to the classroom, and therefore learn to challenge and engage with racism, sexism, ableism, and transphobia on a personal and social level often at the earliest stage of their academic career. These vignettes are not meant to expose the personal lives of students but to underline and recognize the creative ways students negotiate difference and create educational spaces, and sometimes build solidarity to interrogate difficult topics that they don't just study but live out every day. They are neither exhaustive nor comprehensive of the many examples I'm sure my colleagues also have had in their tutorials and classrooms. Some conversations outlined in these vignettes have radicalized me in so many ways and inspired me to rethink decolonial and feminist practice. In vignette #1 I discuss introducing the concept of decolonization to my students and the inherent responsibility of challenging the canon that decolonization brings to the fore. In vignette #2 I discuss what I learned as valuable feminist lessons on care, vulnerability, and unspoken intuitional responsibilities that scholars of colour take on. As I discuss in vignette #3, I have also learned through mistakes about my responsibilities toward my racialized and woman-identified students to not reproduce certain institutional violences. A critical pedagogy approach oriented toward social action can redefine academic engagement between students in the classroom as a site of potential terrain of struggle for decolonization.[1] Jodi Melamed (2018) rightfully points out that the anti-intellectual attacks levelled at universities, weaponized through the rhetoric of free speech, are a product of corporatized post-secondary institutions. However, a pedagogy of dissent can be adapted for social science curricula to seriously engage with settler colonial legacies in our institutional practices, and call for a radical pedagogy, as Melamed articulates, directly concerned with social action.

    These vignettes are a disturbance of the traditional binaries often replicated in post-secondary education such as mind/body, universal/particular, emotional/rational, and so on. I believe that these vignettes offer examples of making space for ways of knowing that are much more comprehensive than conventional binary thinking. These vignettes intend to demonstrate how anti-racist, anti-imperial, decolonial, and feminist pedagogies can challenge the binaries that condition how we value knowledge in academia. The COVID-19 pandemic has changed many institutional dynamics in universities and thrust TAs into the roles of primary instructors, which reveals the true scope of the labour we perform for our students, particularly women, students of colour, queer students, and students with disabilities. I identify as a queer scholar of colour, and while being a cisgender man has protected me of some of the worst aspects of institutional life, other aspects of my identity have provided me with a unique role in the classroom that I did not anticipate when I first became a TA in 2017. Some conversations in the classroom or with individual students have shocked me, some have thrown me off balance altogether. But some of the most memorable experiences have taught me that everyone brings their full selves to the classroom. Nobody leaves their lives, identity, or experiences at the door, and for that reason the classroom space is not only a place for students and instructors to congregate but also can be a radical pedagogical space. Classrooms with tutorial instructors in particular, as not yet institutionalized scholars, negotiate the tension of their place as workers with their commitment to their students and to the process of radical pedagogy. This radical pedagogy approach centres tutorials as a space of learning oriented toward decolonial thought and practice and fosters an imagination for direct social action. This is not true for every TA, or every classroom, but the vignettes I share are my experiences of that radical negotiation.

Vignette 1: What's Decolonial About Pedagogy?
"What does 'decolonizing' mean?" asks one student. "Like, we throw the word around so much and we've been using it all class, but what does it actually mean?" At first, I was taken aback by the question, as if I was already convinced it had a straightforward answer. I was wary that the student didn't actually want to know or was concealing the question under a veil of polite vindictiveness. I paused and felt the eye roll of the classroom, and this made me realize that it is one of the most profound questions he could have asked in a class on political theory. This student had always been interested in dissecting the concepts and theories we engaged with. Other students had often dismissed his inquiries or challenges on the basis that he spoke with a prohibitive stutter and often took time to express himself. There was a not so hidden exhaustion on the part of other students, repeatedly rolling their eyes when he spoke, that I read as an expression of ableism and took note of early on. As the tutorial

instructor, I felt I had a responsibility to ensure he had the proper space and recognition for his contributions to the classroom. To borrow from Sara Ahmed, I didn't want the room to reorient itself toward able-bodied students, excluding him in the process and leaving an ableist imprint on the space itself (2006, 563).

In the few seconds I took to pause, I realized the expansive depth of his question, and that I couldn't answer it in the five minutes left before the end of class. While I opened it up for the class to engage with some Indigenous scholars we had read from that week, I made a commitment to them that we would dedicate the entirety of next tutorial on that exact question. The following week, I began with a series of questions that I believed would prime students for the issue. What does decolonization "look" like? Building on Glen Coulthard and Audra Simpson, authors we had read, what does it entail? Lastly, I asked students, citing Simpson (2016), what role do settlers have in decolonization? I asked this question not to decentre Indigeneity but to make settler students in the class critically reflect on their role in perpetuating and benefitting from colonialism. As the conversation progressed, settlers' responsibility in decolonizing our own psychic and material lives became clearer. In all my classes I remind my students that racism is not racialized peoples' problem; it's a white problem. The burden of dismantling dominant and violent epistemes cannot just be Black, Indigenous, or people of colour's responsibility, because the institution of white supremacy is enacted by the function of whiteness. Motivated by this idea, I decided to not only engage in decolonial thought but also tried to articulate ways we can think of decolonial practice.

Simpson (2016) draws on Darryl Leroux's argument that white Canada is complicit in the disappearance of Indigenous women. She writes, "Darryl Leroux made a careful, and simultaneously impassioned plea in the *Huffington Post* for white Canadians to think about the history that they inhabit, the benefits that they incur from Indigenous dispossession—as Indigenous dispossession is, as I have just argued, foundational for Canada (and of course, the United States)" (2016, 8). Simpson also reflects on her own relationship with teaching as a research professor. She expresses that even though she is a research professor, she expends so much energy on her teaching and her relationship with students to the point of sickness because she sees the need for decolonial pedagogy in the classroom (11). She commits to teaching because of the high stakes of teaching these very subjects, on this land, rubbing against the "canonical" texts that continue to justify dispossession and disavowal of Indigenous land. This is where radical pedagogy enters a scene of urgency. As Simpson points out, because Indigenous and decolonial literature is not curricular, if she does not teach this material, her students may never come across this information. They may never learn, in any other of the dozens of classes throughout their university careers, the history of and continued colonial dispossession. I learn from Simpson and others that decolonial pedagogy is not just an addition; it is crucial to transform students' knowledge and the knowledge-producing institutions students attend. The student who asked "What does 'decolonizing' mean?" was inspired by the subsequent conversations we had. Other students said that they wanted to see this type of inquiry mainstreamed in other courses outside of the social sciences and discussed what that might look like. The recurring theme of our conversation was the lack of Indigenous theory and broader theorization of colonialism in the canonical texts in other social science courses. Students also expressed a dismay in the persistent efforts in canonical political theory texts to erase colonial history (see discussion in Coburn et al., this volume). As settler students, educators, and scholars who live and work on Indigenous land, we are responsible in interrogating colonialism's afterlife through our pedagogical methods and methodologies. This is not limited to those who are concerned with feminist inquiry; the epistemic questions raised by decolonial research and pedagogy can, to borrow from Linda Tuhiwai Smith, offer an opportunity for "breakage" or to push back on modernity's imperialist reach into our ways of thinking (2012, 24). Radical pedagogies call on us to break with canonical thinking. Decolonial and anti-imperialist epistemes question modes of knowledge production that place liberal abstraction above other forms of knowledge, often excluding feminist, decolonial, and leftist knowledge in favour of institutionally apologetic scholarship legitimized in preserving historical structures of white supremacy and sexism.

This vignette points to radical pedagogies that centre decoloniality, offering up not only an alternative curriculum to that of standardized political science, but also truly engaging with the lived experiences students bring to the classroom. Lived experiences that are fundamentally intertwined with the institutional processes of ongoing colonization, when allowed room in a space of critical exchange, can transform the circulation of stories, and knowledge dissemination in the classroom as a form of decolonial practice. Rather than uncritically perpetuate the canonical liberal texts that historically functioned as the standard bearers of imperial conquest, a radical pedagogical method that centres decolonial inquiry can offer up a crucial vantage point into history for what it is, and how it is expressed in students' lives. Part of that decolonial practice is achieved through collaborative work among teaching teams and students to build relational ways of learning and acting.

Vignette 2: Care As a Feminist Pedagogical Practice
Educators are not just teaching politics; we are doing politics in the classroom. We are not just teaching about race, but we are engaging in the element of race in the practice of the classroom. The goal of my radical pedagogy is rooted in practicing feminism and critical race theory in the classroom in post-secondary education. I hope educators see this work not as additional to but necessary in advancing social justice and in depicting a more accurate history of social scientific and political thought if political science is to maintain any relevance. If the COVID-19 pandemic has taught me anything about academia, it is that vulnerability is a beautiful and necessary form of feminist pedagogy. As I'm writing this chapter, I am beginning my third semester as a TA for a fully online course. Many of my students are working abroad in different time zones. Some of my students have contracted COVID-19, some have lost several family members to the virus and suffered immense grief during a time of intense emotional duress. The institutional messaging of my university executive calls for solidarity and support amongst each other as we navigate this highly unequal social terrain, and my students are the attrition in this academic crossing. As both a student and TA, I have witnessed and felt, like all of my colleagues, at times the insurmountable emotional toll that working in isolation has had on our health, while working to meet pre-pandemic deadlines. Consistently throughout the semester I had to convince myself, and my students in an exercise of self-assurance, that we are going through a period of extreme crisis and that our previous standards of productivity have to be abandoned. I worked to trust that my work still holds value, but that my previous standards of productivity in a pre-pandemic world no longer do. That world is definitively

gone, and probably for the better, but I've used the classroom as a space to practice feminist pedagogy of patience, forgiveness, and vulnerability for both myself and my students. It was possibly the hardest lesson to collectively learn in our two semesters together. I do not have immediate caring responsibilities for children or elders, unlike many of my colleagues and students; however, COVID-19 challenged all previous, and already broken, arrangements of social reproduction. Therefore, scholars concerned with feminist pedagogical methods, such as myself, the teaching team, and professors I have worked with had to learn to create new spaces that recognized and respected so much of the reproductive labour our students took on while pursing education.

Vulnerability in the Academy
During the fall and winter semesters of 2020–21, I was assigned to an introductory social sciences course focused on teaching the history of modernity and political economy. The anxiety of my students was palpable, and it was clear that a pedagogical approach that foregrounded the collective trauma we were going through was critical in giving meaning to the content we were teaching. Not only to advance our teaching goals that provide them with introductory knowledge of political economy, but to treat these theories as issues of justice, as they expressed themselves in the everyday lives of students. Care in this context is more than affective labour; it is also a political statement that is charged with radical potential for reconstituting our world that is unfolding and being marked by a permanent change.

I asked my students in the second tutorial, "How are you feeling at this very moment? What is going through your mind?" Immediately words such as *grief*, *fear*, and *anxiety* came to the surface. A call for a caring space, a pedagogical method centred on care, seemed necessary to speak truth to the matter of the content we were about to study. Concepts such as divisions of labour, capitalist development, and modernity could not escape the practical setting we were studying as digitized reflections of ourselves negotiating our private lives collapsed in the same space of our academic work. I strategized with the teaching team about ways to express care in the classroom, but also the theoretical work to move beyond the insular text divorced from the meaning of lived experience. Here, feminist practice came into motion. The personal is obviously political, and the personal is practiced as a political endeavour to build community in a time of crisis.

Grief is something that grips and does not let go; for some of us, it can be all consuming. The COVID-19 pandemic is a form of collective grief, and for anyone who has grieved profound loss, it can also be accompanied by a loss of a sense of purpose. Some of my students said that they did not understand the purpose of continuing school as if it were normal circumstances. Grief brings out a variety of responses in how people cope. Some of my students expressed anger, some fear, others depression and loss of place. Others still expressed a sense of denial and saw school as a distraction from the sense of panic they were feeling. It became clear after speaking with them that our tutorials meant different things to each of them, but that a sense of stability, a place of mutual respect and care, provided reprieve and a feeling of being listened to. Knowing that someone cared and created deliberate space for vulnerability from the outset was important for some to anchor themselves. Making space for vulnerability in academic settings is critical to breaking down the walls that have worked so hard to historically exclude a diversity of students I mentioned above. Vulnerability in a historically suffocating space is a radical move to decolonize the space and practice of academia so adamant on Western and masculine standards of proper conduct. Enacting vulnerability is a radical move in academia because academia disciplines us to be rigid. Vulnerability, however, doesn't soften us but transcends the artificial walls between emotion and reason to articulate radical imaginaries through lived experience. In the face of crisis, we need feeling as well as thinking and doing not only to survive but to articulate interventions that give life back to institutions that were already in a state of protracted decay (see also Paterson's discussion of vulnerability and care in this volume).

Valuing Labour in Our Classrooms

In this tutorial we discussed the development of capitalism and the value of reproductive labour in the context of crisis, which allowed students to articulate what had previously seemed like taken-for-granted lived experiences as political realities. One of my students became particularly attached to Silvia Federici's (1975) *Wages against Housework* because she felt recognized in the reproductive labour she and her mother did that she knew was not explicitly socially valued. The value of reproductive labour has been foregrounded for many by the pandemic, but for this student reading feminist literature and engaging with it in dialogue gave her language for something she already understood. She knew that her mother and her took on disproportionate amounts of labour in the home, everything from childcare to maintenance of daily household life. To punctuate the point, I asked the class to define succinctly what reproductive labour actually is. After much pause and difficulty placing the meaning of the term, they provided examples of what can be considered reproductive labour, such as childcare, cooking, cleaning. But I also pressed them to think of how knowledge within their family, their history, and culture gets transmitted from one generation to the next. Who is primarily responsible for conveying lessons, knowledge, and family history to them as children and now young adults? From there, they broadened their definitions to also encompass the affective aspect labour involved in household reproduction. They were more forthcoming in reflecting on their mothers' care in times of need, advice, and emotional support. Collectively, we concluded that reproductive labour is any type of labour that facilitates and supports daily life. Reproductive labour is life-giving work in all its iterations. I hoped this feminist socialist education on labour would generate radical alternatives to social relations. This consciousness matters because a post-secondary education should be oriented toward direct action that transforms our own social relations. Feministing in political science, in this case, is engaging in a feminist education of labour inside and outside the academy. It is rooting our education of labour in our intimate relations, it is challenging the dominant narratives of labour value. Feministing the classroom is also centring the importance of reproductive labour to push back against the artificial division of intellectual labour and the labour of sustaining life as if they are separable. Feminist education is the most adept at providing students in post-secondary institutions pedagogy directly concerned with their lived experiences and intimate relations as groundwork for institutional transformation.

For this reason, opening up that vulnerable space in tutorial, recognizing the crisis of care work accentuated by the COVID-19 pandemic pushing against their academic lives, was important to several students because it gave theory a material meaning to their lives. For the one student, reproductive labour was not an abstraction; it was a concrete lived experience that she had to take up, and she corporeally understood the challenge and punitive nature of academia for people with caring responsibilities. To go on and teach without concern or attention to the crisis of care work and the collapse of dimensions of the public/private divide would have not been possible; it would have gutted the purpose of teaching about political economies that are fundamentally built on life-giving labour. One student's concluding words in our final tutorial summed up what I'd hoped would be achieved through a class focused on care. In our final goodbye of tutorial, she said, "Thank you for not giving up on us." The gratitude I felt in that moment meant more than being a successful TA, because I wanted to thank them for taking care of all of us.

Vignette 3: Name It for What It Is
Part of feminist pedagogical praxis is embracing the conflict in the classroom and providing students with analytical resources to navigate the tension. As a racialized doctoral student who researches, writes, and teaches about race, I have learned that race is unsettling and disruptive. Sometimes simply being a racialized person in an exclusively white space is disruptive and unsettling. As Ahmed has noted, I know that the mere presence of a person of colour can be an unhappy complication to a previously cohesive state of affairs (2007, 158). I know that many of the students in my tutorials, particularly Black and Indigenous students, at times find themselves alone in their identity and are very aware of this fact. Simply walking through the door is an act of transgression for many spaces, and academia is no exception. The simple mention of Black Lives Matter or Land Back initiatives can lead to a palpable tension in the air. For the majority of the Western academy, there have been deliberate efforts to keep BIPOC faculty, students, and staff outside of their buildings. In an era with the highest enrolment of women and racialized students in universities ever, most BIPOC people can still feel the jagged edges of the institution. I scarcely even like to use the term *introducing* race into courses on capitalism, political economy, or labour, because I cannot conceptually imagine them apart. To introduce race and racism is having to retell the accurate and sincere story that had been previously erased. This is the premise with which I begin with my students. You cannot think of capitalism outside of slavery and colonization. To imagine them as

seperate or additional to the story is to erase five hundred years of history. This very premise can ring in a deafening discomfort in the silence of the classroom. The radical negotiation with professors over who should be included in the syllabus, the negotiation with my students who come from diverse backgrounds and experiences, and my own lived experiences with racism all come into collision in the classroom.

At the very end of one tutorial I was teaching, one white student raised his hand following a heated conversation about misogynoir and gender-based violence. He raised his objection with a noticeably shaken voice to say, "We can't solve racism, if we keep saying f*ck all white people." I was wondering why he felt he had to drop this explosive statement in the middle of the room one minute before the end of class, realizing only after the power of having the last word. Immediately, and predictably, impassioned students wanted to intervene to explain why that statement was so hurtful, including Black women who were in the class. At the time I was afraid of opening up this box that would seemingly never close. I tried for a weak and brief attempt to address the comment and the necessity of anti-racist work that sputtered into a decision to revisit the issue in the next tutorial. However, I still regret having left that comment to be the final word we all walked away with. I realized later that I had protected white fragility and a violent statement like that at the cost of silencing Black students. This was an early personal and pedagogical lesson in maintaining space for the voices of BIPOC students and trusting their knowledge to transform the conversation.

Radical pedagogy is messy and riddled with mistakes, but that cannot be an alibi to avoid it. As educators and researchers concerned with knowledge production and dissemination, we are responsible for taking these challenges head on, acknowledging that this labour is not equally distributed. I have made it my commitment to my students and to myself to not shy away from discomfort in the classroom, because I have learned that discomfort can be a sign that learning is occurring.

In one instance, we had been discussing racial hierarchies in the workplace. In this particular tutorial, all of the students who were present were racialized. The tutorials where only racialized students were present made me realize how much guarding we do as people of colour in predominantly white spaces. How many fine lines we tread in measuring our words to protect white feelings, and how much silent communication is being translated between us when we do not feel as if we can be sincere in telling our experiences. Many of my white students expressed a desire to learn more about race politics in Canada, and various expressions of it in different domains of society. However, something about an exclusively POC space opens a door that is so rarely available to scholars of colour that I often forget their value until I find myself in one. This was the case for this particular tutorial and all of my students had some story to share of their experiences as a person of colour in the workplace. This proved to be not just a space of academic exchange but a moment of solidarity building as we exchanged stories of difficult decisions we made navigating racism in the workplace. This proved to me that a care-centred approach in the classroom, one focused on students' lives, is the starting point for theorizing social phenomena. Our exchanges of tips, experiences, and grievances in dealing with racism were powerful movements of pedagogy for social action taking place in this fleeting space.

Another memorable conversation had to do with the latest developments in gene editing of babies. Some students had raised ethical concerns about this new technology, citing histories of eugenics that worked to exterminate so many racialized populations. The new genetic technology, for some, seemed like an opening for a political economy of white babies and the desirability of white children, a concern I shared with them. One student of colour in the class, however, mentioned that parents should be able to opt for white skin or blue eye colour, for example, because they might reflect on the hardships their child might go through with Brown skin. To frame the concern, I asked in this case if white supremacy was the issue or Brown skin, when another woman of colour quickly intervened to say, "the problem is white supremacy." The learning moment here reminded me that experiences with racism can and do condition people of colour to associate an easier life with white skin. It is based in the reality of the brutalities of white supremacy that privilege white life and bring down violence on racialized bodies. The concerns of the first student, who was also a woman of colour, were not misplaced but were expressed in this thought exercise as a theoretical desire for white skin because of the ease it brings, the feeling of finally being able to relax your shoulders.

Discussions in the classroom were not unlike some conversations of colourism that I've had with friends in my personal life. A desire I once also shared and thought of a lot of as a child. The envy for that feeling of ease, of not being the unhappy discomfort for other people in the room. That creeping feeling of realizing you are a disruption in a peaceful state of white affairs. As an adult and a PHD student concerned with questions of critical race, I now know that sting of resenting yourself a little for making people uncomfortable was in fact internalized white supremacy, a pernicious but invasive force. Almost all people of colour at some point or another, consciously or unconsciously, have tried to reduce their racial difference and increase their proximity to whiteness. That is because all children, but particularly young, racialized children, are taught to devalue their skin and find beauty only in whiteness. That small but potent interaction reminded me of ongoing debates reflected again in my students' lives and found its expression in this unique space we could hold for each other. Not so many years ago, I felt that feeling of disruption and unsettling, but I've learned to embrace it for its radical possibilities. I embrace it because pedagogical discomfort, as an act of subversiveness, is also an act of self-love that is fundamentally radical practice for decolonizing the mind. More so, I hope to have taught my students what I learned with hardship—that embracing that disruptive presence can be a subversive act of resistance and embracing it is a radical power that undermines white supremacy.

Concluding Thoughts
Universities are experiencing an equity, diversity, and inclusion moment. Within this rubric, feminist aspirations of gender equity, addressing intersectional concerns of workplace inclusion, and ending sexual and gender-based violence in our universities have received at least formal recognition by institutions. However, mainstreaming feminist orientations into our pedagogical content and methods remains contested by anti-intellectual cultural debates. Beyond this challenge, the anxieties of mainstreaming or institutionalizing feminist pedagogy does require pause for critical reflection on the harms of institutional co-optation of radical practices and values. On the one hand, introducing feminism into the discipline of political science through pedagogy presents opportunities for challenging dominant power relations in universities that maintain colonial violence. Formalizing the content of feminism in our pedagogical syllabi and methods preserves the hard-won achievements of bringing

feminism from the margin to the centre. On the other hand, anxieties of diluting the critical edge that feminism brings to the table are warranted, because universities do adopt and disarm subversive frameworks for their own institutional needs in self-preservation. The paradox presented here is not new. Mainstreaming feminism into formalized processes and academic pedagogical content has both the potential to dismantle violent relations of power, and/or work as an institutional alibi that preserves ongoing violence (Dhamoon 2015, 29). Feminist, anti-racist, and decolonial scholars then can be understood as trespassers in this context.[2] As trespassers in academic settings, we can often be met with the sharp edges of institutional violence. But subversive academics also hold a special position of insider/outsider knowledge and imagination to decolonize the classroom. I would like to make three points below to present a way forward in feministing our classrooms.

First, as an early career scholar, I am more economically precarious than other more experienced colleagues. However, I am subject to less disciplinary pressure in my ability to research more broadly and freely, with little oversight and pressure for publication, disciplinary practice, and expectations. I emphasize these factors here to highlight the uneven distribution of labour that trespasser academics carry. Women, queer, POC, racialized scholars writ large are tasked with an unwritten script of responsibilities that burden them more than others. However, it is precisely at this juncture that I have personally found the subversive potential of decolonizing the university. I centre decoloniality and feminist thought in my tutorial seminars not just to introduce an alternative syllabus to the standard course option, but to expose my students to radical and transformative thought that they would otherwise not encounter in the majority of their courses. Foregrounding colonization and the slave trade in any discussion of capitalism and modernity is not just about providing a different analytic vantage point into standard political science; it is telling a more accurate and critical reading of modern history. Introducing an epistemic vantage point from feminist and decolonial studies is necessary to address the epistemicide that continues in standard political science syllabi and to advance a pedagogy centred on radical transformation (Loureiro 2020, 51).

The second point I have raised in these vignettes is the need to build social relations of care with my students and colleagues. At the outset of this chapter, I introduced the need to destabilize assumed categories of universality and stable binaries. As Black feminist scholar Patricia Hill Collins has articulated, our particular experiences can refashion individual or group experiences into universalisms and produce new lines of epistemic inquiry (2009, 268). The particular experiences and standpoints of, say, queer, or Black, or women academics inform lines of inquiry and interventions previously excluded from academic knowledge. Collins (2009) further points out that they can generate social justice-oriented knowledge and action moving beyond abstraction. The very terms of what can be inquired and investigated, what merits value for inquiry and the ability to account for those ramifications on societies' most marginalized become possible through the dual life that trespasser academics have. Previously assumed universals of political science and political thought can be destabilized by centring the experiences of trespasser academics. Displacing false universalisms can only be achieved through collective care and uncomfortable solidarities within our classrooms. I have attempted to prioritize insurgent knowledges in my own research and pedagogical practice by repositioning traditional political science within a critical race, anti-imperialist, and feminist framework of discussion. I have done so by providing the necessary space for my students to bring their lived experience to the classroom as political and epistemic engagements. As social scientists concerned with feminist questions, we must always remember that their lives are already implicated in our theoretical discussions.

The final point I bring here is the necessity of facilitating an education that is directly concerned with social action. Our students are already implicated in various social and material relations by virtue of their identities, histories, and material conditions. Our students already have a material stake in the political contestations being debated in political science. On this point, I am still working in collaborations with colleagues formally and informally in imagining the possibilities and exploring the creative and subversive ways of implicating my students in bringing their experiences of social action to the class. I have also reflected on what can be achieved in bringing social action to our students. These prescriptions are by no means comprehensive or useful in every context but reflect some attempts I have made at radicalizing my pedagogy.

At the centre of my pedagogy in the social sciences is always thinking through ways to critically investigate the legacies of slavery, colonialism, and gender-based violence in the very social sciences we are researching and teaching. We cannot separate the university space that we work in from those histories of violence. They are inseparable because it is universities, the global industry of knowledge production, and the relations of production between imperial centre and periphery that birthed the institutions of modernity we inhabit. What I've learned through my limited teaching experience, however, is that students are aware of this history. As I'd hoped to demonstrate through these vignettes, they taught me pedagogical and personal lessons in care and vulnerability. They taught me the importance but also the *means* of creating caring spaces. My students pushed me to really think through what decolonial practice means not only in pedagogy but in daily life. Students have inspired me more, taught me more than I can offer back in living and teaching for dissent. However, learning to teach for dissent is riddled with mistakes. Learning to teaching toward decolonization has been imperfect, but it is that humility that is critical in decolonizing the university. Dismantling the disciplinarity of university spaces requires a level of humility that isn't always present in academic posture, but that our students can teach us. Part of decolonizing the university is rethinking *how* we teach and for *whom* we teach, because students' lived experiences are not neutral nor are they sperate from the history of the brick and mortar we are trying to inhabit as research professionals. Decolonizing the classroom is only one step to decolonizing our relations and building new ones based in mutual care.

Notes

1. I'm inspired by Jodi Melamed's (2018) definition of critical pedagogy, citing Kandace Chuh, as a method of dissent. Critical pedagogies can be oriented toward collective action as a collaborative site that fosters deep relationality.
2. I credit my conversations with Fiona MacDonald for bringing this concept to my attention and providing a new vantage point in subversive academic practices.

References

Ahmed, Sara. 2006. "Orientations: Toward a Queer Phenomenology." *GLQ: A Journal of Lesbian and Gay Studies* 12 (4): 543–74. https://doi.org/10.1215/10642684-2006-002.

Ahmed, Sara. 2007. "A Phenomenology of Whiteness." *Feminist Theory* 8 (2): 149–68. https://doi.org/10.1177/1464700107078139.

Collins, Patricia Hill. 2009. *Black Feminist Thought: Knowledge, Consciousness, and the Politics of Empowerment*, 2nd ed. New York: Routledge.

Dhamoon, Rita Kaur. 2015. "A Feminist Approach to Decolonizing Anti-Racism: Rethinking Transnationalism, Intersectionality, and Settler Colonialism." *Feral Feminisms*, no. 4, 20–37. https://feralfeminisms.com/rita-dhamoon/.

Federici, Silvia. 1975. *Wages against Housework*. Berlin: Falling Wall Press.

Loureiro, Gabriela Silva. 2020. "To Be Black, Queer and Radical: Centring the Epistemology of Marielle Franco." *Open Cultural Studies* 4 (1): 50–58. https://doi.org/10.1515/culture-2020-0005.

Melamed, Jodi. 2018. "The Proliferation of Rights-Based Capitalist Violence and Pedagogies of Collective Action." *American Quarterly* 70 (2): 179–87. https://doi.org/10.1353/aq.2018.0013.

Simpson, Audra. 2016. "The State Is a Man: Theresa Spence, Loretta Saunders and the Gender of Settler Sovereignty." *Theory & Event* 19 (4). https://www.muse.jhu.edu/article/633280.

Smith, Linda Tuhiwai. 2012. "Imperialism, History, Writing and Theory." In *Decolonizing Methodologies Research and Indigenous Peoples*, 2nd ed., 21–47. London: Zed Books.

15

Reworlding the Canadian University

Centring Student Leadership in Institutional Transformation

JAMILAH A.Y. DEI-SHARPE and
KIMBERLEY ENS MANNING

THE JURY IS IN: the last thirty years of equity work in the Canadian academy has failed to transform the structures that prevent Black, Indigenous, Asian, and other peoples racialized as "coloured," or members of the global majority, from fully entering and flourishing in our universities (Henry et al. 2017). According to the most comprehensive study of race and Indigeneity in the Canadian academy, Canadian universities are even less representative than they were during the early 1990s (Henry et al. 2017, 310). Canadian universities, like many other Western academic institutions, have responded to institutional inequities by initiating a proliferation of administration-led task forces, equity policies, and equity offices that have, in some ways, concealed (Ahmed 2012) rather than addressed, fundamental inequities (Henry et al. 2017). Today, the failure of equity, diversity, and inclusion programs (see, e.g., Tungohan, this volume), that we will refer to as EDI or inclusion politics, has become glaringly apparent by the persistence of inequities illuminated by the global pandemic, and the social movements that have gathered increasing force, including Black Lives Matter, Indigenous mobilizations, and anti-Asian hate movements, to name a few.

While past top-down approaches to institutional transformation have faltered, if not outright failed, students, educators, and staff from the global majority have continued to push for and realize much-needed change. If the university is going to undo the structural racism at its base, it will be because leadership by the global majority is supported, resourced, and made central to the processes of transformation. In this chapter we focus on the critically important but often undervalued role that racialized student leaders play in advancing anti-racist educational reform in Canadian universities. Racialized students provide a constant flow of emotional and intellectual labour inside and outside the classroom. As Meghan Gagliardi (forthcoming) argues, the neoliberal university wields an "empowered student" narrative, in which the equity work of racialized students is oversolicited, un(der)compensated, and ultimately undermined by short timelines and other conditions of structural precarity. From the day they enter the university, student leaders respond to systemic racism by challenging microaggressions from classmates and faculty, questioning white syllabi, populating university EDI committees, and working with peers to overturn unjust academic practices.

Racialized students are often tasked with assuming the role of anti-racist experts. As equity tasks proliferate, equity work further renders racialized students subject to precariousness and disempowerment. At worst, the lack of institutional support enables universities to gain access to a consistent flow of free labour to fill equity-related gaps. At best, universities celebrate the contributions of "star" racialized student leaders with awards and media coverage, and the occasional gift of financial recognition. We challenge the inclusive politics of adding racialized bodies and expertise as a means of reform without fundamentally transforming the current system of exclusion. Instead of cultivating reform through a politics of representation or celebration, we suggest a third model: *anti-racist coalition building*, in which university faculty, staff, and administrators assume the role of equity brokers and partner with racialized student leaders. In these pages, we unpack the potential for anti-racist coalition building to yield transformative change by drawing from the tenants of coalition building by women of colour (WOC) feminists, and our individual and joint experiences as a Black PHD student leader (Jamilah) and a white tenured professor and department head (Kimberley). As articulated by feminists of colour, coalition building requires all parties to accountably and "politically commit to disrupting oppressive systems of domination" together (Taylor 2018, 127), mobilizing next-generation expertise with the structural resources needed for institutional transformation.

In this chapter we identify anti-racist coalition building as one means of reworlding the university. Gayatri Spivak (1985) introduces "worlding" as a form of material and ideological conquest through which "colonized consciousness can apprehend itself only in and through colonial systems and knowledges" (Muthyala 2006, 2). Drawing on John Muthyala, we define reworlding as a form of interrogation that disturbs and realigns "the relations among space, time, and memory that create and sustain official, hegemonic culture by managing and policing those communities, cultures, and histories that threaten their power" (2006, 2–3). To reworld the university is to engage in intentional practices that enable the flourishing of racialized peoples—students, faculty, and staff—while simultaneously dismantling the colonial logic at the bedrock of the academy. We see reworlding generally, and coalition building specifically, as a means to disrupt the current Eurocentric worldview/order that dominates higher education.

We begin by arguing that anti-racist coalition building, grounded in a vision of reworlding, holds the potential to break the exploitation of racialized students within the academy, by fundamentally challenging the historical foundations of white supremacy in the modern university. We next turn to the key role that racialized students play in institutional transformation. For true anti-racist coalition building to become realized, we argue that racialized student mobilizers must be recognized, centred, and compensated through new forms of sustainable academic infrastructure. In the context of universities, a "student mobilizer" is a student undertaking an undergraduate or graduate degree while they are actively leading pedagogical initiatives that mobilize marginalized knowledges, reform inequalities in teaching and learning, and increase opportunities for racialized students within the university.[1] In this effort, we argue, that an "equity broker" can also play a key role. We define an equity broker as a university faculty or staff member who actively supports the equity leadership of racialized students in a manner not entirely dissimilar to those who act as an institutional "sponsor" (Hewlett 2013) or "champion" (Henry et al. 2017) of racialized and Indigenized faculty. In the final two parts of the chapter, we deepen these arguments with a fuller discussion of the ethical and material foundations necessary for equity brokers to learn from and with racialized student leaders, in coalitional efforts to reworld the university.

Contextualizing the Field
Anti-Racist Coalition Building: Theory and Practice

In the 1980s, WOC feminists, including Black feminist Audre Lorde, and Chicana feminist Gloria Anzaldua, popularized the notion of coalition and coalition building within the social sciences (Taylor 2018, 121). WOC feminists created coalitions as a civil rights practice in which reciprocal alliances are forged between diverse peoples with a shared commitment to combatting systemic racism and oppression (Taylor 2018, 121). Coalition building is further grounded in a self-reflexive political commitment to engage in a long-term, mutually beneficial partnership despite any unresolved division; to have greater force and support to achieve the systemic transformation desired (Taylor 2018, 122, 124). Unlike traditional inclusive politics, coalitions are not about being a "supportive ally" or increasing representation. Rather, coalitions are grounded in the urgent need for all parties to make demands, make changes, learn and unlearn, and to give and receive love and care (Taylor 2018, 124, 127). In our work together, as a Black graduate student and a white tenured faculty member, we have looked to anti-racist coalition building as an aspirational model to spearhead our shared goals of sustainably resolving inequities, erasure, and exclusion at the bedrock of Canadian universities.

We hold different roles and responsibilities in the academy and yet share a political commitment to institutional transformation. As a graduate student mobilizer, Jamilah uses her position to leverage connections between students and administrators, the community, and the academy. As a faculty broker, Kimberley uses her position to amplify the work of student leaders through funding, connections, and institutional resources. In 2020 we established the Anti-Racist Pedagogy Project (ARPP)—a public database of educational videos and accompanying resources on systemic racism and COVID-19 designed to assist educators and students with the integration of anti-racist education and pedagogy into their teaching and research. Under the leadership of Jamilah, the project evolved into a Respond to Crisis initiative (R2C) and open-source Anti-Racism Video Library housed on the Decolonial Perspectives and Practices Hub (DPPH) webpage, which is now supporting the anti-racist pedagogical aspirations of instructors across Montreal and Canada. As we have reflected upon our work together, we have realized that our capacity to develop a sustainable anti-racist initiative derived from the politically synergic, reciprocal, and hierarchically challenging coalition that we built.

Our coalitional work began in 2018, when we met at a graduate student African studies conference. Addressing the lack of non-Western scholarship in the core graduate curriculum, the conference centred scholarship by African scholars on African politics and society. Jamilah attended the African studies conference as the founder of the DPPH,[2] at the time, a coalition of students invested in social justice education who organized events to sustain dialogue on decolonization and the curricular incorporation of anti-colonial, marginalized, and queer knowledges within Concordia University. Kimberley attended the conference as a faculty supporter as a part of her journey of accountability: she was deeply aware that the Comparative Politics graduate seminar she had previously taught contributed to a collective experience of the Eurocentric whiteness in her home discipline. At that time, she was also working on Critical Feminist Activism and Research (CFAR), a three-year pilot project dedicated to cultivating anti-oppressive and anti-racist approaches to equity, inclusion, and representation on campus.

After working closely with CFAR's two graduate student coordinators, Annick Maguile Flavien and Meghan Gagliardi, and learning more about the challenges faced by racialized students and faculty, Kimberley was continually rethinking about institutional transformation. Connecting with Jamilah, who was already reshaping pedagogical thinking and practice at Concordia, opened a new opportunity to participate in and support the DPPH. Upon introduction, we gradually began to form an ongoing collaboration based upon the WOC coalitional ethics that Liza Taylor defines as reciprocity, renumeration, and respect (2018, 124). An ethos of reciprocity and mutuality has grounded our shared commitment to institutional change, including the determination to transgress the "saviour complex" by strategically acknowledging and leveraging our differing expertise, experience, and access to power and resources.

The first stage of our collaboration emerged in the classroom, when Jamilah and Kimberley worked together on an introductory course in women's studies. Although the relationship began as one of professor and teaching assistant, Jamilah rapidly assumed an increasingly important role in the development and delivery of the course. A dynamic of growing trust, in turn, enabled us to respond to the unprecedented challenges that commenced with the onset of the COVID-19 pandemic and the globalization of Black Lives Matter. Specifically, in summer 2020 we proposed to launch the ARPP, with Jamilah assuming the role of project manager. By this time, we trusted that our collaboration would not be marred by tokenism but geared toward sustainable change.

The key to sustaining the coalition has involved consistently drawing from our reciprocal, activist, and care-driven relationship to deepen the reach, uptake, and accessibility of our work, and maintaining and deepening our commitment to reduce the unequal power relations that mark professor and student. It is important to note, however, that our relationship is nonetheless shaped through the hierarchical imperatives of the university. Right from the outset, Kimberley had privileged access to resources and networks that were not available to Jamilah. The simple fact that Kimberley was in a financial position to initiate our early collaborations reinforced the racial, institutional, seniority, and age differentials between us. This dynamic is not atypical: indeed, the university is built upon the expectation that faculty and administrators initiate, and students follow, rendering anti-racist coalition work in institutions unreliably dependent on individual desires and unlikely mandates for systemic change.

Racialized Students and the Academy: A Fraught History
As several scholars have argued, the contemporary North American university is rooted in a colonial and genocidal logic to erase and assimilate Indigenous and African bodies, and histories into Western European and white supremacist ideals (Ashwar 2015; De Lissovoy 2010; Jones and West 2002; Stein 2016). In the North American context, the European colonial project murdered and exiled Indigenous Peoples and established settlements on Indigenous lands (Land 2015). The histories and cultures of African peoples were also subject to violent disruption: histories in which peoples racialized as Black were murdered or forcefully enslaved to build Western civilization on stolen Indigenous lands (Jones and West 2002). Khalil Saucier and Tyron Woods remind us that it is central to colonial logics to conceive of racialized bodies as fungible—as objects to be used to serve certain ends, then replaced and discarded (2014, 8). Philip Howard (2021) highlights these realities by asserting the ways that North American universities are intrinsically built upon an anti-Black pedagogy.

In the nineteenth century, universities were reserved for "whites only." In the twentieth century, universities became racially segregated, offering students of colour subpar educational resources; the Western model of higher education also globalized—standardizing the exclusionary colonial academy across the world (Mignolo 2007). Today, in the West—Europe, Canada, and the United States—academic institutions promote themselves as "diverse and inclusive" by visibly celebrating the attendance of racialized and international students, and yet the knowledges and pedagogies of the institution itself remain largely anchored in a colonial, anti-Black, anti-Indigenous, Eurocentric history. According to Howard (2023), multiculturalism in Canada is a mirage concealing a history of anti-Black racism. Similarly, Canadian institutions have a hidden curriculum that is anti-Black. The "hidden curriculum" bars Black bodies from academic settings via hiring and admissions in the name of credentials and quotas, while the "null curriculum" includes the misconstrued and absent representations of Blackness in institutions which uphold devaluation and exclusion of all peoples categorized as "coloured" (Howard 2023).

Diversity and inclusion efforts are often presented as an antidote to the deep-seated racial exclusion within universities. However, as Gagliardi (forthcoming), Howard (2023), and Saucier and Woods (2014) argue, the currently constituted diversity and inclusion efforts maintain racialized exploitation and exclusion. According to Taylor, diversity and inclusion are too often understood as actions to render racialized people more visible, rather than to build reciprocal relationships based on trust, love, and shared investments for change (2018, 127). We are situated in Quebec, where EDI efforts proliferate alongside provincial mandates that allow educators to use racial slurs and insensitive teaching materials in the classroom—in the name of academic freedom. In 2019 Quebec also banned certain public servants, including public school teachers, from wearing religious symbols, a legislative decision that has profoundly affected hijab-wearing students, among others (Elbourne, Manning, and Kifell 2022). We believe that if the needs of racialized students and faculty were centred in efforts to realize institutional equity, it would address potential harm, beyond visibility and labour extraction.

Similarly, initiatives launched by racialized student leaders are undermined by stakeholders who fail to fundamentally support and incorporate these efforts into a larger vision of systemic transformation (Gagliardi, forthcoming; see also Bernhardt, this volume). Because there are no structures in place to institutionalize the anti-racist work of student leaders, student initiatives risk dissolving as soon as students graduate and enter the job market. And yet student leadership has always played a pivotal role in challenging academic inequities. Whether one considers the desegregation of schools, or student critiques of the use of the N-word on course assignments, student leaders have been a core force, if not *the* core force, in institutional transformation. Our home institution is a case in point. Before Concordia University was established, one of its institutional predecessors, Sir George Williams College, found itself at the epicentre of anti-racist struggle (Cummings and Mohabir 2022), in which Black student leaders were subject to racist insults and criminal charges (Forsythe 1971). What became later known as "The George Williams Affair" turned into the largest student occupation in Canadian history.

While host universities benefit from the strategies and insights they extract from the leadership of racialized students, and from the increased interest and admissions that follow, sustainable infrastructure to support the student practitioners leading anti-racism and equity initiatives continues to be lacking. Howard (2023) argues that educators must move beyond individual efforts to diversify without remedying the structures that uphold dehumanization, specifically the reliance on anti-Black pedagogy. Drawing from Howard (2023), we urge educators to consider the possibilities of a fugitive pedagogy—a pedagogy of Black freedom that dismantles oppressive structures and offers meaningful ways for racialized people to take up space, find joy, and flourish in the university (Howard 2023). We invite you to join us in the quest of radically reconfiguring the university as we know it: building new ways of learning, new objectives, and new metrics as to what counts as value and knowledge. Instead of providing a misleading list of plug-and-play guidelines to fix centuries-long white supremacy and oppression, we call on readers to re-envision and reimagine one of the foundational cornerstones of the contemporary Canadian university: the relationship between racialized student leaders and the academy.

Reworlding Student Leadership

Given the historically central role that students have played in demanding and achieving institutional accountability, it is surprising that little scholarship has examined the role that students, faculty, and staff play in equity work within academic institutions (Adserias, Charleston, and Jackson 2019). The bureaucratic work of equity, diversity, and inclusion seemingly operates in a rarified space: above and external to the daily grind of student activists struggling to realize the implementation of a Black studies programs, for example, or student activists denouncing sexual harassment—a huge problem, given that as Malinda Smith (2017, 261) notes, most mid- and senior administrative positions in the social sciences are held by white men. When crises occur, as they have done with increasing urgency in recent years, students may be incorporated into consultative processes or asked to join committees that are initiated from above. But the basic infrastructural hierarchy of the university precludes students from accessing university resources to address problems, structurally and sustainably, that students themselves identify as requiring urgent redress.

From Jamilah's experiences as a student leader in equity work, it is racialized students, and trans- and gender nonbinary students, who disproportionately do equity work in the academy. Since the mainstreaming of the Black Lives Matter movement in June 2020, Jamilah has been increasingly solicited to participate on panels, in interviews, and in consultations. She was invited, for example, to speak on the "Black community's response to George Floyd's execution," and to speak to the state of the anti-Black racism movement at Concordia and "whether Black Concordians are satisfied." While Jamilah appreciates the well-intentioned visibility and opportunities, she does not stand for the tokenism culture that calls on only a few Black students, educators, and community organizers to speak on behalf of the feelings and experiences of *all* Black people.

To avoid tokenism, Jamilah has continually sought to build coalitions with institutional partners—taking equity work into her own hands by leading independent projects and initiatives. She champions her university, network, and stakeholders. However, she is privy to the challenges faced by racialized student leaders within the academy, which lacks systems to incorporate student-led equity work sustainably and structurally. Canadian universities as they currently exist do not have systems in place to institutionalize, secure, and sustainably renumerate a student who is, in Jamilah's case, completing a degree while working full-time at the university as an educator and curriculum consultant; a workshop facilitator;

a student rights and responsibilities advocate; a project manager for a public educational resource database showcasing the anti-racist and social justice work of university and local leaders; a community outreach coordinator building collaborations between the university and community organizations; all the while running an educational organization (DPPH) in her home institution.

We bring attention to Jamilah's multiple commitments not to shine a light on Jamilah's multiple contributions, per se, but rather to spark a larger conversation about what and who is recognized as constituting change in the university: What are the boundaries between full-time and part-time educators and students "educating"? What forms of encouragement and sustenance are required to enable student leaders to transform institutional culture and policies? How can Canadian universities be better equipped to train students to be changemakers in society at large? Jamilah is one of many racialized student leaders whose role as a student and educator is blurred in a manner that is unrecognized and undefined in academic bureaucracy. Student leaders in equity work are thus subject to a liminal status where there is a disparity between an insistent demand for and recognition of their labour. Reworlding institutional support for student leaders does not mean renumerating and recognizing only the most active students, on an ad hoc basis. Rather, reworlding student leadership means enabling student leaders to initiate and contribute to equity and anti-racist work in fundamental and ongoing ways. Reworlding student leadership means conceiving of sustainable positions for racialized student leaders that incorporate their work and expertise exposing equity gaps related to curriculum, classrooms, hiring and admissions, and policing—positions that can annually be filled with new students ready to reworld the university for the next generation.

Reworlding Renumeration and Brokering
The equity labour of graduate students is often neither recognized nor rewarded by universities, an obstacle CFAR sought to address, in no small part, through funding student-led initiatives and guiding students on how to successfully apply for institutional grants. But even if institutional funding is available to support an activity, compensating the labour of students driving the initiatives and leading other forms of training, requires an additional layer of advocacy. A line in a CV is welcome but not

commensurate to the amount of time required to develop and give a presentation, sit on a committee, or lead a new institutional initiative.

Sustainably funding student labour, we argue, is thus the first and most important ingredient to enabling anti-racist coalitional work to emerge in the academy. While it is true that many graduate students, including Jamilah, benefit from funding provided by the Tri-Council (a federal body that prioritizes the training and mentorship of graduate students in the allocation of successful grants), the problem is that none of this money is available for the anti-racist initiatives that racialized students often take up alongside their core graduate studies. When it comes to anti-racist work, racialized student leaders often end up working off the side of their desk, with little or no direct support from faculty, who are themselves often exhausted by the heavy demands of teaching, research, and service. This institutional infrastructure, we contend, essentially shapes the student and faculty relationship into a prefigured pattern of power, from which it is difficult to develop alternative possibilities.

The coalitional relationship that we developed is rare, first and foremost because of structural barriers. To start, brokering, unlike graduate student supervision, is not generally recognized as a form of academic work. Indeed, brokering does not fall under "service" or "supervision" as typically understood within academic institutions and as such it can remain unaccounted for in reviews for promotion or pay increases. Brokering involves a multitude of efforts by a faculty member or a senior administrator to alleviate institutional barriers for student equity projects to be realized, renumerated, and sustained within the university. Consequently, brokering can amplify the structural precarity for racialized untenured faculty who have less institutional leverage yet are most likely to support the research and equity projects of graduate and undergraduate students. Indeed, the often unrecognized support that untenured and racialized faculty provide to racialized students can negatively impact the development of their careers (Henry and Kobayashi 2017, 134–35). But while brokering poses risks for early career, racialized faculty, the risks are even greater for racialized student mobilizers.

Indeed, the ad hoc nature of coalitional work can, in turn, introduce a measure of indeterminacy and vulnerability for students navigating graduate and undergraduate education who do not benefit from institutional power if problems arise. There were several unexpected challenges that arose in Kimberley and Jamilah's coalition that threatened to unspool their work. The ARPP was originally proposed by Kimberley as a summer 2020 project. But what started as a short-term project that had the backing of the Office of the Faculty of Arts and Science quickly mushroomed into a much larger initiative involving multiple stakeholders from across the institution, and required more and more of Jamilah's attention and leadership. The project became institutionally supported and housed by one of the university centres. A year after Jamilah started working on the ARPP, the project itself was jeopardized when Kimberley went on sabbatical. While Kimberley sought to establish institutional support for the project well in advance of her departure, another unexpected departure and ongoing institutional transitions suddenly put the project into peril.

At the end of the day, it was Jamilah who managed the challenges and found the eventual solution: making the management of ARPP independent of the university itself and rebranding it as a larger R2C initiative for her educational organization, DPPH. In keeping with the realities of social justice work, the project's transition involved years of labour for Jamilah and Mawunyo Dei, a family member who volunteered to be an emergency website designer. Together they worked to ensure that the important work was not lost amid bureaucratic constraints at Concordia University. Today, the project prevails, faculty across Canada download the videos and curricular aids, and Jamilah delivers workshops and seminars for diverse educational institutions on integrating the resources into classrooms.

During the evolution of the project, Kimberely was present, offering emotional support and exposure, from initially designing and fundraising the project to providing the opportunity to conference and publish the legacy of the work. We learned that transformational work requires both parties' dedication to the coalition, especially in times of challenge and change: Jamilah's dedication as a graduate student mobilizer to cultivate spaces and strategies for decolonial and anti-racist education, and Kimberley's dedication as a broker to facilitate opportunities for equity work to be sustained and showcased. The unexpected scope and departures that occurred during the project illuminated that coalitions for institutional transformation are fragile and require both parties to develop inventive strategies for problem-solving, often without guidance. It requires both parties to be driven to fulfill a shared objective—in this case, making a project on anti-racist education sustainable and impactful. It requires both parties to have deep trust that the commitment to the coalition will not falter even if one party has to take a break. The collaboration on the writing of this chapter, for example, has deepened our coalitional efforts to deconstruct the academy and bring visibility to the project in another format.

Looking back, the rebranded R2C website went live on March 11, 2022, nearly two years after Jamilah began building the initial ARPP. On May 10, 2023, over a year after this development, the independent R2C website was dissolved, and the resources were reconfigured into an Anti-Racism Video Library on the DPPH website for greater accessibility and visibility. The reality is, social justice work, especially when it is taken up from *within* institutions will always evolve, require revisions, endure constraints, delays, and setbacks. However, as we reflect, there are a few key considerations that we are taking away from our work together thus far, which we hope are informative. First, creating educational resources for online teaching is time consuming and yet raises new ethical considerations regarding accessibility, property rights, and bandwidth—university webpages have less space for videos, for example, than independent platforms. Second, every university has its own approach to equity work and that approach can determine the boundaries of new projects or initiatives. Third, coalitional efforts must strive for sustainability between students, faculty, and the administration that anticipates the eventual graduation of graduate student mobilizers. Fourth, anti-racist education is sensitive: Who is sanctioning content? Students who lead this work are not usually granted the authority to make key decisions regarding content and process. Whether you agree with or want to challenge this current reality, it is important to keep in mind the institutional hierarchies that continue to shape anti-racist-education.

All in all, the project lays bare the fundamental need for institutional transformation that recognizes student leadership as a key form of academic work, worthy of institutional recognition and renumeration over the long term. For coalitional work to flourish, student leaders require administrative and faculty brokers who can support student-driven projects through respectful exchange and deep institutional investment. The project also lays bare the fundamental need for both faculty and administrative brokers to engage in a constant praxis of reflection in ways that uphold student leadership as the centre and not the sidenote of institutional transformation.

Reworlding Expertise and Knowledge

The knowledge and expertise that racialized students and educators bring to equity work is often classified as "lived experience" and, as such, is exempt from the formal respect and recognition granted to other contributions recognized as "scientific" within the academy. bell hooks (1992) and Nelson Maldonado-Torres (2007) attribute this devaluation to the colonial logic that expertise and knowledge reside solely in scientific rationality by white, Western, largely heteronormative men. This bias is often attributed to the seventeenth-century scientific revolution in the West—where scientific positivism denigrated community/land/spiritual forms of learning and knowledge central in Indigenous and racialized communities (hooks 1992; Maldonado 2007). In what Maldonado terms the "coloniality of being," European settlers dehumanized the nonwhite others, rending their lived experiences inconsequential (2007, 4).

Jamilah has frequently experienced the high interest in racialized experiences and voices at times when topics on systemic inequalities and equity work are trending, which binds racialized students and educators in a conundrum. On the one hand, racialized peoples are over-solicited to lead equity work from perceptions that their lived experiences make them more knowledgeable in the field. On the other hand, lived experiences are invalidated by positivist standards, reducing their contributions to disgruntled personal endeavours (Collins 2019; Land 2015). Jamilah's experiences as a racialized student in equity work backs this up. As she remarks, "there is always someone who approaches you saying...yes, but..." Yes, you are a student leading anti-racist advocacy within the university, but what about your research and coursework? Jamilah refers to equity work as a dark comedy—where in her experience it does not matter how much a racialized student may achieve, they are always viewed as being superhuman and not needing support because anti-racist work is expected to be intrinsic to their existence. At the same time, anti-racist work is invariably deemed "not enough" for professional success. Indeed, anti-racist work is devalued as extracurricular, outside of the student's degree and scholarly accreditation—even if that work has fundamentally challenged and transformed pedagogy and the curriculum in their respective schools. A colonial dichotomy thus emerges: lived experience and extracurricular activities versus "real" knowledge and "credentials." For decades, anti-colonial scholars have been on a quest to "pluralize" knowledge in the academy to delink this colonial dichotomy (Biko 1978; Dhareshwar 2012; Freire 1970; Jones and West 2002; Silko 1981).

The notion of pluralizing is popularly defined by Walter Mignolo as an epistemic delinking of universal knowledge to make space for multiple worldviews and approaches to co-exist (2007, 450–53). Leslie Marmon Silko (1981) and Audra Simpson (2014), for example, have showcased oral history as a collaborative practice for knowledge production. In application, educators can opt for story sessions with guest lectures over reviewing scholarship and guiding students to share and produce stories as non-written assignments. Practices that pluralize knowledge can serve to legitimize the role of racialized peoples in equity work as intellectual skill-based labour contributing to the academy's knowledge production, which then warrants recognition and renumeration. The ARPP, for example, was born out of our desire to recognize, compensate, and integrate the knowledge of community leaders battling racism under COVID-19.

The colonial dichotomy of knowledge production within higher education also reveals the urgent need to disrupt the very origin of expertise in the faculty-student relationship. Whether it is in the classroom or in the context of research, the professor drives the agenda, providing opportunities for students to benefit from the professor's knowledge and or/ engagement in their field of study. Of course, most faculty will acknowledge that they benefit and learn from their students as well, but this return is nonetheless still structured within a pre-existing arrangement of knowledge production in which the professor leads and the student follows, and is highly dependent upon faculty funding.

Supporting students with funding and guidance is a critically important academic enterprise, but it is important to recognize that these engagements are necessarily contingent on the faculty member's own career trajectory, availability, and willingness to engage with the interests of a graduate student. The hierarchical nature of professor-student relations is even more problematic given the lack of diversity of the professoriate in Canada today and the lack of expertise addressing systemic racism within the Canadian academy. Insofar as these constraints systematically impede the possibility for anti-racist coalition building, we suggest fundamentally rethinking the role of the faculty member in institutional transformation. The materialization of the equity broker is one way to disrupt the normalization of "faculty expertise." Brokers actively seek out the funding, connections, and institutional resources necessary to realize and support student initiatives over the long term. Brokers also work to make student leadership visible and recognized in the academy. To make the contributions of equity brokers institutionally legible and recognized, academic institutions must, in turn, recognize brokerage activities as commensurate to traditional supervision activities, during contract renewal and promotion. Also key: the involvement and commitment of administrative equity brokers who govern the resources necessary for equity projects to succeed.

We also imagine structural innovations that would delink the anti-racist initiatives of student leaders from faculty-led research, so that university funding directly recognizes and supports innovative student-led projects. The establishment of a multi-stakeholder student equity program, for example, might begin to address some of the structural problems outlined above. Granted on an annual basis with possibility for renewal by a committee made up of faculty, staff, and students, student equity funding would be allocated to student-led projects and initiatives that address equity gaps in the university. As a multi-stakeholder initiative, the student equity program would bring together a diversity of committed individuals dedicated to renumerating, recognizing, and providing administrative support for student-led projects. Student-led initiatives would also be given the jurisdiction to replace rather than solely reform inequitable practices and procedures. Establishing such a process would enable the work of racialized student leaders to be financially and institutionally recognized, both imperatives for generating openings for change over the long term.

Concluding Reflections
In this chapter we have shown how we have strategically sought to activate our different positionalities as a Black graduate mobilizer (Jamilah) and white faculty broker (Kimberley) to achieve our objectives through a shared and reciprocal commitment to institutional transformation. This effort has required us to reimagine and reinvent our relationship with one

another, all the while seeking to transform the institution—gradually horizontalizing and leading to new opportunities to realize our shared politics: shifting from an event organizer (J) and event participant (K), course instructor (K) and teaching assistant (J), to project supervisor (K) and project manager (J), to project collaborators, co-presenters, and then co-authors on this chapter.

Our collaboration has over time become less that of professor and student, and more that of peers working collaboratively toward common goals. But this outcome is not guaranteed. Rather, it requires an intentional praxis that seeks to transform the relationship between student leadership and the academy, knowledge and expertise, and remuneration and employment as a means of enacting structural change within the university.

Eduardo Mendieta reminds us that the best remedy for systemic racism and oppression is to harness a "decolonial imaginary" (2020, 15). Like Mignolo's "coloniality of being and knowledge" (2007, 451), Mendieta argues that the practice of imagining has also been "colonized"—where the past, present, and future are solely conceived within the inequitable, material constraints available. Beyond dreaming for better days, Mendieta argues that imagining is a practice to envision new solutions to old problems that are not conceivable with material thinking (15). To overcome the material, Mendieta argues, we can draw from Maria Lugones's (2010) "decolonial feminism,"[3] and the "feminist imaginary," which together enable the psyche to imagine counterhegemonic systems. By projecting this standpoint immaterially, Mendieta argues that resisters gain the capacity to project themselves and environments into a myriad of possibilities (16). A new imaginary is urgently needed in the academy: coalition building to reworld the university is but one experiment in imagining and then implementing new possibilities that have not yet been conceived.

Notes

1. We recognize the important work that undergraduate student mobilizers also play in pushing for change in the university. In this chapter we focus our discussion on the specific leadership role that graduate student mobilizers play as educators and practitioners in training.
2. The DPPH is a student-led initiative turned nonprofit organization dedicated to creating spaces within academic institutions to unpack exclusionary educational practices and cultivate anti-colonial strategies to use in curriculum and learning environments. The

DPPH is known for its syllabus deconstruction events, social gatherings, a short oral historic film celebrating Black Canadian history, Anti-Racism Video Library, a youth mentorship program, inspired research, and publications.
3. Lugones introduces "decolonial feminism" as a theoretical and conceptual standpoint that works to disrupt the colonial legacy and modernity by countering its heterosexist assumptions, known as the coloniality of gender (2010, 743, 748, 754).

References

Adserias, Ryan P., LaVar J. Charleston, and Jerlando F.L. Jackson. 2019. "What Style of Leadership Is Best Suited to Direct Organizational Change to Fuel Institutional Diversity in Higher Education?" In *Building the Anti-Racist University*, edited by Shirley Anne Tate and Paul Bagguley, 26–42. New York: Routledge.

Ahmed, Sara. 2012. *On Being Included: Racism and Diversity in Institutional Life*. Durham, NC: Duke University Press.

Ashwar, Meera. 2015. "Decolonizing What? Categories, Concepts, and the Enduring 'Not Yet.'" *Cultural Dynamics* 27 (2): 1–13. https://doi.org/10.1177/0921374015585231.

Biko, Steve. 1978. *I Write What I Like*. London: University of Chicago Press.

Collins, Patricia Hill. 2019. *Intersectionality As a Critical Social Theory*. Durham, NC: Duke University Press.

Cummings, Ronald, and Nalini Mohabir. 2022. "Protests and Pedagogy: The Legacies of Caribbean Student Resistance and the Sir George Williams Protest, Montreal 1969." *TOPIA: Canadian Journal of Cultural Studies* 44 (March): 1–24. https://doi.org/10.3138/topia-44-001.

De Lissovoy, Noah. 2010. "Decolonial Pedagogy and the Ethics of the Global." *Discourse: Studies in the Cultural Politics of Education* 31 (3): 279–93. https://doi.org/10.1080/01596301003786886.

Dhareshwar, Vivek. 2012. "Framing the Predicament of Indian Thought: Gandhi, Gira and Ethical Action." *Asian Philosophy* 22 (2): 1–19.

Elbourne, Elizabeth, Kimberley Manning, and Zackary Kifell. 2022. "The Impact of Law 21 on Québec Students in Law and Education: Executive Summary of Findings." https://www.concordia.ca/content/dam/concordia/now/docs/The-Impact-of-Law-21-on-Quebec-Students-in-Law-and-Education-Executive-Summary.pdf.

Forsythe, Dennis. 1971. *Let the Niggers Burn: The Sir George Williams Affair and It's [sic] Caribbean Aftermath*. Montreal: Black Rose Books.

Freire, Paulo. 1970. *Pedagogy of the Oppressed*. New York: Continuum International Publishing Group.

Gagliardi, Meghan. Forthcoming. "Wielding the 'Empowered Student' Narrative: Examining How the Responsibility for Anti-Racism Is Assigned and Denied in the Neoliberal University." In *Teaching in the 21st Century: Reflections on Pedagogy and Curriculum from the Gender and Sexuality Studies Classroom*, edited by Natalie Kouri-Towe. Montreal: Concordia University Press.

Henry, Frances, Enakshi Dua, Carl E. James, Audrey Kobayashi, Peter Li, Howard Ramos, and Malinda Smith. 2017. *The Equity Myth: Racialization and Indigeneity at Canadian Universities*. Vancouver: UBC Press.

Henry, Frances, and Audrey Kobayashi. 2017. "The Everyday World of Racialized and Indigenous Faculty Members in Canadian Universities." In *The Equity Myth: Racialization and Indigeneity at Canadian Universities*, by Frances Henry, Enakshi Dua, Carl E. James, Audrey Kobayashi, Peter Li, Howard Ramos, and Malinda Smith, 115–54. Vancouver: UBC Press.

Hewlett, Sylvia Ann. 2013. "Mentors Are Good, Sponsors Are Better." *New York Times*, April 13, 2013. https://www.nytimes.com/2013/04/14/jobs/sponsors-seen-as-crucial-for-womens-career-advancement.html.

hooks, bell. 1992. *Black Looks: Race and Representation*. New York: Routledge.

Howard, Philip S.S. 2023. *Performing Postracialism: Reflections on Antiblackness, Nation, and Education through Contemporary Blackface in Canada*. Toronto: University of Toronto Press.

Howard, Philip. 2021. "More than a Diverse Reading List: Challenging an Antiblack Pedagogy (Dr. Philip Howard)." Spring Perspectives on Teaching Conference keynote, Centre for Teaching and Learning, Western University, May 12, 2021. YouTube video. https://www.youtube.com/watch?v=j5eS7Le4wJM.

Jones, Lee, and Cornel West. 2002. *Making It on Broken Promises: Leading African American Male Scholars Confront the Culture of Higher Education*. Sterling, VA: Stylus Publishing.

Land, Clare. 2015. *Decolonizing Solidarity: Dilemmas and Directions for Supporters of Indigenous Struggles*. London: Zed Books.

Lugones, Maria. 2010. "Toward a Decolonial Feminism." *Hypatia* 25 (4): 742–59. https://www.jstor.org/stable/40928654.

Maldonado-Torres, Nelson. 2007. "On the Coloniality of Being: Contributions to the Development of a Concept." *Cultural Studies* 21 (2): 240–70. https://doi.org/10.1080/09502380601162548.

Mendieta, Eduardo. 2020. "Toward a Decolonial Feminist Imaginary: Decolonizing Futurity." *Critical Philosophy of Race* 8 (1–2): 237–64. https://doi.org/10.5325/critphilrace.8.1-2.0237.

Mignolo, Walter D. 2007. "Delinking: The Rhetoric of Modernity, the Logic of Coloniality and the Grammar of De-coloniality." *Cultural Studies* 21 (2): 449–514.

Muthyala, John. 2006. *Reworlding America: Myth, History, and Narrative*. Athens: Ohio University Press.

Saucier, Khalil P., and Tyron P. Woods. 2014. "Hip-Hop Studies in Black." *Journal of Popular Music Studies* 26 (2–3): 1–27. https://doi.org/10.1111/jpms.12077.

Silko, Leslie Marmon. 1981. *Storyteller*. New York: Seaver Books.

Simpson, Audra. 2014. *Mohawk Interruptus: Political Life across the Borders of Settler States*. Durham, NC: Duke University Press.

Smith, Malinda S. 2017. "Disciplinary Silences: Race, Indigeneity, and Gender in the Social Sciences. In *The Equity Myth: Racialization and Indigeneity at Canadian Universities*, by Frances Henry, Enakshi Dua, Carl E. James, Audrey Kobayashi, Peter Li, Howard Ramos, and Malinda Smith, 239–63. Vancouver: UBC Press.

Spivak, Gayatri Chakravorty. 1985. "The Rani of Sirmur: An Essay in Reading the Archives." *History and Theory* 24 (3): 247–72. https://doi.org/10.2307/2505169.

Stein, Sharon. 2016. "Rethinking the Ethics of Internationalization: Five Challenges for Higher Education." UCLA *Journal of Education and Information Studies* 12 (2): 1–25.

Taylor, Liza. 2018. "Coalition from the Inside Out: Women of Color Feminism and Politico-Ethical Coalition Politics." *New Political Science* 40 (1): 119–36. https://doi.org/10.1080/07393148.2017.1416447.

16 Photovoice as Feminist Pedagogy

FIONA MACDONALD

DRAWING ON Paulo Freire's theory of "education for critical consciousness" ([1974] 2005), photovoice projects have been used by researchers and activists with various community groups since the 1970s (Wang and Burris 1994, 171). In general, photovoice methodology involves the structured use of photographs to identify and analyze salient issues from standpoints that are often unheard or underrepresented, particularly youth (Gant et al. 2009). As such, it offers an approach to, "grasping what is going on at the point in people's lives where biography and society intersect" (Booth and Booth 2003, quoted in Walton et al. 2012, 168). It also facilitates an understanding of the classroom as a community in which everyone's presence is acknowledged and valued (hooks 1994, 8). As the chapters from David Semaan and Nick Dorzweiler in this volume reveal, assisting students in finding and building community in the oft-isolating, anxiety-riddled, and depression-inducing neoliberal institution is an essential aspect of feminist pedagogy.

Photovoice is deeply intersectional. Engaging with intersectionality via self-inquiry facilitates the capacity to see others with the same complexity as one sees oneself. As such, it fosters an "analysis of the in-between" or, "a both/and frame," rather than either/or "binary thinking" consistent with intersectional feminism(s) developed by Patricia Hill Collins and Sirma Bilge (2016, 27) and Vivian May (2015). A relational focus shifts the emphasis away from what distinguishes or separates entities and towards interconnections fostering what May refers to as "heterogeneous commonality"—a concept founded on understanding both individuals and groups as internally heterogeneous. From this perspective, "groups can be characterized by their potential to organize around 'heterogeneous commonality,'" as the notion of the subject is not only "multiple" but also "coalitional" (May 2015, 41). Photovoice is an ideal method for challenging the homogeneity of "dominant imaginaries" by revealing heterogeneous commonality through narratives that bring together both personal and structural knowledge. As such, it is a valuable process through which to foster meaningful connection and community building.

I've been including photovoice projects as assignments in my introductory course to political science and two of my upper-level seminar courses—the Politics of Multiculturalism, and the Politics of Sex, Gender and Women in Political Thought—since 2015, during my tenure as a faculty member at the University of the Fraser Valley (UFV) in Abbotsford, British Columbia, and am now doing the same in my new position at the University of Northern British Columbia in Prince George. In the introductory course, students create an image and write a complementary five-page reflection informed by course readings of their choice that explains how the image reflects a politics they experience in their day-to-day lives. This assignment is consistent with my overarching approach to the first-year course that is centred on revealing and investigating how *everything is political.*

In the two upper-level seminar courses, students create an image and a two-page narrative informed by course material that reflects their experience(s) with "the politics of multiculturalism, diversity, and/or race" and "the politics of gender and/or sexuality." These assignments are shorter in large part to make the projects shareable in art-gallery-style exhibits where students and members of the broader community can engage with the projects. Recently, these gallery events have been a part of International Women's Day events at UFV and the University of Northern British Columbia, as well as events at Abbotsford City Hall as part of a CityStudio collaboration on diversity in the community.[1]

My original motivation for including the projects was to respond to student feedback requesting smaller assignments in my classes. I decided to pilot it as a small project in one upper-level course. These assignments were submitted only to me and were submitted electronically so the images could be shared easily and without printing costs. Upon reviewing these assignments, I was struck by the level of introspection, insight, vulnerability, and trust communicated in the projects. By listening to, and reflecting on, student feedback I had stumbled upon a powerful method through which students integrated course material and their own lived experience and knowledge. I decided to try the assignment in additional classes and to pilot sharing the upper-level assignments in an art gallery format as a reflection on our particular classroom community as well as the many broader communities of which we are a part. These events have now become a cornerstone of my teaching philosophy and approach to the classroom as a community of learning, care, and connection.

This approach is also consistent with conceptualizing the university as a caring institution. As Joan Tronto argues, "Good care in an institutional context has three central foci: the purpose of care, a recognition of power relations, and the need for pluralistic, particular, tailoring of care to meet individuals' needs. These elements further require political space within institutions to address such concerns" (2010, 58; see also Orsini, this volume). As revealed in the next part of this chapter, photovoice projects meet all three of these criteria. The purpose of the projects is to express, validate, reflect on, and share the particular lived experiences of participants and to recognize these experiences as valuable sources of knowledge for both individuals and collectivities. Sharing the assignments in a gallery format creates a political space for all observers (including students, faculty, staff and administrators, family, and community members) in which to access unique insights into the politics the participants experience in their day-to-day lives. These experiences are highly diverse and often reveal highly differential and, at times, conflicting experiences in the same communities as well as points of commonality and/or coalition. The potential impact(s) of these opportunities to exchange narratives should not be underestimated. As experiments by Joshua Kalla and David Broockman (2020, 2021, 2022) demonstrate, the non-confrontational exchange of narrative can reduce exclusionary and/or prejudicial attitudes by facilitating "perspective getting." In other words, learning one another's stories is a powerful avenue to humanization and transformation.

The second section of the chapter examines students' experiences with photovoice and explores the themes that emerged for them through their use of this methodology in my classroom. The discussion is based on a dialogue that brought together six current and former undergraduate students who participated in one or more of these projects at the University of the Fraser Valley between 2015 and 2021. I distributed open-ended guiding questions for the discussion on August 5, 2020, and we met via Zoom on August 12, 2020. The meeting was recorded and subsequently transcribed.

Following an introduction of the participants, the remainder of this chapter is an edited representation of the discussion organized by theme, including how photovoice centres experiential knowledge, reveals the value of particularity and self-representation, demonstrates learning through self-inquiry, fosters engagement and community building, and creates the opportunity to do feminist praxis in the classroom and beyond. Woven throughout are images and text from the photovoice projects. The chapter concludes with reflections on photovoice as a means of feministing in the classroom.

Contributor Bios (2020–2021)

Janel Jack

Janel's ancestral name is HELIKELWET. She is from the W̱SÁNEĆ (Saanich) unceded traditional territories where her father carries the Hereditary Chief title (Chief Vern Jack). She is also from the Stó:lō Nation unceded traditional territories from her mother's side where her great-grandfather carried the Hereditary Chief title (Richard Malloway). Janel is fortunate to have three children, Gordon D. Elliott Jr., Cecelia V.E. Chapman, and Ernest H. Andrew. Her daughter granted her two beautiful grandchildren, Sianna and Joey Jr. These humans are the reason she lives and strives for the best. Janel currently works as an Aboriginal support worker in Richmond School District # 38 and recently completed her BA with a major in political science and minor in communications at UFV.

Harleen Mann

Harleen graduated from UFV with a major in criminal justice and a minor in political science. As a student she volunteered with the Abbotsford Police and Big Brothers and Big Sisters. Both programs support at-risk youth. Due to her passion for the environment, she spends much of her free time volunteering in the community with tree planting and cleaning spaces from litter. Harleen plans to continue to give back to the community and advocate for human and environmental rights.

Tracy Morrison

Tracy graduated with distinction in December 2020 with a BA degree, major in political science at UFV. Her educational journey began when her son was just ten months old, and she graduated with a teenager in tow.

As a single parent, Tracy has navigated her way through a certificate in applied business technology, a diploma in liberal arts, and now a bachelor's degree. Tracy is currently the manager of the Research Office at UFV and hopes to one day find a career where she can contribute to empowering disadvantaged people from all backgrounds and cultures.

Graham Koshman

Graham is a political science major and math minor at UFV. His interests include gender identity/expression, disability rights, anti-colonialism/anti-imperialism/anti-racism, and socialism. Many of these interests show themselves in his photovoice assignments. He takes inspiration from writers including James Baldwin, Karl Marx, Sylvia Rivera, and Fred Hampton. He plans to pursue a career in policy analysis to better advocate for marginalized people.

Christina Ross

Christina is a fifth-year political science student at UFV. Their research interests include queer politics, feminism, and political participation. While attending university, Christina has worked at the Inclusivity Center for their school's Student Union Society. As the pride commissioner, they identified issues that queer students faced and provided solutions to any discrimination.

Raveena Walia

Raveena graduated with distinction from the UFV in 2019 with a bachelor of arts degree, double major in political science and history. Raveena also worked as a research assistant at the UFV, including on the Feminist University Initiative, which aims to foster an equitable and inclusive environment for students of all abilities, genders, sexual orientations, and racial and ethnic backgrounds. Raveena is now in law school at the University of Ottawa and will graduate in 2023.

Theme 1: Doing Political Science Differently by Centring Experiential Knowledge

Photovoice is centred on the lived experiences of participants. The projects discussed here are written in the first person and focus on how each participant experiences politics in their day-to-day life. Two references to concepts from course readings are also required; however, participants have a choice of any two concepts from any of the readings listed on the syllabus. Because this assignment is very different from "typical" political science assignments, students can find the projects challenging as well as exciting.

> *What were your thoughts when you first learned of the assignment?*
> A bit hard to wrap my head around at first, because every university course I've taken they've always said don't write in the first person, keep your personal experiences out of it, and so it was really hard for me to reverse the process. It was kind of hard to write about a personal experience and be so open knowing other people were going to see it...but I really enjoyed it once I got into it.—Tracy

I was really nervous. I wasn't sure how to approach it having learned in every other class not to talk about yourself and your experiences and I was worried about people reading it...I was worried about what people would think and I was unsure about how to go about doing it as well. I guess how to share my experiences and how to connect them to the readings. I wasn't sure how to do that at first. Once I started it, it became more straightforward.—Raveena

I think I was more excited than scared because for the first time we were putting our personal experiences into what we were learning and actually applying the learning towards our life. It was an opportunity to express things that we normally don't get to express. I think in a lot of classes you just get told things, but you don't really get to put it into real life, or you don't get to bring things in real life into the classroom. And it's kind of disconnected, but this way it becomes more interconnected.—Harleen

This discussion reveals the binary between intellectual knowledge and personal experience is alive and well throughout much of our discipline and the academy in general. This binary often prevents students from making important connections between the knowledge they acquire and hold as a person in the world with the knowledge they acquire and hold as a student. Deconstructing this binary is a necessary part of welcoming students into a caring institution that is open to learning with and from

FIGURE 16.1 My personal lived experience with oppression and marginalization as a First Nations woman has been a challenging one. I fight to keep my head above water and work towards decolonizing my worldview. I believe that I am currently experiencing a resurgence within the Western society's educational system while I am looked at through the rear-view mirror of many people around me. My lived experiences of being a First Nations woman of Canada is a true reflection of resistance and resilience as I move forward to empowering myself through social justice and understanding the concept of self-determination.—Janel
(Used with permission from Janel Jack.)

them. It is also a means of shifting away from a transactional understanding of learning and towards a relational one.

Theme 2: The Value of Particularity and Being Seen on Your Own Terms
A foundational part of the projects and gallery events is the opportunity for participants to be seen on their own terms. This element also brings both nervousness and excitement.

What was the most challenging part of the project?
Probably everybody reading my personal thoughts about myself. Being kind of insecure with what other people thought about me. Really when it got

down to it, I thought, "Well, I did actually do a good job." So it boosted my confidence...other people seeing how I see myself.—Janel

If you were to describe this assignment in one word, what would it be?
I know some instructors don't like the personal experiences, especially what I have to say...in this assignment you could make it political if you want or you could make it personal. I chose to make it political.—Janel

I think *intersectional* would be a good word. Especially because most of what I talked about were my disability and gender identity or expression stuff, which are significant aspects of my life experience to me and I think often get somewhat looked over in political discussion. So I think *intersectional* is the term that comes to my mind.—Graham

The word *empowering* comes to my mind. Most of my projects were focused on how I'm a single parent, and just living in a lot of oppression from other people's viewpoints and from society as being a single parent, which you wouldn't think there was that much around but apparently there's a lot. It definitely felt empowering for me to be able to have that voice and to have that stance and to actually relate my viewpoints to the politics of the material.—Tracy

I think *opportunity* would be a good word because it gives you the chance to say things that you've never really been able to say before, and tie together things that you normally wouldn't be able to and to have people see or hear your voice in ways that you normally don't get the chance to.—Harleen

Can I have two words? I would say it's a chance to be creative, which is really rare in political science classes. I also found it really challenging because I'm not used to sharing personal experiences in classes. It's something I wasn't comfortable with at first but then later I ended up really enjoying the assignment. But it was challenging in that it got me to think about the readings in a different way. It also challenged me to share my own experiences and connect them with the readings, which is not something that I would normally have done or normally would have shared, but I did in this instance.—Raveena

FIGURE 16.2 When I was only eighteen years old, I was asked why my parents had not yet arranged a marriage for me. This woman "thought" that all girls of South Asian descent were typically married off at a young age and wanted to know why I remained unmarried at eighteen years old. Not only was this an inappropriate inquiry into my marital status, it was an inquiry based on assumptions about my cultural background. Women are meant to be allies within the women's movement, all fighting for equality, and yet in assuming that I came from a "backwards" culture...this woman separated her experience as a woman from my own, whether she meant to do so or not. This is why intersectionality within the women's movement is so important.—Raveena (Used with permission from Raveen Walia.)

Creating spaces for students to take supported risks by sharing vulnerabilities, frustrations, and personal insights also works to facilitate care in the institution. In this way, knowledge is understood to be both personal and political. As revealed in the examples, care or lack of care is often present in the narratives that accompany the images. More specifically, moments of misrecognition, marginalization, and exclusion are common topics of discussion. These discussions are often framed in contrast or comparison to moments of empowerment, self-reflection, and mobilization.

Vulnerability is a central part of the project and participants choose their level of vulnerability based on their own comfort level and intention. Many participants take the opportunity to share very personal and significant experiences, emotions, and thoughts.

This vulnerability is the reason the names of participants are not included on the projects in the public art gallery displays. In the age of doxing, anonymity is an important part of ensuring a safe experience for all participants. At the same time, participants choose their level of risk, and it is not uncommon for participants to use their own likeness in their projects.

How important is anonymity in the public exhibit?
I think it's really important to have anonymity. I think that helps people to be a bit more open about what they'll talk about, because if someone can attach the name to it, then it can be a bit of a stress…I guess there can be some fear of embarrassment. So I think it's good for it to be anonymous, although I appreciate that some do not have this fear and would like to be more open.—Graham

I actually used my picture because I'm a First Nations woman who's been marginalized all my life. I would like to put whatever I have to say out in public for people to understand exactly where I'm coming from in my life. And to be able for them to see that and have me write whatever I need to say about my life. It was a healing process really, for me. Where I'm not going to be sitting in a shame-based community and being put down and whatever else. This is who I am, and accept it.—Janel

I really liked that it was anonymous. I like that I had the choice of telling people it was mine, like my friends in the class or whoever. And I was glad that random people wouldn't know that it was mine, because while I would've been comfortable sharing it with the class, or most of my classmates, I don't know that I would've been comfortable sharing with people walking by or people just looking at it.—Raveena

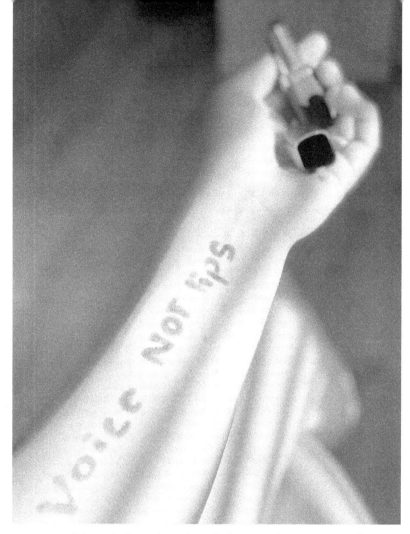

FIGURE 16.3 Being called a prude made me feel pressured to engage sexually. Being called a hoe made me feel guilty for loving my body and what it had to offer. Many people overlook and brush off these words and expect you too as well. They individualize the issue. The responsibility is on me to deal with the way I am valued as a person and the answer is always to just ignore what other people think and say. How are you supposed to ignore what people think when it prevents you from speaking your mind and having your ideas heard? All because you aren't being measured for what's inside your head but for simply having a body that is subject to discernment at every look.—Harleen (Used with permission from Harleen Mann.)

For some people sharing something personal can be a little bit difficult, but it can also be a part of your identity. To put your name on something makes you internalize it a little bit more as well...I wouldn't necessarily have a problem with putting my name on something because of how strongly I believe what I say, and I want people to know. I think it truly depends on the person and their comfort zone and not necessarily something you can just put a blanket answer to.—Harleen

Theme 3: Learning through Self-Inquiry

Self-inquiry is a powerful method of integrating course material in a particular and contextual way. Photovoice methodology fosters a reflective relationship with the scholarship that is personally meaningful. It can also facilitate new feminist understandings and/or articulations of past events, experiences, or viewpoints as political. In so doing it can facilitate the identification of what Sara Ahmed (2017) calls "brick walls," which she defines as "the hardening of history" and "the building materials of power" (91).

> *Did you learn anything new about yourself doing this project?*
> What really stuck out to me was the intersectionality, especially with my lived experience. Living on a reservation, or in an urban area, all that. I've experienced so much that I don't want the next generation to actually have to put up with all that racism and discrimination...When I go in and I dive into something it has to be really from the heart. That's how I was raised as a First Nations woman...Because we're not spoken about often as First Nations women and I like to put it out there. Okay, this is actually how it is to live as the Indigenous women of Canada.—Janel

I learned about the extent to which my disability has affected my current left-wing political views, and the fact that I feel judged and stared at in public. I think also, I don't know that I actually put it in my assignment, but when I was a bit younger I had certain political views I no longer hold, like very right-wing sort of stuff reactionary views on gender and sexuality, for example, which I think was partially a result of me trying to repress gender and sexuality questionings. I think it sort of helped me be more reflective about that stuff, and I am more willing to critique myself.—Graham

I also want to bring up belonging and acceptance as a First Nations woman from the Rez who is also educated on a lot of things in our white society, our European society. I'm not accepted within my own reservation because

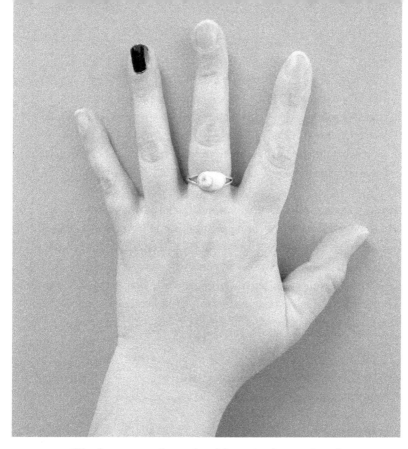

FIGURE 16.4 Why do we accept the gendered dynamics that continue the oppression of women? Because that is what the marriage system is: a form of power and control over women to continue their submission and to continue isolation and impoverishment, according to Cynthia Enloe. The marriage system sustains patriarchy, and many people don't question it, just conforming to its process...Why do we accept one finger to determine our status? *Miss*, *Mrs.*, and *Ms.* versus *Mr.* Three to one. For me I'm just a human and don't need everyone knowing my marital status at any given moment. As for you, patriarchy, you can take a look at my next finger.
—Tracy (Used with permission from Tracy Morrison.)

I'm too educated, and I'm not accepted within the European education because of being First Nations. So it's a sense of belonging, too, that this photovoice has given me. I don't really have to belong somewhere, because when I accept myself that's where I stand. I don't have to belong somewhere. I just know that where I'm coming from is accepted by myself and by other people who view me.—Janel

I felt that it helped me to learn that it's okay to have those open opinions. Like to be a feminist killjoy in my everyday life, and how much feminism relates to politics. It gave me that safe space to have those conversations with other people outside of the classroom and just to have that open mind as well that the conversation could go either way. But it's okay for me to have that voice.—Tracy

Theme 4: Engaging in Conversation and Building Community
While self-inquiry is an integral part of making the projects meaningful, sharing the work in a communal setting is also an important part of creating meaningful impact for participants as well as other observers/community members invited to gallery exhibits. How to facilitate equity is at the heart of feminist praxis. As mentioned earlier, Kalla and Broockman's (2021) work demonstrates that the non-confrontation exchange of narratives, or "hearing about the experiences of an outgroup member," can significantly transform viewpoints and facilitate long-term shifts away from previously held prejudices (2021, 186). Perhaps most importantly, these attitude changes are not temporary but long term.

Was there value in seeing the work of other students?
I believe that we live in a shame-based society, where if you were to represent yourself as an individual, your own identity, you don't follow the protocols, the whatever. I am tired of living in a shame-based society. I'm going to be fifty next year and it's like, no, that's not how I want to raise my children or my grandchildren...To me, in politics, that's what it is. We go around shaming each other to be on top...What it all comes down to is "I'm not alone on how I feel." And when people bring out their own individuality in their work it makes me go, "okay, I'm not the only one that feels like this in this world."—Janel

It was nice to see other students' individuality coming through and seeing all the different ways all of our lives and how they intersect and kind of brought us to that same point. It was also really interesting just to see what others had been through to get to that point too, because also in a university there's a patriarchal structure. It's all hierarchy and the student struggle is always there, but it was so interesting to see where everyone was coming from and then being able to relate to that as well. I really liked

FIGURE 16.5 My pink women's cardigan represents my gender identity and speaks to the way in which patriarchy can harm many who were assigned male at birth such as trans women, nonbinary people, and gender-nonconforming men. As a trans woman who previously identified as the latter two, I have experienced the struggles faced by each group. As a gender-nonconforming man, I felt I was not living up to some expectation of maleness, as a nonbinary person I worried that my identity was a phase, and currently I worry about the potential for others to now victimize me. Patriarchy contributes to this as it affects society's expectations of both men and women to play a specific part, and those who step out of line are often mocked or attacked.—Graham (Used with permission from Graham Koshman.)

to see the creativity and it definitely…gave me more confidence to push back.—Tracy

I just thought it was really cool to read everyone's work because we're all doing the readings in the class and just to learn how people relate those readings to their lives in ways I could relate to and in ways that I can't relate to as well. So I thought that was very valuable. It helped me engage with the readings a lot deeper than I could just on my own.—Christina

It helped me realize a lot of other people who are assigned male at birth struggle with internalized patriarchy and how it affects one's mental health...Unlearning one's toxic masculinity and feeling a bit more free afterwards is an important but often difficult process for people...Reading the experiences of other gender-nonconforming people and reading Susan Faludi's *Stiffed* helped me identify better with those people, but also to identify with the gay men who were worried that if they allowed trans women into their groups that they'd be seen as not worth taking seriously. I don't agree with that view, but just because of stuff I've internalized in the past about expression or identity, especially a fear of being viewed as weak or too feminine, I can sympathize with that and better understand where they're coming from.—Graham

As discussed above, vulnerability is an integral part of the decision-making process participants engage in when choosing how to respond to the assignment. Because the assignment is quite different from most assignments typical in political science, there is value in participating in more than one gallery event. The experience of seeing the works together in a gallery setting offers a unique experience for participants to see their projects in dialogue with one another and generates a feeling of community. Returning to the assignment in another class allows participants to build on this experience and adjust their level of vulnerability and/or risk taking.

Was there value in participating in more than one project/gallery event?
The first exhibit I was a part of made me really nervous thinking other people were going to read it even though my name wasn't on it. And...I think I censored myself a lot more. And then after seeing other people's projects, when I did the assignment again in another course, I just let myself go, took out all the stops and put everything I had into it. I felt so much more comfortable. I just wanted people to hear my voice and put my thoughts to paper and my true thoughts, and not censoring myself at all. And I just wanted to put it out there even if there was negative or positive reactions, it was starting a conservation. So I was very hesitant with the first one but the second one I felt much more confident and much more comfortable. I felt like it related to the material a lot better too doing it that way.—Tracy

Some of you participated in the last exhibit focused on diversity and inclusion in the city that was on display at City Hall. Did knowing it would be in this forum influence your decisions about your project?
I think when you hear that somebody who has the power or the ability to make change in society, there's this pressure when you have the opportunity to tell them something about your experiences, to say something meaningful that will direct change. So just finding the balance between being able to express yourself and say something that maybe the other person will understand and will take into account and make a thing out of it.—Harleen

I didn't feel a pressure to have to deliver, but I took the opportunity knowing that people working at City Hall were seeing my work to say something. So I made sure I was, in my project—talking about stuff specifically, my experiences in the city because I don't live in that city, but I go to school there. It did affect what I talked about...they don't know you're specifically saying it because it's anonymous, so I think it is valuable to share something with people who hold power in a city you live in or that you experience life in.—Christina

Theme 5: Doing Feminist Praxis in the Classroom and Beyond
Overall, the experiences and insights shared in this dialogue reveal photovoice as a powerful methodology for political communication and feminist praxis. As Joyce Green argues, "feminism is both theoretically informed ideology and methodology—the two are inseparable, as feminism is directed at transformative action—based on a political analysis that takes women's experiences seriously" (2017, 7).

Would you say that this project impacted in some way how you think about politics?
I think it did. It made me realize how little literature there is on trans or nonbinary stuff, specifically in political science. This is in spite of people from all parts of the gender spectrum being interested in politics and standing to benefit from better representation. Similarly, there's a lack of literature in political science that talks about disabilities. And also, that politics doesn't have to be super impersonal. You can talk about your own experiences, and sometimes it's very good to do that, because I think it can

FIGURE 16.6 The image I chose to represent my experience of gender as a lesbian is a pair of broken heels, which represents the disconnect I feel from womanhood. Being seen and treated as a woman my whole life, I have been fed these ideas on how I should look and act. Once coming to terms with my sexuality, I have been able to examine what womanhood means to me and reconsider the importance of marriage to me as a gay person.—Christina (Used with permission from Christina Ross.)

sort of help other people think differently about stuff. Sort of see through someone else's eyes.—Graham

I didn't realize how much of my life relates to politics, and I didn't ever think of feminism as really being interrelated, or sexualities or gender to a lot of politics. It definitely opened my eyes a lot there, and now I can see that in almost everything to do with politics as well.—Tracy

Would you describe this project as feminist?
Well, when you put yourself out there and it's like an equal stance. You stand there on an equal level and go, "Okay, I'm putting my vulnerability out there, who's going to stand with me?"—Janel

One thing I liked the most about it was that it gave an opportunity to see the diversity in the class. The diversity of everyone's experiences and how they engage with the readings and how it's different from how I would engage with the readings, and how their experiences shaped their lives.—Raveena

I think it comes from how open the project is. You just relate it to some course readings, and the rest is up to you. How you interpret the readings, how you interpret the specifics of the project, which I think's really good. Like, it can kind of scary maybe, especially if you're used to, like, university classes being extremely structured, but I think ultimately it needs to be open for this kind of a project to work and be meaningful.—Christina

Conclusion

One of the most fulfilling and impactful ways to practice feminism in political science is in the classroom. My approach to feminist pedagogy has developed both intuitively and strategically throughout my career and is rooted in a vision that challenges the traditional ways in which expertise, evidence, objectivity, and power inform and circulate in the classroom. This vision is consistent with theories of feminist pedagogy that conceptualize the classroom as a community of learning, care, and connection (hooks 1994; Shrewsbury 1987). While care is often positioned in our society as a set of practices free from contest or criticism, feminist approaches to pedagogy are founded on the knowledge that empowerment and liberation are cultivated through a process of critical engagement in a context free of shame and domination. Photovoice is a powerful tool through which this context can be created.

   Practising feminist pedagogy in the classroom through photovoice fosters a classroom that engages with politics on a number of levels and from a variety of standpoints. It fosters a classroom community that is deeply relational and particular. This practice is consistent with theories of feminist pedagogy that conceptualize the classroom as a community of learning, care, and connection by embracing differences, making space for conflicting politics, and creating opportunities for the transformation of viewpoints by exchanging narratives. It's also a creative and engaging practice of feminist methodology that can offer important insights and gaps in the field of political science. As Caroline Ramazanoğlu and Janet Holland observe, "Experiences and how they feel remain central to understanding similarities and diversity in gendered lives, and to investigation of inequalities, injustices, and institutionalized power" (2002,

123-24). As the above dialogue demonstrates, engaging with experiential knowledge through self-inquiry fosters the ability to see the same complexity in the lives of others as one sees in oneself. In so doing, photovoice offers a power vehicle of humanization that reveals imperfect points of intersectional understanding and transformation as well as potential coalitions both inside and outside the classroom. Creating spaces of "heterogeneous commonality" (May 2015, 41) puts intersectionality at the centre of learning and, as such, fosters meaningful connections and community building without any expectation of consensus or homogeneity. The ability to see and engage in this way is a cornerstone in contemporary feminist praxis and a valuable tool in creating caring institutions in postsecondary education and beyond.

Note

1. CityStudio is a partnership program between the City of Abbotsford and UFV. Students and faculty connect with city staff to research, design, and implement projects to develop job skills, experience group processes, and network with sector experts. Participation is facilitated though courses and students receive course credit for their work. See the CityStudio website: https://www.abbotsford.ca/city-hall/engagement-innovation/citystudio.

References

Ahmed, Sara. 2017. *Living a Feminist Life*. Durham, NC: Duke University Press.

Booth, Tim, and Wendy Booth. 2003. "In the Frame: Photovoice and Mothers with Learning Difficulties." *Disability and Society* 18 (4): 432-42. https://doi.org/10.1080/0968759032000080986.

Collins, Patricia Hill, and Sirma Bilge. 2016. *Intersectionality*. Cambridge, UK: Polity Press.

Gant, Larry M., Kate Shimshock, Paula Allen-Meares, Leigh Smith, Patricia Miller, Leslie A. Hollingsworth, and Trina Shanks. 2009. "Effects of Photovoice: Civic Engagement Among Older Youth in Urban Communities." *Journal of Community Practice* 17 (4): 358-76. https://doi.org/10.1080/10705420903300074.

Green, Joyce. 2017. "Taking More Account of Indigenous Feminism: An Introduction." In *Making Space for Indigenous Feminism*, 2nd ed., 1-20. Halifax: Fernwood Publishing.

Freire, Paulo. (1974). 2005. *Education for Critical Consciousness*. London: Continuum.

hooks, bell. 1994. *Teaching to Transgress: Education as the Practice of Freedom*. New York: Routledge.

Kalla, Joshua L., and David E. Broockman. 2020. "Reducing Exclusionary Attitudes through Interpersonal Conversation: Evidence from Three Field Experiments." *American Political Science Review* 114 (2): 410-25. https://doi.org/10.1017/S0003055419000923.

Kalla, Joshua L., and David E. Broockman. 2021. "Which Narrative Strategies Durably Reduce Prejudice? Evidence from Field and Survey Experiments Supporting the Efficacy of Perspective-Getting." *American Journal of Political Science* 67 (1): 185-204. https://doi.org/10.1111/ajps.12657.

Kalla, Joshua L., and David E. Broockman. 2022. "Voter Outreach Campaigns Can Reduce Affective Polarization among Implementing Political Activists: Evidence from Inside Three Campaigns." *American Political Science Review* 1 (7): 1516-22. https://doi.org/10.1017/S0003055422000132.

May, Vivian M. 2015. *Pursuing Intersectionality, Unsettling Dominant Imaginaries*. New York: Routledge.

Ramazanoğlu, Caroline, and Janet Holland. 2002. "Knowledge, Experience and Reality: Justifying Feminist Connections." In *Feminist Methodology*, 123-42. Sage Publications. https://doi.org/10.4135/9781849209144.

Shrewsbury, Carolyn M. 1987. "What Is Feminist Pedagogy?" *Women's Studies Quarterly* 15 (3-4): 6-14. https://jstor.org/stable/40003432.

Tronto, Joan C. 2010. "Creating Caring Institutions: Politics, Plurality, and Purpose." *Ethics and Social Welfare* 4 (2): 158-71. https://doi.org/10.1080/17496535.2010.484259.

Walton, Ginger, Stuart J. Schleien, Lindsey R. Blake, Catherine Trovato, and Tyler Oakes. 2012. "Photovoice: A Collaborative Methodology Giving Voice to Underserved Populations Seeking Community Inclusion." *Therapeutic Recreation Journal* 46 (3): 168-78.

Wang, Caroline, and Mary Ann Burris. 1994. "Empowerment through Photo Novella: Portraits of Participation." *Health Education Quarterly* 21 (2): 171-86. https://doi.org/10.1177/109019819402100204.

17 Learning to Relinquish Silence

Feministing in Political Science as an Ethicopolitical Project

NICK DORZWEILER

Feminist Theory as Disciplinary Critique

In the winter of 2010, during the second year of my PHD program, my depression and anxiety caught up with me and I had another breakdown. Many factors contributed to the episode, as is so often the case, and I won't belabor the story. But it would be fair to say that the immediate cause was graduate school itself. Aside from the professors at my undergraduate institution, I had never known anyone with an advanced degree in political science or a related field, and I'm not sure what I expected when I entered my PHD program. In any case, I was unprepared for what seemed to me its pervasive misanthropy. This was not so much about the workload per se, although that certainly encouraged its fair share of isolation and distress. Rather, it was the larger social environment of the program: the constant competition over professorial attention and institutional resources (I recall one student saying that he was going to "bury" another because they were trying to work with the same advisor); the intellectual jousting that seemed to dominate every gathering (I remember a fight breaking out at a party because one man disagreed with another's interpretation of Marx); and, especially, the expectation of expertise that determined whether one was worthwhile or not (when I said in a first-year seminar that I had never read Plato's *Republic* before, an older student asked, "Why are you here?"). Of course, dynamics like this only begin to scratch the surface of much deeper forces in academia—forces that regularly materialize in far crueler, more oppressive forms for those on the margins. In this sense, my own feelings of alienation in graduate school were unexceptional in degree or kind. And yet, at that moment in 2010, I felt I could not continue.

Prior to all this, feminist theory had already captivated me, both intellectually and politically. Although I had only been introduced to the field as an undergraduate student, what I had read and discussed then had transformed the way I understood the world. During this difficult time in my PHD studies, however, feminist theory engaged me in a new way—it began to change the way I *felt* in the world. For instance, I remember experiencing a sense of emotional relief when I read bell hooks argue that theory must be reconceived as a mode of critical thought "fundamentally linked to processes of self-recovery," rather than an exclusive discourse that affirms "intellectual class hierarchy" (1994, 61, 64). I remember passionately underlining, starring, dog-earing the page on which Elsa Barkley Brown remarked that "few historians are good jazz musicians" (1992, 298). By this she meant that academics, like classical musicians, too often demand silence—"of the audience, of all the instruments not singled out as the performers in this section, even often of any alternative vision [other] than the composer's" (298). And I remember feeling a rush of excitement when I read Wendy Brown's call for the creation of "feminist postmodern political spaces" (1995, 50). Here Brown imagined fields of thought and activity that would disrupt academia's longstanding quests for certainty, universal rationality, and epistemological authority, and instead embrace "as a permanent political condition partiality of understanding, cultural chasms whose nature may be vigilantly identified but rarely 'resolved,' and the powers of words and images to evoke, suggest, and connote rather than transmit meanings" (50).

Certainly, the work of these three scholars differs and even diverges from each other in important ways. But when I read them at this particular moment in my life, I felt that, together, they were articulating a powerful critique of the institutional norms of academia in general, and those of political science in particular. Among other things, they were identifying the stringent demands of hegemonic masculine subjectivity that academic political science tends to inculcate in its practitioners—demands of individualism, competition, certitude, and control. These critiques spoke to me. They gave voice to feelings that I had not been able to articulate to that point, not least because I understood my depression and anxiety as the result of my own intellectual and characterological shortcomings. More than this, though, they instilled in me a desire to experiment with who I was in relation to academia, to identify the possibilities and responsibilities to be a different person and scholar than the one academic political science seemed to deem valuable.

For the past decade or so, then, this has been one important meaning of feministing in political science for me. Inspired by the writings of bell hooks, Elsa Barkley Brown, Wendy Brown, and now many others, I wish to embrace feelings of uncertainty, inexperience, and unknowingness that I once viewed as proof of my inadequacy, forms of being I thought I had to obliterate if I were to fashion myself into a "real" (read: particular kind of white male) academic. This is an ongoing project, to be sure, a conglomeration of iterative efforts to identify and transform the ways in which I have trained myself (and in which my self has been trained) to live like Barkley Brown's classical musician, desiring and demanding the silence of others so that my own compositions not be interfered with. In this respect, it is a fundamentally ethical project. But it is also intertwined with the political, institutional, and epistemological critiques of academia developed by hooks, Barkley Brown, and Brown. For if I am to actually undertake the kind of ethical work I hope to, unknotting the myriad internalized desires and fears that keep me tied to "classical" models of subjectivity, then I must attempt to materialize ways of thinking, speaking, and acting that are different from those instilled by the dominant norms of the discipline in which I work. That is, I have to engage in my labour in ways that keep me employed as a contingent faculty member in a political science department, but which also avoid reproducing forms of hegemonic masculine subjectivity and epistemology that the discipline codes as desirable, if not compulsory.

In the remainder of this chapter, I want to explore how *teaching* can function as a key activity through which to manifest this type of ethico-political experimentation, before reflecting on some of the necessary challenges, fears, and failures involved in this work. As I discuss, some of the most unsettling moments in my efforts materialize this notion of feministing in political science occur when the project intrudes, as it so often does, upon deep-seated norms and expectations that operate at both the institutional as well as the individual level. Importantly, though, this work is not just about disturbance and defeat (however necessary and productive those experiences can be). Thus, in a brief conclusion, I suggest that while challenging entrenched institutional and individual norms and expectations can destabilize deeply held senses of self-worth, it also holds the possibility of materializing many new, joyful, and rejuvenating experiences of teaching and studying politics.

Ethical and Political Possibilities of Teaching

As contingent faculty working at a small liberal arts college in the United States, teaching comprises the bulk of my day-to-day work. This is something I value, not least because I have come to view teaching as one of the most politically significant practices I can engage in as a political scientist. Following the work of bell hooks, as well as that of other critical pedagogues such as Paulo Freire and William Ayers, I believe that the classroom "remains the most radical space of possibility in the academy" (hooks 1994, 12). One reason for this belief is simple accounting. Over the span of my career, my activities as a teacher likely will engage me in sustained communication with far more—and far more diverse—political agents than my published scholarship ever will. But there is more to this than just audience size. I also believe that approaching teaching as a means through which to fashion new understandings of self and world through iterative experimentation with others can help materialize one version of the "jazz" subjectivity for which Barkley Brown so poignantly called. As Barkley Brown notes, one of the unique features of most jazz ensembles is that "each member has to listen to what the other is doing and know how to respond while each is, at the same time, intent upon her own improvisation" (1992, 297). Citing the pianist Ojeda Penn, Barkley Brown calls jazz "an expression of true democracy," since each musician "is allowed, in fact required, to be an individual, to go his or her own way, and yet do so in concert with the group" (1992, 297). In certain moments, I believe that teaching can foster a similar dynamic insofar as it emphasizes ourselves and our world as improvisatory, communal creations. A few experiments from some of my own classes might help illustrate my meaning.

In my Feminist Theory seminar, I usually arrange for students to begin the course in a traditional manner: through assigned readings and instructor-led discussions on key debates and concepts in the field. At this stage, traditional "banking" conceptions of pedagogy remain operative. Some pre-established knowledge about gender, even if critical in nature, is transmitted to pupils who are assumed, rightly or wrongly, to not possess that knowledge prior to the educational encounter. This is not the kind of pedagogical experience for which hooks or Barkley Brown ultimately want us to aim, to be sure. When it comes to the student body with whom I work, however—some are well versed in feminist scholarship, others are confronting it for the first time, still others have had a semester or two of dabbling—I find that offering a preliminary introduction to the field can set the stage for more open-ended experimentation in future classes. And things do become more improvisational after these opening weeks. When we grapple with Judith Butler's *Gender Trouble*, for instance, I often ask everyone (including me) to complete an exercise adapted from hooks's *Teaching to Transgress*: in class, we write autobiographical paragraphs about an experience with a cultural norm concerning gender—that is, a norm we would identify as specific to the cultural environment in which we were raised and that helped define for us what notions of gender were possible (or not) in that particular environment. Each person then reads their paragraph out loud to the rest of the group.

The virtue of this exercise is twofold. First, as hooks notes, "our collective voice listening to one another affirms the value and uniqueness of each voice," while also helping to create a group dynamic—an ensemble composition—as aspects of experiences inevitably weave in and out of others' (1994, 84). And, indeed, while the conversation that results from this activity can be many things—funny, sad, angering—it almost always elicits a spirit of shared vulnerability and attentive engagement with one another's stories. In this sense, the activity becomes one small way of manifesting the kind of self and community "care" that Fiona MacDonald thematizes in her previous chapter in this volume.

Second and more broadly, the exercise provides an opportunity for students to move out of the role of knowledge consumer and into that of knowledge creator. Here, participants are not being told—by an author, a professor, a foundational text—that gender is performative. They are, in their own words and in dialogue with others, testing the degree to which a performance theory of gender accounts for expressions of gender they witness in themselves and others. They are assessing a particular body of knowledge in terms of their selves, considering how their own experience is *itself* a body of knowledge that can be activated to reveal new understandings of the way they move in and are understood by the world. Thus, when a class participant relates how they learned (or unlearned) to perform gender from childhood to adulthood, or how the lessons they have learned have been very different in one setting (e.g., the college gym) than another (e.g., the college classroom), the activity helps materialize a collective exploration—rather than a didactic explanation—of the degree to which gender performativity can be felt or witnessed experientially. To draw once more on MacDonald (this volume), the result is to produce "a reflective relationship with the scholarship" that engenders "new feminist understandings and/or articulations of past events, experiences, or viewpoints *as* political" (emphasis added).

Of course, experiments in knowledge creation that emphasize the contingency and indeterminacy of self and world need not always be so personal in nature. In my Masculinities class, for example, I orient discussion of the gendered nature of militarism around an activity inspired by Krista Hunt's (2015) analysis of war photography in Iraq and Afghanistan. Typically, students in this class consider themselves anti-war (if not anti-US), and when introducing the topic many will state that it is well known that the US only engaged in its Middle East adventures for material reasons (oil, land, money, etc.). At this point, I display a photograph taken by an embedded journalist of an American soldier in Iraq, who is pointing a rifle while entering a building. Before telling them any details of the photo, however, such as the nationality of the soldier, the activity in which they are involved, or the location in which it was taken, I ask the students to describe what the photo is "about." Invariably, the narratives they tell are precisely the ones that the US military hoped embedded journalists would tell: "The soldier is in danger;" "It looks like he is about to shoot terrorists;" "I don't see anyone around him, maybe his unit has been killed and he's on his own." As they look longer, however, they begin to ask questions about the photograph that follow Hunt's own. Do we know, for instance, if the building the soldier is entering is a home or a military installation (there are no markings on the building)? Do we know whether the soldier is pointing his weapon at civilians, at "terrorists," or at anyone at all (the viewer of the photo cannot see beyond the soldier's weapon)? Upon further reflection, students are surprised at how much information is lacking from the photograph, and how easy it was for them to overlay a relatively sympathetic if not heroic reading upon it despite their own antipathies toward US military engagement. The ensuing discussion thus reveals that despite its ostensible capacity for representing reality "as it really is," photography can do considerable "political work" (Hunt 2015, 124). In this case, the US military embedded journalists in combat units in part to prime American media coverage to reinforce conventional narratives about who fights ("heroic men") and why ("to kill bad guys").

But our conversation does not end here. At this stage in the exercise, our class has, as a collective, started to uncover the normative valences of a representation that at first glance appears a mere factual index of reality. This analysis in hand, some students will now suggest that the photo is nothing more than a fabrication, a false portrayal of reality that we must see through in order to grasp the "real" truth. For instance, if the photo is trying to manipulate the viewer to see the soldier as in a situation of heroic danger, students may now say that the soldier was more likely the instigator of the violence. Where the photo wants us to see the soldier as fighting "bad guys," students may now say that there was a good reason why the photographer did not want us to see where his weapon was directed. The impulse makes intuitive sense: if propaganda is an attempt to manipulate us in to holding some particular narrative of reality, then an obvious reaction would be to conclude that the opposite narrative offered by the object of propaganda must be the true one. Yet when given enough time and space, students return to the same questions they asked in the first part of the exercise. Who *is* the soldier pointing his weapon at anyway, and why? The fact is, they conclude, it is impossible to know with any confidence *what* is happening in the photo. Put differently, we simply do not have access to any epistemological certainty about the reality the photograph is presenting to us.

In this sense, the reality the photo is portraying is "unknowable." This does not mean whatever event the photograph captured did not happen. But in carefully describing the picture, in unpacking the near-instantaneous process by which we convert (and are encouraged to convert) interpretation into fact, we can see that trying to understand the photograph as a document of "the real" is to miss the sociopolitical work that any representation of reality can do. Precisely because we cannot have unmediated access to an event as distant and sprawling as the war in Iraq, much less an individual skirmish within that war, our determination of "what is actually happening" in such an event is always the result of interpretation, of political judgment influenced by multifarious and complex—but nevertheless mediated and partial—information. In this case (and others like it), we must acknowledge that seeking a knowing certainty that could ground our thinking beyond doubt is not an option. Doing so would help us to begin to grapple with something like the war on terror as a thoroughly political matter. That is, it is a problem that is unlikely to be meaningfully transformed through appeals to traditional positivist and empiricist principles of truth or certainty, but rather through ongoing, belabored public conversations "about the common" and the values we wish to see materialized therein (W. Brown 1995, 51). Responding to such a problem may not be a "scientific" endeavour, then, in the conventional sense of the term. It may instead require the kind of democratic improvisation and interplay emphasized in Barkley Brown's jazz metaphor.

This point leads to a final, simpler example of a tactic I sometimes employ in my teaching. At several points during a course, I often find it rejuvenating to say to myself and students—out loud—that the point of our work together need not always be to "learn," at least not in the sense of imbuing students with some knowledge that they must possess in order to move from a state of ignorance to truth. Instead, I ask what it might mean to imagine using some our time together to experiment with new ways of experiencing ourselves and our world. Here the challenge of education would not be that of dictating the nature of reality, but to "evoke, suggest, and connote" different meanings of it (W. Brown 1995, 50). They have never said so, but I wouldn't be surprised if some students find this suggestion ridiculous. And it is true that in order to keep my job I sometimes have to employ traditional pedagogical methods—translating student work into a fixed hierarchical grading system, for instance—that belies the idealism of such a vision. For me, however, this is even more reason to give voice to it, to try and maintain the language of a different form of education so that it might find ways of expressing itself within and alongside more conventional ones.

I know that the three pedagogical exercises I have just described may sound simple. Some political scientists might describe them as mundane, or perhaps naïve. In some sense, I think this is quite right: any individual example of a pedagogical practice that emphasizes this kind of experimentation or improvisation is likely to appear small in scope. Given this, one might wonder what impact such exercises could hope to have within the modern neoliberal academy, characterized as it is by social, political, and economic forces that are deep, pervasive, and structural in nature. To my mind, there are at least two responses to this question. The first is that, although any single manifestation of this type of work may be small, the very fact of their existence *does* contradict positivist and empiricist theories of knowledge that remain prominent in political science. Other experiences of knowledge *are* possible. We *can* experience ourselves and our world as contingent, indeterminate, and (therefore) modifiable. The second response is that that the mundanity, modesty, or reiterative quality of improvisatory educational work may be precisely the point. Longing for a type of knowledge that generates a radical political rupture, that brings us into a silent, final consensus upon merely reading or hearing it—this, I think, amounts to an ethical, epistemological, and political attachment that runs contrary to those outlined by feminist theorists such as bell hooks, Elsa Barkley Brown, or Wendy Brown. Hence the form of education I hope to manifest does not fixate on dramatic novelty per se. To return to Wendy Brown's language, I desire to create educational spaces that celebrate contingency as a "permanent political condition," that seek to identify but not resolve "cultural chasms," and that value the power of texts to transform rather than transmit stable meaning (1995, 50). Ultimately, this work just *is* experimental. Thus, while I sometimes fantasize that teaching will yield immediate or stunning transformations in myself and others, it is, like all experimental regimens, usually far more painstaking, repetitive, and rarely—if ever—finished.

Institutional and Individual Challenges

Precisely because this pedagogical approach is experimental, the obstacles one might encounter in attempting to manifest it are likely to vary from individual to individual and institution to institution. Certainly, my own experiences with this work are not universalizable. Some of the institutional difficulties I have experienced may be generalizable to a point, however, perhaps especially for those in employed in the discipline on a contingent basis. I want to attend to a few of those difficulties now, before addressing some that are more individual in nature.

Perhaps the most basic institutional challenge in trying to manifest a form of teaching that deviates from traditional banking models of education is that it is unfamiliar to most students. The notion of pedagogy as skill development is so embedded in contemporary educational discourse that undergraduates are rarely asked to consider whether learning could bear any other meaning. This does not mean that students are "dumb," or lack some basic understanding of reality. But it does mean that if I try to experiment with an alternative educational mode—one that I rarely experienced in my own schooling and therefore am also less familiar with—it may not be immediately understood by my students *as* education. It may instead appear as (and sometimes may in fact be) something else: meandering conversation, uncomfortable silence, a confusing line of questioning. This, when combined with the fact that students often (quite rightly) believe that their future job prospects are a function of how well they navigate conventional models of education, means that alternative forms of learning may only appear as so much time- and tuition-wasting. When this occurs, I cannot manifest the type of education I had hoped, at least not in that moment. Since this form of learning depends upon some level of collective improvisation, an inability or unwillingness of students to engage with it yields failure.

Failure of this sort may generate other, longer-term consequences. Because I am contingent faculty at a college where teaching is paramount, quality (read: "high-scoring") student evaluations matter a great deal to my employability. Hence if I experiment with a type of teaching that confuses or displeases students, I could be putting my job at risk. Fear of this outcome can then intermix with feelings of overwork and burnout—a result of the fact that I, like many contingent faculty, take on extra teaching loads throughout the year to make ends meet—to produce a sometimes irresistible desire to work in a way that feels safer, less demanding, more comfortable. In these moments, the deep-rooted structural pull of the neoliberal academy can be felt especially acutely. Although individual department chairs and administrators at my college rarely demand that faculty conform to any specific pedagogical regime, the way in which labour is assessed, distributed, and compensated at an institutional level does considerable work in determining the educational norms that can be materialized there. This structural power touches everyone who teaches at the college, to be sure. Yet those whose pay is relatively lower and contracts relatively less secure are more likely to be cognizant of its effects.

I hasten to add that I confront these challenges of contingent academic employment as someone who occupies categories of identity that otherwise fulfills many students' "typical" image of college education. For so many others, the institutional consequences of pursuing alternative educational models are likely to be far more severe (hooks 1994, 36–38, 42–43). It would therefore be difficult to understate the dangers in pursuing critical pedagogies for those who are in contingent positions, but who also experience other, potentially overlapping forms of marginalization. Given this, I must acknowledge the relative degrees of latitude I have to experiment with forms of teaching that run contrary to traditional expectations. And yet sometimes this awareness also sits uncomfortably alongside another: That my institution, incentivized by the type of budgetary pressures that face many colleges today, has made abundantly clear that the employability of non-tenure-track faculty is a function of administrative interpretations of curricular need and administrative measurements of "satisfactory performance." To run too closely to the edge of either condition is to court unemployment.

In addition to these institutional challenges, experiments in pedagogical practice can also elicit anxieties of a more personal nature. The autobiographical writing exercise described above offers a helpful illustration. As noted, this activity seeks to create a collective dialogue amongst all participants in the educational encounter, as each participant tests Butler's (1999) performance theory of gender in terms of their own embodied experiences. To foster a truly collective dialogue, then, I must be as willing to engage in this exercise as I ask students to be. I, too, need to reflect on and share experiences of gender that were formative in my own life—such as memories of family dynamics, socialization into norms of toxic masculinity in elementary school, and so on. If I choose not to do this, then I am engaging in a performative contradiction (by calling for communal reflection and then exempting myself from it). To return to Barkley Brown's musical metaphor, this would be to hew closer to the silence of "classical" music than the interplay of "jazz" improvisation. This is not a performance I want to enact. But it is not always an easy one to reject. For to genuinely participate in self-work of this kind, with and alongside students, is to potentially destabilize established norms and, it must be said, entrenched privileges that attend to the institutional identity of "professor." In explicitly speaking of my own experiences, as a subject that is historically, culturally, and politically constructed, I am not only inviting students to see me as something other than the traditional college professor—that is, an "objective mind—free of experiences and biases" (hooks 1994, 17). I am also calling attention to the fact that it is not possible for me to possess knowledge of a subject like gender that my students must accept as universal. This does not mean I have no knowledge at all, or no knowledge worth sharing. But it does mean that whatever knowledge I do have is not the same as truth. I cannot claim access to a position of epistemic privilege that would endow me with the ability to shepherd students from a state of ideological ignorance to one of enlightened freedom.

Identifying and challenging these attachments in the context of my activities as a teacher is not easy. In these moments, I can only describe my experience through an awkward circumlocution: my self often resists myself. The result is fear. Fear that if I reflect on "who I am" in the context of an educational experience—if I bear witness to the extent that I am the product of myriad forces, some of which I have directed but most of which I have not—then the students with whom I undertake this reflection will view me as somehow deficient. Fear, too, that if I publicly acknowledge the limitations of my experiences and my knowledge, then students will realize that I have nothing worthwhile to offer them. These feelings can be uncomfortable to bear, and I cannot pretend that they do not often prevent me from undertaking some educational thought or action I might wish. But experiencing them is necessary. For if I am to do more than *know* that I am an uncertain and contingent self, if I am to experience qualities of existence different from those emphasized by norms of hegemonic masculinity and the neoliberal academy, then it should not be surprising that this work sparks anxiety. And this means that while any individual experiment undertaken in any individual class in any individual semester may be small in scope, each constitutes one piece of a larger effort to uproot the norms and expectations that have led me (and perhaps others) to see Barkley Brown's "classical" model of subjectivity as the necessary or only possible one.

Practicing Improvisation

Having reviewed some of the challenges I have experienced in my experiments with critical pedagogy, I want to emphasize that, despite its unsettling nature, this work does not yield *diminished* forms of selfhood. In this sense, pursuing this kind of pedagogy need not mean I relinquish a desire for a sense of self-achievement—to be, say, a "good" teacher. However, it might mean that I must cultivate an awareness that my notion of "good" teaching necessarily requires that I fail. Similarly, pursuing critical pedagogy does not require that I abandon notions of myself as an agent capable of making judgments in and about the world. But it means acknowledging that my judgments can never be complete or final, that they are nothing more than attempts to engage in public conversation from the vantage point of "explicitly postulated norms and potential common values rather than from false essentialism or unreconstructed private interest" (W. Brown 1995, 51). The purpose of this educational philosophy is not to destroy the self, then, but to help generate *different* modes of subjectivity, ones that seek to embrace rather than expunge differences, interdependencies, and contradictions in experience.

And just as this work yields pluralized (rather than diminished) ways of being, so too must it be undertaken in concert with others (rather than in isolation). Drawing one last time on Barkley Brown's (1992) musical metaphor, this ethicopolitical work involves relinquishing the silences demanded by academia's particular version of "classical music" in favour of potentially messier but also more creative, communal, and improvisatory genres. In undertaking this practice, of course, I run the risk that others will reject my playing. At other times, my own playing will be too clumsy, too out of tune, or in a key that clashes with that of even willing interlocutors. In these moments, the educational improvisations I have in mind will likely produce little in the way of a coherent product. It will be just messy. I may then need to search for new partners to improvise with, as well as interrogate the failures in my own performances. In other cases, however, the mess will coalesce in unexpected ways, and a workable riff will emerge. When these openings do appear, they are incredibly exciting. They impel me to continue playing.

Thirteen years ago, I experienced very few of these moments. Indeed, I hardly even knew it was possible to play in the discipline in this way. But today, I have been discovering more opportunities for meaningful, creative improvisation. Mostly, I continue to find them in the classroom, that "most radical space of possibility in the academy." Increasingly, though, I am also finding them in the course of my scholarly activities, a place I had least expected to do so. In fact, I can now say that some of the most meaningful and heartening of these opportunities have emerged as I have met others in the discipline—not least the editors of and contributors to this volume—whose engagement with related notions of feministing in political science have made me feel much less scared and alone than I did as a graduate student over a decade ago.

In concluding these reflections, however, I do not want to issue a call for every reader to follow the path down which I have (and continue to) stumble. Certainly, I hope aspects of my experiences will resonate with some. Perhaps they too believe that teaching represents a particularly significant practice through which to grapple with norms of hegemonic masculinity that cut across both institutional and individual realms of experience. But I know this view is far from universal. Labour conditions, individual proclivities, academic interests—these and other factors all vary far too widely to offer anything like a prescription for future action. If there is "call" I would like to end with, then, it is necessarily broad: to urge political scientists to foster experimental or improvisatory engagements with some aspect of their academic labour that feels significant as well as accessible to them, and ideally requires them to enter into interdependent relationships with others. If such a call doesn't sound prescriptive enough, that is in some sense the point. While it is certainly possible to design programs aimed at ethical or political absolution, feminist thinkers such as bell hooks, Elsa Barkley Brown, and Wendy Brown teach us that such programs may only reinforce attachments to individualism, competition, certitude, and control that have pervaded this discipline for much of its existence in the North American academy. I therefore am not (and would not want to be) in a position to determine "what is to be done." I can only say that I believe the creation of more collaborative, caring, and democratic public spaces within the academy will require, among other things, improvisations of the self that are undertaken at some risk with and alongside others. And so, I continue to practice.

References

Brown, Elsa Barkley. 1992. "'What Has Happened Here': The Politics of Difference in Women's History and Feminist Politics." *Feminist Studies* 18 (2): 295–312. https://doi.org/10.2307/3178230.

Brown, Wendy. 1995. *States of Injury: Power and Freedom in Late Modernity*. Princeton, NJ: Princeton University Press.

Butler, Judith. 1999. *Gender Trouble: Feminisms and the Subversion of Identity*, 2nd ed. New York: Routledge.

hooks, bell. 1994. *Teaching to Transgress: Education as the Practice of Freedom*. New York: Routledge.

Hunt, Krista. 2015. "The 'War on Terrorism.'" In *Gender Matters in Global Politics: A Feminist Introduction to International Relations*, 2nd ed., edited by Laura J. Shepherd, 116–26. New York: Routledge.

(RE)BUILDING
POLITICAL SCIENCE

18 Towards an Agenda for Feministing Political Science

Intersectional Feminist Pathways

CHAMINDRA WEERAWARDHANA

Making Sense of Feministing Political Science

In the academy, departments of political science have long been far from accommodating towards perspectives that diverge from what is considered mainstream, if not a widely accepted and acclaimed knowledge base and theoretical perspectives, largely developed by (cisgender) men. While feminist politics and feminist international relations (IR) have made it to almost all undergraduate and postgraduate courses in many countries, it is not inaccurate to state that feminist politics still remain at the fringes of the study of politics and IR. In an IR theory course, for example, it is rare to teach feminist IR in the first half of the semester, and even rarer during the first few weeks of the course. Challenges to the development of the field of feminist politics and IR also exist in the form of representation. Despite the popularity of the social media hashtag #representationmatters and an increasing understanding across the board of the importance of ensuring diverse representation in every sector, lack of representation continues to remain a work in progress in the academy. In the political science academy of the territories of Turtle Island we know as Canada, for example, how many Indigenous women occupy secure posts in university departments of political science? The same question can be asked about women at many other diverse intersections of lived experience, including women living with disabilities, women of colour and non-Western backgrounds and/or citizenships, women of trans and gender-diverse experiences, and marginalized people at many other multiple intersections of lived experience.

It is in this context that I—an international politics PHD, a citizen of a South Asian country, an intersectional feminist human rights defender, and researcher who navigates academic and rights defender circles in

Turtle Island and elsewhere on a regular basis—approach the thematic of this tremendously timely volume—feministing political science. I define the verb *feministing* as implying the tedious efforts, past and present, of political scientists (especially women in the academy) to call for, build, and strengthen a focus on feminist politics and IR in what has been (and in many ways continues to be) a very phallocentric academy. In this sense, feministing involves efforts to transform the institutional landscape in terms of representation, coursework, and availability of specialist degree programs, including PHD and postdoc programs in feminist politics and IR. The focus on feministing also involves building upon, and moving beyond, the emphasis on feminist political science as a disciplinary subfield.[1] Most importantly, the full significance and potential of feministing is to be found in a core focus on challenging established ways of doing things, of rattling the system, and calling for meaningful, long-term, and holistic transformation. To reiterate the obvious disclaimer, these latter tasks are inherently very demanding, and the achievable scope is indeed limited, in the capitalist-industrial complex that controls university structures in Turtle Island and elsewhere. Our collective core focus as advocates of feminist politics and IR, then, ought to be to work individually and collectively towards the best possible outcomes, strategizing against the many institutional and corporate barriers ahead of us.

Defining the Feminist in *Feministing*?
One of the foremost challenges in strategizing along an axis of feministing political science is that of how we define the term *feminist*. My reading of the noun *feminism* is that it is not sustainable in the absence of the qualifier *intersectional*. This understanding is informed by my own global work in academic research, grassroots feminist organizing, and human rights advocacy. It is crucial to reiterate the Black feminist roots of the term *intersectionality*, a key analytical tool that facilitates the task of identifying the multiple intersections of lived experience between race, gender, socioeconomic realities, and more.[2] Reflecting upon, and taking into account the many intersecting, interrelated, and inextricably linked forms of oppression that characterize people's lived experiences is a crucial principle of Black feminist thought in Turtle Island. This approach to feminist thought and praxis, developed by many Black feminist thinkers over the years, has notably led to many positive iterations in other

contexts of feminist advocacy, in different parts of the world. Today, the South Asian region, for instance, is marked by a fast-emerging new generation of young intersectional feminist activists and thinkers, whose feminist politics is based on a fulsome acknowledgement of the nonbinary nature of the world. Their advocacy stands in sharp contrast with that of previous generations of feminists in the region, whose discourses have been restrictive, with a highly cisnormative understanding of womanhood. From Turtle Island to Aotearoa and beyond, new generations of Indigenous feminists are reclaiming the feminist traditions and histories of their communities, in that process strongly challenging the patriarchal and misogynist dictates within their own communities (see, e.g., Fiola 2020).[3] In my own work, a key focus on exploring non-cisnormative frontiers of feminist thought—especially trans feminist perspectives on politics and IR—has sought to highlight how such perspectives are closely interconnected with profoundly transformative and decolonial praxes and priorities.[4] These perspectives mark a significant departure from long-established feminist discourses that focus on a binary and highly cisnormative understanding of feminist knowledge generation and advocacy.

Reading the "feminist" in *feministing* along such a progressive intersectional feminist understanding is crucial if the most effective outcomes are to be achieved in ventures that can be described as feministing political science and IR. An understanding of feminism of this nature enables us to take stock of the extremely complex and rich diversities of womanhood in a fundamentally nonbinary world. It facilitates the task of delving into the socially transformative, if not healing potential of intersectional feminist work. Indeed, it is a body of activist praxes and knowledge systems that clearly help us chart a human-rights-focused, humane, and considerate path forward. A path of this nature is of crucial relevance to a world where politics and international affairs continue to be primarily managed, shaped, and gate-kept by cisgender (and largely heteronormative) men.

To take stock of what feministing political science truly involves, it is therefore extremely useful to ground the logic of feministing as an intersectional feminist priority. In this sense, feministing political science, or for that matter any other academic discipline, would involve a central focus on *intersectionally sensitive and informed inclusion*. This does not mean a mere focus on equality and diversity. Instead, this involves a more comprehensive assessment of the multiple ways in which power dynamics operate in the academy. This also involves working towards a deeper understanding—at both individual and collective levels—of what it really means to engage in anti-oppression and anti-racism work within one's professional sphere. This brand of intersectional inclusion calls for critical and counterintuitive engagements with the concepts of power and agency. Who wields more power, for example, in a political science department in a research-intensive Canadian university? What are the relational dynamics between those who have historically held high power/representation/secure jobs/professional recognition versus those who stand at the margins, with less power, less representation, insecure jobs, and a lack of due recognition? As opposed to what is often construed in professional contexts as equity, diversity, and inclusion policies, for instance, this kind of intersectionally inclusive work calls for a deeper, lifelong, and intensely personal commitment to progressive transformation. Critically examining power relations, identifying intersecting lived experiences of oppression, and developing theoretical insights and hands-on praxes to challenge them are all deeply grounded and overarching features of the Black feminist tradition of Turtle Island. In advocating for an approach that centres around intersectionally informed inclusion as a core strategy of feministing political science, I gratefully acknowledge the painstaking work of generations of Black feminist thinkers, activists, and changemakers, for developing one of the most profoundly transformative and transferable knowledge bases on anti-oppression, anti-racism, and gender justice work ever developed in Turtle Island.

Feminist Political Science in/for a New World: On Seedlings of Change
This section reflects upon how we can envisage the task of positively transforming how we teach and research political science and IR by paying increased attention to intersectional feminist thought. In the following, I maintain that one of the ways in which meaningful feministing can be achieved is through the diversification of teaching and learning in the sphere of political science. Across the length and breadth of Turtle Island, for example, teaching feminist political science requires a strong emphasis on Indigenous feminist approaches, knowledge systems, and epistemologies. This is all the more crucial, given the systemic injustices

and challenges that Indigenous communities continue to face. The popular amnesia surrounding the colonial history of Canada is also closely interlinked to the ways in which topic areas such as "Canadian politics," "Canadian federalism," "Canadian multiculturalism," and, in general, Canadian studies, have been taught, especially in university departments of political science. To this point, many in the academy could respond by affirming how attentive they have been to Indigenous perspectives, and how "inclusive" their programs are. However, the point made here is that, given the long and charged past (and present) of violence against Indigenous Peoples, there is a clear need to centre Indigenous ontologies and epistemologies in university departments of political science.[5] This is a much broader objective that goes way beyond the presence of less than a handful of Indigenous faculty members, or courses on Indigenous politics. This body of work imperatively involves a process of recentring knowledge dissemination in university departments of political science.

Attending annual conferences of leading Turtle Island–based learned societies specialized in political science in the pre-COVID-19 years, I have been struck by the reality of how Indigenous politics are discussed in such platforms. At such a gathering in Blackfoot Territory in 2016, a female white settler academic who works on Indigenous politics categorically stated that irate campaigns and calls for rights led by Indigenous people are somewhat futile. Instead, she maintained that Indigenous people ought to focus on "calm and peaceful" approaches, and on dialogue! At yet another event, I vividly recall how a young white settler academic complained about the discontent and discomfort of a class with a majority of Indigenous students, when they learnt that she was their lecturer in a module on Indigenous politics. These are just two everyday examples of how the political science academy can be insensitive towards issues of Indigenous politics and representation. They also indicate a considerable gap between how the Canadian political science academy perceives Indigenous politics and the actual priorities and discourses in Indigenous politics and justice movements today.

The political science academy seeks a certain conformity to ways of being and practices of yesteryear. Outside the academy, Indigenous communities, especially women, gender-diverse people, and youth are transforming their political discourses and liberation praxes along critical feminist and decolonial perspectives. Addressing this gap in departments of political science along a logic of genuine transformation that stems beyond routine tokenizing is a key priority for feministing political science in Turtle Island.

Diversifying Political Science?

What does it mean to engage in feministing political science meaningfully and holistically? In many countries, transforming political science departments along an axis of diversification continues to remain a major challenge. It is no exaggeration that they are spaces marked by high levels of intransigence, and in some cases, a relative lack of preparedness for progressive change. Political science departments remain, by and large, highly cis-heteronormative spaces. Very few non-cisgender people, for instance, make their way to secure positions in such spaces. In my own lived experience, a senior academic in the UK once categorically told me that I should seek opportunities outside the academy, as a woman of trans experience "would stand no chance whatsoever" in obtaining secure employment in (a UK university department of) political science. Views of this nature are well-established realities in the academy. A political science department is a place that produces, develops, and shares knowledge in the areas of politics and IR. This implies that the impact of how they function, and who gets to engage in knowledge production and dissemination in such coveted spaces, have a direct impact on the overall output of such departments. Consequently, it is accurate to note that the ways in which university departments of politics function carry a great deal of significance to the hands-on spheres of local, provincial, and national politics as well as foreign affairs.

A key component of a strategy of feministing political science is indeed that of challenging the centre—if not the power structures—of the political science academy. All across Turtle Island, these power structures continue to be held by individuals with an advantage when it comes to binary gender hierarchies, racial fault lines, and positions of influence. How best can we challenge these dynamics? Incremental strategies of strengthening diversity have long been under way in many departments of political science. However, do such measures alone suffice, if the ultimate objective were to be to restructure power dynamics in political science departments? As Black feminist leaders teach us in relation to their feminist advocacy, this too is a body of work that needs to be understood as a constant process, with no specific end date. The work does not stop at one initiative, one strategy, one coordinated effort to obtain the laurels of an equality and diversity monitoring body, or a reaction at the behest of an outcry from students seeking learning and research options of our times (from an incisive focus on Indigenous politics to politics of intersectional feminisms, including trans and intersex feminist politics).

Feministing political science calls for a manifesto for meaningful transformation, a plan of action with short-, medium-, and long-term priorities. While some measures along a progressive direction are epistemological and ontological, others are pragmatic and practical. As the COVID-19 pandemic transforms the landscape of higher education, these new developments can be deployed effectively to strengthen the intersectional feminist core of political science departments. The possibility of virtual teaching and learning sessions, for example, should be a feminist priority. Such flexibility enables female academics at many intersections of lived experience to engage in professional activity under more flexible circumstances. They can be of special relevance to women in political science who may not possess passports issued by Global North countries and are consequently faced with many immigration hurdles. Indeed, deploying new technologies effectively can have a supportive and positive impact on scholars with caring responsibilities.

Concluding Remarks: Towards a Politics of Progressive Transformation

Fiona MacDonald's (2017) emphatically titled a journal article "Knocking Down the Walls of Political Science" challenges the political science academy to go beyond its focus on the gender binary, which has been strongly upheld in the discipline. This article is a guiding contribution that facilitates a reflection along a new, and refreshingly feministing, axis. The feministing work that lies ahead involves making the political science department a place where concepts such as *Mana Mothuhake* (self-determination) and *Mana Whenua* (rights and sovereignty over land) are no longer alien perspectives, a place where politics and IR-focused research into decolonial feminist methodologies, including trans and intersex feminisms, and in the specific context of Turtle Island, Black feminist thought, are fully welcome.[6] Most importantly perhaps, transformative currents of this nature in political science departments hold the key to positively transforming our political spheres at local, provincial, and national levels, on the long route to meaningful recentring of power-politics and political strategizing, along intersectional feminist principles.

Notes

1. Indeed, feminist political science has long been a presence in the political science academy as a disciplinary subfield, gaining increasing influence over the years (see, e.g., Sawer 2014). However, the parameters of this brand of feminist political science have often been restrictive, in terms of representing a varied range of voices, perspectives, and epistemologies developed by women from a range of diverse backgrounds. It has also been built upon an extremely binary understanding of gender and feminist knowledge-making. The present reflection, together with other contributions to this volume, is an effort to move towards a much more critical, diverse, and transformative approach to the teaching, learning, and dissemination of politics and IR.
2. While the term *intersectionality* is attributed to Professor Kimberlé Crenshaw (1989, 1991), intersectionality as a tool in women's organizing, knowledge generation, and movement building has a rich history in the Black feminist tradition of Turtle Island. Earlier precedents such as the "Combahee River Collective Statement," a key document in Black feminism, outline a template for intersectional feminist solidarity building (Combahee River Collective 1977). Writings of key Black feminist thinkers, from Professors Audre Lorde, Angela Davis, bell hooks, Alice Walker, Barbara Smith, and indeed many others, carry the defining hallmark of an intersectionally informed approach to feminist advocacy, knowledge generation, and movement building (see notably Collins 1990). Some critiques of intersectionality, in favour of relational and constructivist approaches, often depart from a linear understanding of intersectional feminist thought, as a body of work that has been developed over many decades by several generations of Black feminist thinkers and practitioners. Being a legal expert, Professor Crenshaw's reading of intersectionality is indeed intended for a legal audience.
3. This body of work is being principally carried out outside the academy, in the forms of campaigns, such as the Missing and Murdered Indigenous Women campaign and actions in Turtle Island, the Standing Rock, Ihumātao, and Mauna Kea campaigns in Turtle Island, Aotearoa, and Hawai'i, and many initiatives that strive to carve out decolonial paths ahead, from seeking reparations, challenging colonialist public memory, and exploring Indigenous approaches to governance and caring for communities. The central role of youth, especially of Gen Z, in making these processes happen, is evident, for example, in the work of activists such as Kassie Hartendorp (https://samesamebutdifferent.co.nz/writer/kassie-hartendorp/) and India Logan-Riley (https://www.youtube.com/watch?v=Qdxa1H4y-hw). In Aotearoa, this body of work has also made its way to the legislature, in the form of the work of Te Pāti Maōri, which, at the time of writing (February 2022), has two seats in Aotearoa's national legislature in Te Whanganui a Tara.

4. On trans feminist perspectives of feminist organizing and knowledge production, see Weerawardhana 2017, 2018, 2020.
5. In Canada, many constructive dialogues have dealt with the necessity of meaningfully including Indigenous approaches and epistemologies in the academy. Despite the richness of these bodies of work from coast to coast, the institutional realities are such that their practical impacts are only parsimoniously visible in the academy. A discourse on feministing political science can therefore draw much inspiration from critical dialogues on Indigenizing the academy (see, e.g., Brulé and Koleszar-Green 2019).
6. In Te Reo Māori, the terms *Mana Mothuhake* and *Mana Whenua* are widely used in Aotearoa as well as other Pacific islands as fundamental concepts in articulating Indigenous campaigns and actions for equity and justice.

References

Brulé, Elizabeth, and Koleszar-Green. Ruth. 2019. "Cedar, Tea and Stories: Two Indigenous Women Scholars Talk about Indigenizing the Academy." *Cultural and Pedagogical Inquiry* 10 (2): 109–18. https://doi.org/10.18733/cpi29448.

Collins, Patricia Hill. 1990. *Black Feminist Thought: Knowledge, Consciousness, and the Politics of Empowerment*. Boston: Hyman.

Combahee River Collective. 1977. "Combahee River Collective Statement." https://americanstudies.yale.edu/sites/default/files/files/Keyword%20Coalition_Readings.pdf.

Crenshaw, Kimberle. 1989. "Demarginalizing the Intersection of Race and Sex: A Black Feminist Critique of Antidiscrimination Doctrine, Feminist Theory and Antiracist Politics." *University of Chicago Legal Forum*, art. 8, 139–67. https://chicagounbound.uchicago.edu/uclf/vol1989/iss1/8.

Crenshaw, Kimberle. 1991. "Mapping the Margins: Intersectionality, Identity Politics, and Violence against Women of Color." *Stanford Law Review* 43 (6): 1241–99. https://doi.org/10.2307/1229039.

Fiola, Chantal. 2020. "Naawenangweyaabeg Coming In: Intersections of Indigenous Sexuality and Spirituality." In *In Good Relation: History, Gender and Kinship in Indigenous Feminisms*, edited by Sarah Nickel and Amanda Fehr, 136–53. Winnipeg: University of Manitoba Press.

MacDonald, Fiona. 2017. "Knocking Down Walls in Political Science: In Defense of an Expansionist Feminist Agenda." *Canadian Journal of Political Science* 50 (2): 411–26. https://doi.org/10.1017/S0008423916001190.

Sawer, Marian. 2014. "Feminist Political Science and Feminist Politics." *Australian Feminist Studies* 29 (80): 137–47. https://doi.org/10.1080/08164649.2014.930554.

Weerawardhana, Chamindra. 2017. "Profoundly Decolonising? Reflections on a Transfeminist Perspective of International Relations." *Meridians* 16 (1): 184–213. https://doi.org/10.2979/meridians.16.1.18.

Weerawardhana, Chamindra. 2018. "A Transfeminist Perspective on Development Work." In *Routledge Handbook on Development Studies*, edited by Corinne L. Mason, 119–30. London: Routledge.

Weerawardhana, Chamindra. 2020. "Erasure at the 'Tipping Point'? Transfeminist Politics and Challenges for Representation: From Turtle Island to the Global South/s." In *Turbulent Times: Transformational Possibilities? Gender and Politics Today and Tomorrow*, edited by Fiona MacDonald and Alexandra Dobrowolsky, 304–25. Toronto: University of Toronto Press.

19 "Refusal Has Been Really Important in My Life"

Political Science Aunties Discuss Feministing in Political Science

Dialogue with YASMEEN ABU-LABAN, KIERA L. LADNER, REETA CHOWDHARI TREMBLAY, and LEAH F. VOSKO
Edited by ETHEL TUNGOHAN and ALANA CATTAPAN

ON MAY 28, 2021, we gathered together leading scholars in political science who have been groundbreaking in their fields—academic aunties of sorts—to talk about the changing nature of political science, attempting to institute structural changes within the discipline, and the challenges of diversity work. This dialogue highlights the manifold ways one can be part of feministing in political science.

On Self-Care in the Pandemic

ETHEL TUNGOHAN: Let's start by talking about self-care, which is incredibly important, especially during the pandemic.

YASMEEN ABU-LABAN: One thing I have done almost since the start of the pandemic is yoga online. We meet three times per week, which has been fantastic. It's a group that had been meeting face to face before, but I'd say we got to know each other even better during the pandemic. I think all of us are so grateful that our instructor moved the yoga classes online. Our instructor delivers mail for Canada Post and does yoga in addition. She's a very interesting person!

KIERA LADNER: What have I been doing for self-care? Gardening again. I am so happy it is spring or summer or whatever. We had frost and snow just days ago! So I don't know what season it is, but I'm really happy that there's green stuff outside and that I can spend more time in my garden. The winter was long, so I have been trying to take periodic breaks. I just got back from a week off, where I spent lots of time with horses, and that was self-care.

LEAH VOSKO: I've been learning the clarinet. That means practicing for twenty to thirty minutes a day. I'm learning some klezmer, and a bit of jazz, and hopefully given how long it's taking for this pandemic to end, by the time it's over I'll be able to play with someone else beyond my instructor on Zoom.

REETA CHOWDHARI TREMBLAY: I did actually have a tough winter. There was some sickness in my family along with the routine duties we perform as academics. This pushed me to take care of myself. We are so lucky, we live in Victoria, so walking has been good, but I've been teaching myself Persian. I've learned Arabic script, I am good now in Urdu, and I am getting better in Persian! So that's what's going on, but thank you for asking!

On Stasis and Change in Political Science:

ET: The first question that we had as a team was to ask, How has political science changed as a discipline from when you were a graduate student until today? In other words, has the field become more receptive to feminist, anti-racist, Indigenous methods in research? Is the field keeping up with a changing society?

LV: Since I started my graduate studies in the early 1990s, the field has become more multidisciplinary yet, somewhat frustratingly, less intradisciplinary in some ways. We've nurtured separate fields—gender and politics, race and politics, Indigenous politics. This is a great development, but what I find frustrating (especially when I'm developing a syllabus in gender and politics) is the lack of intradisciplinary exchange—to some extent, we have pursued disengagement over mainstreaming, although there is some intradiscplinary recognition in cross-cutting fields such as feminist political economy.

YAL: I think we have had a change and growth of work around issues of race and Indigeneity and gender. We have more scholars doing that, but it hasn't necessarily been integrated into the discipline as a whole, nor has it fundamentally shifted the knowledge hierarchy of the discipline of political science. That's an observation other people have made, and I said the same thing in my Canadian Political Science Association presidential address (see Abu-Laban 2017).

What I would say more positively is that demographically the discipline has really shifted. When I started my graduate work at Carleton university in 1988, I arrived there never having had a political science professor who was a woman. In that period of the late 1980s in US political science, women made up about 15 per cent of the professors, in contrast to sociology, which was 30 per cent of professors. If I fast-forward to today, women make up a third of Canadian Political Science Association members, and also globally, women make up a third of political scientists across the world. These are changes that have happened in my lifetime that I think should also be noted.

RCT: I go back a generation or more before Yasmeen, and there weren't many women at that time in the field of political science. Yes, our profession has changed demographically. My comments will generally pertain to the comparative politics subdiscipline, because that's where I come from. If I were to summarize the changes in the discipline of political science, I would put them in two boxes. One box for me is the dominant, hegemonic one, fundamentally dominated by the US methodology. I wouldn't use the word *positivism*, but basically the adherents of this box have a commitment and an urge to have a scientific political science—a purity of the discipline. Yes, there have been debates about the scientific nature of the discipline, but the hegemonic contours of the discipline remain intact.

In the other box what I would put is the radical rethinking of categories, analytical and methodological categories. I must admit that coming from India to the United States for graduate studies, my bias was already with the critical theory framework, e.g., the Americans did not understand India, and thus we needed to explore the postcolonial scholarship, subaltern scholarship with its origins in the Global South. Getting back to this box, the critical approach has had huge impact in terms of rethinking the analytical categories whether these happened to come from the feminist, or Global South scholars, and postmodernists. Derrida, Foucault, Edward Said, Homi Bhabha were part of it, then later feminism, postfeminism, intersectionality, Indigeneity, and race were added on.

There has been very little interaction between those two boxes. Only those critical approaches have been allowed to enter into the margins of the hegemonic box which accommodate themselves to the existing scientific methodological biases of the discipline.

Political science, the way it is right now in Canada: we teach the hegemonic stuff, make sure that hierarchies of knowledge stay intact, and give the discipline a purity whereas the radical camp just works on its own and plays in its own territory. I must admit that it makes me quite frustrated: Why can not we have an eclectic political science?

KL: I think that there has been a shift. It's a small shift and that the bit of a shift has maintained that same box. Still that box has shifted somewhat to, at least performatively, include different topics within the same institutional and theoretical paradigms.

I remember grad school. I completed my first master's degree at the University of Saskatchewan in 1993–1994. That's a department where there were almost entirely white men. I think that the two faculty members that were not white men struggled horribly. My time there included sitting at my defence of my master's with my supervisor apologizing because he had told me countless times that "you don't study Indians in political science." At my defence! I think that it's come a long way from that—not being looked upon as something to be taken seriously in political science—but as a result I think that we also haven't seen that change as the discipline still marginalizes and ignores Indigenous scholarship. I was talking to some students not long ago for a graduate conference and was laughing at the fact that I've gone from the margins to the mainstream, all within twenty years. But the reason that I've become mainstream in part of the discipline is because I talk about federalism and the constitution. The work is not really mainstream—it just speaks to the mainstream—while a lot of Indigenous scholarship refuses to do so.

ET: If, as Yasmeen said, there has been a demographic shift, why isn't the discipline changing? Or is it that people can see that the structures of power that are still intact, that the field cannot accommodate divergent research interests, divergent methodologies, and that in order to gain traction we use existing tropes in order to be legible? Why hasn't it shifted? And will it ever shift?

LV: I kept thinking "why are we asking about political *science*?" I think all of us engaged in this dialogue, as students of *politics*, as scholars that do feminist politics, attentive to Indigeneity, gender, race, and (dis)ability, feel a degree of discomfort with certain positivist methods, fearing that they might obscure such social relations. In pointing to the dominance of positivist methods, I am not suggesting that it is necessary to replace interpretivism with positivism, but rather to foster multiple methods and dialogic approaches. As students of politics, we might learn certain things looking through a positivist lens, and proceeding in a particular way empirically, but we might simultaneously be able to juggle aspects of interpretivism that are complementary rather than contradictory.

YAL: I would just add another observation, which is that the period that we're talking about, let's say the 1980s to the present, is also one where there's been a lot of shifts in the way that research is funded. There's been a real push, for example, at the Social Sciences and Humanities Research Council of Canada to have policy-relevant research. Many of us see value in that, and being in political science encourages that kind of thinking, and that kind of practicality. But if you're doing policy-relevant work, you might indeed be taking a more positivist approach. I think that might also account for some of the paradoxes we're talking about. My honours BA, my master's degree, and my PHD were all on immigration policy. When I finished my PHD, I might as well have been from Mars! Immigration was just not on the agenda of this discipline. It is now! It's incredible to me how much that has changed and how many people are doing work in that area. It does also have something to do with the changing research landscape, and the funding structure in Canada and internationally. We're not disconnected from those larger, broader trends.

RCT: I think there are a couple of things happening. One is the resistance to change. There's such a huge institutional stickiness, mostly in terms of maintaining the reputation of the scholarship produced by all of us. Where does the reputation factor come from? It's really decided by what kind of journals we publish in, how many citations we have, and their connection to the determination of our promotion and tenure in the academy. We haven't published this yet, but one of my colleagues and I are doing a research project on comparative politics—is there a comparative politics tradition in Canada? We started by looking at how many people really think they're comparativists, how they define themselves, and what are their most cited articles. It is amazing that there's such a hierarchy of reputational factors. Most of us who work on, for example, the "Global South" are identified as working on "soft issues." Much of this work is published in interdisciplinary journals. And guess what? Interdisciplinary journals are not being cited. This results in a hierarchy of reputations. There's a kind of built-in mechanism which is self-defeating or has a self-defeating purpose. I'm hoping by this research to show people that in Canada, we have to figure out how we create a space for ourselves, when we are dealing with this very hegemonic discourse.

A second problem is that we rely upon the reputation factors determined by the American political science community. But what about Canadian scholarship on race, Indigeneity, and decolonization? In Canada we are so privileged to have a strong presence of feminist and Indigenous scholars, and race scholars are emerging, but from where do we still import our knowledge? It's coming from the US. I think we need to seriously take care of this issue. I am hoping the present and the future generations will do that. I find it really shocking that I've been in this profession now for forty-some years and we're still resisting. Yes, we've made lots of positive changes. I'm here, we're here, because of changes, but we're still resisting.

On Diversity and Refusal

ET: Are there attempts at diversifying the profession that excite you? That are actually going to be where we can change the field to be more accommodating of diversity writ large?

KL: I think that while there's been institutional pushback, there's also been an institutional push. Indigenous politics was never discussed much in my undergraduate degree, nor my master's degree in political science, nor my PHD. But there's been an institutional push to get to diversifying, to get Indigenous scholars, because of what has happened in Canada. I think the discipline has been pushed because of the reality of the settler state and the settler colonial project. Things began to shift in the early 1990s following the Charlottetown Accord and Oka, as the discipline started paying attention. The journals started paying attention around the same time. But it's really with the Truth and Reconciliation Commission that every university wanted Indigenous scholars. And every political science department wants at least one Indigenous scholar and wants Indigenous students in their programs. I think that there has been this pushback, but there's also been this push in, and I think that to get Indigenous scholars to stay, there's been a lot of—maybe allowance?—that other BIPOC scholars haven't had the same opportunities. But it hasn't always been that way. When I was interviewed at an institution years ago, I was asked, could I teach something other than Indigenous politics? Well, of course, I'm a Canadianist. But many questioned this too. Then they said, "Well, we'll let you teach Indigenous politics, *if* the courses fill up."

YAL: I think as political scientists we can identify structural obstacles to diversifying the profession in terms of research or teaching. But I also think that whenever we're thinking about structure we want to think about agency. I would say that there are amazing opportunities that were available, and I think are still, for people who want to work collectively. Some of the more meaningful things I've done have involved working collectively, with Kiera, for example, and Abigail Bakan and Daniel Salée and Kathy Brock, and Malinda Smith to have a Race, Ethnicity, Indigenous Peoples and Politics section in the Canadian Political Science Association. Currently, as vice-president of the International Political Science Association, it's been great to have this opportunity to institutionalize attention to gender and diversity by developing a strategic plan, and having changes to policy and procedures, even the constitution. That also involves really collective work and working with others. Whatever situation we find ourselves in, in whatever time period, there are those kinds of opportunities, and it's good to think about what you can do, and what you can do with others who might be like minded.

LV: Like Yasmeen, some of the most inspiring growth moments in my career have involved working collectively with other scholars, in particular, with colleagues inside and outside the discipline and also with practitioners of various sorts in the field—that is, community legal workers, people in precarious jobs, informal reading groups, exchanges I've had over the years with, for example, people connected to the Institute for Political Economy at Carleton, at the University of Alberta, through York's International Political Economy Summer School, scholars working on immigration in Yasmeen's midst, and, of late, Indigenous feminist scholars. I've really valued these interactions and dialogues. In such fora, I've also learned that mentoring works in various ways—one has the opportunity to learn from both one's seniors and one's juniors.

RCT: I don't want to sound pessimistic. I agree with Yasmeen that we've made progress. But I think that in the life of the discipline, there are some very special moments which really shake it up. I think back to when I was a grad student, there was such a moment, because everyone was questioning structural functionalism and modernization theories. Since then, I think we've been making progress. It's been very slow progress, and it's been happening through informal networks, with women taking positions of power, Yasmeen and Kiera have made huge contributions to diversifying both our discipline and profession. And now you folks are undertaking this responsibility. For me, we are precisely in the midst of a critical juncture now. There are key ongoing movements: movements in support of Black Lives because of George Floyd, the #MeToo movement, the movement drawing attention to anti-Asian hate. I think this has shaken our society, and it has opened up an opportunity to bring about some major changes. We are finding that institutions are taking note of it more and more. I think somehow, we have to take advantage of this crucial moment. And if we don't take advantage of this, we will have missed a big opportunity.

YAL: I was just going to agree that there is a need for the informal networks, because there is something going on at universities which sort of intersects with the attention that we've seen over the past year with Black Lives Matter and George Floyd, which is that universities were being pushed by the government to embrace EDI (equity, diversity, and inclusion). EDI has become a bit of a mantra of the modern neoliberal university. And I think on the one hand there are some very positive things about EDI in that it's not just talking about diversity, it's talking about, "What are the institutional elements that could create more equitable outcomes and what are the institutional and cultural things that could create more inclusive outcomes?" In this sense EDI is attuned to social justice.

But the other side of it is that we need those critical voices, and we need people to be having their informal networks of conversation more than ever, because EDI can also translate into more work for racialized minorities, and women, and an expectation that they're going to be doing the work of EDI and making the university "EDI friendly." I also think EDI, like any discourse, can be used in all kinds of ways, and mobilized for all kinds of ends. We need those critical perspectives to ensure that the outcomes of this moment, which are combined with so many other things that are happening—including maybe a level of empathy that hasn't been there, because we're going through a pandemic and that's something that we share—that the outcomes are really good. I do see some mixed things about this particular moment.

KL: We would not have some of the Indigenous scholarship we have without some of the people that supported and moved things. I just read Kathy Walker's PHD thesis for UBC as the defence is coming up next month. I was gobsmacked at where Indigenous scholars are today. What this young Cree scholar did—I couldn't have even dreamed this up twenty years ago when I did my PHD. It's written with language—really, it's written from language. It's a PHD in critical Cree feminist theory. And it's just phenomenal. It wouldn't exist without that institutional support. Those networks are key but really, we also have to think about refusal—the refusal of Indigenous scholars. Because while Indigenous scholars have been kind of let into the discipline, the discipline hasn't really changed, and at times has refused to change. I couldn't get a job teaching Indigenous politics. I couldn't get a job—I went through multiple job interviews, even one that was offering a job in Indigenous politics, and they hired a white guy—they hired someone who was safer. I think that also speaks to our refusal. Because while we've been let in the door, I think all of us have refused to be anything but who we are. And I think that's huge. I look at Yasmeen, I look at Reeta, I look at Leah, I look at the next generation, I look and I go, wow! Especially this next generation refusing to be anything but who you are. It's huge. Refusal is huge.

On Corporatization and Institutional Support

ET: Suddenly all universities are struggling to implement EDI policies; we're going to have targeted Black hires, targeted Indigenous hires, and yet one of the questions that remains unanswered is institutional readiness. We're supportive of these initiatives to decolonize the curriculum, and yet, as scholars of race, of gender, of Indigeneity, of postcolonialism, we see the writing on the wall that the people who we may be recruiting may not be part of a structure that will allow them to thrive. How do we diversify the discipline through these institutional targets, while also recognizing that some institutions simply aren't ready?

YAL: I think these are excellent questions. But again, we have a context that is quickly evolving as we speak. The closures at Laurentian University earlier this year were something I never really imagined happening in Canada (for more on the closures, see Cattapan, this volume). It was unthinkable that you could shut down entire departments and have universities declared insolvent like that. We're also in a period where there's really an unknown future because of the COVID-19 pandemic. Changes have been occurring over the past number of months, and we need to know what it will mean financially and otherwise for universities. I do think that on the ground we're still there and operating, and it behooves universities and departments that do their clustered hiring to ensure that there are appropriate supports put in place. I think it behooves universities and departments even if they're not doing cluster hires but hiring individuals that there are appropriate supports put in place. I think having institutionalized mechanisms to mentor and ensure the success of people that are coming in and moving through the ranks is important.

I think that also for the larger profession, having supports for people is key. That's where something like the Canadian Political Science Association is so important for providing a space for having broader discussions about issues people might be facing that have to do with the profession. I think all those things matter as much if not more than ever. But I just wanted to make the observation that even for myself, I'm in a university where we're being cut and slashed by the current Kenney government (in Alberta) to levels I never imagined happening, especially all at once. We're in a moment where universities are also changing, as much as there may be more attention to issues of racism and anti-racism.

LV: I'm glad you brought up Laurentian, Yasmeen. I feel like we're in a moment of continuity and change. I've been reading and thinking deeply about relationality as it is understood and envisioned by Indigenous feminists a great deal lately. I've been reading this material partly to reflect on institutional dynamics that I find very oppressive and partly to think through how to transform subfields prone to sidelining relational thinking. I think it's important to ask what we can learn, in terms of our practice as professionals in the discipline and in the university system, from thinking relationally to ensure that individuals and social groups aren't isolated, that is, to move towards better, more holistic practices and greater inclusivity.

The case of Laurentian, however, illustrates vividly that while transformative praxes in the academy are growing, there are also continuities, in this instance, evident in privatization. In the pandemic, I've tried to engage in various types of action-oriented research, including promoting the importance of the care economy. Doing this work has revealed the profound consequences of privatization. Hearing from colleagues at Laurentian, which established one of the first midwifery programs, designed to serve northern communities, including many Indigenous women and francophones—despite or perhaps in spite of the importance of such programming, this program got shut down—marking a moment in which the friction between the continuity and the change is remarkably sharp.

RCT: I thought I'd go back to your question about who we may be recruiting who may not be part of a structure that will allow them to thrive and what should we do? I think this is a question we've been asking for a while since we've been hiring women in our profession. I've been dealing with it for the past thirty years. My answer is: once we get into a kind of settled position (tenured), I think our responsibility is to implement the concept of refusal. I think I've followed that in my life, despite the fact that sometimes I've been labelled as an outsider or aggressive. The practice of refusal has been really important in my life.

I have always believed that when you hire someone, you need to take care of them. You have to help them to succeed. That's the responsibility of the people who hired them. Senior colleagues who have had tenure, chairs of departments, deans, whoever is there, have to basically make sure that they take care of the people who are brought in, emotionally, but at the same time ensure that they keep track of the target—the goal is ensuring success in the department and the university. Success is really important, that's how we are judged by others. You are judged through how many things you've published, whether you have taught your courses well, whether you've done this or that. So I think mentorship goes along with it.

I do think the problem goes back to Yasmeen's point as well—the corporatization of the university. In this corporatized world, we are witnessing leadership which is actually quite problematic. With a corporate mentality, accounting comes first, academics come second. You need to save money rather than taking care of your own, what I call your bricks and mortar—your faculty members, students, and staff. That's what the university is about and not only counting the dollars. We need to move away from this neoliberal model of the university.

KL: I think Laurentian scares the bejeesus out of all of us. I still run with the mantra "just do it." You have to publish. I stress that so much to some of the younger colleagues. Publish, publish, publish, publish, publish. But do work that really moves you and do work that is going to be of benefit. And also think in terms of community knowledge mobilization or alternative forms of publication. I'm working with students on some publications, but most of my work is focused on "other" or nonpublication right now. We're working on a big COVID-19 project right now, 90 per cent of what we're doing isn't going to be published in a traditional sense, as it's going to the community, government, and public health agencies. Beyond this, I am working on Missing and Murdered Indigenous Women and Girls (MMIWG), and I just finished with a whole year stint on the national MMIWG committee with the frigging federal government and all of the national Indigenous organizations, spending more time there than I would on a publication, but we have a data strategy and a national action plan coming out. What's more beneficial? I was just writing to my dean before hopping on, arguing that really this eighty-plus-page data strategy and the national action plan should be considered a publication this year. We'll see how it goes.

On Increasing Expectations and Resistance

ET: It almost seems as though the powerbrokers keep pushing back. We keep telling our students and our colleagues, "you've got to publish," but how can they publish in light of corporatization of the university, in light of COVID-19, in light of these racial anxieties that we feel when we look at the Atlanta shootings? So how can we ethically tell our students and our early career scholar friends, just keep publishing because that's what you need to get tenure, when their humanity keeps getting questioned? So where does the resistance lie?

YAL: I'm going to say that of course COVID-19 has had these uneven effects; it has taken a toll particularly on many women, racial minorities, and Indigenous Peoples, and this is also the case in the profession of political science and more broadly the academy. But it has also impacted all of us. As a consequence, I think we also have an opportunity to think about redefining some of this stuff that we do. To do it in different ways. I think this was already happening on the ground, certainly at my university and I think at others, going back to March, April, May of 2020, where there started to be discussions of COVID-19 interruptions and extending the tenure clocks. I think we really could take this further, because if so many of us have had our work impacted by the demand for online teaching, by losing family members, by not having daycare, by having to homeschool children, and so on and so forth, then we really need to think of the cumulative impact this past year has had on people. What I've seen over my career as a political scientist is that every five years or so we sort of ratchet up what the expectations are on people coming into the profession, and what it means to be productive. I would say in all three areas that we're judged on—teaching, service, and research—the expectations of what we're supposed to do as academics have continually gone up, even as supports that we're given as academics have actually diminished at our institutions. I really do think this is a moment where we could be having a better collective conversation, and where the compassion I think many of us have developed, because of what's been happening with COVID-19, may be used for great impact for the university and for how we do our work.

LV: Like Yasmeen, I agree that, on the one hand, COVID-19 provides a great opportunity to reflect upon, challenge, and change our practices—and we should definitely take advantage of it. Yet, on the other hand, I do think it's important to protect critical voices in the academy. I am reluctant to tell my students, "you can take it easy a for a while," because it's hard to anticipate what might happen in universities going forward. Look at what Yasmeen has described is happening in Alberta, and what happened at Laurentian. As a result, I'm inclined to remind my students that "scholarship, especially early career scholarship, is an endurance test. So keep up with your academics and your activism." At the same time, I always want to model both compassion and risk-taking and, especially, to confront the new austerity, as it is manifest in universities and beyond, and its gendered, racialized, and ableist implications.

RCT: I'm with Leah on this one. I think we have to really work hard and help people to endure. Because the standards are not going to change. I also worry that the amnesty which is being given by the university is delaying the process of people getting tenure, and a variety of other implications we have not touched on. For example, young women with children who work in areas outside the mainstream. There are some who work collaboratively with partners, and collaborative work has been really hard during "Zoom time." The amnesty which was intended to increase productivity only delays the process. Going back to Kiera's advice also: you've got to publish and figure out how to do it. I again go back to our responsibility, in terms of tenure and promotion decisions. I have stood up for my junior colleagues, I've opened my mouth questioning, for example, some male colleagues who have put down scholars doing collaborative work saying, "oh, joint authors," therefore it cannot be good work. They don't know how much work it can entail. To edit a whole book is probably more work than anything else. I think the responsibilities will fall on all of you, the ones who have tenure, who feel very comfortable, to call such people out on those things. That's the only way to do it.

KL: It's a tough question. What do I tell my research partners about the work we're supposed to be doing? I think I've just spent this COVID-19 carrying more and more and more of a workload! We just carry the weight, we just do what we can, I think I still just try to show an example by still trying to take some evenings off, and not working weekends (except to catch up on marking if I really need to). We also have to speak out on these tenure committees for this generation coming forward, on the hiring process for this generation coming forward. I have told my grad students that if they can't get their writing done, you know, I understand. I think we also have to press that engaged scholarship is worth as much, whether it's an edited collection with the community, or whether it's community-based, doing more on archiving, working on software developing. Do crazy stuff, but find ways to argue that these are publications. Because at the end of the day, a public form of knowledge mobilization, like the archive itself, is a publication. It's not a tool, it's a publication. I think that we have to start changing the way we think of outside or "other" scholarship, and really press and press and press. It held up my promotion clock for about six years. I went up for promotion six years later than I really should have, and now all these scholars who are far more traditional have gone forward, because their scholarship matters. Or where they publish matters. I think we owe it to those people who go forward after us to have those conversations. I think we just have to keep it moving but we also need to refuse. Two mantras to live by: refusal but also just do it.

ET: These are such important words of wisdom, and I really truly appreciate the space that you have shared with us today. And I like that we are talking about the politics of refusal, the politics of speaking up, even amidst all these structural barriers, so I really appreciate that.

References

Abu-Laban, Yasmeen. 2017. "Narrating Canadian Political Science: History Revisited: Presidential Address to the Canadian Political Science Association Toronto, Ontario May 30, 2017." *Canadian Journal of Political Science* 50 (4): 895–919. https://doi.org/10.1017/S000842391700138X.

Walker, Katherine. 2021. "Okâwîmâwaskiy: Regenerating a Wholistic Ethics." PHD diss., University of British Columbia. https://dx.doi.org/10.14288/1.0398723.

20 En Route to a Black Feminist Praxis

Reflections of a Black Woman Graduate Student

TKA C. PINNOCK

AS AN UNDERGRADUATE STUDENT in political studies, I often spent my free time scrolling through the faculty pages of various departments of politics websites. I would count the number of "Black" faces or "Black-sounding" names that I came across, building an internal ledger of Black political scientists. I continued this practice throughout those four years, expanding my search to include graduate students. It is still something I do now—as a doctoral student in politics. There is, perhaps, a sophisticated psychosocial analysis that can be done on why I do this, but I offer two simple reasons: the first is that at the core of it, I am trying to find *my people*. I was one of three Black students in my undergraduate cohort, again one of three Black students in my master's program, and, not surprisingly, one of three Black students in my doctoral cohort. I have never been taught by a Black faculty member, or better yet, had the opportunity to be taught by Black faculty because, up until recently, none of the departments in which I have studied had a Black professor as part of their faculty complement. The second reason is admittedly much more doleful: the running ledger reminds me of how far the discipline has yet to go and this, to my mind, is a salve for future disappointment.

There are so few of us: Black, Indigenous, and racialized women in political science. A study of the Canadian academy shows that racialized women are the most underrepresented among full-time, full-year university teachers, and experience the highest unemployment rates (Canadian Association of University Teachers 2018). The Canadian discipline of political science, specifically, "remain[s] overwhelmingly White and primarily male" (Smith 2017, 261). Much scholarly attention on and practical interventions to redress issues of racism and inequity in the Canadian academy revolve around the everyday lived experiences of racialized faculty (Henry, Dua, Kobayashi et al. 2017; Henry, Dua, James et al. 2017; Fan et al. 2019), but we must also be attentive to the experiences of racialized graduate students. Anecdotally, we know that few Black students are accepted into doctoral programs, and I reckon even fewer complete them, when stories of Black graduate students who have "exited" their doctoral program to preserve their emotional and mental well-being abound.[1] We cannot adequately address issues of inequity facing racialized and women faculty without attentiveness to the experiences of those in the pipeline.

In this chapter, I reflect on my journey towards enacting a Black feminist praxis, focusing on the everyday space of the classroom. I draw on personal reflections—jottings, streams of consciousness, and journal entries—of a particular incident as a tutorial leader to elucidate the ways in which the simultaneous and multiple relationships a doctoral student has with the university collide and converge to mediate the political and pedagogical commitments of emerging racialized scholars. At the time of writing this, I know of only two publications by Black Canadian women scholars on their experiences as doctoral students—one of whom is in political science (Thomas 2020; Williams 2001). I hope to add to this scant body of literature by sharing my experience as a Black Canadian woman pursuing doctoral studies in political science.

'Membering as Methodology

This chapter is birthed from memory, or more accurately from my reflections on personal experiences that I choose to "remember" and those I choose to "forget." Remembering and forgetting are both emotionally and intellectually purposive for me; deliberate acts meant to purge or protect my spirit and intellectual space (see Shahid 2014). Some stories I have chosen to forget for it is not safe as a graduate student, and especially as a Black woman graduate student, to remember them. The precarity of my position demands that I not give them voice—or any space whatsoever. Yet I 'member it all. *'Membering* is a Caribbean colloquialism for *remembering* and I credit Caribbean Canadian author and poet Austin Clarke (2015) for returning the word to my consciousness. Here I use it not just as a nod to my Afro-Caribbean heritage but to register memories as inseparable and constituent parts of the complex whole that is our identities, histories, and personal politics. My memories—those I remember and those I forget—are always part of me for the lived experience of a thing can never be *un*lived. Like Cynthia Dillard's (2012) concept of (re)membering as used by Kyra Shahid (2014), 'membering is about recognizing and returning to their rightful place those fragments and pieces that have been compartmentalized.

I have found it comforting to put to paper those experiences that have been the most jarring and violent. The act of writing allows me to confront and rid myself of the intensity of the emotions, my incapacity to respond adequately in the moment, and the sometimes existential crisis that accompanies these experiences. The act of writing is "a reorientation," affecting not only the content of my writings, but also how I think and feel (Ahmed 2012, 2). I do not write my experiences to (re)make them as academic writing. Though I am not immune to the "pressure cooker" of scholarly productivity imposed by the demands of the neoliberal academy (Hawthorne and Meche 2016), my 'membering is not a yielding to "the imperative to transform all experience into writing" (Ahmed, 2012, 5). Rather, my 'membering serves as a space from which to think from and about the academy and my relation to it as a Black woman doctoral student. I am giving testimony—bearing witness to—the workings of race and racialization in the institution. And, as Denise Baszile asserts, in my first-person account of what has or is happening, I speak not only on my behalf, but in relationship to my community "from which and because of which [I] narrate...reveal[ing] the extent to which what is or has happened has taken a toll on the lives of real people" (2008, 253). My story is the story of many Black women in academia and other institutional spaces where we are "bodies out of place" (Alexander-Floyd 2015, 466).

My 'membering follows closely the methodological and theoretical approach of Black feminist autoethnography (BFA) as proposed by Rachel Griffin (2012). Marrying Black feminist thought and autoethnography, BFA "offers a narrative means for Black women to highlight struggles common to Black womanhood without erasing the diversity among Black women coupled with strategically 'talking back' to systems of oppression" (Griffin 2012, 143). BFA encourages us as Black women in academia to tell our stories to "expose, politicize, and narrate the 'subjected knowledge' birthed from a standpoint informed by intersectionality" (143). My storytelling is an enactment of BFA. I self-interrogate to make narrative sense of my personal experiences in hopes that the insights I gain will lead to deeper analysis and critique of the systemic forces that shape the lives and life chances of Black women (Nash and Viray 2013).

The stories I 'member—this first act of making the personal public and political—is the beginning of my journey towards a Black feminist praxis.

My Story

Like Griffin, "I speak not for all Black women but for myself in the hopes that my voice will echo and affirm the experiences of women who look like me" (2012, 145).

On a weekday evening, during my early days as a teaching assistant (TA) at a large urban Canadian university, I received an email from a white male student in my tutorial complaining about "issues of sexism, discrimination, and general disrespect" he felt he had experienced at the hands of a Black female student. A few days later, the course director— an older white woman—and I met with the two students. The meeting left me feeling untethered—my mind was racing, and my spirit was unsettled. I felt that I had borne witness to something—though I could not articulate in that moment, what that *something* was. I kept replaying the conversation on my long commute home and settled on journaling to get my thoughts out. In my journal, I wrote,

> The situation between Janelle and John has me thinking.[2] The question that I've been reflecting on is what is my politics in the classroom? Here is a Black woman like me talking about her feelings and experiences of marginalization and anti-Black racism and bursting at the seams with frustration and anger because she just wants acknowledgement that the power relations and dynamics she sees at play are real. She details all the slights, incidents, and ways he has made her feel less than his colleague. She wants him to confirm that he's doing these things, to acknowledge his actions. But she won't get it, because he doesn't see it—white men don't see it! He says all the right things; he talks about feminism and change and intersectionality. He remains calm, and the more frustrated and irate she becomes, the calmer he gets as he repeatedly says, "I don't know why you are so angry?" or "why do you think it's acceptable to speak to me or anybody that way?" He tells her that she has her perspective on things, and he has his, and it's all just a matter of perspective and understanding where each other

is coming from. She blurts out that she hates white men! And as a Black woman, I know what she means. So I say, "what you mean is you hate white privilege and patriarchy." The truth is this is not about perspective, and I really want to say "f! perspective. This is about relations of power." She asks why he thinks it was ok for him to greet her with "wha gwaan" when they first met. He tells her he has an African American best friend and that using ebonics or Jamaican patois doesn't mean anything. His remark pisses her off and frankly, me too, but I'm the TA and the course director is here.

How do I get my white male student to understand the power dynamics at play with all its gender and racial undertones, and help my Black female student productively walk and talk through her experiences? This doesn't seem possible in the moment, but the course director and I have tacitly agreed on the expedient course of action, which is to break up their group. His frequent mentions of "hostile environment," "harassment," and "discrimination" got us both jittery.

I feel so conflicted. I wasn't sure if Janelle left feeling raw, exposed without support or a safety net. That she had bore her soul and frustrations for naught. And I feel like a failure! I'm a Black woman, I get and intimately understand what she felt and was talking about yet I did nothing but try to say things that were politically correct and acceptable because I am a TA and my job is to promote learning for everyone. I wonder if she left that meeting feeling I should have had her back more but didn't. I wonder if she felt that I had worked to further silence her feelings by not calling things out—naming them. I am unsure and this whole ordeal has me really thinking about my role as a TA, what I do in the classroom, and how my embodiment comes into play. While I agree with her sentiments, I am a TA with a particular employment relationship with this institution. I have certain responsibilities. I can't appear to be biased—he would definitely complain about that. But I also have my own politics to consider of calling people "in" as opposed to "out" and having a genuine commitment to ensuring that all my students leave the class with the tools to critically examine the world, themselves, and their positions and thought patterns. I wanted that for both of them. I wanted that to be the resolution of our meeting. Him "getting" his privilege and her understanding how to name privilege and not people. I think I failed in helping them get to that point.

Making It Make Sense

I have returned to this scene on many occasions to make sense of the event and my experience of it. Each visit ends with contemplation of, What does it mean to be *me* in the classroom? What do I represent and to whom? What emotions does my embodiment incite? In the space of the classroom, I am concurrently a Black woman, an instructor, an institutional employee, and a graduate student. Each of these roles positions me differently in relation to the university.

As Black women, both the undergraduate student and I are assumed interlopers in the Canadian academy (Daniel 2018). Our bodies are constructed in particular ways: as the angry Black woman; the caretaking Mammy, and always as the resilient strong Black woman (Daniel 2018; Griffin 2012; Mullings, Gooden, and Spencer 2020). While I watched the young Black woman battle these markings that she felt the young white man had imposed on her, in the moment I was also urgently concerned with how we were both constructing Blackness and Black womanhood. It was not far from my mind how my responses to the unfolding situation would be read—how too assertive a tone would mark me as the angry Black woman—but also how the words and emotions of my student would further mark *her* as an angry Black woman. And this was not simply a matter of respectability politics but a concern for the ways in which Black people's emotions—their anger—is used to delegitimize and invalidate their feelings and concerns. White fear and fragility deny the complexity of Black emotions and read Black anger as violent and unjustified, often responding punitively with surveillance and containment. I did the mental math of possible outcomes; I calculated that if the incident escalated up the university administration ladder, the Black student would be on the losing end for she dared to voice her emotions. Her anger may not be perceived as expressive of hurt, disappointment, and exhaustion; there may not be any compassion for her. My interventions—attempts to rephrase her words, paraphrase her outbursts—were a feeble but instinctive move to neutralize the inevitability of the raced and sexed imagery that accompanies Black women's defence of their emotional and mental well-being. As a Black student and as a Black TA, I find it a herculean task to overcome my hypersensitivity to how my actions are implicated in constructions of Black womanhood in the classroom. To cite bell hooks, we Black women—whether as students or professors—are always acutely aware of the presence of our body in these settings (1994, 135). And if we "want to remain, [we've] got, in a sense, to remember [our]self...to see [our]self always as a body in a system that has not become accustomed to [our] presence or to [our] physicality" (hooks 1994, 135).

I often feel as if I failed the Black student, that I was inadequate in caring for her. Black women in the academy bear the burden of care for themselves, their colleagues, and other students (Love et al. 2021, 8), engaging in practices of other-mothering (Jack-Davies 2018) that have proven to be vital to the success of those typically on the margins. Like Black and racialized faculty, Black graduate students *feel* the demands from Black and other racialized undergraduate students wishing to have mentors and role models whom they believe can relate to them and their lived experiences (Henry, Dua, Kobayashi et al. 2017). I say *feel* because these demands are not always explicit and intellectual, but deeply emotive, expressed in expectant desires and hopes that the racialized instructor shares a certain likeness to them. A likeness that moves beyond the raced and gendered body itself to the location of that body in the particular space of the academy. Black faculty, graduate, and undergraduate students all inherit an implicit knowledge about "our" placement and "our" relation to place. I intimately understood the experiences of this Black woman undergraduate student—of being Black in the university— and desired to care for her but not knowing how.

My position as a TA mediated the intimacy between us as Black women students. Black graduate students—especially women graduate students—are not exempt from what Koritha Mitchell (2021b) calls "know-your-place aggression." Black (and racialized) faculty members, particularly women, have shared their classroom experiences, noting how their legitimacy is often questioned by their (undergraduate) students (Mitchell 2021a, 2021b; Mullings, Gooden, and Spencer 2020). As one Black woman faculty notes in sharing her experience teaching at a large urban Canadian university, "My sense of belonging and legitimacy is always questioned in the classroom...Undergraduate students frequently exert their power over me by challenging my authority; they demand and are granted private meetings with full-time faculty administrators to discuss my classroom management style and abilities without ever addressing their concerns with me first" (Mullings, Gooden, and Spencer 2020, 99). Racialized and women TAs, by virtue of inhabiting a space of authority, are similarly visited with microaggressions in the classroom, ranging from questions about their competence and knowledge to questions about their fairness. My fellow racialized graduate students have shared experiences of undergraduate students' refusal to pronounce their names properly or of male undergraduates attempting to bully their female TAs. And so, I was not surprised that my white male student demanded that I respond to his email or give him a call by the next morning (though he sent his email after 7 p.m.) "or else," or that unbeknownst to me he had forwarded the email he sent me to the course director. These are moments of "stress" for Black graduate students. White bodies—especially white male bodies—do not get "stressed" in their encounters with objects or others, as their whiteness "goes unnoticed" (Ahmed 2007), unnoticed because white men are the somatic norm—"the invisible prototype of those who are seen as rightfully belonging in spaces of power and authority" (Alexander-Floyd 2015, 465).

I read these encounters through the lens of my embodiment and its "in/visibility" in the classroom and hallways of the ivory tower. I am a "space invader"—that is, an individual outside the "somatic norms" of academia, and so like other women and racialized scholars, I am an "in/visible subject" (Puwar 2004 cited in Alexander-Floyd 2015, 465; see also Tungohan, this volume). Space invaders are highly visible, featured for the diversity we represent, yet invisible in terms of our evaluation as competent individuals. Our in/visibility generates super-surveillance and a burden of doubt such that we are never seen to be measuring up (Puwar 2004 cited in Alexander-Floyd 2015, 465). As a Black TA, my goal is to limit contact with the managerial functions of the institution and deter opportunities for my competence and character to be called into question. This thinking—the fear of reprimand—partly animates my actions in the classroom, and shapes interactions with my students.

It is in the classroom that I find my in/visibility most forcefully acts as a disciplinary tool. Sara Ahmed (2007) posits that spaces acquire the "skin of bodies" that inhabit them, and take shape by being orientated around some bodies, more than others. As a collective space, the university classroom is a space where "white bodies gather, and cohere to form the edges of [that] space" (Ahmed 2007, 157). It is a space where whiteness is assumed as a given, and as such, my Black body is exposed and hypervisible. My (hyper)visibility, however, is not just a physical marker; it necessarily has implications for my pedagogical practices and my politics. I want my students to be critical on paper and in real life but, as I confront my own Blackness in the classroom and wider institutional spaces, I wonder if I hold myself to the same level of scrutiny, if institutional expectations as well as a desire to be less exposed temper my politics.

On reflection, my greatest fear as a Black woman scholar is being complicit in (re)producing systemic oppression in academia. I fear that as a Black woman in this space, I too am making invisible and hidden that which I name and call out in other aspects of my life. That my politics and sharp analysis when called upon and needed will be covered in the mud of institutional expectations. I fear that I will fail my most marginalized students by asking or suggesting that they be less angry, less frustrated, use nicer words to name that which maims them; that they understand the theories and analytical frameworks but use them in ways the system deems appropriate (see Bernhardt's discussion of "reasonableness," this volume). Am I replicating our erasure—our marginality?! This fear is real when we consider that the institutionalization of whiteness involves an accumulation of decisions about who to recruit, such that recruitment functions as a technology for the reproduction of whiteness: "The act of recruitment, of bringing new bodies in, restores the body of the institution, which depends on gathering bodies to cohere as a body. Becoming a 'part' of an institution, which we can consider as having a share in it or of it, hence requires not only that one inhabits its buildings, but also that we follow its line...to be recruited is not only to join, but to sign up to a specific institution" (Ahmed 2007, 158). Black graduate students are not immune to these reproductive processes. We are recruited to our departments because our work fits the kind of "critical" and diverse scholarship the institution is trying to include as part of its body. We are the diversity. Yet it simultaneously finds ways to erase and otherwise constrain the scholarship produced by us emerging scholars.

Considering the situation of Black women academics, Patricia Hill Collins has argued, "They know that being an academic and an intellectual are not necessarily the same thing...These women confront a peculiar dilemma. On the one hand, acquiring the prestige enjoyed by their colleagues often required unquestioned acceptance of academic norms. On the other hand, many of these same norms remain wedded to notions of Black and female inferiority" (2000, 16). Black women graduate students face a similar dilemma: we are constantly struggling against our own erasure and for the integrity of our work in the context of ongoing institutionalized whiteness. We fight to keep our intellectual and political commitments, even as the institution and our respective disciplines make it costly for us to do so.

For those of us in political science, the cost can be steep as we face a notably "resistant discipline" (Vickers 2015). Despite the presence of "more women professors, robust politics and gender fields and feminist subfields," the discipline's epistemology, ontology, and methodology have not significantly changed (Vickers 2015, 749). Furthermore, racialized and other minority scholars bear the burden of teaching and researching issues of diversity. A 2012 report by the Canadian Political Science Association's (CPSA) Diversity Task Force found that the systematic exploration of issues of diversity is left almost entirely to members of the groups most directly affected by them;[3] and, that there are "disturbingly low levels of interest" in equity issues as teaching priorities (CPSA Diversity Task Force 2012, 9). The task force concluded that "As in social science analysis of diversity and equity outside the academy, we find indications that women and minority political scientists experience more challenges and disadvantages associated with difference than others do...We take it as particularly significant that members of a few of the groups we have examined are more likely than others to have considered leaving the profession" (CPSA Diversity Task Force 2012, 25). Almost a decade later, Joanna Everitt noted in her Presidential Address to the CPSA, "Although it is clear that Indigenous and racialized scholars are more present in political science than in the past, their numbers remain relatively small, despite the fact that larger cohorts of racialized graduate students have been filling our classrooms for the past few decades" (2021, 759). The discipline's ongoing disinterest in equity and diversity is burdensome for Black, Indigenous, and racialized women faculty and graduate students. We exist in a discipline and profession that is apathetic to both our physical and intellectual presence yet needs us to save it from itself.

The "invisibility of broader representation of diversity" among Canadian university faculty means that racialized students "in many social science and humanities disciplines, in particular, never or rarely experience someone like themselves as university professors, mentors, and leaders, and as researchers and knowledge producers" (Henry, Dua, James et al. 2017, 303). The Canadian academic workforce is not as diverse as the student body (Canadian Association of University Teachers 2018). In the Canadian discipline of political science, despite important changes in the demographics and research foci of faculty and graduate students, faculty composition does not align "with undergraduate student populations especially in relation to gender and race/ethnicity" (CPSA Diversity Task Force 2010, 10). For some racialized students, having a Black or racialized graduate student as tutorial lead or mentor is the closest they may come. The emotional labour demanded of racialized and women faculty by the institution as it diversifies its (primarily undergraduate) student population also extends to racialized and women graduate students, even if to a lesser extent. We, too, mentor, support, and guide racialized students as they navigate the academy. Furthermore, despite their marginalization in the discipline, the research and teaching foci of racialized women faculty and graduate students (along with others from groups that have been historically marginalized) are central to understanding the complex sociopolitical issues of contemporary society, nationally and internationally. *Our* work fuels and is fed by projects of radical futurity. *Our* work makes the discipline relevant in a rapidly changing world. Political science needs *us*. Yet we must be vigilant about the ways our success in the profession requires our complicity in its apathy.

Returning to the encounter between my students, I often think about what my actions in that moment say about my politics. Did my fear of the young white man lodging a complaint with the university or my silence in not naming things mean that I am not critical or radical or truly committed to equity? Would my Black woman counterparts have been more assertive or militant in this situation? I have shied away from sharing this story with other Black graduate students because I am ashamed that my actions fell short of my own—and our collective—political commitment to speak truth to power. As someone who spends her time working and volunteering with Black and diasporic communities, my response in the institution is outside of what I consider to be my norm. Or have I convinced myself of such?

For some, this self-interrogation is indicative of the mental and emotional tax racialized and women scholars pay as "bodies out of place"—and, it is, when driven by a burden of doubt. However, self-interrogation is a sine qua non of enacting a Black feminist praxis. Enactment is never a complete process but always in progress. It requires us to engage in continual reflexivity about our investments in the political and intellectual project that is Black feminism; to be truthful with ourselves about the ways we are complicit in the reproduction of our marginality and in "relational othering" (Dhamoon 2021). It asks us to bear witness to injury caused to bodies and souls, and to seek repair. It reminds us to politicize our presence so that *our being (t)here* is not just additive but transformative, rescripting institutional practices. My enactment of a Black feminist praxis is rooted in questioning—about why I am here and what I (shall) do here.

Why Am I Here?
As I wrote this chapter, I had the privilege of chairing a roundtable of Black women scholars in political science at an international conference. One sister-scholar advised us to ponder the "purpose of our presence" in the academy, especially when we feel defeated or exhausted. In response to the question, "why are we here?" some Black women scholars encouraged us to see our work in the academy in the vein of the Black radical tradition: "Within the oppressive enclave of the Eurocentric academy, the black woman, along with the black man, can fulfill the historic role of freedom fighter" (Benjamin 1997, 4). Others caution against coming to the academy "to save the world," instead advising that we seek to "impact one life at a time" and take resistive comfort in the "ripple effect that is created" by such action (Daniel 2018, 64). Still, others encourage us to be productively "angry"—to be fed up with "the repeated failures of dominant society to respect the humanity of Black women [or] eradicate the harm that Black women have already and continue to endure" (Griffin 2012, 150).

Some days, I do not have an answer to this question: I am too weary, too depleted, too beaten up. I often doubt the intellectual and political value of my work; I wonder if I really have anything to say and if anyone will care about the very small part of the world which I have chosen to study. The precarity of academia crushes my soul. Other days, I am a believer in my choice to pursue doctoral studies. Energized by my community of fellow racialized and women emerging scholars who are bringing their unique brilliance to the world, my purpose becomes clear. However,

I have become comfortable with the uncertainties and struggles that mark my experience as a Black woman in academia. I see these as part of my own journey towards enacting a Black feminist praxis—a continual self-reflexivity on how I can "raise social consciousness regarding the everyday struggles common to Black womanhood; embrace self-definition... humanize Black women" (Griffin 2012, 143) and unearth "complicity and complacency" (151).

So why am I here? I hold on to Black feminism's view that the world is "one in the making" (Collins 2000, 290). And, as such, I have a responsibility to "write not only what I want to read—understanding fully and indelibly that if I don't do it no one else is so vitally interested, or capable of doing it to my satisfaction—*I [will] write all the things I should have been able to read*" (Walker 1983, 13). This is Black feminist praxis.

Concluding Thoughts...For Now

In the present moment, Canadian universities have responded to the global movement against anti-Black racism and calls for truth and reconciliation with Indigenous Peoples by creating EDI administrative positions and circles, through targeted hiring of Black and Indigenous faculty, and increased funding for Black, Indigenous, and racialized students. Yet this moment requires me (and other Black women scholars) to build and enact a Black feminist praxis, for this is the means by which I (we) may authentically exist in academia and in the discipline of political science. We know the moment will pass; we know the backlash will come; and we know we must still fight.

The "emotional evidence" (Williams 2001, 93) of my journey that I have shared with you is deeply personal. I have chosen to do so in the hope that in sharing my experiences, others may see themselves, and allies may be more empathetic to the Black women "beginning scholars" (Williams 2001) in their midst. The journey to a radical praxis is littered with doubt and insecurity, particularly for those of us who are privileged to be in an institution predicated on disciplining and erasing us. I am not sure when I will arrive, but I am en route.

| There are things I have "forgotten" that I will 'member...in time.

Notes

1. Lahoma Thomas (2020) recalls a story of a counterpart "exiting" the doctoral program. I, too, have several examples of Black students' exits due to unsupportive departments, lack of mentorship, and intellectual hostility. Our anecdotal evidence is supported by a 2012 report by the Canadian Political Science Association's Diversity Task Force, which indicated that women and minority political scientists are more likely than others to have considered leaving the profession.
2. Names have been changed to protect the identity of individuals in my narration.
3. In 2006 the CPSA struck a Diversity Task Force with a mandate to examine issues relating to diversity in the profession. Chaired by Yasmeen Abu-Laban, the Diversity Task Force produced two reports: "Report and Analysis of the Questionnaire for Chairs of Departments of Political Science" in May 2010 and "Report and Analysis of the Canadian Political Science Association Member Survey" in May 2012.

References

Ahmed, Sara. 2007. "A Phenomenology of Whiteness." *Feminist Theory* 8 (2): 149–68. https://doi.org/10.1177/1464700107078139.

Ahmed, Sara. 2012. *On Being Included: Racism and Diversity in Institutional Life*. Durham, NC: Duke University Press.

Alexander-Floyd, Nicole. 2015. "Women of Color, Space Invaders, and Political Science: Practical Strategies for Transforming Institutional Practices." *PS: Political Science & Politics* 48 (3): 464–68. https://doi.org/10.1017/S1049096515000256.

Baszile, Denise Taliaferro. 2008. "Beyond All Reason Indeed: The Pedagogical Promise of Critical Race Testimony." *Race Ethnicity and Education* 11 (3): 251–65. https://doi.org/10.1080/13613320802291140.

Benjamin, Lois. 1997. Introduction to *Black Women in the Academy: Promises and Perils*, edited by Lois Benjamin, 1–7. Gainesville: University Press of Florida.

Canadian Association of University Teachers. 2018. *Underrepresented & Underpaid: Diversity & Equity among Canada's Post-Secondary Education Teachers*. April 2018. https://www.caut.ca/sites/default/files/caut_equity_report_2018-04final.pdf.

Clarke, Austin. 2015. *'Membering*. Hamilton, ON: Dundurn.

Collins, Patricia Hill. 2000. *Black Feminist Thought: Knowledge, Consciousness, and the Politics of Empowerment*, 2nd ed. New York: Routledge.

CPSA Diversity Task Force. 2010. "Report and Analysis of the Questionnaire for Chairs of Department of Political Science," May 2010. https://CPSA-acsp.ca/diversity-task-force/.

CPSA Diversity Task Force. 2012. "Report and Analysis of the Canadian Political Science Association Member Survey," May 2012. https://CPSA-acsp.ca/documents/pdfs/diversity/2012_Diversity_Task_Force_Report.pdf.

Daniel, Beverly-Jean. 2018. "Knowing the Self and the Reason for Being: Navigating Racism in the Academy." *Canadian Woman Studies* 32 (1–2): 59–66. https://cws.journals.yorku.ca/index.php/cws/article/view/37695.

Dhamoon, Rita Kaur. 2021. "Relational Othering: Critiquing Dominance, Critiquing the Margins." *Politics, Groups, and Identities* 9 (5): 873–92. https://doi.org/10.1080/21565503.2019.1691023.

Dillard, Cynthia. B. 2012. *Learning to (Re)member the Things We've Learned to Forget: Endarkened Feminisms, Spirituality, and the Sacred Nature of Research and Teaching.* New York: Peter Lang.

Everitt, Joanna. 2021. "Presidential Address: Academic Absences, Disciplinary Siloes and Methodological Prejudices within the Political Science Discipline in Canada." *Canadian Journal of Political Science* 54 (4): 749–68. https://doi.org/10.1017/S0008423921000883.

Fan, Lai-Tze, Anthony Jeethan, Mary Grace Lao, Andrea Luc, and Priya Rehal. 2017. "Navigating Racialized Spaces in Academia: Critical Reflections from a Roundtable." *coMMposite* 49 (3): 69–78. http://www.commposite.org/index.php/revue/article/viewFile/267/199.

Griffin, Rachel Alicia. 2012. "I AM an Angry Black Woman: Black Feminist Autoethnography, Voice, and Resistance." *Women's Studies in Communication* 35 (2): 138–57. https://doi.org/10.1080/07491409.2012.724524.

Hawthorne, Camilla, and Brittany Meche. 2016. "Making Room for Black Feminist Praxis in Geography: A Dialogue between Camilla Hawthorne and Brittany Meche." *Space+Society*, September 13, 2016. https://www.societyandspace.org/articles/making-room-for-black-feminist-praxis-in-geography.

Henry, Frances, Enakshi Dua, Carl E. James, Audrey Kobayashi, Peter Li, Howard Ramos, and Malinda Smith. 2017. *The Equity Myth: Racialization and Indigeneity at Canadian Universities.* Vancouver: UBC Press.

Henry, Frances, Enakshi Dua, Audrey Kobayashi, Carl James, Peter Li, Howard Ramos, and Malinda S. Smith. 2017. "Race, Racialization and Indigeneity in Canadian Universities." *Race Ethnicity and Education* 20 (3): 300–14. https://doi.org/10.1080/13613324.2016.1260226.

hooks, bell. 1994. *Teaching to Transgress: Education as the Practice of Freedom.* New York: Routledge.

Jack-Davies, Anita. 2018. "Navigating Racism: Black Graduate Students Need Support." *The Conversation*, April 30, 2018. https://theconversation.com/navigating-racism-black-graduate-students-need-support-92550.

Love, Bridget H., Emerald Templeton, Stacey Ault, and Onda Johnson. 2021. "Bruised, Not Broken: Scholarly Personal Narratives of Black Women in the Academy." *International Journal of Qualitative Studies in Education.* https://doi.org/10.1080/09518398.2021.1984607.

Mitchell, Koritha (@ProfKori). 2021a. "After 15+ years of university teaching, here's what I know for sure: Some students are convinced that if I'm the professor, 1) the class can't actually require intellectual work from them 2) my authority is illegitimate [She's probably not qualified. You know, affirmative action]." Twitter, May 24, 2021. https://twitter.com/ProfKori/status/1396793722013106176.

Mitchell, Koritha (@ProfKori). 2021b. "3) if they don't get their way, I have evil intentions. [The accusations are no joke!] When this happens, the student is just showing how well they've learned what the USA teaches. This, too, is know-your-place aggression. It comes from all directions." Twitter, May 24, 2021. https://twitter.com/ProfKori/status/1396793723288264704.

Mullings, Delores V., Amoaba Gooden, and Elaine Brown Spencer. 2020. "Catch Me When I Fall! Resiliency, Freedom and Black Sisterhood in the Academy." *Cultural and Pedagogical Inquiry* 12 (1): 91–104. https://doi.org/10.18733/cpi29535.

Nash, Robert J., and Sydnee Viray. 2013. "The Who, What, and Why of Scholarly Personal Narrative Writing." *Counterpoints*, no. 446, 1–9. https://jstor.org/stable/42982209.

Puwar, Nirmal. 2004. *Space Invaders: Race, Gender, and Bodies Out of Place*. Oxford: Berg Publishers.

Shahid, Kyra T. 2014. "Finding Eden: How Black Women Use Spirituality to Navigate Academia." PHD diss., Miami University. http://rave.ohiolink.edu/etdc/view?acc_num=miami1398960840.

Smith, Malinda S. 2017. "Disciplinary Silences: Race, Indigeneity and Gender in the Social Sciences." In *The Equity Myth: Racialization and Indigeneity at Canadian Universities*, edited by Frances Henry, Enakshi Dua, Carl James, Audrey Kobayashi, Peter Li, Howard Ramos, and Malinda S. Smith, 239–62. Vancouver: UBC Press.

Thomas, Lahoma. 2020. "A Black Feminist Autoethnographic Reflection on Mentoring in the Discipline of Political Science." *PS: Political Science & Politics* 53 (4): 788–92. https://doi.org/10.1017/S104909652000044X.

Vickers, Jill. 2015. "Can We Change How Political Science Thinks? 'Gender Mainstreaming' in a Resistant Discipline: Presidential Address Delivered to the Canadian Political Science Association, Ottawa, June 2, 2015." *Canadian Journal of Political Science* 48 (4): 747–70. https://jstor.org/stable/24810960.

Walker, Alice. 1983. *In Search of Our Mothers' Gardens: Womanist Prose*, 2nd ed. San Diego: Harcourt Brace Javoanovich.

Williams, Charmaine C. 2001. "The Angry Black Woman Scholar." *NWSA Journal* 13 (2): 87–97. https://muse.jhu.edu/article/25303.

Conclusions

Towards a Lexicon of Feministing

THE EDITORIAL COLLECTIVE

IN AN OPEN LETTER to researchers, communities, and educators working in the context of settler colonialism, Eve Tuck (2009) calls for the suspension of "damage-based frameworks" that emphasize and reduce Indigenous communities to deficit. She explains, "Desire, yes, accounts for the loss and despair, but also the hope, the visions, the wisdom of lived lives and communities. Desire is involved with the *not yet* and, at times, the *not anymore*" (2009, 417). For Tuck, desire-based frameworks aim to upset settler colonial dynamics by "understanding complexity, contradiction, and the self-determination of lived lives" (416). Desire itself is, of course, complex, adhering to each of us in ways connected to our socio-structural location, which shapes who is most often read through the lens of deficit, pathology, and tokenism. Desire-based frameworks raise important questions about subjectivity and agency; who is desired and on what terms, and who is positioned (as worthy) to articulate desire? What then are the implications if we query desire—an assertion of the "not yet," the "not anymore," and of hope—as a disciplinary question for political science?

It was and is a politics of desire that motivates this collection. As many contributions to the volume suggest, we need to account for the structural violence, loss, and exclusion imbued in the histories and contemporary realities of political science, but we are hopeful in our desire for a discipline that interrogates rather than replicates modes of exclusion and power, that understands the critical nature of experiential knowledge, and recommits to meaningful articulations of justice. As Yasmeen Abu-Laban has described, links between Canadian political science and the power structures animating the state are clear: "We are living in a moment in which we are being reminded about buried and unacknowledged history, as well as about the colonial past and the colonial present...The organizational and ideational evolution of political science is closely interconnected with Canada's history and unequal social relations since Confederation. This is because organized political science in Canada was really at heart a national venture" (2017, 896, 898). In bringing these contributions together, we have worked to collectively think through how to "do" political science and politics differently. For both our editorial collective and the larger group of contributors, this work has required reflecting on our embodied experiences, while at the same time exposing the structural forces at play that (re)produce the power relations underscoring colonial white hetero capitalist patriarchy. The intention here is not to solely name the loss and damage associated with these relations of power, but to also think transformatively. Desire is not a resolution of our politics, but it provides an opening to a political orientation focused on how things could be, that can sustain our myriad intersecting communities and commitments. What possibilities emerge when desire grounds feministing?

It was desire that informed some of our initial objectives as an editorial collective, one of which was to develop some sort of manifesta, or a blueprint for change, drawing from the work of the contributors. But it seemed odd to us—perhaps even antithetical to feministing—to try to speak in unison. We come to this collection with histories, experiences, and positionalities shaped in and through power. While there are lots of points on which we are agreed, there are also points on which we differ. Our experiences, communities, and commitments are distinctly situated, and although our work together is often enriching and generative, the work of feministing across and within contexts of power means that there is frustration and concerns left unresolved. Our perspectives and positionalities are not harmonious, nor did we anticipate them to be. Further, as we made our way through the chapters, the idea of a manifesta seemed misplaced. It didn't feel right to foreclose opportunities for change by imposing a set of actionable items. We were reminded of the promise Jack Halberstam sees in movements like Occupy Wall Street, in which there was "refusal to conjure an outcome…because the outcome will be decided on by the process of dissent, refusal, and carnivalesque failure" (2012, 15). For Halberstam, "all we can know for sure is that the protests signal and announce a collective awareness of the end of normal life" (15). For us, this volume reflects a collective reckoning, an "awareness of the end of normal life," from which we can unlearn, undo, and redo political science.

In this conclusion, we reflect on our collaboration as editors of this volume—our motivations, our struggles, and our orientations to creating space to refuse, to resist, and to desire. Recognizing the differences in our experiences and approaches, we provide these reflections in turn, highlighting the lived lives that have informed the shape of this collection, at least from an editorial standpoint. Then, instead of the manifesta we originally imagined (and its clear vision of actionable items and outcomes), we offer a lexicon of feministing. A lexicon provides a vocabulary or a way of understanding and speaking to the labour of feministing that focuses simultaneously on present-day realities and on future-oriented dreams of reworlding. This temporality is complex; the contributions in this collection show us that ways of doing political science that challenge the mainstream and that contest longstanding forms of power are being practiced daily. Yet we find in these contributions points of contestation and convergence that give us the language to recognize one another's ideas and experiences. A lexicon of feministing gives us—and readers, we hope—a vocabulary to not only imagine and articulate but to affirm other possible futures for the discipline of political science, and, indeed, the academy.

Reflections on Feministing

Nisha on Feministing and the Temporalities of Disruptive Reading

Given the expansive temporality of feministing, that an edited collection invokes a "beginning" and an "ending" warrants pause, particularly as we consider our accountabilities as an editorial collective. As the outcome of a series of intentional, political, and epistemic acts, what is housed within this collection is necessarily delimited, instantiating the tensions of assembling voices, disassembling others, and the risks of "freezing" a selection of interventions as a kind of corpus of knowledge. To move *with* this tension, we note that this collection holds and homes embodied stories and analyses, but also risk. However, if read carefully and critically, this collection also holds and homes a series of possible pathways for resistance, disruption, and refusal, and an important lexicon or set of cues to embolden an ethos of feministing moving forward (Allen, Nath, and Georges 2023).

By intentionally moving to the verb feminist*ing*, this collection invites a pushing back against hegemonic approaches within political science that erase insurgent and resurgent political struggles in their focus on identity and harm (Bhandar et al. 2022; Dhamoon 2006; Nath, Tungohan, and Gaucher 2018). In their chapter, Kelly Aguirre, Mariam Georgis, and Sarah Munawar clearly name that as a discipline, the boundaries of political science are "affirmed through the intentional absenting and appropriation" of some stories. The stakes are high. We reorient by exploring how feministing can render visible the complex labour of doing *politics* and ultimately undoing political science (Dhamoon 2020). This risky boundary transgressive work is not without cost, but as our contributors illuminate, it is integral work that draws a line connecting the epistemic with our relational accountabilities. Thematically then, the pieces in the collection *do* cohere around a set of key commitments wherein feministing involves the epistemic labour of *challenging form and expertise*; the labour of *disruptive pedagogies*; the labour of *unsettling methodologies*; and the labour of *transgression*, of not just the discipline but the logics of the neoliberal white settler colonial academy itself.

In making intentional space for these open renderings of feministing, the collection also lays bare that the very act of assembling this work is not without risk. Indeed, feministing itself is replete with tension in that it is a word that risks erasing and flattening diverse lineages of feminist praxis and struggle; these lineages of praxis are often ones that have been struggling against hegemonic white feminist frameworks. Put differently, while the pieces in this collection coalesce to think and work through feministing, they are not necessarily politically commensurable. As we think through beginnings and endings, and the logics that have shaped the refusal of white colonial feminisms, we would be remiss as a collective if we didn't also engage in a critical and disruptive reframing and (re)witnessing of our work here (IRK Collective, forthcoming). As Elaine Coburn, Rita Kaur Dhamoon, Joyce Green, Genevieve Fuji Johnson, Heidi Kiiwetiniepinesiik Stark, and Gina Starblanket insist in offering their typology of practices to disrupt hegemonies of political science, *this disruption is generative*. Alongside this, Kelly Aguirre gestures towards the steadiness required to enact disruption by likening the witnessing stance to the posture of feminism: "posture is a bearing you must actively sustain, be present to and responsive through." As we reflect together in this concluding chapter, this kind of committed and steady disruption as we interrogate and (re)witness our work here feels necessary. What could have shifted had we put the contributions/contributors into explicit conversation with each other? What or who might we have centred in treating the collection as a pedagogical encounter for contributors as well? Why have we read, experienced, and affectively responded to this collection differently? How is that political? Or, more profoundly, how have we been changed (or unchanged) through the process of engaging with the work of contributors?

Asking and answering these questions can be discomforting because it doesn't satisfy linear impulses towards resolution or prescription—these questions lay bare that the linearity of form belies any linearity of content. In asking you to read disruptively at the introduction to this book, we invited this reading for *both* coherence and disjuncture, including a reading of those rough edges that reveal incommensurabilities, as well as a reading for our gaps and erasures. Moreover, and perhaps most critically to me, this *feministing as disruptive reading* is grounded in the imperative (re)witnessing work that we regularly do for each other but must also extend to ourselves. For example, in reflecting on the audience of this book, we queried who would understand the experiential and embodied knowledges we assembled, the methodological form of narratives and dialogues, and the critical pedagogies articulated, as contributions of both labour *and* research. Critically, this (re)witnessing of the epistemic breadth and depth of our labour within the academy illuminates the form and structure of political science and the politics it seeks to explain. Put differently, this (re)witnessing work enables us to make visible our own institutional labour as epistemic, our relational accountabilities, and how both refuse the long history of disciplinary willful dismissal and backlash against Indigenous, anti-racist, and feminist scholarship. As readers, we can witness and "take care of the stories" that are shared, as Sarah Munawar describes. Moreover, as Tka Pinnock asserts in her chapter, this kind of (re)witnessing work requires a posture of vigilance about our complicity in the discipline's broader apathy. As a collective then, we can name that had we done things differently, another collection might have been possible. But, this is precisely one of the generative openings of feministing—that it necessitates an ongoing labouring that honours the complexity of the multiplicities we are always holding as we enact our politics. In the doing of this collection, we also expose otherwise ways things can be done.

Fiona on Experiential Knowledge and Collective Space

For me, this collection, and the notion of feministing itself, is about creating and taking space to centre the experiential knowledge carried by feminists in the discipline. What is it like to be in the discipline or—*be disciplined*—cognitively, materially, affectively, and emotionally? How can we combat the isolation, self-doubt, self-blame, loneliness, and fear that operates in our neoliberal institutions and our disciplinary structures? This book asks readers to listen and reflect deeply as the contributions in this collection reveal important departure points in responding to these questions.

At this stage in my career, having been on faculty at three institutions, having been department head and a representative on University Senate, I have come to think of listening as a rare and radical act. This collection invites deep listening to the varied and, at times, conflicting, narratives of feministing in political science. As such, it invites readers to reflect on the meaning of these experiences as potential sources of validation and recognition as well as critical directives for refusal, transformation, coalition building, and reworlding.

In creating a collective space to recognize the value of our experiences, a space that moves these conversations out of the bathroom stalls in which they so often occur, I hope this volume offers a sense of community and critical reflection on our roles and responsibilities in said community. The notion of community has been a topic of debate and disagreement amongst the editorial team. For me, however, recognizing and learning from our experiences collectively is at the heart of transforming the discipline. Being in community does not mean, nor require, a shared experience or shared perspective. The value of being in community lies in large part, in the divergences, disagreements, and debates that operate within and between collectivities—collectivities constituted through complex structures and processes that operate beyond our individual positionalities but that profoundly shape our individual experiences in ways only made clear through collective reflection.

Making space to hear these divergences and taking the time to listen and reflect deeply is intersectional feministing in action. The emphasis on action, of *doing*, as Nisha highlights above, is key. Intersectionality, as a concept, is interpreted and invoked in many different, and at times, highly contested or conflicting ways. As Alexandra Dobrowolsky and I discuss elsewhere, understanding intersectionality as a lens to uncover and/or create pathways for transformation is rooted in the activism(s) of Black women of the nineteenth century, including Maria Stewart and Sojourner Truth, and the varied global activist movements of the 1960s and 1970s (2020, 8). Drawing on this legacy, scholars of intersectionality, such as Patricia Hill Collins and Sirma Bilge (2016), as well as Vivian May (2015), invoke a relational lens that shifts the focus away from what distinguishes or separates entities and towards interconnections. This process fosters what May terms "heterogeneous commonality"—a concept that reflects an understanding of individuals and groups as internally heterogeneous. From this perspective, "groups can be characterized by their potential to organize around 'heterogeneous commonality,'" as the notion of the subject is not only "multiple" but also "coalitional" (May 2015, 41). As I discuss in my chapter in this volume, a complex, contextual focus on interconnections and coalitions underlines the importance of exchanging narratives in pursuit of transformation. This collection, grounded in the complex lived experiences of feminists in our field at this moment, is a valuable resource for challenging the homogeneity of "dominant imaginaries" of feminism(s), feminists, political science, and political scientists, by revealing heterogeneous commonality through narratives that bring together both personal and structural knowledge (May 2015). As such, it offers readers various connections and entry points through which to foster meaningful connections, coalitions, and strategies for resistance, refusal, and, most importantly, reworlding.

Alana on Struggle as Feministing

We began our collaboration on this volume prior to the COVID-19 pandemic, and through the long months that followed, the editorial collective and our contributors, like so many others, struggled to find time and space to do our work, while we navigated isolation and anxiety. The daily tasks of avoiding illness, and of taking care of our families, our students, and ourselves are an undercurrent in this volume, written in stolen moments late at night and past proposed deadlines. In our (virtual) classrooms, research, academic commitments, and personal lives, we struggled—we struggle—to engage in the time-consuming work of feministing, while trying to stay afloat (Bisaillon et al. 2020).

I've been thinking a lot lately about what it means to struggle. To struggle, as I understand the term, is to push back, and contest constraint or restriction, trying to be free, or at least more free than when the fight began. Struggle is a critical part of resistance, insofar as it is the affective, burdensome work of making change. If resistance is about what one does in the face of adversity, struggle is, at least in part, how the labour of resistance *feels*. To this end, to struggle presumes great effort and energy and, importantly, it does not presume any measure of success.

As the contributions to this volume demonstrate, feministing in political science is an ongoing struggle. It is not only the time and effort it takes to do the work, but the time and effort it takes to have that work counted and seen, with no promise that the efforts will be rewarded. And our experiences of the struggle differ widely—as the contributions to the volume and the perspectives of the editorial collective in this conclusion suggest—our visions of potential futures are not and cannot be the same.

The idea of struggle here is an important one. It is an idea that, for me, underpins the work of *Feministing*, as a verb, as a book, and as an ongoing intellectual project. The idea of struggle for me is bound up with anti-capitalist critique and an understanding of the need for revolution. What is struggle if not a recognition that the effort is worth it, and that we must recognize those experiencing exploitation and poor working conditions to organize for collective action?

Solidarity is a critical counterpart to struggle; and for me, this volume is one that allows us to find one another, not only to commiserate, but to build towards better, more generative, and more fulsome lives. As I suggest in my chapter on the spider and the fish, justice-oriented academics working in the contemporary university at once experience the constraints of an institution increasingly oriented towards corporate interests while finding solidarity and collaboration with one another. Feministing too is an exercise in contradiction; we invest our time and energy (intellectual, emotional, and otherwise) in institutions built on the backs of marginalized communities in the name of a more equal world. What does it mean to undo an institution from within? To reimagine, or as Jamilah Dei-Sharpe and Kimberley Ens Manning suggest in their chapter, to reworld it? Or, as Alison Mountz and colleagues (2015) suggest, to simply slow down?

Sara Ahmed, whose work informs so many of the chapters in this volume, writes about solidarity that it "does not assume that our struggles are the same struggles, or that our pain is the same pain, or that our hope is for the same future. Solidarity involves commitment and work, as well as the recognition that even if we do not have the same feelings, or the same lives, or the same bodies, we do live on common ground" (2004, 189). The very different experiences chronicled in this volume by no means paint a complete picture of the struggles of engaging in feministing in political science. We have not, for example, included perspectives from those who found their struggles too difficult to bear, or who were otherwise pushed out of the discipline. As Ethel points out in her reflections below, our volume includes limited reflections on parenting and domestic work and how it might shape the possibilities of feministing from the first. But this volume offers, following Ahmed, a view into different struggles, different pain, and different hopes for different futures and the common ground we may find therein.

Ethel on the Possibilities of/for Other Worlds
When contemplating the possibilities of a feminist other world, I am reminded of what Patricia Pessar and Sarah Mahler (2003) write as the importance of cognitive imaginings as a way for us to continue subsisting in our current world. Over the years, I have always jokingly discussed with my community of feminist academics how much better our lives would be if we could create our *own* university. We could teach, read, learn, research, create, celebrate, theorize, and explore, untethered by the demands of the academic industrial complex. For me, one way I have tried to make peace in the academy is by encouraging people, including the readers of this book, to think of *how else* the university could look and to recognize that there are other ways of doing things, and other worlds to be built.

    Recognizing that there are different ways to disrupt, to do things differently, to destroy in order to build anew, can enable us to think outside the silos that we are placed in by universities and departments and disciplines and fields. What I want readers to get out of this volume is to recognize that there are possible pathways in front of them that they may not have considered, pathways that can help them change their everyday realities and that may even scale up and lead to structural transformation. I also want readers to understand that feministing is also about unlearning feelings of indebtedness and beholden-ness and gratitude, of reclaiming our time and our energy and ourselves, of prioritizing our and our community's needs. Ultimately, feministing is about acts of refusal. Here, we are indebted to Black and Indigenous feminist theorizations on the politics of refusal. By calling for change that goes beyond policies of inclusion into institutional spaces (whether the state, the university, and other such spaces), the politics of refusal seeks structural transformation and calls on Black and Indigenous women not to "sell themselves short" (Karera 2021, 109; see also Simpson 2007).

Our path towards transformation is invariably imperfect. In fact, there are failures in this volume. In discussing failures, I do so as a deliberate feminist tactic, yet I proceed cautiously because I know that failure has, as Shaista Patel notes, "real repercussions for Black, Indigenous and people of color in particular...Always our presence in these white neoliberal institutions is a threat" (2022, 213). My purpose in listing these failures is to ensure that we continuously remain self-reflexive and that we don't eschew accountability in favour of keeping the peace.

The first failure I note is the composition of the editorial collective. What filters do we bring when curating this collection? Would the collection look different if the editorial collective, which consists of five cis, het women in tenured or tenure-track positions in universities in the Global North, included precariously employed academics? Graduate students? Scholars from the Global South? Queer and trans scholars? Although we made every effort to include chapters from scholars with a range of experiences and with different intersecting social locations, we invariably bring with us filters that affect our judgment on whose work merits inclusion.

Despite being a volume on feministing, it is odd to me, too, that we did not have a chapter addressing domestic and care work. In focusing on work, whether in terms of research, or teaching, or everyday encounters in the academy, the volume might inadvertently appear to prioritize transforming public life (i.e., work) when much of the inequities that feminists have sought to mitigate take place in private. Responsibilities for childcare, elder care, and care for the community are invariably gendered. When my darkest moments since starting my faculty position in 2016 involved, first, having to work through postpartum depression and, second, finding out that institutions do not offer paid leave for women who are recovering from miscarriages—and when my happiest moments took place when both professional and personal worlds collided, such as the time I took my kids with me when doing fieldwork—not having a chapter directly recognizing care work is a failure. And finally, perhaps we have failed in curating articles that focus on challenges, that focus on the dark side of academia, that focus on sadness. Have we been able to capture the *joy* that comes with feministing? Have we captured the desires underpinning our work, to paraphrase Tuck (2009)?

True to the observation made by Global South, postcolonial, Black, and Indigenous feminists that feminist movements sometimes hold as universal the experiences of white women, I am aware that the actions that some can take remain inaccessible or even dangerous for others. Engagements in the political sphere, for example, may be more fraught for Black, Indigenous, and women of colour, given the additional layers of racist vitriol (on top of the already expected gendered violence) that they face. Trusting that change *can* take place within institutions is another difference. I do not think, ultimately, that one unified feminist movement is possible or even desirable, or that there is one roadmap to "feminist." But I do think that opening up a praxis of *mutual* accountability and decolonial care can possibly bring everyone closer to our collective liberation.

Stephanie on Un/learning, Reflexivity, and Complicity

Upon reading and rereading the contributions in this volume, I am struck by the cross-cutting themes: themes of exclusion, community building, and transformation. I am also struck by the emotional complexity articulated across the chapters, revealing anger and frustration, but also (or perhaps resulting from) hope and desire for a better way. For me, the text reveals the constructive and generative possibilities of *unlearning*. Halberstam describes "unlearning" as "learning, in other words, how to break with some disciplinary legacies, learning to reform and reshape others, and unlearning the many constraints that sometimes get in the way of our best efforts to reinvent our fields, our purpose, and our mission. Unlearning is an inevitable part of new knowledge paradigms if only because you cannot solve a problem using the same methods that created it in the first place" (2012, 10). Unlearning, then, asks us to identify what's not working and for whom, and to look outside of current practice to think critically about change.

For Halberstam (2011), unlearning comes from failure, which provides opportunities to recreate meanings of success and opens space for new questions and ways of knowing, freed of disciplinary norms. Discussing anti-disciplinarity, Halberstam writes, "In some sense we have to untrain ourselves so that we can read the struggles and debates back into questions that seem settled and resolved" (2011, 11). Failure and unlearning offer possibility—possibility to define transformation on our own terms. As Ethel reminds us above, identifying failure, specifically the silences and omissions in this volume, is a feminist tactic, not to undermine success or to dole out reprimands; rather, it comes from a place of critique and reflexivity.

Opening up to failure and unlearning, then, necessitates a reflexive engagement with the text, turning inward to interrogate our own assumptions and understandings about the topics explored throughout the book. How did we respond to particular texts? What resonates with us and why? What makes us sad, angry, discouraged, hopeful, and so on? In undertaking this critical reading and reflection, I also invite readers to locate themselves. Where are *you* in this volume? Many, like myself, are caught in that complex matrix of both penalty and privilege. We can use these chapters to create community and strategize for change, but we also need to reckon with our own roles within oppressive institutions. Where are we complicit? Where can we trouble? How can we build consensual alliances (Yee 2009) to press for change?

In my own reading of the text, I was particularly struck by the stories of exclusion. To be clear, this isn't just about imposter syndrome, but rather processes and practices of exclusion that work to silence or invisibilize particular experiences and subjectivities. These experiences not only speak to me on a personal level, through my own feelings of exclusion, but also prompt me to reflect on the ways I'm complicit in the silencing and invisibilizing and vulnerabilizing of others. Those times, for example, when I didn't speak up and when I didn't show up, when I was too worried about getting it perfect rather than just doing it, and especially those times when I didn't even see it. My hope is that this volume will encourage readers to be introspective and reflexive as they read through and respond to the chapters. It is this troubling of institutions and structures and our respective roles therein that promises change.

Towards a Lexicon of Feministing

Our individual reflections offer insights into how each of us interpreted and navigated the volume. As readers will see, we each came to—and leave from—this project from different positionalities and carry different perspectives on what needs to be done. What readers might *not* see is how our process with each other has been a constant site of learning and exchange. For us, discordance is not necessarily a stumbling block, but rather it has sparked an ongoing set of generative encounters that make it possible for us to come together in coalition to undo and redo political science. As many contributors write, finding community and/or solidarity can be decidedly non-linear, messy, and, as such, feel unresolved as we are speaking to a way of continually (re)enacting a politics that is bound up in relations of power. This tension at the core of this collection may analytically foreclose us from offering a series of prescriptive changes, but this tension is also simultaneously why the analytic of feministing enables so many contributors to find an opening here to articulate a politics of complexity.

In light of this complexity and our resistance to proposing a singular blueprint for change, we are drawn towards identifying a lexicon of feministing that can identify the relationships between our contributions, particularly as we reflect upon some of the shifts we can witness in our own writing and thinking as a group. Moreover, in returning to the work of the contributors, we see patterns across the texts related to, but that reach beyond, the organization of the collection around key themes: temporality and the case for transformation; relationality, community, and care; the "real" world of politics; gatekeeping, mentoring, and pedagogy; and rebuilding political science. Together, the contributions go beyond the thematics we set out, and call attention to transgressive interventions and practices that seem to be fertile ground for a common framework for conversation—an orienting vocabulary, a lexicon (Allen, Nath, and Georges 2023). We focus here on a few critical ideas that emerge from the volume—challenging form and expertise; unsettling methodologies through experiential knowledge and narrative; disruptive pedagogies; refusal; accountabilities; struggle and solidarity; unlearning and otherworlding; and emotionality—although there are many more, and these ideas, as evidenced below, intersect and overlap. As opposed to attaching programmatic or prescriptive readings of these words/phrases, in our focus on labour, refusal, resistance, coalition building, and desire as epistemic, we turn towards the idea of a lexicon to identify the conceptual terrain upon which we are feministing, and to raise questions for future (re)orientation. Put differently, as we engage in meaning-making, separately and together, we expose other ways things can be done. What would political science look like if *these* were the grounds or terrain of contestation?

Challenging Form and Expertise
As we work towards an analytic of feministing, we recognize that the personal *is* political science. For example, in her chapter on storying with Kelly Aguirre and Mariam Georgis, Sarah Munawar describes political theory as the care-based knowledge she has learned from her kin and her deen. Her theorizing on who is a person, the ways of living that are considered meaningful, *and* her orientation to hold political theory accountable emerged *through* her epistemic care work for her father. Munawar's understanding highlights the fact that experiential knowledge *is* expertise, as we push back on how the discipline privileges certain forms of knowledge and silences others, as is also described by Jeanette Ashe and as emerges in the dialogue between Melanee Thomas, Nadia Verrelli, and Kimberley Ens Manning about the implications of their work in politics on their lives as political scientists. In this reorienting of what we understand as expertise, we need to ask questions, such as:

- How do we write our research? When and where does our research start and end?
- How do we write ourselves into our research? Who are we always in collaboration with, even when they are not formally identified as collaborators?
- How might we challenge the pressure to be legible to political science/scientists, or rather how do we demand accountability that political science is legible to us?
- How do we challenge academic and disciplinary gatekeepers?

Unsettling Methodologies: Experiential Knowledge and Narrative
Relatedly, our methodologies are decidedly political, reflecting the values we hold as researchers. In her chapter, for example, Tka Pinnock writes

of 'membering as methodology, the "first act of making the personal public and political," and writes of the emotionally and intellectually purposive acts of remembering and forgetting—a method that puts into place lived experience that "can never be *un*lived." Our methodologies have the potential to shape and, consequently, undermine or nurture relationships within the academy and between the academy and communities. The letters written by Julianne M. Acker-Verney, Alana Cattapan, Alexandra Dobrowolsky, Tammy Findlay, and April Mandrona explore how we might disrupt research-related hierarchies of the "knowers" and the "known." Towards this end, we might ask,

- How do methodologies shape the questions that can be asked and answered within our discipline?
- How do social location and proximity matter in research?
- How do our methodologies render us (il)legible in political ways?
- What does an intentionally expansive understanding of ethical and relational accountability look and feel like within academia?

Disruptive Pedagogies
Disruptive pedagogies ask us to rethink how we teach political science and facilitate knowledge. We see the classroom—and our students—as sites of change, offering hope and opportunities to instill the critical importance of unmaking these institutions together, as explored in both David Semaan's and Nick Dorzweiler's contributions. In her chapter, Fiona MacDonald, together with her students, reveals how resistance can be cultivated in the classroom, where students individually and together can envision other worlds. Important questions to ask include

- Who do we centre in our teaching, and how does this shape the pedagogical arc of our teaching?
- What kinds of canons are we assembling?
- Where does teaching and learning temporally and spatially occur?
- To whom are we accountable to in our teaching?

Refusal
The politics of refusal comes from a long line of Black and Indigenous scholarship that vividly reveals the (re)generative possibilities of refusal

(Arvin 2019), as well as what's at stake with a politics of recognition (e.g., Simpson 2014, 2017). As universities have embarked on equity, diversity, inclusion, and decolonization initiatives and Canadian political science has begun advocating for Indigenization of the discipline, we must situate ourselves critically, making visible the various effects produced by such interventions. This is clear in Emily Grafton's chapter, for example, in which she interrogates what is at stake in the work of Indigenization as a site of simultaneous resistance and co-optation. The chapters by Nicole Bernhardt and Tka Pinnock and the dialogue between Yasmeen Abu-Laban, Leah Vosko, Reeta Chowdhari Tremblay, and Kiera Ladner speak as well to the competing imperatives of both being part of damaging and troublesome institutions and spaces in order to survive, but also refusing it where and when possible. These initiatives, often smokescreens of inclusion, also potentially silence those who seek to challenge them, for fear of being "unreasonable" or "ideological." Refusing is messy and the challenge of when to refuse and when to comply is never easy, particularly for those with less social privilege or who occupy more precarious positions within the academy. After all, opportunities to be "difficult" are not equally distributed. Resisting and refusing these liberal forms of inclusion and representation is risky. Things we should be attuned to include the following questions:

- What constitutes refusal?
- Who can refuse? What are the risks of refusal and for whom?
- What does our own refusal look like?
- How can we nurture a politics of refusal?
- How is refusal ongoing?
- How can we create and assert the validity of our own spaces?
- How can we be relationally accountable to refusals, in particular those of Indigenous and Black colleagues and students?

Accountabilities

As feminists working within the academy, our accountabilities are complicated in structural, ethical, and relational ways. We acknowledge our hierarchical, structural accountabilities to our employers, but this need not be our priority, even as our institutional affiliations are what bring us to the discipline. For us, thinking about accountability entails much more than our place in the ivory tower. It entails being accountable to communities, in terms of both our research communities and our colleagues through listening and witnessing, and creating spaces of meaning, for sharing and support, and to identify pathways and mobilize for change. It can also involve accountability to our circles outside of the institution, and to ourselves as we run ourselves ragged for institutions "that don't love us back." Kelly Aguirre, Mariam Georgis, and Sarah Munawar describe this as an ethics of receptivity, in which we must be emboldened to be willfully accountable and hold others to account, while also being open to refusal, exit, and the need to grieve. Elaine Coburn, Rita Kaur Dhamoon, Joyce Green, Genevieve Fuji Johnson, Heidi Kiiwetiniepinesiik Stark, and Gina Starblanket also speak to a relational accountability in their invitation that we not move too swiftly out of the discomfort produced by a feminist politics of disruption; they orient us towards feministing as responsibility and activism, noting that this responsibility manifests in the "hard work of transforming the discipline." There is also a generational dimension, in that we see ourselves as accountable to future generations of scholars. These dimensions include things like citational justice rooted in citational practices that acknowledge the scholarly and community lineage of our work, particularly the work of Black, Indigenous, and women of colour, resisting audit culture with its emphasis on codifying measures of efficiency and success, and engaging in meaningful, impactful work that is geared towards social change beyond simply citation indices and publications. As academics, we are in conversations with other political scientists, but siloing across the discipline and the persistent distinction between "mainstream" and "marginal" looms large. We can use those critical conversations with others to call out the ways in which the mainstream has not done enough to adequately capture politics, as well as the willful ignorance that allows it to continue. In thinking about accountability and feministing, we ask,

- To whom are we accountable?
- Who is accountable to us?
- How do we push back against institutional harm and violence?
- How do we resist co-optation, and choose language that won't be used against us, as Black feminists remind us?
- What is our responsibility to the discipline?
- What are the limits of accountability?

Struggle and Solidarity

We are trying to make change within fundamentally flawed institutions, but there is hope, and joy, in our persistence. Despite the knowledge that structural inequities are deeply embedded in institutional practices and in disciplinary norms, we nevertheless find spaces of meaning when "pulling back the curtain." In doing so, we find new bases of solidarity and coalition building that enable us to create supportive spaces and sites of repair. In her chapter, Alana Cattapan evokes struggle in describing feministing as a "project of persistence," but also critically links this to an anti-capitalist posture that requires that we think about the university as a corporate or neoliberal entity, trading in an economy of knowledge. As many of our contributors describe, this struggle is *labour*, be it the interpretive labour Sarah Munawar identifies, the relational work in finding community, as Lindsay Larios and Manon Laurent discuss in relation to their friendship of feminist solidarity, and as Amanda Bittner explains in building community online, or the institutional work of challenging power, as explored in Ethel Tungohan's, Jamilah Dei-Sharpe and Kimberley Ens Manning's, David Semaan's, and Nicole Bernhardt's respective chapters. These communities, however, are not defined by damage. It is oftentimes baffling to us that feminists are seen as dour killjoys when, in reality, feminist communities that are brought together by a shared desire for subversion delight in each other and in our common agenda and find hope in being part of such a collective.

Yet we recognize, of course, the unevenness of each other's fraught journeys in the academy mean that being in solidarity with each other entails deliberate and careful self-reflection on the possibilities and limitations of that solidarity, as indicated by both Michael Orsini and Chamindra Weerawardhana. While there are sites of convergence in our respective journeys, many of us take very different paths, and it is important, then, not to assume a singular solution to our challenges. A praxis of feminist solidarity encourages us to ask the following questions:

- What can we build together?
- How do retain a practice of critical hope when being part of progressive movements for change that respond to persisting structural inequities (Tungohan 2023)?

- Within coalitions, how can we ensure that the perspectives of communities that face the biggest challenges are continuously centred?
- Is it my/our voices that should be centred at this junction?

Unlearning and Other-Worlding

As noted above, unlearning requires us to break out of disciplinary silos to see the world differently. It requires us to acknowledge current structures and to identify and call out the disciplinary gatekeepers, as well as the ruse of academic freedom; it requires us to understand how institutions are disciplinary, limiting spaces for pushback. At the same time, however, unlearning offers an exchange of new ideas and new ways of doing things; it offers new bases of solidarity and enables us to re-vision metrics of success.

We therefore see unlearning as the basis of other-worlding. Other-worlding necessitates the abolition of our current structures and creating new ones. But it can also involve shifting relationalities, like the kind of dissident friendships and labouring *for* each other that emerges in Kelly Aguirre, Mariam Georgis, and Sarah Munawar's work, or building anti-racist coalitions that challenge conventional hierarchies that Kimberley Ens Manning and Jamilah Dei-Sharpe describe, or the supportive networks that Amanda Bittner has built and found in times of isolation. Our experiences as teachers and students too are sites of unworlding, as we can rethink longstanding hierarchies by inspiring one another. As we work towards broader transformation, what keeps us in the struggle, rife with desire for a different discipline, institution, and world, are the incremental changes we can make, that may accrue over time, together slowly turning the tide. Questions we can ask include

- What's not working?
- Where do we look for inspiration, and how can we apply that in political science?
- What new world(s) do we wish for?
- What are our hopes (and fears) for the future?
- What kinds of changes can be made to work towards that?
- Who can we work with to make that happen?

Emotionality

The chapters in this volume speak from a range of emotional registers, encompassing hope, joy, frustration, and anger, sometimes all at the same time. Emotions shape and are shaped by our work; they also shape the spaces we hold and the relationships we nurture, or not. But emotions don't emerge out of nowhere; they arise within particular institutions and structures and are often the basis of toxic relationships therein. As such, they are also disciplinary, determining who can get emotional and what emotions are legitimate, and for whom, within particular spaces and contexts, as Stephanie Paterson highlights. They can be used in manipulative—and silencing—ways that stymie progress and sustain power relations. Put differently, non-relational understandings of emotions can centre people in dominant positions in really problematic ways. Through feministing, we are attempting to navigate the tensions of honouring and recognizing the affective, while also understanding the emotions that are not devoid of power; emotions get weaponized by the university (and those of us within the university) in assertions of collegiality that often expect an abandonment of our politics.

Yet, as contributors to this collection make clear, the emotive, affective, and somatic are, and can be, a compass that tells us when something is amiss. When we are frustrated and exhausted, emotions can signal that a moment of pause is needed, and that this exhaustion may be our bodies anticipating problems that are emerging given the knowledges we've gained through our experiences of oppression. Listening to the emotive, affective, and somatic can thus be necessary sustaining work, not only pointing to the necessity of rest but also helping us reorient ourselves towards those things that bring us joy. We can ask,

- How do we feel about our work?
- What brings us joy and hope or, conversely, anger and frustration?
- Are our relationships within the academy fulfilling? If not, why, and what can we change?
- How do emotions inform what we know?

Conclusion

As we reach the final pages of this collection, we view it as neither a starting point or an end. The project of feministing can't (and shouldn't) be so neatly bounded. Feministing is a normative goal, a set of reflective questions, and a messy and an ongoing project. The collection is also a curation of both the ongoing barriers to flourishing, and a recognition of many possible visions of a different discipline, academy, and world. Our reflections indicate that the collection, and the broader project of feministing, is not stable, but rather a site of conversation, contestation, and solidarity, and the lexicon shared here serves as a conceptual and rhetorical terrain from which to continue to survive and to continue our work.

By coming to this lexicon through an orientation to refusal and desire, this collection offers multiple readings of these political postures: refusal to determine specific outcomes and define a singular path to get there; refusal to surrender the terrain of political science; refusal as a site of regeneration (Arvin 2019); that refusals invoke more than reaction, repair, and rehabilitation, and are de facto disciplinary questions (Nath 2022); and that desire can include the desire to burn it down and rebuild, collectively and individually, but always in solidarity and/or coalition. As Ashon T. Crawley has so carefully written, Black, Indigenous, and queer folx have "never submitted to the ideal of a '*the* world' as a kind of individual thing, an only thing" (2020, 27). Rather, "otherwise possibility is not utopic…but it *is* the elaboration of the fact that alternatives exist…This is why, for me, *there are worlds*" (29). Learning from Crawley, our articulation of a politics of desire is grounded in an assertion of "not yet," "not anymore," and "but still."

As we note in the introduction to the collection, it is in dreaming and supporting one another's visions of other possible worlds that we are able to find solidarity and ensure that "we are not left complacent or defeated." The paths leading to other possible disciplines, universities, and worlds, are multiple, diffuse, and often divergent. Feministing is about the ethics, politics, and processes that enable us to dream. It is in this dreaming, this imagining, that we find strength to keep struggling together, to keep disrupting the status quo, to unlearn and contest the boundaries of what counts as a "good" academic, and to create space to articulate our experience. In brief, it is in this work that we keep fighting, to keep feministing.

References

Abu-Laban, Yasmeen. 2017. "Narrating Canadian Political Science: History Revisited." *Canadian Journal of Political Science* 50 (4): 895–919. https://doi.org/10.1017/S000842391700138X.

Ahmed, Sara. 2004. *Cultural Politics of Emotion*. New York: Routledge.

Allen, Willow Samara, Nisha Nath, and Trista Georges. 2023. "Antiracist Interventive Interviewing with Public Sector Workers: Subverting Colonial Interventions." *International Journal of Qualitative Methods*, no. 22. https://doi.org/10.1177/16094069231166655.

Arvin, Maile. 2019. *Possessing Polynesians: The Science of Settler-Colonial Whiteness in Hawai'i and Oceania*. Durham, NC: Duke University Press.

Bhandar, Davina, Rita Dhamoon, Anita Girvan, and Nisha Nath. 2022. "Insurgent and Resurgent Workshop Call for Papers for Race, Ethnicity, Indigenous Peoples and Politics Panel." Canadian Political Science Association Annual Conference, York University, Toronto, May 30–June 1, 2022.

Bisaillon, Laura, Alana Cattapan, Annelieke Driessen, Esther van Duin, Shannon Spruit, Lorena Anton, and Nancy S. Jecker. 2020. "Doing Academia Differently: 'I Needed Self-Help Less Than I Needed a Fair Society.'" *Feminist Studies* 46 (1): 130–57. https://doi.org/10.1353/fem.2020.0010.

Collins, Patricia Hill, and Sirma Bilge. 2016. *Intersectionality*. Cambridge, UK: Polity Press.

Crawley, Ashon T. 2020. *The Lonely Letters*. Durham, NC: Duke University Press.

Dhamoon, Rita Kaur. 2006. "Shifting from 'Culture' to 'the Cultural': Critical Theorizing of Identity/Difference Politics." *Constellations* 13 (3): 355–73. https://doi.org/10.1111/j.1467-8675.2006.00406.x.

Dhamoon, Rita Kaur. 2020. "Racism as a Workload and Bargaining Issue." *Socialist Studies* 14 (1). https://doi.org/10.18740/ss27273.

Halberstam, Jack. 2011. *The Queer Art of Failure*. Durham, NC: Duke University Press.

Halberstam, Jack. 2012. "Unlearning." *Profession*, 9–16. http://www.jstor.org/stable/41714132.

IRK Collective. Forthcoming. "Breaking Daymares, Weaving Daydreams: Care at the Insurgent/Resurgent Knowledges (IRK) Lab." *In Care to Dream: Practices and Daydreams of Caring through Crisis*, edited by Amanda Watson and Reema Farris. Vancouver: UBC Press.

Karera, Axella. 2021. "Black Feminist Philosophy and the Politics of Refusal." In *Oxford Handbook of Feminist Philosophy*, edited by Asta and Kim Q. Hall, 109–19. Oxford and New York: Oxford University Press.

MacDonald, Fiona, and Alexandra Dobrowolsky. 2020. "Introduction: Transforming and Transformational Gender Politics in Turbulent Times." In *Turbulent Times, Transformational Possibilities: Gender and Politics Today and Tomorrow*, edited by Fiona MacDonald and Alexandra Dobrowolsky, 1–20. Toronto: University of Toronto Press.

May, Vivian M. 2015. *Pursuing Intersectionality: Unsettling Dominant Imaginaries*. New York: Routledge.

Mountz, Alison, Anne Bonds, Becky Mansfield, Jenna Loyd, Jennifer Hyndman, Margaret Walton-Roberts, Ranu Basu, Risa Whitson, Roberta Hawkins, Trina Hamilton, and

Winifred Curran. 2015. "For Slow Scholarship: A Feminist Politics of Resistance through Collective Action in the Neoliberal University." *ACME: An International Journal for Critical Geographies* 14 (4): 1235–59. https://acme-journal.org/index.php/acme/article/view/1058.

Nath, Nisha. 2022. "Introduction—Roundtable on Enacting Refusals: Reflecting on Political Science, Research Ethics and Settler Colonialism." Annual Meetings of the Canadian Political Science Association, York University, Toronto, May 30–June 1, 2022.

Nath, Nisha, Ethel Tungohan, and Megan Gaucher. 2018. "The Future of Canadian Political Science: Boundary Transgressions, Gender and Anti-Oppression Frameworks." *Canadian Journal of Political Science* 51 (3): 619–42. https://doi.org/10.1017/S0008423918000197.

Patel, Shaista. 2022. "Talking Complicity, Building Coloniality." *Journal of Curriculum and Pedagogy* 19 (3): 211–30. https://doi.org/10.1080/15505170.2020.1871450.

Pessar, Patricia R., and Sarah J. Mahler. 2003. "Transnational Migration: Bringing Gender." *International Migration Review* 37 (3): 812–46. https://www.jstor.org/stable/30037758.

Simpson, Audra. 2007. "On Ethnographic Refusal: Indigeneity, 'Voice' and Colonial Citizenship." *Junctures*, no. 9, 67–80. https://junctures.org/index.php/junctures/article/view/66.

Simpson, Audra. 2014. *Mohawk Interruptus: Political Life across the Borders of Settler States*. Durham, NC: Duke University Press.

Simpson, Audra. 2017. "The Ruse of Consent and the Anatomy of 'Refusal': Cases from Indigenous North America and Australia." *Postcolonial Studies* 20 (1): 18–33. https://doi.org/10.1080/13688790.2017.1334283.

Tuck, Eve. 2009. "Suspending Damage: A Letter to Our Communities." *Harvard Educational Review* 79 (3): 409–28. https://doi.org/10.17763/haer.79.3.n0016675661t3n15.

Tungohan, Ethel. 2023. *Care Activism: Migrant Domestic Workers, Communities of Care and Movement-Building*. Chicago: University of Illinois Press.

Yee, Jessica. 2009. "Allyship and Youth." *Our Schools / Our Selves* 18 (2): 101–06.

Contributors

YASMEEN ABU-LABAN is a professor of political science and Canada Research Chair in the Politics of Citizenship and Human Rights at the University of Alberta. She is also a fellow at the Canadian Institute for Advanced Research. Her published research addresses themes relating to ethnic and gender politics; nationalism and globalization; immigration policies and politics; surveillance and border control; and multiculturalism and anti-racism. She served as president of the Canadian Political Science Association (2016–2017), and as vice-president of the International Political Science Association (2018–2021). She is currently the founding chair of Research Committee 46 (Migration and Citizenship) in the International Political Science Association.

JULIANNE M. ACKER-VERNEY embraces her life as a woman with disabilities, sharing the adventure with her partner in Halifax, Nova Scotia, where she is currently completing a PHD in educational studies at Mount Saint Vincent University. She is an experienced community-based and academic researcher. Her MA thesis focused on supporting the full participation of diverse women with disabilities in research. Julianne is active in social justice initiatives and organizations, including as a past member of the Alexa McDonough Institute for Women, Gender and Social Justice steering committee. Publishers of her research include *Third World Thematics* and *Canadian Public Policy*.

KELLY AGUIRRE is an assistant professor in the Department of Political Science at the University of Victoria where she also received her PHD (2019). She is a queer and autistic mestiza of Nahua, ñuu savi, German-Russian, and Welsh settler ancestry. Her areas of scholarship and interest are Indigenous and decolonial politics, methodological ethics, rhetoric and poetics, as well as critical theory and the roles of theorists as witnesses and storytellers of political life. Recently she has begun work considering IBPOC experiences of disability and neurodiversity in academia and entanglements of race, gender, Indigeneity and disability in political theory and decolonial movements; including Indigiqueer and neuroqueer interventions on issues of normativity and contributions to otherwise political imaginaries.

JEANETTE ASHE holds a PHD from Birkbeck, University of London, teaches politics at Douglas College, BC, and is visiting faculty at the Global Institute for Women's Leadership, King's College, University of London. Recent publications include her book *Political Candidate Selection: Who Wins, Who Loses and Under-Representation in the UK* (Routledge, 2019), and book chapters "The Implementation of Equality-Based Candidate Selection Decisions in the British Labour and Conservative Parties," "Gender Sensitizing Parliaments: A Seven-Step Field Guide," "Canada's Political Parties: Gatekeepers to Parliament," and "Gender Sensitivity under Trudeau: Facebook Feminism or Real Change?" Her scholarship can also be found in the *Canadian Journal of Political Science*, *Party Politics,* and *British Politics.*

NICOLE S. BERNHARDT is an assistant professor in political science at the University of Toronto Scarborough. Her research focuses on human rights policy as a response to structural racism. She received her PHD in politics from York University, for which she was awarded an Ontario Graduate Scholarship and the Abella Scholarship for Studies in Equity. Nicole has worked as a policy advisor for the Anti-Racism Directorate and as a human rights officer for the Ontario Human Rights Commission. She teaches courses on Canadian government and public policy, and currently serves on the executive for the Black Canadian Studies Association.

AMANDA BITTNER is a professor in the Department of Political Science and director of the Gender and Politics Lab at Memorial University. She specializes in elections, voting, and public opinion, with a focus on gender, political institutions, and survey research. She's committed to raising kind, feminist kids, loves drinking coffee and wine with friends, and her ideal day is spent either hiking along the ocean or lounging on the couch with a good book and her little dog, Data, at her feet.

ALANA CATTAPAN is the Canada Research Chair in the Politics of Reproduction and an assistant professor in the Department of Political Science at the University of Waterloo. She is also an adjunct professor at the Johnson Shoyama Graduate School of Public Policy at the University of Saskatchewan. She studies gendered inclusion in policy-making, identifying links between the state, the commercialization of the body, and reproductive labour.

ELAINE COBURN is an associate professor of international studies and director of the Centre for Feminist Research, York University. Her writing is concerned with unjust inequalities and how to challenge them. Her scholarship is published in the *Canadian Review of Sociology*, *International Feminist Journal of Politics*, *International Sociological Review*, and *Political Studies*, among other journals. She writes for *Canadian Notes and Queries*, *Herizons*, and the *Literary Review of Canada*.

JAMILAH A.Y. DEI-SHARPE is a Ghanaian Jamaican Canadian PHD candidate in sociology at Concordia University, Montreal. She specializes in critical race and gender relations in North America and critical approaches to higher education, focusing on Black Canadian history, the African diaspora, men and masculinities, and decoloniality. She is a SSHRC Joseph Armand Bombardier Award recipient for her doctoral research on Black Masculinities in Canada. She is also a Queen Elizabeth Scholar in the Advanced Scholars West Africa program. She is a sociology instructor, an educational consultant, an avid community organizer, and critical pedagogue. She co-founded the National Black Graduate Network, is co-organizer for the Canadian Sociological Association's Race and Ethnicity cluster, founded the Decolonial Perspectives and Practice Hub, and is the project architect for the Anti-Racist Pedagogy Project.

RITA KAUR DHAMOON (she/her/their) is an anti-racist feminist with over thirty years of experience working with various communities to confront inequities and build spaces of support. Inspired by other members of the Insurgent/Resurgent Knowledges (IRK) Lab (Davina Bhandar, Nisha Nath, and Anita Girvan), Rita aspires to do more creative art, learn the dhol, and gain a better understanding of gardening. She has also published in the areas of critical race politics, anti-racist feminism, and anti-colonialism; critiques of liberal multiculturalism; intersectionality and its possibilities and limits; the relationship between Indigenous people and non-Black, non-Indigenous people of colour; and Sikhs in Canada. She is also an associate professor in the Department of Political Science at the University of Victoria.

ALEXANDRA DOBROWOLSKY, professor of political science at Saint Mary's University, specializes in Canadian; comparative; and women, gender, and politics. She has published in a range of national and international journals. Her recent contributions include articles and chapters on equality and multiculturalism; public engagement; sexuality and constitutionalism; and feminist governance in North America. She is one of the co-editors of the *Finding Feminisms* special issue of the *Canadian Journal of Political Science* (June 2017) and has written and co-edited six books on topics of representation, constitutionalism, social policy, immigration, and citizenship, including *Women and Public Policy in Canada: Neo-liberalism and After?* (Oxford University Press, 2009), and *Turbulent Times, Transformational Possibilities? Gender and Politics Today and Tomorrow* (University of Toronto Press, 2020), co-edited with Fiona MacDonald.

NICK DORZWEILER is Senior Professor of the Practice of Political Science and Women's and Gender Studies at Wheaton College (Massachusetts), and an instructor for the Chicago Field Studies program at Northwestern University. His research interests include contemporary political theory, the history and philosophy of social science, and the politics of popular culture. His recent scholarship has appeared in *Contemporary Political Theory*, *Constellations*, and *Polity*. His current book project, which has been supported by two American Council of Learned Societies Project Development Grants, investigates the mid-twentieth-century political scientist Harold Lasswell and his creation of a mass psychotherapy radio program for the National Broadcasting Corporation.

TAMMY FINDLAY is a professor in the Department of Politics, Economics, and Canadian Studies at Mount Saint Vincent University. Her research focuses on feminist intersectionality and social policy, child care policy, women's representation, and democratic governance. She is the author of *Femocratic Administration: Gender, Governance, and Democracy in Ontario* (University of Toronto Press, 2015), and co-author of *Women, Politics, and Public Policy: The Political Struggles of Canadian Women*, 3rd ed. (Oxford University Press, 2020). She is a research associate with the Canadian Centre for Policy Alternatives–Nova Scotia and was the 2021–2022 president of the Canadian Research Institute for the Advancement of Women.

MARIAM GEORGIS is an assistant professor of global Indigeneity in the Department of Gender, Sexuality. and Women's Studies at Simon Fraser University. She is Assyrian, Indigenous to present-day Iraq, and currently living on and sustained by the unceded traditional territories of the Coast Salish Peoples, including the Tsleil-Waututh, Kwikwetlem, Squamish, and Musqueam Nations. Grounded in embodied decolonial feminist epistemologies, her scholarship is located at the nexus of global politics, critical Indigenous studies, and Middle East studies. Her research interests include issues of global security; global colonialism(s), Indigeneities, and decolonization; and politics of southwest Asia.

EMILY GRAFTON (Métis Nation) has a PHD in Native studies from the University of Manitoba (Winnipeg). As a researcher and educator, her work concerns critical discourse analysis of settler colonialism, gender and feminist theories, and the politics of reconciliation and the state. Emily has held several senior positions in politics (provincial, municipal, and Indigenous). She was the research-curator, Indigenous content, at the Canadian Museum for Human Rights (Winnipeg) and the Indigenous research lead and executive lead, Indigenization, at the University of Regina. She is currently an associate professor of politics and international studies, University of Regina.

JOYCE GREEN is professor emerita in the Department of Politics and International Studies at the University of Regina. Her work deals with Indigenous-state relations; Indigenous feminism; citizenship; identity and racism in Canada's political culture; and Indigenous human rights in Canada. Recently, she has immersed herself in Ktunaxa language and Nation matters. She is the editor of *Making Space for Indigenous Feminism* (Fernwood, and Zed Books, 2007) and *Indivisible: Indigenous Human Rights* (Fernwood, 2014). Dr. Green is English, Ktunaxa, and Cree Scottish Métis, and her family's experiences have inspired much of her scholarly and political work. She now lives in a·kiskaq i?it, in ʔamakʔis Ktunaxa (Cranbrook, BC, in Ktunaxa territory).

GENEVIEVE FUJI JOHNSON is a Yonsei settler of Japanese and Irish ancestry on Turtle Island (Canada). Although proud of her family's history of resilience, she is reckoning with their four generations of Indigenous dispossession. It is thus with gratitude and respect that she divides her time between the traditional and unceded territories of the Musqueam, Squamish, and Tsleil-Waututh Nations and those of the Tla-o-qui-aht Nation. Dr. Johnson is a professor of political science at Simon Fraser University. Her current work focuses on issues of sex work governance and sex worker rights.

KIERA L. LADNER is a distinguished professor in political studies and the Canada Research Chair in Miyo we'citowin, Indigenous Governance, and Digital Sovereignties at the University of Manitoba (Winnipeg). Her current research focuses on comparative Indigenous constitutional law politics, digital sovereignties, missing and murdered Indigenous women and girls, and treaty federalism.

LINDSAY LARIOS holds a PHD in political science from Concordia University (Montreal) and is an assistant professor in the Faculty of Social Work at the University of Manitoba (Winnipeg). Her research focuses on the politics of pregnancy and birth, and precarious migration as an issue of reproductive justice in the Canadian context. She is a research affiliate of the Centre for Human Rights Research and the Canadian Centre for Policy Alternatives–Manitoba. She also sits on the Board of Directors for the Women's Health Clinic and is a member of the Healthcare for All Manitoba Coalition.

MANON LAURENT is a postdoctoral fellow at the Chair of Creative Work at Collège de France. She has a PHD in sociology from Université Paris Cité and in political science from Concordia University (Montreal). Her research explores state-society relations in urban China. Her thesis focuses on how the commodification of educational resources and the integration of China into a global normative space transform parents into political actors. She has taught at Nanjing University, Concordia University, and the Université de Paris. She has published in the journals *Pacific Affairs*, *Mouvements*, and *Urbanités*; and in three collective volumes, *Disciplines scolaires et cultures politiques* (PUR, 2018), *Social Welfare in India and China: A Comparative Perspective* (Palgrave Macmillan, 2020), and *Asia in Care* (CNRS Editions, 2024).

FIONA MACDONALD is an associate professor specializing in gender politics at the University of Northern British Columbia. She co-edited the *Finding Feminisms* special issue of the *Canadian Journal of Political Science* (June 2017), which includes her article "Knocking Down Walls in Political Science: In Defense of an Expansionist Feminist Agenda." Her other publications can be found in the journals *Hypatia*, *Citizenship Studies*, *Constellations*, and *Canadian Public Administration*. Her article "Indigenous Peoples and Neoliberal 'Privatization' in Canada: Opportunities, Cautions and Constraints" won the 2012 John McMenemy Prize for the best article published in volume 44 of the *Canadian Journal of Political Science*. Her co-edited book (with Alexandra Dobrowolsky), *Turbulent Times, Transformational Opportunities? Gender and Politics Today and Tomorrow*, was published with University of Toronto Press in 2020.

APRIL MANDRONA is an associate professor at NSCAD University. She received a doctorate in art education from Concordia University (Montreal) and was a Social Sciences and Humanities Research Council postdoctoral fellow at McGill University in the Department of Integrated Studies in Education. She has published articles and book chapters on young people's visual culture, rurality, ethics, and participatory visual research. Her most recent edited volume is *Ethical Practice in Participatory Visual Research with Girls: Transnational Approaches* (Berghahn, 2021). Her SSHRC-funded community art education research with historically excluded groups focuses on the social roles of artistic production and innovative approaches to understanding narrative, belonging, well-being, and participation.

KIMBERLEY ENS MANNING is principal of the Simone de Beauvoir Institute and professor of political science at Concordia University (Montreal). Dividing her time between the territories of theLəkʷəŋən (Songhees and Esquimalt) Peoples and the Un-Ceded Traditional Lands and Waters of the Kanien'kehá:ka Nation, Kim's research focuses on gender and politics in state formation and pedagogical efforts to deepen equity in health care and education. A founding Board Member of Gender Creative Kids, Kim also conducts research with parent advocates of transgender young people. She is the author of *The Party Family: Revolutionary Attachments and the Gendered Origins of State Power in China* (Cornell, 2023) and has previously published in the *Canadian Journal of Political Science*, *Gender and History*, and *The China Quarterly*.

SARAH MUNAWAR is a Muslim and settler living on and sustained by the occupied and unceded lands and waters of the Musqueam, Tsleil-Waututh, and Squamish nations. She earned her PHD in political science from the University of British Columbia. She is a political science instructor at Columbia College (Vancouver) and a visiting professor at the Elizabeth Rockwell Center for Ethics and Leadership at the Hobby School of Public Affairs at the University of Houston. Her research interests include Muslim-feminist thought, decolonial epistemologies, health equity, comparative care ethics, and disability justice. Her scholarship is deeply embedded in her responsibilities and her relations as a mother, as a caregiver for her father, and as a Muslim woman.

NISHA NATH (she/they) is an associate professor of equity studies at Athabasca University living in amiskwaciwâskahikan (colonially known as Edmonton) in Treaty 6. Her work looks at the intersections of citizenship, race, security, and settler colonialism. In addition to collaborating on the Insurgent/Resurgent Knowledges (IRK) Lab and a co-authored manuscript titled *The Letters: Writing Lives through and against the University* with Drs. Rita Dhamoon, Anita Girvan, and Davina Bhandar, she is engaged in a Social Sciences and Humanities Research Council–funded research project on discretion and the settler colonial socialization of public sector workers (with Dr. Willow Samara Allen).

MICHAEL ORSINI is a professor in feminist and gender studies and political studies at the University of Ottawa. A critical policy scholar, his work foregrounds the perspectives of people marginalized from policy-making. Michael has completed research on autism, HIV/AIDS, and the link between art and disability. His work has appeared in several journals, including *Sociology of Health and Illness*, *Social Policy and Administration*, *Sociological Review*, and *Critical Policy Studies*. He has co-edited six books, including *Seeing Red: HIV/AIDS and Public Policy in Canada* (University of Toronto Press, 2018), *The Handbook of Critical Policy Studies* (Edward Elgar, 2021), *Mobilizing Metaphor: Art, Culture and Disability Activism in Canada* (UBC Press, 2016), and *Worlds of Autism: Across the Spectrum of Neurological Difference* (University of Minnesota Press, 2013).

STEPHANIE PATERSON is a professor in the Department of Political Science at Concordia University (Montreal), where she specializes in feminist and critical policy studies. Her research centres on the effects produced when states take up and deploy feminist knowledges and expertise, which has led to substantive expertise in feminist and critical policy studies; feminist governance, state feminism, and gender mainstreaming; and the politics of pregnancy, childbirth, and motherhood. Her work appears in journals such as *Critical Policy Studies*, *Gender, Work and Organization*, the *Canadian Journal of Political Science*, and *Politics & Gender*.

TKA C. PINNOCK is a PHD candidate in the Department of Politics, and a research associate at the Centre for Research on Latin America and the Caribbean at York University. Her research interests lie at the intersection of feminist political economy, political ecology, globalization, and critical development studies where she explores the everyday politics of "life-work." Her dissertation project explores the ways in which the life-work of marginalized workers is (re)shaped by and in response to contemporary economic development processes, using the tourism sector in Jamaica as a case study. Her community work also gives rise to an interest in diaspora studies and community-based research.

DAVID SEMAAN is a PHD candidate in the Department of Politics at York University. His work engages in anti-imperialist, decolonial, and feminist analyses of contemporary Canadian public policy, especially as it concerns securitization, policing, and prison. David's research maps Canada's position in the circulation of political economies of surveillance and carcerality. He aspires to develop methods of community-engaged research to speak with BIPOC activists in the queer community in Canada and in South West Asian and North African countries.

GINA STARBLANKET is an associate professor in the Indigenous Governance program at the University of Victoria and former Canada Research Chair in the Politics of Decolonization at the University of Calgary. Gina is Cree and Saulteaux and a member of the Star Blanket Cree Nation in Treaty 4 territory. She is the principal investigator of the Prairie Indigenous Relationality Network, and her research takes up questions of treaty implementation, prairie Indigenous life, gender, and Indigenous feminism.

HEIDI KIIWETINEPINESIIK STARK (Turtle Mountain Ojibwe) is an associate professor of Indigenous governance. Her research interests include Indigenous law and governance, Treaty rights, and Indigenous politics in the United States and Canada. She is the co-editor of *Indigenous Resurgence in an Age of Reconciliation*, with Aimée Craft and Hōkūlani K. Aikau (University of Toronto Press, 2023), and *Centering Anishinaabeg Studies: Understanding the World through Stories*, with Jill Doerfler and Niigaanwewidam Sinclair (University of Manitoba Press, 2013). She is the co-author of the third and fourth editions of *American Indian Politics* and the *American Political System* with David E. Wilkins (Rowman & Littlefield, 2010, 2017).

MELANEE THOMAS is a professor in the Department of Political Science at the University of Calgary. Her research addresses the causes and consequences of gender-based political inequality, focusing on Canadian political parties, elections, and political institutions; gender and politics; and the politics of energy transition. Her scholarship appears in *Electoral Studies*, *Political Communication*, *Politics and Gender*,

Political Behavior, *Energy Politics*, and the *Canadian Journal of Political Science*.

REETA CHOWDHARI TREMBLAY is professor emerita of comparative politics and former provost/vice-president academic at the university of Victoria. She is past president of the Canadian Political Science Association and Canadian Asian Studies. Her research interests include secessionist movements in South Asia and the politics of subaltern resistance and accommodation in postcolonial societies. Her recent publications include *The Political Economy of Natural Resource Funds* (co-edited with Eyene Okpanachi, Palgrave Macmillan, 2021); *Religion and Politics in Jammu and Kashmir* (co-edited with Mohita Bhatia, Routledge, 2020); "India: Federalism, Majoritarian Nationalism, and the Vulnerable and Marginalized" (in Victor Ramraj, ed., *COVID-19 in Asia*, Oxford, 2020); and *Modi's Foreign Policy* (co-authored with Ashok Kapur, Sage, 2017).

ETHEL TUNGOHAN is the Canada Research Chair in Canadian Migration Policy, Impacts, and Activism and an associate professor of politics at York University. Her book *Care Activism: Migrant Domestic Workers, Movement-Building, and Communities of Care* (University of Illinois Press, 2023) examines migrant care worker activism in Canada from 2009 until 2022. She has written widely on immigration policy, social movements, intersectionality, gender, and "diversity" politics, and socially engaged research. She is an enthusiastic proponent of socially engaged research and has a long history collaborating on research projects with migrant organizations in Canada such as Migrant Resource Centre Canada, Migrante Canada, and Gabriela Ontario.

NADIA VERRELLI, PHD, is an associate director (part-time) at the Institute of Intergovernmental Relations, Queen's University and an associate professor in Law and Justice at Laurentian University. Her research interests focus on federalism, secession, and Canadian institutions. She has published articles and chapters on Canadian institutions, the Canadian Constitution, and federalism in various journals and edited books. Currently, she is writing a book titled

"Reference re Secession of Quebec?" She is also interested in violence against women and children. She continues to research court, government, and media responses to domestic violence. She is the co-author of *No Legal Way Out: R v. Ryan, Domestic Abuse, and the Defence of Duress* (with Lori Chambers, UBC Press, 2021). In 2021, Dr. Verrelli was the federal NDP candidate for the riding of Sudbury, Ontario.

LEAH F. VOSKO, fellow of the Royal Society of Canada, is a professor of politics and Canada Research Chair in the Political Economy of Gender and Work at York University. Her current research, using the lens of feminist political economy, examines employment standards and their enforcement, access to rights among workers labouring transnationally, and international mobility programs. Her latest sole-authored book, *Disrupting Deportability*, was published by Cornell University Press in 2019, and her latest co-authored book, *Closing the Employment Standards Enforcement Gap: Improving Protections for People in Precarious Jobs*, was published in 2020 with University of Toronto Press.

CHAMINDRA WEERAWARDHANA, PHD, a is a researcher and political analyst. Her work focuses on intersectional feminist international relations, conflict resolution, and gender politics. She is the co-founder of the Consortium for Intersectional Justice, and has held research and teaching assignments in several French, British, Dutch, and Canadian universities. Outside the academy, she has worked in international human rights advocacy and political organizing. In addition to her monograph *Decolonising Peacebuilding* (Cambridge Scholars Publishing, 2018), her work has appeared in academic journals and book chapters. *Crisis Dispatches*, a collection of selected political commentaries, will be published in 2024.